Modern East Asia:
From 1600

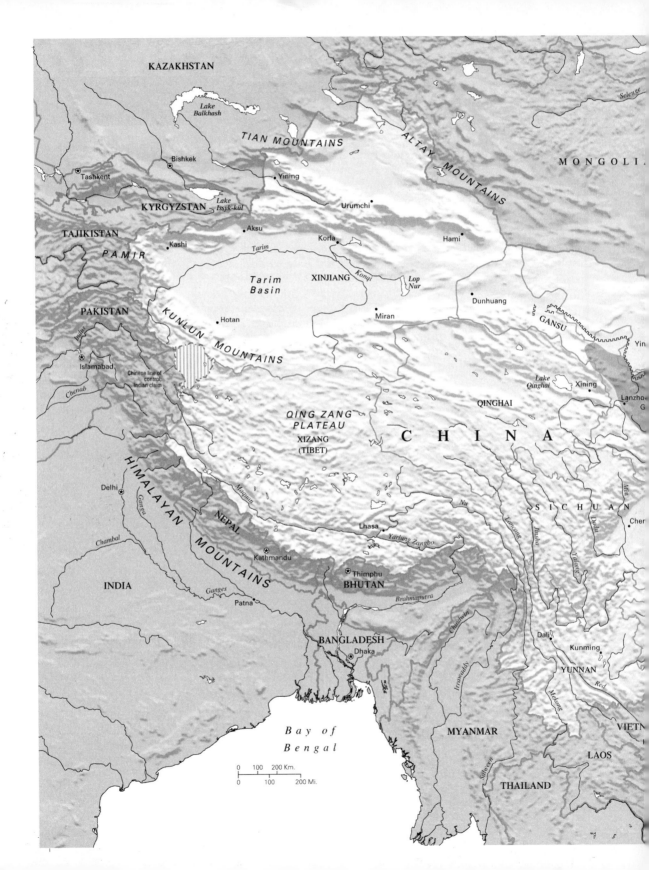

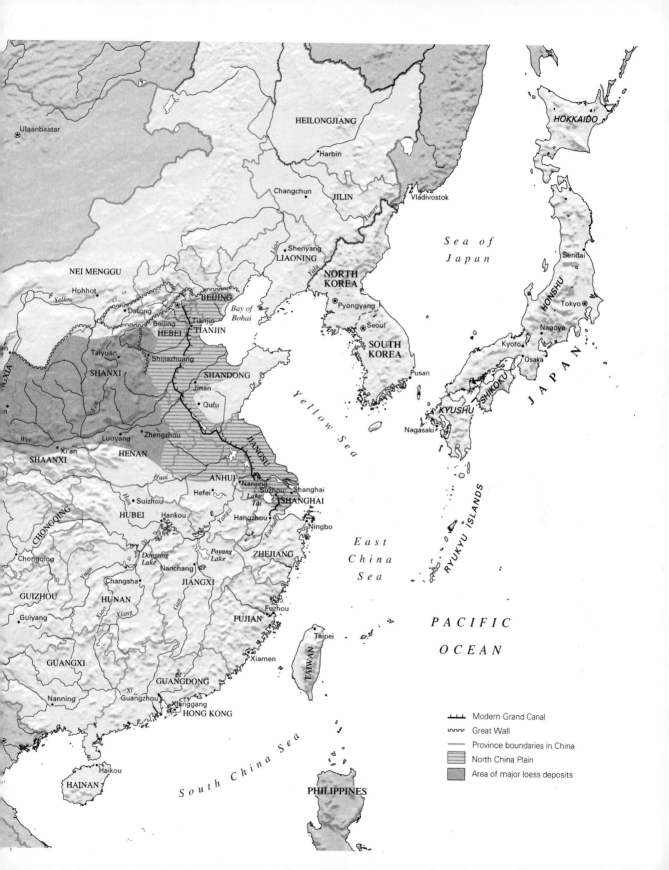

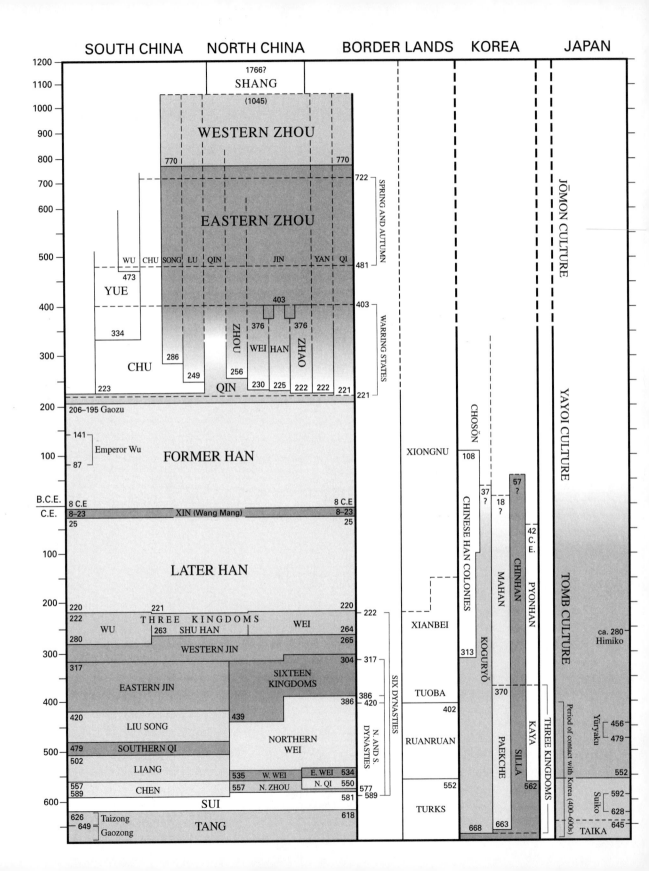

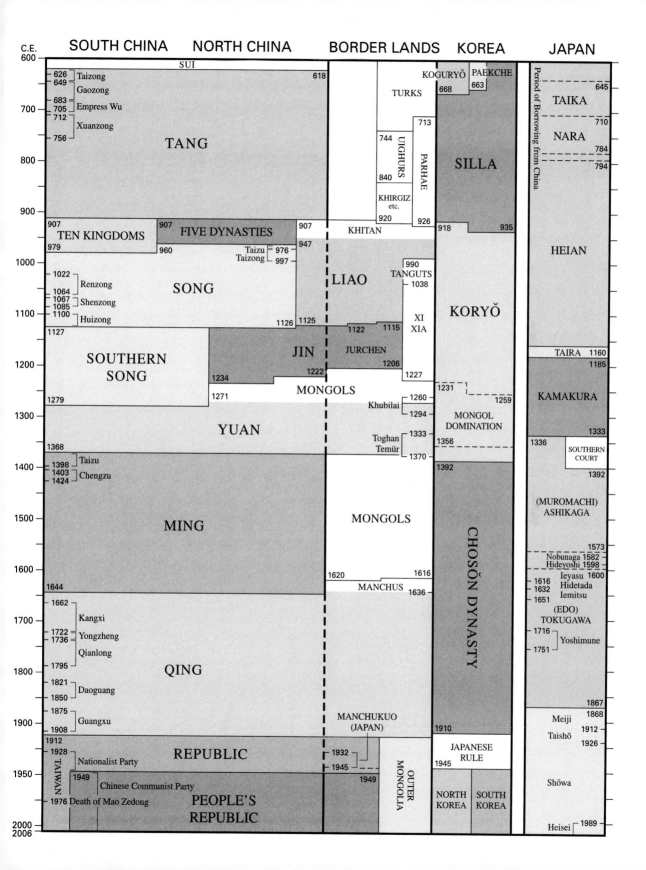

Modern East Asia: From 1600

A Cultural, Social, and Political History

PATRICIA BUCKLEY EBREY
University of Washington–Seattle

ANNE WALTHALL
University of California–Irvine

JAMES B. PALAIS
University of Washington–Seattle

HOUGHTON MIFFLIN COMPANY
Boston   New York

Publisher: Charles Hartford
Senior Sponsoring Editor: Nancy Blaine
Senior Development Editor: Julie Swasey
Senior Project Editor: Jane Lee
Editorial Assistant: Kristen Truncellito
Senior Art and Design Coordinator: Jill Haber
Senior Photo Editor: Jennifer Meyer Dare
Composition Buyer/Manufacturing Coordinator: Chuck Dutton
Senior Marketing Manager: Sandra McGuire
Marketing Assistant: Molly Parke

Cover image: Caption: *The General and His Wife (shamanistic deities),* Korea, Chosŏn Dynasty, ink and color on paper. Credit: With permission of the Royal Ontario Museum © ROM.

Text credits appear on page 625.

Printed in the U.S.A.

Library of Congress Control Number: 2001133247

ISBN: 0-618-13385-2

123456789-MP-09 08 07 06 05

CONTENTS

MAPS AND FIGURES

PREFACE

THERE ARE MANY REASONS TO LEARN about East Asia. A fifth of the world's population lives there. Every day newspapers carry articles on the rapid transformations of the world economy that make China, Japan, and Korea a growing presence in our lives. Globalization means that not only are people crossing the Pacific in ever increasing numbers, but also that American popular culture draws from many sources in East Asia, from Korean martial arts to Japanese anime and Chinese films.

But why approach East Asia through its history, rather than, say, its economy or contemporary culture? Many reasons can be offered. One cannot gain an adequate understanding of modern phenomena without knowing the stages and processes that led up to them. Moreover, all of the countries of East Asia are strongly historically-minded. To a much greater extent than in the United States, people know and identify with people and events of a thousand or more years ago. In all three countries, people still read for pleasure *The Three Kingdoms,* a novel written in fourteenth century China about the leaders of three contending states in third century China. Historical consciousness also underlies the strong sense of separate identities among the people of China, Korea, and Japan. The fact that time and again Korea was able to protect its independence despite the attempts of both China and Japan to conquer it is a central part of Korean identity today. Yet another reason to learn about East Asia in the past is its comparative value. As a region that developed nearly independently of the West, East Asia sheds light on other ways human beings have found meaning, formed communities, and governed themselves, expanding our understanding of the human condition.

When the three authors of this volume were students themselves (in the 1960s and 1970s), the fullest and most up-to-date textbook on East Asia was the two-volume set published in 1960 and 1965 by Houghton Mifflin, *East Asia: The Great Tradition* and *East Asia: The Modern Transformation,* written by Edwin O. Reischauer, John K. Fairbank and Albert M. Craig. Not only did we learn the basic political chronology from these books, but they introduced us to such central issues as the dynastic cycle, the interplay of the Chinese and "barbarians," the ways Korea and Japan adapted features of the Chinese model, the challenge posed by the West in the nineteenth century, and modern revolutionary movements. When it came time for us to develop our own research agendas, these books still cast a shadow as we pursued questions that they did not pose or delved more deeply into topics that they covered only superficially.

It was because we respected these books that we were willing to listen when Nancy Blaine of Houghton Mifflin approached us about doing a new history of East Asia for the current generation of students. We knew that the task would be daunting. Could we take into account the wealth of scholarship that had been published in the forty-odd years since the original *East Asia* books and yet produce the leaner, more visual book wanted by students and teachers today? As we discussed how to meet these challenges, we came up with a plan for this book.

COMPARABLE COVERAGE OF KOREA

The growth of Korean studies over the last quarter century now makes it possible to give

Korea comparable coverage to China and Japan (we ended up giving China about 50 percent of the space, Japan 30 percent, and Korea 20 percent). We know that many teachers have been frustrated in their attempts to cover Korea in their East Asia courses for lack of suitable materials and hope that our efforts prove useful to both them and their students.

A BROAD FOCUS: *CONNECTIONS* CHAPTERS

A second key decision we made was to search for ways to keep in mind the larger whole as we told the separate stories of China, Korea, and Japan. Our solution was to periodically zoom out to look at the wider region from a global or world-historical perspective. Thus, every few chapters we have inserted a mini-chapter on developments that link the societies of East Asia both to each other and to the larger global context. We have labeled these mini-chapters "Connections" because they put their emphasis on the many ways each society was connected to what went on outside it. For instance, the origins and spread of Buddhism are of great importance to all of the societies of East Asia, but much of the story can be told as a common story that connects East Asia with the rest of Asia. Similarly, many books write about World War II in East Asia in entirely different ways in their China and Japan chapters. By stepping back and writing about the war from a more global perspective, we can help students see the larger picture.

BALANCED CULTURAL, SOCIAL, AND POLITICAL HISTORY

Even though the volume of scholarship on East Asia has increased many-fold since the original *East Asia* set was written, we decided to honor its example of striving for balanced coverage of the different strands of history. A basic political narrative is essential to give students a firm sense of chronology and to let them think about

issues of change. Moreover, there is no denying that the creation of state structures has much to do with how people lived their lives. Even the fact that people think of themselves as "Chinese," "Korean," or "Japanese" is largely a by-product of political history.

We also believed that students should gain an understanding of the philosophies and religions of East Asia. Confucianism and Buddhism have both been of great importance throughout the region, but in very diverse ways, as the historical context has continually changed. Other elements of high culture also deserve coverage, such as the arts of poetry and calligraphy.

Yet we did not want to neglect topics in social, cultural, and economic history, where much of our own work has been concentrated. Even if the state is important to understanding how people lived, so were families, villages, and religious sects. We also wanted to bring in the results of scholarship on those who had been marginalized in the traditional histories, from laborers and minorities to women at all social levels.

A NARROW FOCUS: BIOGRAPHIES, DOCUMENTS, AND MATERIAL CULTURE

The danger of trying to cover so much is that we would have to stay at a high level of generalization. To keep our readers engaged and bring our story down to earth, we decided to devote three or four pages per chapter to closer looks at specific people, documents, and material objects.

Biographies

Many chapters have a one-page biography, about someone who would not normally be mentioned in a history book. Although we found few truly ordinary people to write about for the earlier periods, we still ended up with a diverse set of individuals. The people sketched range from the most accomplished (such as the eminent Chinese poet Du Fu and the Korean philosopher Yi

Chehyŏn) to remarkably ordinary people (such as a woman whose job was to mind the neighborhood telephone). Three military men are portrayed; others were physicians, entrepreneurs, and founders of religious sects. We also have included some agitators and revolutionaries, and even a winning volleyball coach.

Documents

In our chapters we frequently cite short passages from primary sources, but thought that students would also benefit from texts long enough for them to get a sense of the genre, the author's point of view, and the circumstances described. A few of those we have included were written by famous writers, such as Fukuzawa Yūkichi and Lu Xun. Some are excerpted from well-known pieces of literature, such as the play, *The Peony Pavilion*. Others will be less familiar to teachers and students alike. Legal documents have been selected for what they reveal of ordinary people's lives. Religious texts of several sorts were chosen to help us see religion and popular beliefs in action. Many authors are utterly serious, complaining bitterly of war or corruption, for instance; others have well-developed senses of humor. All of the documents selected prompt active involvement and critical interpretation as they get readers to listen to the concerns of people of the past.

Material Culture

Texts are not our only sources for reconstructing the past; there is much to be discovered from material remains of many sorts. To give focus to this dimension of history, for each chapter we have selected one element of material culture to describe in some detail. These range from the most mundane—food, drink, clothing, houses, and means of transportation—to objects of art, including specific paintings, sculptures, or performing arts. Many of the objects discussed have economic significance, for example, fertilizers, periodic markets, and the Grand Canal. Others are examples of ingenuity, such as the Korean water clock. Most of the features for the late nineteenth or twentieth century bring out ways material culture has changed along with so much else in modern times—from changes in the food people eat, to streetcars and political posters.

THINKING LIKE A HISTORIAN

The "Documents" and "Material Culture" features challenge students to draw inferences from primary materials much the way historians do. Another way we have tried to help students learn to think like historians is to present history as a set of questions more than a set of answers. What historians are able to say about a period or topic depends not only on the sources available, but also the questions asked. To help students see this, we begin each chapter with a brief discussion of the sorts of questions that motivate contemporary historians to do research on the time period. Most of these questions have no easy answers—these are not questions students will be able to answer simply by reading the chapter. Rather they are real questions, ones interesting enough to motivate historians to sift through recalcitrant evidence in their efforts to find answers. The earliest chapter on Korea, for instance, poses the question of how the three states on the Korean peninsula were able to survive in the face of Chinese power. The chapter on early nineteenth century Japan points out that historians have studied the period for clues to the causes of the Meiji Restoration, wanting to know the relative weight to assign to foreign pressure and domestic unrest. For the chapter dealing with China under the Nationalists, readers are told that the desire to explain the Communist victory in 1949 has motivated historians to ponder such questions as why May Fourth Liberalism lost its appeal and whether the economic politics of the Nationalists could have brought prosperity to China if Japan had not invaded. We hope that posing these questions at the beginning of each chapter will help readers see the significance of the topics and issues presented in the chapter.

USING THIS TEXT IN CLASS

East Asian history is taught many ways, as a one-semester or one-year course, or as linked courses on China and Japan (and sometimes also Korea). To fit the needs of these different approaches, this text is available in three formats: comprehensive, divided by country, and divided chronologically. Since those who divide chronologically might prefer to break either at the end of Part Three (1600) or at the end of Part Four (1800), Part Four appears in both of the chronologically-divided volumes. Similarly, the separate volumes on China and Japan each include all of the Connections mini-chapters.

Those who wish to supplement this text with other readings will find many suggestions at the end of each chapter.

ACKNOWLEDGMENTS

Many people have contributed to the shaping of this book. The three authors have been teaching about the societies of East Asia for two or three decades, and the ways they approach their subjects owe much to questions from their students, conversations with their colleagues, and the outpouring of scholarship in their fields. As we worked on this text, we received much advice from others, from early suggestions of possible collaborators, to critiques of our original proposal and reviews of the drafts of our chapters. The reviewers' reports prompted us to rethink some generalizations, urged us not to weigh the book down with too much detail, and saved us from a number of embarrassing errors. We appreciate the time and attention the following reviewers gave to helping us produce a better book:

James Anderson, University of North Carolina at Greensboro; R. David Arkush, University of Iowa; Craig N. Canning, College of William and Mary; Sue Fawn Chung, University of Nevada, Las Vegas; Anthony DeBlasi, University of Albany; Ronald G. Dimberg, University of Virginia; Franklin M. Doeringer, Lawrence University; Alexis Dudden, Connecticut College; Karl Friday, University of Georgia; Karl Gerth, University of South Carolina; Andrew Goble, University of Oregon; John B. Henderson, Louisiana State University; Jeff Hornibrook, SUNY Plattsburgh; William Johnston, Wesleyan University; Fujiya Kawashima, Bowling Green State University; Ari Daniel Levine, University of Georgia; Huaiyin Li, University of Missouri-Columbia; Angelene Naw, Judson College; Steve Phillips, Towson University; Jonathan Porter, University of New Mexico; Wesley Sasaki-Uemura, University of Utah; S. A. Thornton, Arizona State University; Lu Yan, University of New Hampshire; Ka-che Yip, University of Maryland, Baltimore County; Theodore Jun Yoo, University of Hawaii at Manoa.

We also are grateful for all the work put into this book by the editorial staff at Houghton Mifflin: Nancy Blaine originally convinced us to take on this job; Julie Swasey went through all of our drafts, arranged the reviews, and made numerous suggestions; Linda Sykes secured the photos; Penny Peters handled the art; and Jane Lee managed the production details.

The division of work among the three authors was primarily by country of specialization, with Patricia Ebrey writing the parts on China, Anne Walthall those on Japan, and James Palais those on Korea. The Connections chapters we divided among ourselves chronologically, with Patricia Ebrey taking the early ones (on prehistory, Buddhism, Cultural Contact Across Eurasia, and the Mongols), Anne Walthall taking the early modern and modern ones (on Europe Enters the Scene, Western Imperialism, and World War II), and James Palais doing the final one on East Asia in the Twenty-First Century.

CONVENTIONS

Throughout this book names are given in East Asian order, with family name preceding personal name. Thus Mao Zedong was from the Mao family, Ashikaga Takauji from the Ashikaga family, and Yi Sŏnggye from the Yi family.

Both Japanese and Korean have phonetic scripts (Japanese a syllabary, Korean an alphabet), though Japanese additionally makes extensive use of Chinese characters. There are standard ways to transcribe these scripts into our alphabet (the Hepburn system for Japanese and the McCune-Reischauer for Korean with a few modifications, primarily placing priority on pronunciation rather than orthography). Chinese does not have a phonetic script, and more than one system of transcribing it has been commonly used. The romanization system used here is the pinyin system.

The basic vowels, *a*, *e*, *i*, *o*, and *u* in all three languages are pronounced as in Italian, German, and Spanish.

a as in f*a*ther

e as in *e*nd

i as the first *e* in *e*ve (in Chinese often like the *e* in sh*e*)

o as in *o*ld (shorter in length and with less of the *ou* sound of English)

u as in r*u*de (shorter in length than English)

Diacritical marks over vowels change the pronunciations:

ŏ in Korean is like the *o* in r*o*t, except shorter in length than English

ŭ in Korean is something like he *oo* in f*oo*t

The macron over the *ō* or *ū* in Japanese indicates that the vowel is "long," taking twice as long to say, as though it were doubled. Macrons have been omitted from common place names

well known without them, such as Tokyo and Kyoto.

ü in Chinese (used only after *l* or *n*) is like the German *ü*

The three languages are not so similar when one vowel follows another. In the case of Japanese, each vowel is pronounced as a separate syllable. In Chinese, they create a (one syllable) diphthong (e.g., *mei*, which is pronounced like may). In Korean, two vowels also form diphthongs, but with some special pronunciations; *ae* is like the *a* in *a*dd; *oe* like the *ö* of German; and *ŭi* like the *uee* in q*uee*r.

Consonants for Japanese romanization are close enough to English to give readers little difficulty. In the case of Korean, voiced consonants (*j*, *g*, *b*, *d*) are like English. However, aspirated consonants (*ch'*, *k'*, *p'*, *t'*) marked by a marked exhalation of air, and unaspirated consonants (*ch*, *k*, *p*, *t*) are like English but without any aspiration at all. In the Chinese case, divergence between how an English speaker would guess a pronunciation and how the word is actually pronounced is even greater. The most confusing consonants are listed below:

c   ts in tsar

z   dz in adze

zh   j in jack

q   ch in chin

x   sh

In the case of Chinese, the romanization system does not convey tones, which are also an important element in pronunciation. Another complication is that pinyin has only become the standard system of romanization in recent decades. Some earlier spellings were based on dialects other than Mandarin (Peking, Canton, Sun Yat-sen). More often the Wade-Giles system of romanization was employed. From context, if nothing else, most readers have inferred that Mao Zedong is the same person whose name used to be spelled Mao Tse-tung, or that Wang Anshi is the pinyin form of Wang An-shih. Two older spellings have been retained in this book because they are so widely known (Sun Yatsen and Chiang Kaishek). Charts for converting pinyin to Wade-Giles and vice versa are widely available on the Internet, should anyone want verification of their guesses (see, for instance, http://www.loc.gov/catdir/pinyin/romcover.html; http://www.library.ucla.edu/libraries/eastasian/ctable2.htm; or http://oclccjk.lib.uci.edu/wgtopy.htm).

Modern East Asia:
From 1600

PART FOUR

Growth and Stability (1600–1800)

Europe Enters the Scene

TRADE ROUTES FLOURISHED BETWEEN Northeast and Southeast Asia long before European merchants and Catholic missionaries entered the South China Sea. Lured by Asian silks, ceramics, and spices, ships under the Portuguese flag were the first to risk the voyage in the early sixteenth century. The Spanish, British, and Dutch followed. In early seventeenth-century Japan, early eighteenth-century China, and early nineteenth-century Korea, rulers put a stop to missionary activities, albeit for different reasons. Trade between Europe and East Asia continued, but it was confined to Guangzhou in China and Nagasaki in Japan.

Hemmed in by Spain, Portugal relied on trade to fill royal coffers. At the beginning of the fifteenth century, Portuguese ships started exploring the west coast of Africa in search of gold. African gold then financed a voyage around the Cape of Good Hope in 1488. From there, the Portuguese established a colony at Goa on the west coast of India and followed Muslim and Indian trade routes to the Spice Islands of Indonesia. Once Queen Isabella and her husband, Ferdinand, captured Grenada, the last Muslim emirate in Spain, in 1492, they funded Christopher Columbus's voyage across the Atlantic in hopes of finding an alternative route to China. In 1494, the pope divided the world beyond Europe between Spain and Portugal. Spain's sphere included most of the western hemisphere except Brazil; Portugal went east.

China's contact with Portugal began in 1511 when Admiral Alfonso de Albuquerque captured the Chinese entrepôt of Malacca near the tip of the Malay Peninsula. With this as a base, the first official Portuguese embassy followed traders to

China in 1517. It behaved badly by refusing to conform to Chinese customs. Ship captains acted more like pirates than traders. Few Portuguese were willing to risk the long voyage in tiny ships around the Horn of Africa, across the wide expanse of the Indian Ocean and through the Strait of Malacca to Macao. Most were neither officials dispatched from the Portuguese court nor explorers seeking glory and territory. What they had in limited resources and manpower had to go toward making a profit in an already thriving commercial milieu (see Map C5.1).

Periodic prohibitions on maritime travel by Ming emperors at Beijing did not stop the Portuguese or seafaring people on the south China coast who made little distinction between trade, smuggling, and piracy. In 1521 the Ming tried to ban the Portuguese from China. Two years later an expeditionary force commissioned by the Portuguese king and charged with negotiating a friendship treaty defeated its mission by firing on Chinese warships near Guangzhou. In 1557, without informing Beijing, local Chinese officials decided that the way to regulate trade was to allow the Portuguese to build a trading post on an uninhabited bit of land near the mouth of the Pearl River. This the Portuguese called Macao. It became the first destination for all Europeans going to China until the nineteenth century, and it remained a Portuguese settlement until 1999.

The only significant new products Portuguese traders brought to networks that had already developed in East Asia were firearms and New World crops such as corn, sweet potatoes, and tobacco. They reached Japan by accident in 1543 when a typhoon blew three ships with a mixed crew of Southeast Asians to a small island called Tanegashima. The islanders helped repair their ship and bought their cargo. Among the goods exchanged for Japanese silver was the harquebus, a clumsy ancestor of the musket. The island's ruler ordered his retainers to study its operation and manufacture and distributed samples to more powerful mainland warlords. In 1570, Japanese troops deployed the Tanegashima harquebus in battle. In the meantime, Portuguese traders profited from the Ming ban on Japanese ships because they had raided the coast. The Portuguese carried 20 metric tons of Japanese silver a year to China in exchange for silk, sugar, medicine, and dye.

Trade between China and Europe increased in the late sixteenth century through an economic conjuncture that included the Americas. China needed silver because its monetary system depended on it and domestic production had declined after 1430. Chinese merchants bought Japanese silver carried on Portuguese ships. China also absorbed 50 percent of silver mined in Mexico and Bolivia and carried in Spanish ships to Manila, founded in 1571 when Spain made the Philippines a colony. Disruptions in the flow of silver from Japan and the western hemisphere in 1639 contributed to the fall of the Ming. Spanish silver bought manufactured goods—Chinese silk, porcelain, and lacquer—that dominated the luxury trade in Europe and funded Spain's wars against multiple enemies for generations.

Portuguese merchants seeking profits in East Asia faced competition from their government when the Portuguese viceroy at Goa made the Japan trade a royal monopoly in 1550. The Ming approved because their officials also wanted to see trade regularized. Each year a captain major appointed by the crown sent ships to Japan where warlords competed to attract the ships to their ports. (See Color Plate 19.) The governor of Macao forbade the sending of goods to Japan on private ships via third countries, especially the Philippines. His directives were futile; Portuguese and Spanish traders with crews drawn from all over East and Southeast Asia found Manila too convenient to abandon.

Catholic missionaries seeking converts who followed the traders hoped to keep the religious wars that undermined the pope's spiritual hegemony secret from Asia. The first were Jesuits, from the order founded by Ignatius Loyola in 1534 to promote Catholic scholarship and combat the Protestant Reformation initiated by Martin Luther in 1517. Jesuits insisted that Christianizing China and Japan was not to be done with the intent to conquer, as had been the case in the western hemisphere. As individuals, they displayed a rare sensitivity to other cultures. They were willing to find universal principles of belief outside a European context, but they served an institution that refused to compromise with indigenous beliefs and practices. Despite the efforts of charismatic missionaries, the Catholic church never gained the ascendancy in East Asia enjoyed by that other foreign religion, Buddhism.

The Jesuit priest Francis Xavier had worked in India and the Indies before China and Japan attracted his attention. After many misadventures, he landed on Satsuma in 1549. The Satsuma lord hoped that by treating Xavier well, he would attract the official Portuguese trading ships the next year. When the ships went instead to the island of Hirado, the lord expelled Xavier's party. Xavier traveled throughout western Japan as far as Kyoto, proselytizing wherever warlords gave permission. Asked why the Chinese knew nothing of Christianity if it was indeed an ancient and true religion, Xavier decided that Japan would become Christian only if China led the way. His efforts to enter China ended when he died on an uninhabited island off the China coast in December 1552.

Jesuits and Dominicans soon joined the missionaries and converts Xavier left behind in Japan. In 1565 Louis Frois met Oda Nobunaga who befriended the Jesuits to discomfort his Buddhist enemies. In 1580 Jesuits acquired Nagasaki from a warlord interested in promoting trade with Portuguese ships. In 1582, four young Kyushu samurai left Nagasaki for Lisbon and Rome, where they helped Jesuits get a papal bull that put Japan off limits to other orders. It proved to be ineffective, and quarrels between the Catholic orders over how best to present Christianity to East Asia damaged the missionaries' credibility in the eyes of Asian rulers.

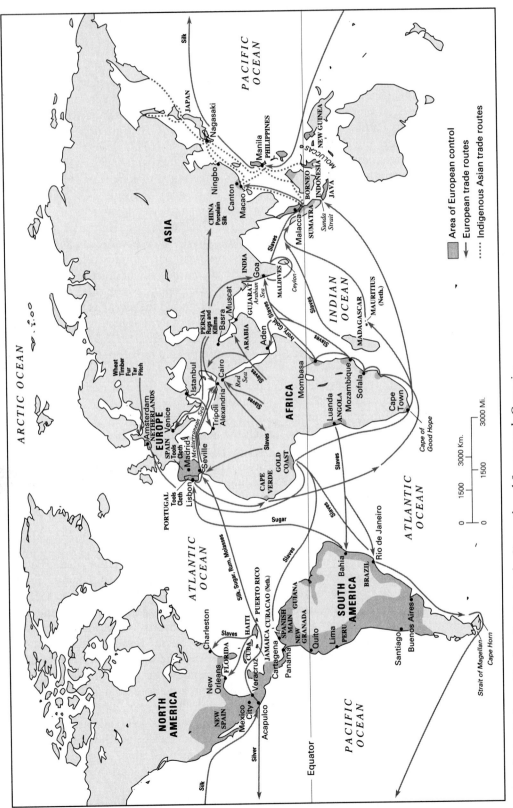

Map C5.1   Seaborne Trading Empires in the Sixteenth and Seventeenth Centuries

Warlords trying to unite Japan under secular authority became increasingly suspicious of Christianity. If an absolute god demanded absolute loyalty, where did that leave the bonds between lord and retainer? Repression began in 1587 and intensified nine years later when the pilot of a ship wrecked on the Japanese coast allegedly pointed out that soldiers had followed Spanish missionaries to the Philippines. In 1614 Tokugawa Ieyasu decided that missionaries undermined the social order and were not essential to foreign trade. He ordered them expelled under threat of execution. He also tortured and killed Christian converts who refused to apostatize. Among the martyrs were Koreans who had been brought to Japan as slaves during Toyotomi Hideyoshi's invasions in the 1590s. The shogunate broke off relations with Catholic countries in 1624. The remaining Christians practiced their religion in secret by crafting statues of the Virgin Mary in the guise of Kannon, the Buddhist goddess of mercy.

Christianity arrived later in China. Not until 1583 did the Jesuit Matteo Ricci receive permission to move farther inland than Macao. Once he had educated himself in the style of Chinese literati, he set himself up in Nanjing. In 1601 he received tacit imperial permission to reside in Beijing. From him the Chinese learned western-style geography, astronomy, and Euclidean mathematics. In the years after Ricci's death in 1611, Jesuits regulated the Chinese lunar calendar. They suffered occasional harassment from xenophobic officials, but they retained their standing with Chinese literati during the turmoil that led to the collapse of the Ming Dynasty and the founding of the Qing in 1644. Catholic mendicant orders allowed into China in 1633 criticized Jesuits for aiming their efforts at the ruling class and trying to fit Christian ideas into the Chinese world-view rather than remaining European in approach and appealing to the masses.

Ricci and his Jesuit successors believed that Confucianism as a philosophy could be assimilated to monotheism. Confucianists and Christians shared similar concerns for morality and virtue. Rites of filial piety performed for the ancestors did not constitute a form of worship,

Matteo Ricci. Matteo Ricci is shown here in a French lithograph holding a map of the world to which he offers the crucified Christ. *(The Granger Collection)*

which made them compatible with Christianity. Mendicant orders disagreed. In 1715, religious and political quarrels in Europe exacerbated by longstanding antagonism to the Jesuits resulted in Ricci's accommodation with Chinese practices being deemed heretical. Angry at this insult, the Kangxi emperor forbade all Christian missionary work in China, although he allowed Jesuits to remain in Beijing to assist with the calendar. A Jesuit portrait painter later proved popular at the courts of his son and grandson. The outcome of the rites controversy over whether converts should be allowed to maintain ancestral altars, exacerbated by accusations that missionaries had meddled in the imperial succession, led the Qing to view all Europeans with suspicion.

China's rulers also tried to limit trade for strategic reasons. Between 1655 and 1675 the Qing banned maritime trade and travel to isolate Ming loyalists on Taiwan. In addition to official trade at the state level, the Qing permitted merchants to trade with foreigners, but only under tight control. After 1759, all maritime trade, whether with Southeast Asia or Europe, was confined to Guangzhou. Merchants put up with burdensome restrictions because in exchange for silver, China provided luxury items and tea, a bulk ware, introduced to Europe in 1607.

The profits to be made in East and Southeast Asia lured traders from Protestant countries following the religious wars of the latter half of the sixteenth century. Determined not to allow their Catholic rivals to dominate the world, Protestant nations sent explorers across the oceans. Britain's defeat of the Spanish Armada in 1588 began Spain's long decline. Early in the seventeenth century, the Dutch started their assault on Portuguese trade and colonies, especially in what is now Indonesia. Both nations established East India Companies in 1600 whose ability to capitalize trade far exceeded that of the merchants of Spain and Portugal.

Like Qing emperors, seventeenth-century Japanese shoguns tried to regulate foreign trade by confining it to specific harbors. In contrast to the sixteenth century, they also tried to prevent the increasingly short supply of precious metals from leaving the country by practicing import substitution for silk and sugar. A Dutch ship carrying a mixed crew of men from Europe and the western hemisphere arrived in 1600. (Of five ships with a crew of 461 men, only one ship and twenty-five men survived to reach Japan.) The next ships that arrived in 1609 received permission to set up quarters on Hirado, as did the British, who arrived in 1613. Both the Dutch and British arrived as representatives of trading companies, not their governments. Disappointed with scant profits, the British soon shut down their quarters. Unhappy with what it deemed smuggling, in 1635 the shogunate issued a maritime ban that forbade all Japanese from sailing overseas and ordered those who had migrated to Southeast Asia to return home or face permanent exile. The thriving Japanese community at Hoi An in Vietnam disappeared. In a further attempt to control unregulated trade and piracy, the shogunate later banned the building of ocean-going ships. In 1641 it ordered the Dutch to move from Hirado to the artificial island called Dejima in Nagasaki bay originally constructed for the Portuguese. The annual visits by Dutch ships allowed an exchange of information, continued Japan's connections with Southeast Asia, and opened the door to western science and medicine.

Korea proved inhospitable to merchants and missionaries alike. In the early seventeenth century British and Dutch traders made several attempts to insert their goods into the Japanese trade route through the islands of Tsushima, but memories of piracy, fear of unregulated trade that smacked of smuggling, and suspicion of European intentions led the government to refuse entry to their goods. Korean scholars in residence at the Chinese court read the Jesuits' religious, scientific, and mathematical treatises and took them back to Korea, where they attracted a small following for Catholic Christianity. The converts soon became embroiled in the factional infighting that characterized politics in eighteenth century Korea. No European missionary or merchant tried to visit Korea until three French priests landed illegally in 1836–1837. The Korean court had them and their converts executed in 1839 for spreading the "evil teaching" that ran counter to the dictates of filial piety.

SUGGESTED READING

For Southeast Asian networks, see A. Reid, *Southeast Asia in the Age of Commerce: 1450–1680*, vols. 1 and 2 (1988, 1993). For a recent book that compares trade in Europe and Asia, see K. L. Pomeranz, *The Great Divergence: China, Europe, and the Making of the Modern World* (2000). For the Jesuits in China, see J. Spence, *The Memory Palace of Matteo Ricci* (1984). For Japan see M. J. Cooper, *They Came to Japan: An Anthology of European Reports on Japan, 1543–1640* (1965); G. Elison, *Deus Destroyed* (1974); and D. Massarella, *A World Elsewhere: Europe's Encounter with Japan in the Sixteenth and Seventeenth Centuries* (1990).

The Creation of the Manchu Empire (1600–1800)

The seventeenth and eighteenth centuries were the age of the Manchus. As the Ming Dynasty fell into disorder, the Jurchens put together an efficient state beyond Ming's northeastern border and adopted the name *Manchu* for themselves. After they were called in to help suppress peasant rebellions, the Manchus took the throne themselves, founding the Qing Dynasty (1644–1911). Many Chinese did all they could to resist the Manchus out of loyalty to the Ming, but by the eighteenth century, Chinese and Manchus had learned to accommodate each other. In many ways the eighteenth century was the high point of traditional Chinese civilization. The Manchus created a multiethnic empire, adding Taiwan, Mongolia, Tibet, and Xinjiang to their realm, making the Qing Empire comparable to the other multinational empires of the early modern world, such as the Ottoman, Russian, and Habsburg Empires.

Many historians have been attracted to research on the seventeenth and eighteenth centuries because it provides a baseline of traditional China before the rapid changes of the modern era. Besides the usual questions of why the Ming fell and the Qing succeeded, scholars have recently been asking questions about the Manchus themselves. Who were they, and how did their history shape how they ruled China? How did they compel the allegiance of peoples of different backgrounds? How did they manage to give traditional Chinese political forms a new lease on life? Other historians have focused more on what was going on among the Chinese during these two crucial centuries. Was population growth a sign of prosperity? Or was it beginning to cause problems? How did scholars respond to Manchu rule?

THE MING DYNASTY LAPSES INTO DISORDER

After 1600 the Ming government was beset by fiscal, military, and political problems. The government was nearly bankrupt. It had spent heavily to help defend Korea against a Japanese invasion (see Chapters 13 and 15), had to support an ever-increasing imperial clan, and now had to provide relief for a series of natural disasters.

The bureaucracy did not pull together to meet these challenges. Officials diagnosed the problems confronting the dynasty in moral terms and saw removing the immoral from power as the solution, which led to fierce factionalism. Accusations and counteraccusations crossed so often that emperors wearied of officials and their infighting. Frustrated former officials who gathered at the Donglin Academy in Jiangsu province called for a revival of orthodox Confucian ethics. They blamed Wang Yangming for urging people to follow their innate knowledge, which seemed to the critics as equivalent to urging them to pursue their personal advantage.

At this time a "little ice age" brought a drop in average temperatures that shortened the growing season and reduced harvests. When food shortages became critical in northern Shaanxi in 1627–1628, army deserters and laid-off soldiers began forming gangs and scouring the countryside in search of food. By 1632 they had moved east and south into the central regions of Shanxi, Hebei, Henan, and Anhui provinces. Once the gangs had stolen all their grain, hard-pressed farmers joined them just to survive. Li Zicheng, a former shepherd and postal relay worker, became the paramount rebel leader in the north. The ex-soldier Zhang Xianzhong became the main leader in the central region between the Yellow and Yangzi rivers. The Ming government had little choice but to try to increase taxes to deal with these threats, but the last thing people needed was heavier exactions. Floods, droughts, locusts, and epidemics ravaged one region after another. In the Jiangnan area tenants rose up against landlords, and urban workers rioted. Meanwhile, the two main rebel leaders were in a race to see which of them could topple the Ming and found a new dynasty.

Part of the reason people rioted over rents was that real rents had risen due to deflation, itself brought on by a sudden drop in the supply of silver. In 1639 the Japanese authorities refused to let traders from Macao into Nagasaki, disrupting trade that had brought large quantities of silver to China. Another major source of silver was cut off a few months later when Chinese trade with the Spanish in the Philippines came to a standstill after a slaughter of Chinese residents. For China the drop in silver imports led to hoarding of both silver and grain, creating artificial shortages.

In 1642 a group of rebels cut the dikes on the Yellow River, leading to massive flooding. A smallpox epidemic soon added to the death toll. In 1644 Li Zicheng moved through Hebei into Beijing, where the last Ming emperor, in despair, took his own life. Zhang Xianzhong had moved in the opposite direction, into Sichuan, where his attacks on Chongqing and Chengdu led to widespread slaughter. Both Li and Zhang announced that they had founded new dynasties, and they appointed officials and minted coins. Neither, however, succeeded in pacifying a sizable region or ending looting and violence.

THE MANCHUS

The Manchus were descended from the Jurchens who had ruled north China during the Jin Dynasty (1127–1234). Although they had not maintained the written language that the Jin had created, they had maintained their hairstyle. Manchu men shaved the front of their head and wore the rest of their hair in a long braid (called a queue). The language they spoke belongs to the Tungus family, making it close to some of the languages spoken in nearby Siberia and distantly related to Korean and Japanese.

During the Ming Dynasty the Manchus had lived in dispersed communities in what is

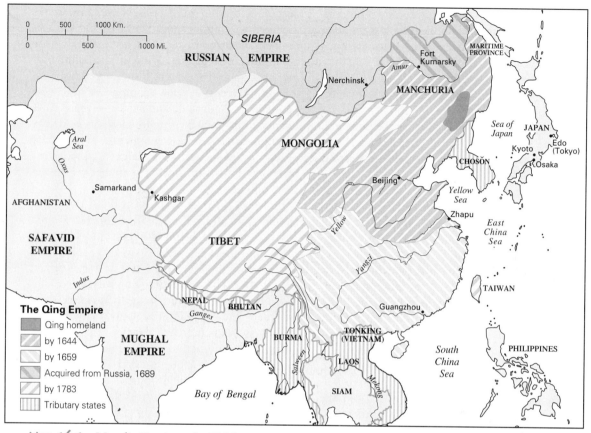

Map 16.1 **Manchu Empire at Its Height**

loosely called Manchuria (the modern provinces of Liaoning, Jilin, and Heilongjiang). In the more densely populated southern part of Manchuria, Manchus lived in close contact with Mongols, Koreans, and Chinese, the latter especially in the Ming prefecture of Liaodong (see Map 16.1). The Manchus were not nomads, but rather hunters, fishermen, and farmers. Like the Mongols, they had a tribal social structure and were excellent horsemen and archers. Also like the Mongols, their society was strongly hierarchical, with elites and slaves. Slaves, often Korean or Chinese, were generally acquired through capture. From the Mongols, the Manchus had adopted Lamaist Buddhism, originally from Tibet, and it coexisted with their native shamanistic religion. Manchu shamans were men or women who had experienced a

spiritual death and rebirth and as a consequence could travel to and influence the world of the spirits.

Both the Chosŏn Dynasty in Korea and the Ming Dynasty in China welcomed diplomatic missions from Manchu chieftains, seeing them as a counterbalance to the Mongols. Written communication was frequently in Mongolian, the lingua franca of the region. Along the border with the Ming were officially approved markets where Manchus brought horses, furs, honey, and ginseng to exchange for Chinese tea, cotton, silk, rice, salt, and tools. By the 1580s there were five such markets that convened monthly, and unofficial trade occurred as well.

The Manchus credited their own rise to Nurhaci (1559–1626), who in 1583 at age twenty-four became the leader of one group of

Manchus. Over the next few decades, he was able to expand his territories, in the process not only uniting the Manchus but also creating a social-political-military organization that brought together Manchus, Mongols, and Chinese. When the Korean Sin Chung-il traveled to Nurhaci's headquarters in 1595–1596, he encountered many small Jurchen settlements, most no larger than twenty households, supported by fishing, hunting for pelts, collecting pine nuts or ginseng, or growing crops such as wheat, millet, and barley. Villages were often at odds with each other over resources, and men did not leave their villages without arming themselves with bows and arrows or swords. Interspersed among these Manchu settlements were groups of nomadic Mongols who lived in yurts in the open areas. Sin observed that Nurhaci had in his employ men from the Ming territory of Liaodong who could speak both Chinese and Manchu and could write in Chinese. Nurhaci's knowledge of China and Chinese ways was not entirely second-hand, however. In 1590 he had led an embassy to Beijing, and the next year he offered to join the Ming effort to repel the Japanese invasion of Korea. Nurhaci and his children married Mongols as well as Manchus, these marriages cementing alliances.

> ### Early Manchu Rulers and Their Reigns
>
> | | |
> |---|---|
> | Nurhaci (Tianming) | 1616–1626 |
> | Hong Taiji (Tiancong) | 1627–1635 |
> | (Chongde) | 1636–1643 |
> | Fulin (Shunzhi) | 1644–1661 |
> | Xuanye (Kangxi) | 1662–1722 |
> | Yinzhen (Yongzheng) | 1723–1735 |
> | Hongli (Qianlong) | 1736–1795 |

Like Chinggis, who had reorganized his armies to reduce the importance of tribal affiliations, Nurhaci created a new social basis for his armies in units called *banners*. Each banner was made up of a set of military companies, but included the families and slaves of the soldiers as well. Each company had a captain, whose position was hereditary. Many of the commanding officers were drawn from Nurhaci's own lineage. Over time new companies and new banners were formed, and by 1644 there were twenty-four banners (eight each of Manchu, Mongol, and Chinese banners). When new groups of Manchus were defeated, they were distributed among several banners to lessen their potential for subversion.

In 1616 Nurhaci declared war on the Ming Empire by calling himself khan of the revived Jin Dynasty and listing his grievances against the Ming. In 1621 his forces overran Liaodong and incorporated it into his state. After Nurhaci died in 1626, his son Hong Taiji succeeded him. In consolidating the Jin state, then centered on Mukden, Hong Taiji grudgingly made use of Chinese bureaucrats, but his goal was to replace them with a multiethnic elite equally competent in warfare and documents. In 1636 Hong Taiji renamed his state Qing ("pure"). When he died in 1643 at age forty-six, his brother Dorgon was made regent for his five-year-old son, Fulin, the Shunzhi emperor (r. 1643–1661).

The distinguished Ming general Wu Sangui (1612–1678), a native of Liaodong, was near the eastern end of the Great Wall when he heard that the rebel Li Zicheng had captured Beijing. Dorgon proposed to Wu that they join forces and liberate Beijing. Wu opened the gates of the Great Wall to let the Manchus in, and within a couple of weeks they had occupied Beijing. When the Manchus made clear that they intended to conquer the rest of the country and take the throne themselves, Wu joined forces with them, as did many other Chinese generals.

MING LOYALISM

When word reached the Yangzi valley of the fall of Beijing to the Manchus, Ming officials selected a Ming prince to succeed to the throne and shifted the capital to Nanjing, the Ming secondary capital. They were thus following the strategy that had allowed the Song Dynasty to continue to flourish after it had lost the north in 1126. The Ming court offered to buy off the Manchus, as the Song had bought off the Jurchens. Dorgon, however, saw no need to check his ambitions. He sent Wu Sangui and several Manchu generals to pursue the rebel forces across north China. Li Zicheng was eliminated in 1645, Zhang Xianzhong in 1647.

At the same time, Qing forces set about trying to defeat the Ming forces in the south. Quite a few able officials joined the Ming cause, but leadership was not well coordinated. Shi Kefa, a scholar-official who had risen to minister of war in Nanjing, took charge of defense and stationed his army at Yangzhou. Many other generals, however, defected to the Manchu side, and their soldiers were incorporated into the Qing armies. As the Qing forces moved south, many local officials opened the gates of their cities and surrendered. Shi Kefa refused to surrender Yangzhou, and a five-day battle ensued. The Manchu general was so angered at Shi's resistance that he unleashed his army to take revenge on the city, slaughtering hundreds of thousands. As cities in the south fell, large numbers of Ming loyalists committed suicide, their wives, mothers, and daughters frequently joining them.

In the summer of 1645, the Manchu command ordered that all Chinese serving in its armies shave the front of their heads in the Manchu fashion, presumably to make it easier to recognize whose side they were on. Soon this order was extended to all Chinese men, a measure that aroused deep resentment and made it easier for the Ming loyalists to organize resistance. When those newly conquered by the Qing refused to shave their hair, Manchu commanders felt justified in ordering the slaughter of defiant cities such as Jiading, Changshu, and Jiangyin. Still, Ming loyalist resistance continued long after little hope remained. The Manchus did not defeat the two main camps until 1661–1662, and even then Zheng Chenggong (Koxinga) was able to hold out in Taiwan until 1683.

Ming loyalism also took less militant forms (see **Biography: Printer Yu Xiangdou and His Family**). Several leading thinkers of this period had time to think and write because they refused to serve the Qing. Their critiques of the Ming and its failings led to searching inquiries into China's heritage of dynastic rule. Huang Zongxi (1610–1695) served the Ming resistance court at Nanjing, and followed it when it had to retreat, but after 1649 he lived in retirement at his home in Zhejiang province. The Manchu conquest was so traumatic an event that he reconsidered many of the basic tenets of Chinese political order. He came to the conclusion that the Ming's problems were not minor ones like inadequate supervision of eunuchs, but much more major ones, such as the imperial institution itself. Gu Yanwu (1613–1682) participated in the defense of his native city, then watched his mother starve herself rather than live under Manchu rule. He traveled across north China in search of a better understanding of Ming weaknesses, looking into economic topics Confucian scholars had rarely studied in depth, such as banking, mining, and farming. He had only disdain for scholars who wasted their time on empty speculation or literary elegance when there were so many practical problems awaiting solution. He thought that the Ming had suffered from overcentralization and advocated greater local autonomy. Wang Fuzhi (1619–1692) had passed the provincial exams under the Ming, but marauding rebels made it impossible for him to get to Beijing to take the *jinshi* exams in 1642. After Beijing fell to the Manchus two years later, Wang joined the resistance. He raised troops in his native Hunan province and for a while held a minor post at the court of the Ming pretender, but fell victim to factional strife and in 1650 withdrew to live as a retired scholar. Wang saw an urgent need not only to return Confucianism to its roots, but to protect Chinese civilization from the "barbarians." He insisted that it was as important to distinguish Chinese from barbarians as it was to distinguish superior men from petty men. It is natural for rulers to protect their followers from intruders:

BIOGRAPHY   Printer Yu Xiangdou and His Family

The Qing conquest impinged on the lives of people of all walks of life, though in different ways. The printers in Jianyang in western Fujian province supported the Ming loyalist cause and published books with Ming dates well after 1644, which not surprisingly turned the Qing authorities against them, leading to the decline of their industry.

The Yu family of Jianyang in western Fujian began publishing books in the Song Dynasty, and the town where they lived eventually came to be called "Book Market." By late Ming there were several related Yus who operated publishing companies. One of the most successful of them was Yu Xiangdou. His grandfather had established a family school, and there had been hopes that Xiangdou would become an official, but by 1591 he gave up trying to pass the civil service examinations and concentrated on making money in the book business.

Yu did not merely solicit manuscripts and hire carvers for the wood blocks; he also wrote, annotated, and edited books himself. He compiled two collections of Daoist stories and another three of court-case fiction. He published versions of major novels, sometimes abridged, sometimes with commentaries. Sometimes he claimed that he had written or compiled a work that now we can see he merely copied, as there was nothing like copyright protection in his day.

Yu did not hide his presence in his books. At least three times, he included a portrait of himself in the book. In these portraits, he presents himself much as scholars were presented in the illustrated fiction he published: writing at a desk with servants in attendance or standing in a pavilion looking at the reflection of the moon on the water.

For twenty or more of his books, Yu wrote the preface himself. In a 1628 book on geomancy, which he published jointly with his son and nephew, he included a diagram of the burial sites of his parents and earlier ancestors. He also claimed that one of his ancestors, after recognizing the geomantic advantages of the place, encouraged his family to take up printing.

Yu published all sorts of books he thought would sell well. As aids to examination candidates, he published simplified histories and collections of selected literary pieces. Other reference works were explicitly addressed to the "four classes of people" and included information on farming, weaving, strange countries, medicine, music, chess, and the like, all with illustrations. Yu also published morality books by Yuan Huang, a well-known advocate of the Three Teachings (Confucianism, Buddhism, and Daoism). Yu was particularly active in publishing illustrated fiction, especially historical novels. The format he popularized had the illustrations run across the top of the page, with captions beside it, and the text below, allowing one to glance at the picture while reading the story. One of his historical novels proved so popular that the wood blocks wore out after several reprintings and he had to have them totally recarved.

Although Yu Xiangdou's son and grandson followed him in the book trade, Qing government efforts to eliminate Ming loyalism hurt their business and Jianyang rapidly declined as a book center.

"Now even the ants have rulers who preside over the territory of their nests, and when red ants or flying white ants penetrate their gates, the ruler organizes all his own kind into troops to bite and kill the intruders, drive them far away from the anthill, and prevent foreign interference."[1] The Ming rulers had failed in this basic responsibility.

THE QING AT ITS HEIGHT

For more than a century, China was ruled by just three rulers, each of whom was hard working, talented, and committed to making the Qing Dynasty a success. The policies and institutions they put into place gave China a respite from war and disorder, and the Chinese population seems to have nearly doubled during this period, from between 150 and 175 million to between 300 and 325 million. Population growth during the course of the eighteenth century has been attributed to many factors: global warming that extended the growing season; expanded use of New World crops; slowing of the spread of new diseases that had accompanied the sixteenth-century expansion of global traffic; and the efficiency of the Qing government in providing relief in times of famine. Some scholars have recently argued that China's overall standard of living in the mid-eighteenth century was comparable to Europe's and that the standards of China's most developed regions, such as the Jiangnan region, compared favorably to the most developed regions of Europe at the time, such as England and the Netherlands. Life expectancy, food consumption, and even facilities for transportation were at similar levels. The government in this period had the resources to respond to famines and disasters; indeed, during the eighteenth century, the treasury was so full that four times the annual land tax was cancelled.

Kangxi

After the Shunzhi emperor died of smallpox (which struck many Manchus after they settled in Beijing), one of his sons who had already survived the disease was selected to succeed. Known as the Kangxi emperor (r. 1661–1722), he lived to see the Qing Empire firmly established.

The Kangxi emperor proved adept at meeting the expectations of both the Chinese and Manchu elites. At age fourteen, he announced that he would begin ruling on his own and had his regent imprisoned. He could speak, read, and write Chinese and appreciated the value of persuading educated Chinese that the Manchus had a legitimate claim to the Mandate of Heaven. Most of the political institutions of the Ming Dynasty had been taken over relatively unchanged, including the examination system, and the Kangxi emperor worked to attract Ming loyalists who had been unwilling to serve the Qing. He undertook a series of tours of the south, where resistance had been strongest, and held a special exam to select men to compile the official history of the Ming Dynasty.

The main military challenge the Kangxi emperor faced was the revolt of Wu Sangui and two other Chinese generals who in the early years of the conquest had been given vast tracts of land in the south as rewards for joining the Qing. Wu was made, in effect, satrap of Yunnan and Guizhou, and it was his armies that had pursued the last Ming pretender into Burma. When the Qing began to curb the power of these generals in 1673, Wu declared himself the ruler of an independent state, and the other two "feudatories" joined him. Although the south was not yet fully reconciled to Qing rule, Wu, as a turncoat himself, did not attract a large following. Although it took eight years, the military structure that the Qing had put together proved strong enough to defeat this challenge. At the conclusion of these campaigns, Taiwan, where the last of the Ming loyalists had held out, was made part of Fujian province, fully incorporating it into China proper.

By annexing Mongolia, the Kangxi emperor made sure the Qing Dynasty would not have the northern border problems the Ming had had (see Map 16.1). In 1696 he led an army of eighty thousand men into Mongolia, and within a few years Manchu supremacy was accepted

---

1. W. Theodore de Bary and Richard Lufrano, *Sources of Chinese Tradition: From 1600 Through the Twentieth Century* (New York: Columbia University Press, 2000), p. 35.

there. Qing forces were equipped with cannons and muskets, giving them military superiority over the Mongols, who were armed only with bows and arrows. They thus could dominate the steppe cheaply, effectively ending two thousand years of northern border defense problems.

The Qing also asserted its presence in Tibet. This came about after a group of Western Mongols tried to find a new place for themselves in Tibet. The army the Qing sent after them occupied Lhasa in 1718. In the 1720s, the Qing presence in Tibet was made firm with the establishment of a permanent garrison of banner soldiers. By this time, the Qing Empire was coming into proximity of the expanding Russian Empire. In 1689 the Manchu and the Russian rulers approved a treaty—written in Russian, Manchu, Chinese, and Latin—defining their borders in Manchuria and regulating trade. Another treaty in 1727 allowed a Russian ecclesiastical mission to reside in Beijing and a caravan to make a trip from Russia to Beijing once every three years.

The Kangxi emperor took a personal interest in the European Jesuit priests who served at court as astronomers and cartographers and translated many European works into Chinese. However, when the pope sided with the Dominican and Franciscan orders in China who opposed allowing converts to maintain ancestral altars (known as the "rites controversy"), he objected strongly to the pope's issuing directives about how Chinese should behave. He outlawed Christian missionaries, though he did allow Jesuit scientists and painters to remain in Beijing.

Qianlong

The Kangxi emperor's heir, Yinzheng, who ruled as the Yongzheng emperor (r. 1723–1735), was forty-five years old when he took the throne. A hard-working ruler, he tightened central control over the government. He oversaw a rationalization of the tax structure, substituting new levies for a patchwork of taxes and fees. The Yongzheng emperor's heir, Hongli, the Qianlong emperor (r. 1736–1795), benefited from his father's fiscal reforms, and during his reign, the Qing government regularly ran surpluses.

It was during the Qianlong reign that the Qing Empire was expanded to its maximum extent, with the addition of Chinese Turkestan (the modern province of Xinjiang). Both the Han and Tang Dynasties had stationed troops in the region, exercising a loose suzerainty, but neither Song nor Ming had tried to control the area. The Qing won the region in the 1750s through a series of campaigns against Uighur and Dzungar Mongol forces. Like Tibet, loosely annexed a few decades earlier, this region was ruled lightly. The local population kept their own religious leaders and did not have to wear the queue.

The Qianlong emperor put much of his energy into impressing his subjects with his magnificence. He understood that the Qing capacity to hold their empire together rested on their ability to speak in the political and religious idioms of those they ruled. Besides Manchu and Chinese, he learned to converse in Mongolian, Uighur, Tibetan, and Tangut and addressed envoys in their own languages. He was as much a patron of Lamaist Buddhism as of Chinese Confucianism. He initiated a massive project to translate the Tibetan Buddhist canon into Mongolian and Manchu. He also had huge multilingual dictionaries compiled. He had the child Dalai Lamas raised and educated in Beijing. He made much of the Buddhist notion of the "wheel-turning king" (cakravartin), the ruler who through his conquests moves the world toward the next stage in universal salvation (see Color Plate 20).

To demonstrate to the Chinese scholar-official elite that he was a sage emperor, Qianlong worked on affairs of state from dawn until early afternoon, when he turned to reading, painting, and calligraphy. He took credit for writing over forty-two thousand poems and ninety-two books of prose. He inscribed his own poetry on hundreds of masterpieces of Chinese painting and calligraphy that he had gathered into the palace collections. He especially liked works of fine craftsmanship, and his taste influenced artistic styles of the day. The Qianlong emperor was ostentatiously devoted to his mother, visiting her daily and tending to her comfort with all the devotion of the most filial Chinese son. He took several tours down the Grand Canal to the Jiangnan area, in part to emulate his grandfather, in part to entertain his mother. Many of his gestures were costly. His southern tours cost ten times what the Kangxi emperor's had and included the construction of temporary palaces and triumphal arches.

For all of these displays of Chinese virtues, the Qianlong emperor still was not fully confident that the Chinese supported his rule, and he was quick to act on any suspicion of anti-Manchu thoughts or actions (see **Documents: Fang Bao's "Random Notes from Prison"**). When he first took the throne, he reversed the verdict on the case of a Chinese named Zeng Jing who had been persuaded by an anti-Manchu tract to try to start an uprising. His father, the Yongzheng emperor, had treated Zeng leniently, preferring to persuade him of Manchu legitimacy than to punish him. The Qianlong emperor had him dragged back to Beijing, retried, and executed. More than thirty years later, when rumors reached the Qianlong emperor that sorcerers were "stealing souls" by clipping the ends of men's queues, he suspected a seditious plot and had his officials interrogate men under torture until they found more and more evidence of a nonexistent plot. A few years after that episode, the Qianlong emperor carried out a huge literary inquisition. During the compilation of the *Complete Books of the Four Treasuries,* an effort to catalogue nearly all books in China, he began to suspect that some governors were holding back books with seditious content. He ordered full searches for books with disparaging references to the Manchus or previous alien conquerors. Sometimes passages were omitted or rewritten, but when the entire book was offensive, it was destroyed. So thorough was the proscription that no copies survive of more than two thousand titles.

The Qianlong emperor lived into his eighties, but his political judgment began to decline in his sixties when he began to favor a handsome and intelligent young imperial bodyguard named Heshen. Heshen was rapidly promoted to posts normally held by experienced civil officials, including ones with power over revenue and civil service appointments. When the emperor did nothing to stop Heshen's blatant corruption, officials began to worry that he was becoming senile. By this time, uprisings were breaking out, especially in the southwest, where the indigenous Miao were being pushed out of the river valleys by Han Chinese migrants. Heshen supplied the Qianlong emperor with rosy reports of the progress in suppressing the rebellions, all the while pocketing much of the military appropriations himself.

The Qianlong emperor abdicated in 1795 in order not to rule longer than his grandfather, the Kangxi emperor, but he continued to dominate court until he died in 1799 at age eighty-nine.

The Banner System

The Kangxi, Yongzheng, and Qianlong emperors used the banner system to maintain military control and preserve the Manchus' privileges. In the first few decades of the Qing, as the country was pacified, banner forces were settled across China in garrisons, usually within the walls of a city. All of the Chinese who lived in the northern half of Beijing were forced out to clear the area for bannermen, and Beijing became very much a Manchu city. In other major cities, such as Hangzhou, Nanjing, Xi'an, and Taiyuan, large sections of the cities were cleared for the banners' use. The bannermen became in a sense a hereditary occupational caste, ranked above others in society, whose members were expected to devote themselves to service to the state. They were also expected to live apart from nonbanner Chinese and were not allowed to intermarry with them.

Outside the cities, lands were expropriated to provide support for the garrisons, some 2 million acres altogether, with the densest area in the region around Beijing. In China proper bannermen did not cultivate the fields (as they had in Manchuria), but rather lived off stipends from

DOCUMENTS

Fang Bao's "Random Notes from Prison"

As more and more varied types of sources survive, it becomes possible to get better glimpses of the less pleasant sides of life. The ordeal of judicial confinement was hardly new to the eighteenth century, but it was not until then that we have so vivid a depiction of it as that provided by Fang Bao (1668–1749). In 1711 he and his family members were arrested because he had written a preface for the collected works of one of his friends whose works had just been condemned for language implying support for revival of the Ming Dynasty. After Fang spent two years in prison, he was pardoned and went on to hold a series of literary posts. Despite this brush with imperial censorship, Fang was willing in his account of his time in prison to point to the inhumane way people not yet found guilty of a crime were treated and the corruption of prison personnel, who demanded cash in exchange for better treatment.

In the prison there were four old cells. Each cell had five rooms. The jail guards lived in the center with a window in the front of their quarters for light. At the end of this room there was another opening for ventilation. There were no such windows for the other four rooms and yet more than two hundred prisoners were always confined there. Each day toward dusk, the cells were locked and the odor of the urine and excrement would mingle with that of the food and drink. Moreover, in the coldest months of the winter, the poor prisoners had to sleep on the ground and when the spring breezes came everyone got sick. The established rule in the prison was that the door would be unlocked only at dawn. During the night, the living and the dead slept side by side with no room to turn their bodies and this is why so many people became infected. Even more terrible was that robbers, veteran criminals and murderers who were imprisoned for serious offenses had strong constitutions and only one or two out of ten would be infected and even so they would recover immediately. Those who died from the malady were all light offenders or sequestered witnesses who would not normally be subjected to legal penalties.

I said: "In the capital there are the metropolitan prefectural prison and the censorial prisons of the five wards. How is it then that the Board of Punishment's prison has so the rents, paid part in silver and part in grain. The dynasty supported banner soldiers and their families from cradle to grave, with special allocations for travel, weddings, and funerals. Once the conquest was complete, the banner population grew faster than the need for soldiers, so within a couple of generations, there were not enough positions in the banner armies for all adult males in the banners. Yet bannermen were not allowed to pursue occupations other than soldier or official. As a consequence, many led lives of forced idleness, surviving on stipends paid to a relative. By the time of the Qianlong emperor, this had become enough of a problem that he had most of the Chinese bannermen removed from the banner system and reclassified as commoners, increasing the Manchu dominance of the banner population.

Bannermen had facilitated entry into government service. Special quotas for Manchus allowed

many prisoners?" [My fellow prisoner, the magistrate] Mr. Du answered: ". . . The chiefs and deputy heads of the Fourteen Bureaus like to get new prisoners; the clerks, prison officials, and guards all benefit from having so many prisoners. If there is the slightest pretext or connection they use every method to trap new prisoners. Once someone is put into the prison his guilt or innocence does not matter. The prisoner's hands and feet are shackled and he is put in one of the old cells until he can bear the suffering no more. Then he is led to obtain bail and permitted to live outside the jail. His family's property is assessed to decide the payment and the officials and clerks all split it. Middling households and those just above exhaust their wealth to get bail. Those families somewhat less wealthy seek to have the shackles removed and to obtain lodging [for the prisoner relative] in the custody sheds outside the jail. This also costs tens of silver taels. As for the poorest prisoners or those with no one to rely on, their shackles are not loosened at all and they are used as examples to warn others. Sometimes cellmates guilty of serious crimes are bailed out but those guilty of small crimes and the innocent suffer the most poisonous abuse. They store up their anger and indignation, fail to eat or sleep normally, are not treated with medicine, and when they get sick they often die.

"I have humbly witnessed our Emperor's virtuous love for all beings which is as great as that of the sages of the past ages. Whenever he examines the documents related to a case, he tries to find life for those who should die. But now it has come to this [state of affairs] for the innocent. A virtuous gentleman might save many lives if he were to speak to the Emperor saying: 'Leaving aside those prisoners sentenced to death or exiled to border regions for great crimes, should not small offenders and those involved in a case but not convicted be placed in a separate place without chaining their hands and feet?'" . . .

My cellmate Old Zhu, Young Yu, and a certain government official named Seng who all died of illness in prison should not have been heavily punished. There was also a certain person who accused his own son of unfiliality. The [father's] neighbors [involved in the case only as witnesses] were all chained and imprisoned in the old cells. They cried all night long. I was moved by this and so I made inquiries. Everyone corroborated this account and so I am writing this document.

———
Source: From Pei-kai Cheng, Michael Lestz, and Jonathon D. Spence, *The Search for Modern China: A Documentary Collection* (New York: Norton, 1999), pp. 55–58, slightly modified.

them to gain more than 5 percent of the *jinshi* degrees, even though they never exceeded 1 percent of the population. Advancement was also easier for bannermen, since many posts, especially in Beijing, were reserved for them, including half of all the top posts. In the middle and lower ranks of the Beijing bureaucracy, Manchus greatly outnumbered Chinese. One study suggests that about 70 percent of the metropolitan agencies' positions were reserved for bannermen and less then 20 per-

cent for Chinese (the rest were unspecified). In the provinces, Manchus did not dominate in the same way, except at the top level of governors and governors-general, where they held about half the posts.

Bannermen had legal privileges as well. They fell under the jurisdiction of imperial commissioners, not the local magistrate or prefect. If both a Chinese and a Manchu were brought into court to testify, the Chinese was required

Imperial Bodyguard Zhanyinbao. Dated 1760, this life-size portrait was done by a court artist in the European-influenced style favored by the Qianlong emperor. *(The Metropolitan Museum of Art, The Dillon Fund, 1986 [1986.206])*

emperor also tried resettling Manchus back in Manchuria, but those used to urban life in China rarely were willing to return to farming, and most sneaked back as soon as possible.

Within a generation of settling in China proper, the Chinese dialect of the Beijing area became the common language of the banner population. The Qing emperors repeatedly called on the Manchus to study both spoken and written Manchu, but it became a second language learned at school rather than a primary language. Other features of Manchu culture were more easily preserved, such as the use of personal names alone to refer to people. (Manchus had names for families and clans but did not use them as part of their personal names.)

The elements of Manchu culture most important to the state were their martial traditions and their skill as horsemen and archers. Life in the cities and long stretches of peace took a toll on these skills, despite the best efforts of the emperors to inspire martial spirit. The Qianlong emperor himself was fully literate in Chinese, but he discouraged the Manchu bannermen from developing interests in Chinese culture. He knew the history of the Jin Dynasty and the problems the Jurchens had faced with soldiers living in China taking up Chinese ways, and he did everything he could think of to prevent this. Although the Qing court was as sumptuous as any other in Chinese history, the emperor tried to convince the bannermen that frugality was a Manchu characteristic, to be maintained if they were not to lose their ethnic identity.

Perhaps because they were favored in so many ways, the bannermen proved a very loyal service elite. Unlike their counterparts in other large empires, the banner armies never turned on the ruling house or used the resources that had been assigned to them to challenge central authority.

to kneel before the magistrate but the Manchu could stand. If each was found guilty of the same crime, the Manchu would receive a lighter punishment—for instance, wearing the cangue (a large wooden collar) for sixty days instead of exile for life.

Despite the many privileges given to Manchu bannermen, impoverishment of the banner population quickly became a problem. Although the government from time to time forgave all bannermen's debts, many went bankrupt. Company commanders sometimes sold off banner land to provide stipends, which made it more difficult to provide support thereafter. The Qianlong

CONTACTS WITH EUROPE

The Qing regulated its relations with countries beyond its borders through a diplomatic system modeled on the Ming one. Countries like Korea, Ryukyu, Japan, Vietnam, and many of the other states of Southeast Asia sent envoys to the court at Beijing. Europeans were not full players in this system, but they had a marginal presence.

Trading contacts with Europe were concentrated at Guangzhou in the far south (see **Connections: Europe Enters the Scene**). Soon after 1600, the Dutch East India Company had largely dislodged the Spanish and Portuguese from the trade with China, Japan, and the East Indies. Before long, the British East India Company began to compete with the Dutch for the spice trade. In the seventeenth century the British and Dutch sought primarily porcelains and silk, but in the eighteenth century, tea became the commodity in most demand. By the end of the century, tea made up 80 percent of Chinese exports to Europe.

In the early eighteenth century, China enjoyed a positive reputation among the educated in Europe. China was the source of prized luxuries: tea, silk, porcelain, cloisonné, wallpaper, and folding fans. The Manchu emperors were seen as wise and benevolent rulers. Voltaire wrote of the rationalism of Confucianism and saw advantages to the Chinese political system as rulers did not put up with parasitical aristocrats or hypocritical priests.

By the end of the eighteenth century, British merchants were dissatisfied with the restrictions imposed on trade by the Qing government. The Qing, like the Ming before it, specified where merchants of particular countries could trade, and the Europeans were to trade only in Guangzhou, even though tea was grown mostly in the Yangzi valley, adding the cost of transporting it south to the price the foreign merchants had to pay. The merchants in Guangzhou who dealt with western merchants formed their own guild, and the Qing government made them guarantee that the European merchants obeyed Qing rules. In the system as it evolved, the Europeans had to pay cash for goods purchased and were forbidden to enter the walled city of Guangzhou, ride in sedan chairs, bring women or weapons into their quarters, and learn Chinese.

Great Pagoda at Kew Gardens. A taste for things Chinese led to the construction of a ten-story, 162-foot tall octagonal pagoda in Kew Gardens in London in 1762. It was originally very colorful and had eighty dragons decorating its roofs. *(The Art Archive)*

As British purchases of tea escalated, the balance of trade became more lopsided, but British merchants could not find goods Chinese merchants would buy from them. The British government also was dissatisfied. It was becoming suspicious of the British East India Company, which had made great fortunes from its trade with China, and wanted to open direct diplomatic relations with China in part as a way to curb the company. To accomplish all this, King George III sent Lord George Macartney, the former ambassador to Russia and former governor of Madras. Macartney was instructed to secure a place for British traders near the tea-producing areas, negotiate a commercial treaty, create a desire for British products, arrange for diplomatic representation in Beijing, and open Japan and Southeast Asia to British commerce as well. He traveled with an entourage of eighty-four and six hundred cases packed with British goods that he hoped would impress the Chinese court and attract trade: clocks, telescopes, knives, globes, plate glass, Wedgwood pottery, landscape paintings, woolen cloth, and carpets. The only one of the British party able to speak Chinese, however, was a twelve-year-old boy who had learned some Chinese by talking with Chinese on the long voyage.

After Lord Macartney arrived in Guangzhou in 1793, he requested permission to see the emperor in order to present a letter to him from George III. Although the letter had been written in Chinese, its language was not appropriate for addressing an emperor. Still, the British party was eventually allowed to proceed to Beijing. Once there, another obstacle emerged: when instructed on how to behave on seeing the emperor, Macartney objected to having to perform the kowtow (kneeling on both knees and bowing one's head to the ground).

Finally Macartney was permitted to meet more informally with the Qianlong emperor at his summer retreat. No negotiations followed this meeting, however, as the Qing court saw no merit in Macartney's requests. It was as interested in maintaining its existing system of regulated trade as Britain was interested in doing away with it.

Several of the members of the Macartney mission wrote books about China on their return. These books, often illustrated, contained descriptions of many elements of Chinese culture and social customs, less rosy than the reports of the Jesuits a century or two earlier. The official account of the embassy, prepared by George Staunton, depicted Chinese women as subjugated: "Women, especially in the lower walks of life, are bred with little other principle than that of implicit obedience to their fathers or their husbands." Although the wives of the peasantry worked very hard at domestic tasks and did all the weaving in the country, they were treated badly: "Not withstanding all the merit of these helpmates to their husbands, the latter arrogate an extraordinary dominion over them, and hold them at such distance, as not always to allow them to sit at table, behind which, in such case, they attend as handmaids."[2] From books like these, Europeans began to see more of the complexity of China. The Chinese, by contrast, did not learn much about Europe or Britain from this encounter.

SOCIAL AND CULTURAL CROSS CURRENTS

During the late Ming, Chinese culture had been remarkably open and fluid. Especially in the cities of Jiangnan, new books of all sorts were being published; the theater flourished; and intellectuals took an interest in ideas of Buddhist, Daoist, or even European origin and, encouraged by Wang Yangming's teachings, pursued truth in individualistic ways.

With the collapse of the social order in the early seventeenth century and the conquest by the Manchus, many in the educated class turned against what had come to seem like a lack of standards and commitments. Early Qing Confucian scholars often concluded that the Ming fell as a result of moral laxity. Wang Yangming and his followers, by validating emotion and spontaneity, had undermined commitment to duty and respect for authority. The solution, many thought, was to return to Zhu Xi's teachings, with their emphasis on objective standards outside the individual.

This conservative turn was manifested in several ways. Laws against homosexuality were made harsher. Because literati argued that drama and fiction were socially subversive, theaters were closed and novels banned. Qian Daxian, a highly learned scholar, went so far as to argue that the vernacular novel was the main

---

2. George Staunton, *An Authentic Account of an Embassy from the King of Great Britain to the Emperor of China* (London: W. Bulmer, 1798), 2:109.

threat to Confucian orthodoxy. The cult of widow chastity reached new heights, with local histories recording more and more widows who refused to remarry, including those who lived their entire lives as the celibate "widows" of men to whom they had been engaged but who had died before they had even met.

The conservative turn in scholarship fostered a new interest in rigorous textual analysis. Some Confucian scholars turned back to the Han commentaries on the classics, hoping that they could free their understandings of the texts from the contamination of Buddhist and Daoist ideas that had infiltrated Tang and Song commentaries. Others wanted to rely solely on the classics themselves and to concentrate on verifiable facts. Yan Ruoju compiled a guide to the place names in the Four Books and proved that the "old text" version of the *Book of Documents* could not be genuine. Research of this sort required access to large libraries, and it thrived primarily in Jiangnan, with its high densities of both books and scholars.

There are always those who resist calls for decorum and strenuous moral effort, and in the eighteenth century, both the Manchu rulers and the Chinese intellectual elite provided room for the less conventional to contribute in creative ways. Exploration of the potential of ink painting for self-expression reached a high point in the eighteenth century with a closely affiliated group of painters known as the Eight Eccentrics of Yangzhou (see **Material Culture: Jin Nong's Inscribed Portrait of a Buddhist Monk**). These painters had no difficulty finding patrons, even among social and cultural conservatives. Similarly, Yuan Mei, on familiar terms with the great classicists and philologists of his day, was willing to risk their censure by taking on women as poetry students. One of his female poetry students, Luo Qilan, wrote in 1797 to defend him from charges of impropriety, arguing that if Confucius had believed in the principle that words spoken inside a chamber must stay indoors, he would have removed poems by women from the *Book of Poetry*.

The Dream of Red Mansions

Women with poetic talents figure prominently in an eighteenth-century novel, *The Dream of Red Mansions* (also called *Story of the Stone*), considered by many the most successful of all works of Chinese fiction. Concerned with the grand themes of love and desire, money and power, life and death, and truth and illusion, it is at the same time a psychologically sensitive novel of manners. The author of the first eighty chapters was Cao Xueqin (1715–1764). He died before it was completed, but another writer added forty chapters to complete it before it was published in 1791. Cao Xueqin came from a Chinese family that had risen with the Manchus. Bondservants of the ruling house, they were in a position to gain great wealth and power managing enterprises for the rulers. In the eighteenth century, however, the family lost favor and went bankrupt.

The *Dream* portrays in magnificent detail the affairs of the comparably wealthy Jia family. The central characters of the novel are three adolescents: Jia Baoyu and his two female cousins of other surnames who come to live with his family. One of the cousins, Lin Daiyu, is sickly and difficult; the other, Xue Baochai, is capable and cheerful. A magnificent garden is built in the family compound in order to receive a visit from Baoyu's sister, who had become an imperial consort. After the visit Baoyu and his cousins and their personal servants move into the garden, an idyllic world of youth and beauty. This magical period comes to an end when Baoyu is tricked into marrying Baochai (thinking he is marrying Daiyu). While the wedding is taking place, Daiyu is on her sickbed, dying of consumption. The novel ends with Baoyu passing the *jinshi* examinations, only to leave his wife and family to pursue religious goals.

Much of the power of *Dream* comes from the many subplots and the host of minor characters from all walks of life—officials, aristocrats, monks and nuns, pageboys, gardeners, country relatives, princes, gamblers, prostitutes, actors,

MATERIAL CULTURE

Jin Nong's Inscribed Portrait of a Buddhist Monk

Chinese painters often combined words and images, sometimes inscribing poems or explanations of the occasion that gave rise to the painting on the painting itself. The highly individualistic painters of the eighteenth century known as the Eight Eccentrics of Yangzhou sometimes carried this practice to its limit, filling all the space on a painting with their writing. The painting shown here, by Jin Nong (1687–1764), is dated 1760. Writing in his highly distinctive calligraphy, Jin Nong fills the space around the Buddha with a history of the painting of images of Buddhas followed by personal remarks:

> I am now a man beyond seventy years of age who has no false ideas and desires. Though physically I am in the dusty world, I earnestly try to live cleanly. I wash my ten fingers, burn incense, and hold the brush to record the dignity and seriousness of humanity. What I do is not far from the ancient tradition. I offer good wishes to all men on earth.
>
> In the second lunar month, 1760, on the date when Buddha achieved enlightenment, I painted several Buddha images, four Bodhisattvas, sixteen Lohans, and distributed these sacred materials. These works are the product of my deep conviction, not in the style of famous masters of the Jin and Tang. My inspiration came from the Longmen caves that were carved a thousand years ago. When my priest friend, Defeng commented, "These paintings found [a new school] and will be followed by the coming generations," I roared with laughter.[1]

Portrait of a Monk. This hanging scroll, painted by Jin Nong in 1760 in ink and colors on paper, measures 133 by 62.5 cm. *(Collection of the Tianjin History Museum)*

———

1. Tseng Yuho, trans., *A History of Chinese Calligraphy* (Hong Kong: University of Hong Kong Press, 1993), p. 94, slightly modified.

and innkeepers. The seamier side of political life is portrayed through memorable cases of abuse of power. The machinations of family politics are just as vividly captured through numerous incidents in which family members compete for advantage. The maids in the family are often unable to keep the lustful men away, in the process attracting the anger of their wives. A concubine of Baoyu's father plots demon possession against both Baoyu and his sister-in-law, the household manager Xifeng. One of Baoyu's mother's maids commits suicide after Baoyu flirts with her. This incident, coupled with Baoyu's dalliance with an actor, provokes his father into administering a severe beating.

At one point Baochai notices that Daiyu has unconsciously quoted a line from a play. She then confesses that since she was seven or eight, she and the other children in her family had read plays:

All of us younger people hated serious books but liked reading poetry and plays. The boys had got lots and lots of plays: The Western Chamber, The Lute-Player, A Hundred Yuan Plays—*just about everything you could think of. They* used *to read them behind* our *backs, and we girls used to read them behind theirs. Eventually the grown-ups got to know about it and then there were beatings and lectures and burnings of books—and that was the end of that.*[3]

SUMMARY

How different was China in 1800 than it had been in 1600? China was part of a much larger empire—the largest since the Mongol Empire. For the first time, China was administered as part of the same polity as Tibet and Xinjiang. It was the most populous and economically dominant part of the empire, but politically the Manchus were in control. The Manchus depended on Chinese officials and soldiers to help administer their empire, but they perfected ways to ensure that the Manchus would maintain their dominance.

Although a large segment of the educated elite alive during the conquest did everything in their power to resist the Manchus, in deep dread of another "barbarian" dynasty, the Manchus proved to be very different sorts of rulers than the Mongols had been, and by 1800 Chinese of all social levels had gotten used to Manchu rule. The Manchu rulers made a point to patronize Chinese culture, and many facets of Chinese culture thrived during this period, ranging from historical research to manufacturing technology. The standard of living in the mid-eighteenth century was high, and the population was growing. The Manchu rulers were highly sensitive to ethnic slights, however, which may have made Chinese in high office especially cautious.

SUGGESTED READING

W. Peterson, ed., *The Cambridge History of China*, vol. 9, part 1, covers the early Qing. A. Hummel, ed., *Eminent Chinese of the Ch'ing Period (1644–1912)*, 2 vols. (1943), is a useful reference work. Good overviews of Qing history are found in F. Wakeman, *The Fall of Imperial China* (1975), and J. Spence, *The Search for Modern China* (1990). On the Ming-Qing transition, see F. Wakeman, *The Great Enterprise* (1985); J. Spence and J. Wills, eds., *From Ming to Ch'ing: Conquest, Region, and Continuity in Seventeenth-Century China* (1979); and L. Struve, *The Southern Ming, 1644–1662* (1984). On the Manchus, see P. Crossley, *The Manchus* (1997) and *A Translucent Mirror: History and Identity in Qing Imperial Ideology* (1999); M. Elliott, *The*

---

3. Cao Xueqin, *The Story of the Stone*, vol. 2, trans. David Hawkes (New York: Penguin Books, 1977), p. 333.

Manchu Way: The Eight Banners and Ethnic Identity in Late Imperial China (2001); and E. Rawski, *The Last Emperors* (1998).

On how China fits into global change in the seventeenth and eighteenth centuries, see K. Pomeranz, *The Great Divergence: China, Europe, and the Making of the Modern World Economy* (2000); R. Wong, *China Transformed: Historical Change and the Limits of European Experience* (1997); and J. Waley-Cohen, *The Sextants of Beijing: Global Currents in Chinese History* (1999). China's population growth is reexamined in J. Lee, *One Quarter of Humanity: Malthusian Mythology and Chinese Realities* (2000).

On the Qing court and government, see J. Spence, *Emperor of China: Self Portrait of K'ang Hsi* (1974); H. Kahn, *Monarchy in the Emperor's Eyes: Image and Reality in the Ch'ien-lung Reign* (1971); A. Zito, *Of Body and Brush: Grand Sacrifice as Text/Performance in Eighteenth-Century China* (1997); and J. Hevia, *Cherishing Men from Afar: Qing Guest Ritual and the Macartney Embassy of 1793* (1995). On the Qing fears of anti-Manchu sentiments, see L. C. Goodrich, *The Literary Inquisition of Ch'ien-lung* (1935); K. Guy, *The Emperor's Four Treasuries: Scholars and the State in the Late Ch'ien-lung Era* (1987); P. Kuhn, *Soulstealers: The Chinese Sorcery Scare of 1768* (1990); and J. Spence, *Treason by the Book* (2001).

For Early Qing social history, see J. Spence, *The Death of Woman Wang* (1978); S. Naquin and E. Rawski, *Chinese Society in the Eighteenth Century* (1987); B. Elman and A. Woodside, eds., *Education and Society in Late Imperial China, 1600–1900* (1994); G. W. Skin-ner, ed., *The City in Late Imperial China* (1977); and S. Naquin, *Peking: Temples and City Life, 1400–1900* (2000). Biographies offer excellent insight into the life of the elite. See A. Waley, *Yuan Mei, Eighteenth Century Chinese Poet* (1956); D. Nivison, *The Life and Thought of Chang Hsüeh-ch'eng (1738–1801)* (1966); and W. Rowe, *Saving the World: Chen Hongmou and Elite Consciousness in Eighteenth-Century China* (2001).

For Qing intellectual and cultural history, see B. Elman, *From Philosophy to Philology: Intellectual and Social Aspects of Change in Late Imperial China* (1984), and K. Chow, *The Rise of Confucian Ritualism in Late Imperial China: Ethics, Classics, and Lineage Discourse* (1994). Contact with European ideas and religion is treated in J. Gernet, *China and the Christian Impact: A Conflict of Cultures* (1985), and D. Mungello, *The Great Encounter of China and the West, 1500–1800* (1999).

China's greatest novel is available in an excellent translation by D. Hawkes and J. Minford, *The Story of the Stone*, 5 vols. (1973–1982). Another important and entertaining eighteenth-century novel is *The Scholars*, trans. H. Yang and G. Yang (1973). On women in the seventeenth and eighteenth centuries, see D. Ko, *Teachers of the Inner Chambers: Women and Culture in Seventeenth-Century China* (1994); S. Mann, *Precious Records* (1997); F. Bray, *Technology and Gender: Fabrics of Power in Late Imperial China* (1997); E. Widmer and K. Chang, eds, *Writing Women in Late Imperial China* (1997); and K. Chang and H. Saussy, eds., *Women Writers of Traditional China: An Anthology of Poetry and Criticism* (1999).

CHAPTER SEVENTEEN

Edo Japan
(1603–1800)

Tokugawa Settlement

Material Culture: Night Soil

Documents: Ihara Saikaku's "Sensible Advice on Domestic Economy"

Biography: Tadano Makuzu

Maturation and Decay

The social and political order imposed under the Tokugawa shoguns consolidated trends long in the making. The demarcation of villages as corporate communities, the separation of samurai from commoners, the creation of bounded domains, and the growth of and restrictions on commerce all had antecedents in the late sixteenth century. The structure of family life, in particular the emphasis on primogeniture and the custom of brides serving their husbands' families, continued practices already apparent in the fourteenth century. Yet peace also made possible economic developments that some historians deem proto-industrialization, unprecedented urbanization, and a flourishing of theater, fiction, poetry, and intellectual life.

What distinguished the Tokugawa shogunate from previous military regimes? What were the consequences of the political settlement for economic and demographic growth? To what extent did shogunal efforts to restrict foreign contact isolate Japan? What did samurai do without battles to fight? How did urban and rural commoners make their presence felt?

TOKUGAWA SETTLEMENT

The cadastral surveys and separation of warriors from the land begun under Hideyoshi and continued in the seventeenth century aimed at ordering society according to unchanging criteria. The Tokugawa brought an end to the conflicts caused by sibling rivalry by insisting on strict primogeniture for the military ruling class and confiscating domains rived by succession disputes. As a result, a ruler's personality and level of competence mattered less than his office, and the retainers' loyalty focused on the position, not the individual. The monarch and his court lived, according to popular parlance, "above the clouds" in Kyoto. Samurai stood at the top of the official status order, followed by commoners in order of their contributions to society. In principle no one was to change residence or status, nor was marriage permitted across status lines. In reality, status boundaries were fluid. Since changing names changed identity, a commoner woman took an aristocratic name when serving a military household. Individual actors and prostitutes became celebrities, and the exclusive right to work with animal skins made some outcasts wealthy.

Tokugawa Social Hierarchy

Core Social Statuses	Other Social Groups (Between Statuses)	Outcasts
Samurai	Priests	Blind Female Entertainers
Cultivators	Doctors	Beggars
Artisans	Monks	Prostitutes
Merchants		Actors
		Non-Humans (Hinin)
		Polluted Ones (Kawata)

This status order restricted rural communities to cultivators. In the seventeenth century, most villages had at least one dominant family, often descended from a rusticated warrior, which monopolized the position of headman. A council of elders comprising landholding cultivators known as *honbyakushō* provided a sounding board for matters pertaining to village affairs. The *honbyakushō* households included family members, house servants, and fieldworkers. In central and eastern Japan, villages contained complex lineage systems with multiple branches. Across Japan social, economic, and political inequality structured village life. The men who claimed descent from village founders expected to be treated with deference, they claimed the largest and best fields, and they dominated village politics. Their wives shared their prestige; a male of lesser standing had to treat such women with respect.

Villages divided up the countryside. A village contained residential plots, rice paddies, and dry fields, each assigned to households. In some regions the agricultural lands periodically rotated from family to family. These households cooperated in doing the heavy work of leveling rice paddies and building dikes, managing irrigation networks, and transplanting rice seedlings into the paddies. Women performed this last backbreaking task in a carryover of medieval religious beliefs that sanctified it as a fertility ritual. Beyond this basic level, each household was on its own to prosper or to fail. Village boundaries also enclosed wastelands and forests with access to their products carefully regulated by the village council. As a corporate entity embodied by the headman, the village was collectively responsible for paying taxes, both the yearly tribute measured in units of rice (*koku*—1 koku equals 5.1 bushels of rice, the amount needed to feed one man for a year) and various ancillary exactions, for example, fees for the privilege of exploiting forest resources.

Bounded, contiguous villages constituted the building blocks of domains ruled by daimyo that typically were bounded and contiguous. The shogun had the largest domain concentrated chiefly in eastern and central Japan totaling approximately one-fourth of the total agricultural base. Vassal daimyo (*fudai*) were hereditary retainers. They governed domains; they also served as the shogun's chief advisers and his first line of defense against potential foes. According to a decree of 1634, only vassals whose domains contained over 10,000 *koku* enjoyed the status of daimyo. The shogun's retainers with smaller fiefs, often made up of parcels in several villages, were called *hatamoto* ("beneath the banner"). In addition the shogun commanded the services of thousands of housemen who received stipends from the shogun's warehouses. Daimyo who had been shogun Tokugawa Ieyasu's rivals or peers were deemed outside lords (*tozama*). Fewer in number than the vassal daimyo, the mightiest controlled large domains that functioned almost as nations. Some of the shogun's collateral relatives also numbered among the daimyo. They were neither wealthy nor politically powerful, but they enjoyed great prestige. All daimyo, who numbered between two hundred fifty and two hundred eighty, had retainer bands to be supported and employed.

Government

The government pieced together by the Tokugawa shoguns over some forty years developed an elaborate bureaucratic structure (later called a *bakufu*—tent government). The senior councilors—four to five men who rotated on a monthly basis, each of them a vassal daimyo worth at least 30,000 *koku*—took responsibility for policy decisions, personnel matters, and supervising the daimyo. Their assistants, also vassal daimyo, handled matters relating to the shogun's retainers. The *hatamoto* staffed the administrative positions, beginning with the magistrates in charge of finances, cities, and temples and shrines. Finance magistrates supervised the intendants responsible for seeing that the villagers paid their taxes and general agrarian affairs. They also managed the increasingly futile task of balancing expenditures with income. Their staff, and those of the other magistrates, included an array of functionaries, guards, and servants. Although the shogun tried to reduce the size of his army in the seventeenth century, he was never able to provide more than part-time employment to his retainer: 42 percent of *hatamoto* (1,676 in 1829) served in the fatigue regiment, the default category for men without office. Each daimyo likewise had an overly abundant staff of advisers, accountants, liaison officers, attendants, tax collectors, doctors, teachers, guards, servants, and placeholders.

The shogunal and domainal governments developed the most complex, sophisticated, and coherent administrative systems Japan had ever seen. Retainers learned to wield a brush as well as a sword, understand high finance, and accustom themselves to routinized office jobs. Administrative systems also retained distinctly unmodern bureaucratic elements. The shogun bestowed his former family name of Matsudaira on important *fudai* and *tozama* daimyo, both as an honor and as a reminder that rulers were kin. Opportunities for promotion depended on hereditary rank; men born of guards stayed guards. The senior councilors may have been policy experts, but they were also the shogun's vassals. Their duties included watching him perform ancestral rites, lecture on the Chinese classics, and dance in Nō. When he left the castle to go hawking or visit one of their number, they and their subordinates had to attend him. The shogun maintained a large staff of palace women ordered in a female bureaucracy to serve him, his wife, and his mother in the great interior (*ōoku*). Their responsibilities included a yearly round of ceremonies and managing gift exchanges with the Kyoto court and daimyo families.

Although the daimyo ran their domains as they saw fit, the shogunate started to issue decrees to regulate their behavior in 1615. It limited the number of guns allowed per castle and restricted castle repairs. The daimyo could not harbor criminals, collude against the shogun, or marry without the shogun's permission. All daimyo had the responsibility of contributing men and money to the shogun's building projects, and they could be relocated from one region to another at the shogun's pleasure. Most important, the shogunate issued increasingly stringent guidelines governing the daimyo's attendance on the shogun. Known as *sankin kōtai* and formalized in 1635, this system stipulated that each daimyo spend half of his time in his domain and half in the shogun's capital at Edo. Each daimyo's wife and heir had to reside in Edo as hostages. Designed to keep the daimyo both loyal to the shogun and effective in local administration, the system balanced the centrifugal forces that had weakened the Kamakura regime and the centripetal tendencies that had destroyed the Ashikaga. *Sankin kōtai* also had the inadvertent consequence of stimulating trade, encouraging travel, and spreading urban culture to the hinterland.

The shogunate appropriated certain national responsibilities to itself. It refurbished the highway

system with post stations and checkpoints to
keep guns out of Edo and female hostages in.
For its own defense, it forbade the building of
bridges over major rivers. It oversaw the development of coastal shipping routes, took over the
mines for precious metals, and minted copper,
silver, and gold coins. It initiated an official
handwriting style for documents. It forbade the
practice of Christianity and set up a nationwide
system of temple registration to ensure compliance. In 1635 it forbade Japanese to travel overseas and banned foreign books. In 1639 it
regulated relations with the West by allowing
only the Dutch to trade at Nagasaki. It dele-
gated the oversight of trade and diplomacy with
neighboring countries to three domains: Satsuma for the Ryukyus, Tsushima for Korea, and
Matsumae for the Ainu and the north. The
shogunate supervised trade with China that
took place at Nagasaki; it had less control over
the Chinese goods that arrived indirectly
through the Ryukyus and Hokkaido.

Under the Tokugawa regime, people inhabit-
ing the Ryukyu Islands found themselves forced
into much closer proximity to Japan. An independent kingdom with tributary ties to China as
well as Japan in the sixteenth century, the
Ryukyus suffered invasion by Satsuma in 1609.
Although the king survived and trade with
China continued, he had to surrender control
over his islands' diplomatic and economic
affairs, to the detriment of the islanders' well-
being. Intellectuals in the Ryukyus tried to craft
a new identity by claiming that although they
were politically subservient to Japan, they
achieved moral parity with both Japan and
China by cultivating the way of the Confucian
sage.

Relations with the Ainu in Hokkaido evolved
differently. There the shogunate had the Matsumae family with longstanding ties to the
region establish a domain on the island's southern tip. The Matsumae received the privilege of
monopolizing trade with the Ainu in exchange
for a pledge of loyalty. In 1669, conflict between
Ainu tribes over access to game and fish escalated into a war to rid Hokkaido of the Japan-

Ainu Feeding a Hawk. This mid-nineteenth century
drawing of an Ainu feeding a hawk depicts the
bird as almost as large as its captor. The Ainu is
stereotypically hairy with full beard and heavy
eyebrows. *(Brett Walker/Collection for Northern
Studies, Hokkaido University Library)*

ese. Following its bloody suppression, the Ainu
and the Japanese solidified distinct ethnic identities that incorporated elements of the other—
eagle feathers and otter pelts for the Japanese
ruling class and ironware, rice, and sake for the
Ainu. Between 1590 and 1800, the Ainu became
increasingly dependent on trade with the Japanese for their subsistence, while periodic epidemics brought by traders ravaged their
population. Many ended up working as contract
laborers in fisheries that shipped food and fertilizer to Japan.

The Tokugawa shogunate survived for over
250 years not simply because it dominated Japan
militarily but because, like Oda Nobunaga and
Toyotomi Hideyoshi, Ieyasu and his heirs recognized the importance of ideology in transforming power into authority. Nobunaga claimed
that he acted on behalf of the realm (*tenka*), not
his private, selfish interests. Governance of his
domain became public administration (*kōgi*).
He also built a shrine to himself; Hideyoshi
actively promoted a cult to his own divinity.

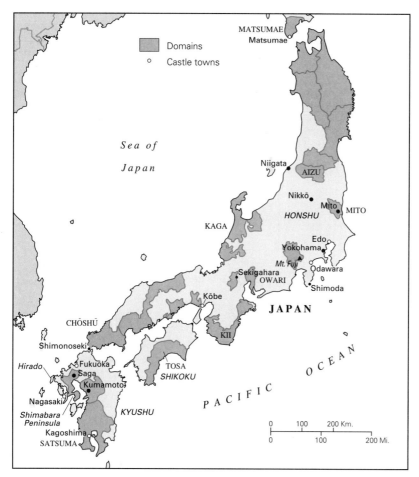

Map 17.1   Tokugawa Japan, 1600–1868

Ieyasu's posthumous title apotheosized him as *Tōshō daigongen*—the Buddha incarnate as the sun god of the east. Enshrined at Nikkō, he protected the shogunate from malignant spirits and worked for the good of all people. (See Map 17.1.) The third shogun Iemitsu claimed that the shogunate manifested a just social order that followed the way of heaven (*tendō*). This way is natural, unchanging, eternal, and hierarchical. The ruler displays the benevolence of the Buddha, the warrior preserves the peace, and the commoners are obedient. The fifth shogun, Tsunayoshi, tried to domesticate the warriors by codifying mourning rituals, lecturing on Confucian classics, and forbidding the killing of ani-

mals, especially dogs (used for target practice). His successor reversed the last stricture, and the eighth shogun Yoshimune sought to revive the martial arts. One aim of later reforms between 1787 and 1793 was to redress the balance between brush and sword, suggesting that for samurai, how to follow the way of heaven was not self-evident.

Agricultural Transformations and the Commercial Revolution

Cultivators, merchants, artisans, and rulers quickly exploited the peace dividend. Large- and small-scale reclamation projects, often funded

Artisans. Cottage industries relied on families. Both the pattern dyers depicted on the screen to the right and the weavers shown on the screen to the left employed men and women, children and grandparents. (*LEFT: Werner Forman/Corbis; RIGHT: Sakamoto Photo Research Laboratory/Corbis*)

by merchants at a daimyo's behest, opened rice paddies and expanded arable land by 45 percent. Rivers were diked and new channels dug to bring irrigation water to fields. Countless building projects, partly to repair the ravages of war in Kyoto but mainly to build the plethora of daimyo mansions, shogunal palaces, and merchant quarters in the new capital at Edo and the castle towns, seriously depleted forests. By the end of the seventeenth century, floods sweeping down denuded mountains threatened hard-won fields. The shogunate led the way in regulating the use of forestry products, but the agricultural base continued to press against ecological limits. (See **Material Culture: Night Soil.**)

The introduction of better seeds and new crops intensified the use of land and labor. The accumulation of small innovations based on observations of soil types and climatic condi-

tions led to the development of rice varieties suited for specific local conditions. Fast-ripening rice spread cultivation into the marginal lands of the northeast. Farther south, it allowed the sowing of a second crop, often wheat, although some paddies in Kyushu supported two rice crops a year. Corn, tobacco, and sweet potato, products of the western hemisphere, became dry field staples along with barley and millet. In a trend that continued throughout the Tokugawa period, seventeenth-century agronomy experts traveled Japan building social networks of like-minded experimenters, seeking the most advanced methods for increasing crop yields, and disseminating their findings in books.

Cultivators also grew cash crops and developed products based on Chinese technology. The spread of cotton growing in western Japan beginning in the sixteenth century reduced the

MATERIAL CULTURE

Night Soil

The Edo city government left waste disposal in the hands of individual landlords. Daimyo and *hatamoto* contracted with nearby villages to bring fresh vegetables to their compounds and remove waste. Communal toilet facilities in each commoner ward also had to be cleaned.

In the eighteenth century, cultivators planted crops where they had once foraged for green fertilizer. The more intensive use of land forced them to look outside their communities for soil amendments. Vegetable farmers near Edo carted away night soil and other organic wastes to supplement the manure they produced themselves. Separated into solids and liquid and cooked in its own heat to kill harmful organisms, night soil became a valuable commodity.

In the late eighteenth century, townspeople expected cultivators to pay for the privilege of collecting night soil. Landlords insisted that tenants use their toilet facilities and tried to sell their product to the highest bidder. Transactions between subcontractors, wholesalers, and middlemen raised costs. Regional alliances of cultivators petitioned the shogunate to keep prices down.

The value placed on night soil reflected status inequality. Landlords segregated toilets by sex because men's excrement was valued more highly than women's. Samurai received more for their waste than did commoners. An eighteenth-century farmhouse had a toilet for samurai made of polished wood. The tenant farmers and family members used an open pit.

Toilets. The photo on the left depicts a toilet for the use of samurai officials next to the formal reception room at a village headman's house. On the opposite side behind the stable is the pit for family and servants to use (right). *(Photos courtesy of Anne Walthall)*

hours women had to spend preparing cloth for their families while revolutionizing clothing and bedding. During the seventeenth century, Japan imported Chinese silk and sugar. By the 1730s for silk and the 1830s for sugar, domestic production provided substitutes. The daimyo competed in developing products for export to fund

their mandated trips to Edo. They hired teachers to show cultivators how to harvest lacquer, make paper, and raise silkworms. They promoted distinctive styles of wooden combs, paper hair ties, and ceramics. Merchants supplied the capital, and cultivators supplied the labor, although a few rural entrepreneurs managed to profit from the distribution of raw materials and the transportation of goods. Lights fueled by rapeseed oil enabled work to continue into the night. Increases in agricultural productivity spurred demand for nonagricultural goods produced by rural households. The growth of cottage industries diversified income sources and led to a virtuous cycle of interaction between agriculture and manufacturing. Neither entrepreneurs nor domains tried to set up large-scale production units. Instead they emphasized quality and variety, trying to beat the competition by producing regional specialties found nowhere else.

The agricultural and commercial revolutions meant higher per capita productivity and a trend toward smaller families. After almost a threefold increase in the seventeenth century, Japan's population remained surprisingly stagnant. In villages the extended families characteristic of earlier times broke down by the end of the seventeenth century into main families and branches or landlords and tenants. Most households cultivated parcels just big enough to support a stem family of grandparents, parents, and children. There was not enough to bestow on more than one heir. Historians have supposed that cultivators practiced abortion and infanticide lest they have more children than they could afford. Even if the heir died, the ease of adoption meant that a family could usually find someone to carry on the family line. Other factors were also at work. Men often left their homes for months at a time to work in towns and cities, especially during the winter. The female age at marriage went up in central Japan because women increasingly worked to gain experience before settling down. Disease mattered: smallpox, for example, can reduce male fertility by 50 percent. Syphilis struck urban populations. Periodic famines hit some regions harder than others. In the early nineteenth century, population decline in the impoverished northeast offset growth in the more commercially developed and prosperous west.

One characteristic of Japan's early modern growth was that while labor remained in the countryside, capital largely concentrated in the cities. Not until the late eighteenth century did rural entrepreneurs amass significant amounts of capital, and they often depended on urban merchants for financial backing. Daimyo traveling on *sankin kōtai* marketed rice they collected in taxes to merchants in Osaka who advanced them currency and letters of credit. These promissory notes, redeemable at the merchant's branch in Edo, served as Japan's first paper money. Domains later printed their own currency, modeled on religious talismans to gain users' trust. Merchants either advanced the money to make specialty products or bought them at a discount to sell to urban consumers. Some merchants acted as purveyors to daimyo and their women, stimulating the desire for high-quality laborintensive goods. Others catered to the broader market by selling cotton cloth, lamp oil, and soy sauce. At the end of the seventeenth century, a few Osaka and Edo merchants had become extremely wealthy, and a number of daimyo found themselves deeply in debt.

Urban Life and Culture

Edo's spatial layout mirrored the shogun's strategic concerns. Taking advantage of technological advancements in fortifications, the shogun's castle was enclosed behind multiple stone walls surrounded by moats. The shogunate drained the swamp on which the city was built through canals that provided transportation for goods and people. Bridges over the moats were faced with guardhouses, forcing the traveler to make a sharp turn, and no roads led directly to the castle. Vassal daimyo and the shogun's retainers lived in its immediate vicinity, providing another ring of protection. The wealthy *tozama* daimyo had large compounds containing barracks for their retainers, storehouses, mansions, and gardens. None was allowed moats and stone walls, and quarters for the vassal daimyo surrounded them. Each daimyo maintained multiple compounds; the total number was over one thousand. The ruling class took the salubrious highlands for itself, leaving the lowlands directly east and south of the castle for commoners. Scattered throughout the city were shrines and temples. Daimyo castle towns followed a similar pattern of segregating people according to status and occupation.

The seventeenth century saw an unprecedented increase in urban growth, from little more than 1 percent of Japan's population to almost 15 percent after 1700. In addition to the castle towns were three metropolises: Kyoto became a manufacturing center of luxury goods, Osaka served as Japan's chief market, and Edo's swollen population of daimyo and bureaucrats made it a consumption center. Urbanization stimulated the growth of commercial publishing that created and fed a reading public hungry for knowledge and entertainment. It provided space for exhibitions from religious icons to botanical specimens and for private salons where scholars, artists, and writers met patrons. Urban residents paid for services—hairdressing, amusements—that had once been provided by servants. They bought processed food and cloth that their ancestors had made themselves. Labor and leisure were oriented toward the market, and purchasing finished products saved time. This transformation stimulated a consumption revolution—the increased demand for a greater variety of goods from durable luxury items such as elaborately carved transoms to drug foods such as sake and tobacco.

Unprecedented urban prosperity culminated in the Genroku era (1688–1704), the heyday of townsman (*chōnin*) culture, justly celebrated in art and literature. Ihara Saikaku wrote stories about the samurai passion for boys, but most of his works focused on the foibles of the townspeople in books such as *Five Women Who Loved Love* and *The Life of an Amorous Man*. He also wrote books on how to make and keep money. (See **Documents: Ihara Saikaku's "Sensible Advice on Domestic Economy."**) Matsuo Bashō raised the seventeen-syllable verse form known as haiku to a fine art, in the process making poetry accessible to commoners in town and country. Chikamatsu Monzaemon wrote librettos for the puppet theater that explored the complex interplay between social obligations and human feeling, as when a young man in love with a prostitute wants to buy the contract that indentures her to the brothel owner but lacks the resources to do so without causing irreparable harm to his family's business. Caught between love and duty, the couple resolves the dilemma by committing double suicide. Although Chikamatsu wrote for puppets, the literary artistry of his scripts endeared them to amateur performers and raised the quality of theatrical performances.

Two pleasure zones are associated with the Genroku era: the brothel district and the theaters, often located in close proximity to each other on the margins of respectable society. These constituted the "floating world" (*ukiyo*), celebrated in woodblock prints of courtesans and actors along with pornography. In the early seventeenth century, entrepreneurs in the three metropolises petitioned the shogunate to establish districts for prostitution where it could be regulated and controlled. A moat and walls surrounded Edo's Yoshiwara with a main gate where guards noted the men who entered and prevented women from leaving. The earliest customers were daimyo and samurai. Merchants whose lavish spending brought them great renown soon eclipsed them. In this status-conscious society, courtesans too were ranked.

Kabuki began in the early seventeenth century on a riverbank in Kyoto where a prostitute erected a stage on which to sing and dance to attract customers. Fights over her charms led the shogunate to forbid women to appear on stage in 1629. Boys then replaced them as actors and prostitutes. Again the shogunate stepped in to quell disorder, banning all but mature men from performing in public. To make up for what they lacked in sex appeal, actors developed the techniques of acting, singing, and dancing performed on elaborate and frequently changing sets that made kabuki the spectacle known today. It became enormously popular, with the highest acclaim reserved for the men who specialized in playing women. It staged reenactments of the scandals arising in

DOCUMENTS

Ihara Saikaku's "Sensible Advice on Domestic Economy"

Ihara Saikaku (1642–1693) is often considered Japan's first professional author because he lived by his pen, writing haiku, short stories, novels, and essays that described life in Osaka during the heyday of the townspeople. Here he feeds the merchants' obsession with the making and saving of money by focusing on the details of daily life and the qualities desired in a wife.

"The immutable rule in regard to the division of family property at the time of marriage," said the experienced go-between from Kyoto, "is as follows: Let us suppose that a certain man is worth a thousand *kan*. To the eldest son at his marriage will go four hundred *kan*, together with the family residence. The second son's share will be three hundred *kan*, and he too is entitled to a house of his own. The third son will be adopted into another family, requiring a portion of one hundred *kan*. If there is a daughter, her dowry will be thirty *kan*, in addition to a bridal trousseau worth twenty *kan*. It is advisable to marry her off to the son of a family of lower financial status. Formerly it was not unusual to spend forty *kan* on the trousseau and allot ten *kan* for the dowry, but because people today are more interested in cash, it is now customary to give the daughter silver in the lacquered chest and copper in the extra one. Even if the girl is so ugly that she can't afford to sit near the candle at night, that dowry of thirty *kan* will make her bloom into a very flowery bride!"

"In matchmaking, money is a very important consideration. If thirty *kan* of silver is deposited with a trustworthy merchant at six-tenths percent interest per month, the income will total one hundred and eighty *momme* monthly, which will more than suffice to support four women: the bride, her personal maid, a second maid, and a seamstress. How unselfish must be the disposition of a bride who will not only look after the household faithfully, meantime taking care never to displease her husband's family, but also at the same time will actually pay for the food she eats! If you are looking merely for beauty, then go where women are made up solely to that end, to the licensed quarters. You are free to visit them any time of night you may wish, and thoroughly enjoy it, but next morning you will have to pay out seventy-one *momme*—which is not in the least enjoyable!"

"It is better on the whole to give up dissipation in good time, for a roué is seldom happy in later life. So even if life at home seems dry and tasteless, you'd better have patience with a supper of cold rice, potluck

townspeople's society, but it became best known for swashbuckling melodramas set in the past, for the shogunate forbade any discussion of its own affairs or those of contemporary samurai society.

Intellectual Trends

The Edo period saw an explosion in intellectual life. Deprived of the opportunity to gain fame in

battle, some samurai turned to scholarship and made serious efforts to understand society. In the seventeenth century, Hayashi Razan formulated the Tokugawa ideology in neo-Confucian terms that saw the social order as a reflection of the visible natural order in that both realized an underlying metaphysical principle. Among his students was Yamaga Sokō, famous for defining a way for samurai to survive during a time of peace: "The

bean curd, and dried fish. You may lie down whenever you like, at perfect ease, and have a maid massage you down to the very tips of your toes. If you want tea, you may sip it while your wife holds the cup for you. A man in his own household is the commander supreme, whose authority none will dare to question, and there is none to condemn you. There's no need to seek further for genuine pleasure."

"Then, too, there are certain business advantages to staying home. Your clerks will stop their imprudent visits to the Yasaka quarters and their clandestine meetings at that rendezvous in Oike. And when in the shop, since they can't appear to be completely idle, maybe they'll look over those reports from the Edo branch office, or do some other work that they have been putting off doing—all to the profit of you, the master! The apprentice boys will diligently twist wastepaper into string, and in order to impress you, the master, sitting in the inner room, they will practice penmanship to their profit. Kyushichi, whose habit it is to retire early, will take the straw packing from around the yellowtail and make rope on which to string coins; while Take, in order to make things go more smoothly tomorrow, will prepare the vegetables for breakfast. The seamstress during the time you're at home will take off as many knots of Hino silk as she ordinarily does in a whole day. Even the cat keeps a wary watch in the kitchen and when she hears the least sound in the vicinity of the fish hanger she will mew to scare away the rats. If such unmeasured profit as this results from the master's remaining at home just one night, think how vast will be the benefits that will accrue within the space of a whole year! So even if you are not entirely satisfied with your wife, you have to exercise discretion and realize that in the gay quarters all is but vanity. For a young master to be well aware of this is the secret of the successful running of his household."

Such was the counsel offered by the veteran go-between.

Be that as it may, let me say that the women of today, under the influence of the styles of the gay quarters, dress exactly like professional entertainers. Prominent drapers' wives, who in public are addressed as mesdames, are so attired as to be mistaken for high-class courtesans; while the wives of small shopkeepers, who once served as clerks of the drapers, look exactly like courtesans one grade lower. Again, the kimono worn by wives of tailors and embroiderers who live on the side streets bear a startling resemblance to those of the women employed in teahouses. It is fun to spot them in a crowd dressed in conformity with their respective degrees of fortune.

Source: Saikaku Ihara, *This Scheming World*, trans. Masanori Takatsuka and David C. Stubbs (Rutland, Vt.: Charles E. Tuttle Company, 1965), pp. 54–57 (modified).

business of the samurai consists in reflecting on his own station in life, in discharging loyal service to his master . . . in deepening his fidelity in associations with friends, and . . . in devoting himself to duty above all."[1] Kyoto scholar Itō Jinsai likewise began as a neo-Confucianist, only to reject the notion of metaphysical principle in favor of studying Confucius himself. For him, the purpose of scholarship was to show how to put morality based on benevolence and love into practice, a goal achievable by commoners as well as samurai. Such was the cachet of Chinese philosophy that any man who had pretensions of becoming

1. Ryusaku Tsunoda et al., eds., *Sources of the Japanese Tradition* (New York: Columbia University Press, 1959), 1:390.

learned had to employ Chinese categories of thought. Women were not subject to this restriction, but for that reason, they had no formal access to scholarship beyond the study of Japanese poetry. (See **Biography: Tadano Makuzu**.)

Ogyū Sorai gained influence by attacking the neo-Confucian Hayashi school and Itō Jinsai. He argued that only the most ancient Chinese texts, those that predated Confucius, were worthy of study because they contained the teachings of the sage kings, the creators of civilization. The social order did not reflect the unchanging natural order of beasts; instead it was an artificial construct, made in history, and that was a good thing. Men needed rules lest their passions run away with them. Japan was fortunate that its own sage king Ieyasu had created the shogunate, and his deeds were not for mere mortals to challenge. Sorai's rational bureaucratic view of government called on the samurai to devote themselves to public duty. In 1703 forty-seven retainers from the Akō domain assassinated their dead lord's enemy (an incident dramatized as "The Treasury of Loyal Retainers," *Chūshingura*) because, they claimed, their honor as samurai left them no choice. Sorai applauded the deed but acceded to the official position that since they had broken the law against private vendettas, they had to atone by committing suicide. As long as people obeyed the law, government had no business interfering in their private lives.

The eighteenth century saw a proliferation of schools and thinkers. Dazai Shundai explored the ramifications of political economy. He urged daimyo to supplement the flat revenues derived from an agrarian tax base by promoting the production of goods for export. Kaiho Seiryō took Shundai's ideas a step further by arguing that all social relationships are predicated on the measured exchange of goods and services, a principle understood by merchants but not, unfortunately, by samurai. Andō Shōeki claimed that Sorai's sage kings were thieves and liars who created governments to deceive and cheat the cultivators. In his eyes, the samurai were no better than parasites.

Merchants pondered business ethics. Troubled by the excesses of the Genroku period

when some financiers had gone bankrupt through lavish spending and making too many bad loans to the daimyo, Ishida Baigan founded the Shingaku school (literally, study of the heart). He argued that merchants deserved to make a just profit because their profit was equivalent to the samurai's stipend. They should devote themselves to their enterprises with the same devotion a samurai showed to his lord, and like the samurai they should strive for moral perfection. Texts and teachers could guide this quest, but it could be completed only through meditation and the practice of diligence, thrift, and fortitude. Baigan and his followers had no political agenda; the idea that merchants might have something to say to samurai was left to the merchant academy in Osaka, the Kaitokudō, founded in 1724. Its teachers denied that merchants caused the ills of famine and indebtedness through their pursuit of profit. Merchants, they argued, played a crucial role in society by facilitating the circulation of goods based on objective and accurate calculations. When they applied this principle to domain finances, their advice regarding fiscal policy ought to be followed. A number of them gained coveted positions as advisers to daimyo and shogun.

Other thinkers found inspiration in the Japanese past. The greatest of them was Motoori Norinaga, whose prodigious memory enabled him to decipher the patterns of Chinese characters used to write *Kojiki*, Japan's most ancient history. Through the study of history and literary classics, he affirmed Japan's unique position in the world as the sole country ruled by descendants of the sun goddess, and he celebrated the private world of the individual. Based as they were on the spontaneity of human feeling, Japanese values were superior to those of other peoples. "In foreign countries, they place logic first, even when it comes to revering the gods . . . all this is but shallow human reasoning." The Chinese had introduced rules that while they might be necessary in China where people were naturally inclined toward error, were entirely unsuited to Japan, where people were intrinsically perfect in their possession of the "true

BIOGRAPHY Tadano Makuzu

Male intellectuals focused on morality, politics, and economics; Tadano Makuzu (1763–1825) drew on her observations and experience as a daughter of the samurai to analyze human relations.

Born Kudō Ayako, she grew up in a lively and prosperous family of parents, her father's mother, and seven siblings. At age nine she insisted that her mother teach her classical Japanese poetry. Ayako enjoyed her grandmother's company because she was a cheerful and attractive woman who loved kabuki. To complete her education, at fifteen Ayako became an attendant to the lord of Sendai's daughter, a position she held for ten years.

Ayako's father, Heisuke, had many friends who shared his interests in medicine, botany, foreign trade, and western countries. He hoped to arrange a good marriage for Ayako should his proposal of 1780 for the colonization of Hokkaido and trade with Russia lead to a position with the shogunate. The fall of his patron in 1786 stymied his career and his plans for his daughter.

When Ayako left service, she was too old to make a good match. In 1789 she was married to a man so decrepit that she cried until she was returned to her parents. In 1797 her father found her a husband in a widower with three sons, Tadano Iga Tsurayoshi, a high-ranking Sendai retainer with an income four times that of the Kudō family. Marrying Iga meant that Ayako had to leave the city of her birth for Sendai, a move she likened to "the journey to hell." There she spent the remainder of her life visited only occasionally by her husband, who remained on duty in Edo.

Signed with the pen name Makuzu, "Solitary Thoughts" (*Hitori kangae*) encapsulates Ayako's views on her society distilled during her years of isolation in Sendai. She bemoans her ignorance of Confucianism because her father thought it inappropriate knowledge for a woman. It was of little use even for men, she believed, because it was too clumsy to regulate the niceties of Japanese behavior. Like other intellectuals of her day, she pitied the samurai for not understanding the principle of money. Instead of a well-ordered harmonious society, she saw competition, hatred, and strife: "Each person in our country strives to enrich him or herself alone without thinking of the foreign threat or begrudging the cost to the country." Townspeople despised warriors: "They take secret delight in the warriors' descent into poverty, hating them like sworn enemies." Antagonism governed even relations between the sexes: "When men and women make love, they battle for superiority by rubbing their genitals together."

Source: Janet R. Goodwin, Bettina Gramlich-Oka, Elizabeth A. Leicester, Yuki Terazawa, and Anne Walthall, "Solitary Thoughts: A Translation of Tadano Makuzu's *Hitori Kangae*," *Monumenta Nipponica* 56 (Spring 2001): 21, 25, 36; 56 (Summer 2001): 179.

---

heart" (*magokoro*).[2] Even when he was asked by a daimyo to comment on the conditions of his day, Norinaga took a resolutely apolitical position, claiming that rulers should live in accordance with the way of the gods discernable in the study of history and poetry.

Official interest in western studies began in 1720 when Shogun Yoshimune lifted the ban on western books so long as they did not promote Christianity. Japanese doctors and scientists

2. Sey Nakamura, "The Way of the Gods: Motoori Norinaga's Naobi no Mitama," *Monumenta Nipponica* 46 (Spring 1991): 39.

attracted to what was called "Dutch studies" paid little attention to western philosophy; their enthusiasm was for practical matters, in particular the study of human anatomy, astronomy, geography, and military science. Sugita Genpaku discovered that a Dutch human anatomy book provided names for body parts not found in Chinese medical texts. In 1771 he watched the dissection of a criminal's corpse, a fifty-year-old woman, performed by an outcast. Although this was not the first dissection performed in Japan, the evidence of his own eyes plus the Dutch text led him to invent Japanese terms for pancreas, nerve, and other body parts; these terms were later exported to China. The belief in empirical reason and the efficacy of experiment promoted by the Chinese "practical learning" school already constituted one strand of Japanese intellectual life; the opportunity to engage with western scientific texts developed it further. Sugita spread his ideas through his writing and salons, whose members ranged from merchants to daimyo. Western instruments such as the telescope and microscope fascinated intellectuals. The insights they gained into the natural world percolated into popular culture when Utagawa Kunisada drew pictures of greatly magnified insects to illustrate a story about monsters.

MATURATION AND DECAY

Following the excesses of the Genroku period, shogunal and domainal officials fretted over the state of government finances and their retainers' morale. The miserly Ieyasu had left stores of gold bullion, but his heirs spent them so freely that by the 1690s, the shogunate had to devalue the currency. Creeping inflation eroded the value of tax revenues and samurai stipends, while the growing availability of consumer products stimulated demand. Shogun Yoshimune responded by instituting reforms in the 1720s. To aid the samurai who received their stipends in rice, he supported rice prices even though urban consumers complained. He assessed a "voluntary contribution"

from all daimyo of a rice donation in proportion to their domain's size in return for spending less time in Edo on *sankin kōtai*. Instead of basing taxes on each year's harvest, he tried to eliminate fluctuations in revenues by establishing a fixed tax rate. He allowed villages to open new fields in regions previously set aside to provide forage and fertilizer and encouraged the cultivation of cash crops. To reduce expenditures, he issued sumptuary legislation and cut the staff of palace women. He inaugurated a petition box, already tried in some domains, to allow commoners' suggestions and complaints to reach his ear. A famine caused by a plague of locusts in western Japan in 1732 brought the reform period to an end.

Popular Culture

In contrast to the ruling class, urban commoners generally enjoyed the benefits of the consumption revolution. By 1750 Edo's population had reached well over 1 million inhabitants, making it perhaps the largest city in the world at the time. A fish market dominated the hub of the city at Nihonbashi; the surrounding streets were lined with shops selling goods of every sort. Restaurants catered to people for whom dining out had become a pleasure. Innkeepers who specialized in accommodating plaintiffs became proto-lawyers in an increasingly litigious society. The draper Echigoya innovated a fixed price system for cash (see Color Plate 21). The world's first commodity futures market opened in Osaka. Kabuki actors incorporated advertisements into their routines starting in 1715. In 1774 a popular actor affixed his name to cosmetics sold in his store, mentioned his products on stage, and placed them in woodblock prints. Best-selling authors accepted money to praise products such as toothpaste and pipes.

The spread of commerce made education both possible and necessary. In thousands of villages across Japan, priests, village officials, and rural entrepreneurs opened schools to provide the rudiments of reading and mathematics. Coupled with the private academies in castle towns and cities for samurai and merchants, their

School Children and Teacher. In this early nineteenth cartoon by Hokusai, the teacher listens to three boys recite. Another student counts on his toes; rough housing turns into a fight. *(Corbis)*

efforts led to impressive rates of literacy by the mid-nineteenth century: approximately 40 percent for men and between 10 and 15 percent for women. Students studied didactic texts; those for women emphasized docility, modesty, and self-restraint lest the young working woman slip from seamstress to prostitute. Publishers supplied a growing market with one-page almanacs and Buddhist mandalas as well as pamphlets giving advice on agriculture and etiquette. Some students learned to read well enough to enjoy multivolume works of historical fiction, but for many, the aim was more practical: to learn when to plant crops and calculate profit and loss.

The national road system designed to bring daimyo to Edo began to attract increasing numbers of commoners in the eighteenth century. Although the shogunate prohibited travel in the interests of preserving order, it allowed pilgrimages, visits to relatives, and trips to medicinal hot springs. With a passport issued by a local official giving name, physical description, and destination, travelers set off, usually on foot, always in groups, accompanied by neighbors to see them to the community border. Many traveled in confraternities that raised money to send a few members on pilgrimage each year. The most popular destination was Ise, with its outer shrine to the god of agriculture. Since few trav-

elers were likely to repeat the pilgrimage experience, they were determined to see as much as possible. They took enormous detours through temple circuits and stopped in Edo and Osaka for sightseeing and theater. Men traveled in the prime of life; women traveled either before they were married or after they had a daughter-in-law to raise the children and run the household. Rather than suffer the invasive inspection procedures required at checkpoints, women hired guides to show them byways. Men and women bought quantities of souvenirs to ship back home and distribute to those who had given them money before they left. They kept diaries of their trip; some were little more than expense accounts, and others were lengthy descriptions of things seen and heard.

Not every pilgrim was literate or had the permission of his or her local official. Fired, they said, with the imperative to make a pilgrimage to Ise or some other sacred spot, they escaped from parents or employers with nothing but the clothes on their backs. They depended on the charity of strangers who hoped to accrue some of the merit of making the pilgrimage by giving alms. They also fell prey to bandits and procurers. At approximately sixty-year intervals, thousands of people, men and women alike, left towns and villages to make a thanksgiving pilgrimage (*okage mairi*) to the inner shrine of the sun goddess at Ise. Many never returned home. Instead they found their way to cities, where they joined a floating population of day laborers and prostitutes.

Hard Times and Peasant Uprisings

The underside to prosperity, continuing inequities, and injustice gave rise to thousands of incidents of rural protest. The corporate structure of the village meant that protest was organized collectively. When cultivators lodged complaints against unjust officials or pleas that the tax burden be reduced following a crop failure, they petitioned the lord to show compassion to the honorable cultivators because their hardships threatened their survival. As the village's representative, the headman was supposed to take the responsibility for seeking redress from samurai officials dealing with rural affairs. If officials deemed the matter worthy of consideration, they passed it up the chain of command. If at any point an official decided not to trouble his superiors, those below had no legal recourse. According to rural lore, in the seventeenth century a few brave headmen, epitomized by Sakura Sōgorō, made a direct appeal to the daimyo, or, in Sōgorō's case, to the shogun. Sōgorō paid for his audacity by suffering crucifixion along with his wife and saw his sons executed before his eyes. Although historians doubt his existence, he became Japan's most famous peasant martyr.

Few headmen in the eighteenth century were willing to risk their families to help their neighbors. Instead of an individual groveling before his superiors, cultivators marched together to assert their grievances en masse. They called their deeds *ikki,* harking back to the leagues that had bedeviled political authorities in the sixteenth century. In 1764, approximately two hundred thousand cultivators marched toward Edo to protest new demands for forced labor to transport officials and their goods on the national roads. Smaller outbursts roiled domains, peaking at times of economic hardship. Seldom did any district erupt more than once, and protestors wanted redress, not revolution. Yet fear that rural protest would expose such weaknesses in domainal administration that the shogun would transfer the daimyo or simply dispossess him limited efforts to expropriate the products of cultivators' labor.

The 1780s brought hard times to Japan. Mount Asama erupted in 1783, spewing ash that blocked sunlight all summer. Widespread crop failures exacerbated by misguided governmental policies led to famine, a catastrophe repeated in 1787. It is said that the population declined by nine hundred twenty thousand. In the eyes of many sufferers, the cause of their plight was not so much natural disaster as human failing. Unlike earlier rural protests that had demanded tax relief and government aid, the majority of incidents in the 1780s focused on commercial issues and the perfidy of merchants accused of hoarding grain while people starved. Commoners rioted for five days in Edo, punishing merchants by smashing their stores, trampling rice in the mud, and pouring sake in the street.

The famine exposed problems at all levels of society. The shogunate had struggled for years with an inadequate tax base and the increasing competition between daimyo, merchants, and cultivators for access to commercial income. Under the aegis of senior councilor Tanuma Okitsugu, it had proposed schemes to force merchants to buy shares in guilds granted a monopoly over trade in a specified item. The guild then paid regular fees in "thank you" money to the shogun. These monopolies angered those excluded, manufacturers forced to accept lower prices for their products, and daimyo who had their own schemes for profiting from trade. Following the Edo riot, the shogunate launched a second reform led by essayist, novelist, and staunch neo-Confucian Matsudaira Sadanobu to rectify finances and morals. He established new standards for bureaucratic conduct that endured to modern times. His "Edo first" policy ensured that the city remained quiescent for almost eighty years.

Sadanobu's reforms also had a darker side. A floating population of men without families or property worked as day laborers in fields and cities. Sadanobu had those in Edo rounded up and confined to an island in the bay. From there they were transported to the gold mine on Sado in the Japan Sea, where most of them died within two or three years. The harshness of this measure brought universal condemnation, and it was not repeated. Instead governments encouraged urban wards and rural villages to police themselves.

SUMMARY

By the beginning of the nineteenth century, the Japanese people had enjoyed almost two centuries of peace. Most cultivators seldom saw

**Color Plate 17
Rice Planting.** This sixteenth-century painting of *Rice Planting* depicts it as a fertility festival with men providing the music while women work.
(Tokyo National Museum/ DNP Archives.com)

**Color Plate 18
The Garden of the Master of Nets.** A large pond is the central feature of the *Garden of the Master of Nets* in Suzhou. Notice the use of plants, rocks, and walkways.

Color Plate 19

Arrival of the Portuguese. This six-panel folding screen depicts the *Arrival of the Portuguese*—soldiers in short pants, merchants in balloon pants, and priests in black robes accompanied by African servants.

(Musee des Arts Asiatiques-Guimet, Paris, France/RMN/Art Resource, NY)

Color Plate 20

The Qianlong Emperor Receiving Tribute Horses. This detail from a 1757 painting by the Italian court painter Giuseppe Castiglione (1688–1768) shows the reception of envoys from the Kazakhs. Note how the envoy, presenting a pure white horse, is kneeling to the ground (performing the kowtow).

(Musee Guimet, Paris/The Art Archive)

Color Plate 21
Dry Goods Store in Surugacho. In this painting entitled *Dry Goods Store in Surugacho, Edo,* customers take off their shoes to enter the shop. Male clerks serve female customers while others gather around the manager. The owner is at the back of the store.

(Corbis)

Color Plate 22
Women at the Tano Festival, by Sin Yunbok (1758–?), Chosŏn Dynasty. This painting captures the eroticism that is frequently associated with Sin Yunbok's depiction of women. Notice the two boy monks stealing a glance at the women from behind the rocks.

(Kansong Museum of Fine Arts, Seoul)

Color Plate 23
Procession for Crown Prince Sado. Procession returning from a visit to Hwasŏng (modern Suwŏn) to Seoul in 1795 led by King Chŏngjo with his mother, Lady Hyegyŏng, to honor the 60th birthday of his father, Crown Prince Sado, who had been murdered by his own father, King Yŏngjo, in 1762.

(Han Yong'u, *Tasi ch'annun uri yoksa* [*Our History, Rediscovered*], p. 11 left)

Color Plate 24
The Foreign Quarter in Guangzhou. Before the Opium War, foreign traders in Guangzhou were not to leave the small strip of land outside the city where their "factories" were located. They could live there only while arranging shipments and had to return to Macao once their ships were loaded.

(Winterthur Museum)

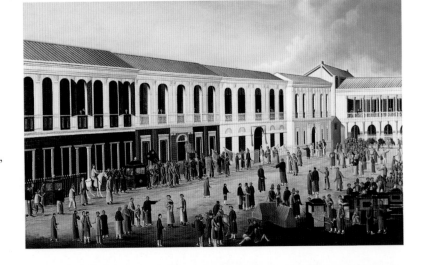

samurai officials. Despite the village and ward notice boards hung with placards admonishing commoners to refrain from luxuries, people let their pocketbooks regulate their behavior. To be sure, cultivators suffered under heavy taxes. Merchants had to accept arbitrary restrictions on commerce and pay ad hoc forced loans to meet the governments' endemic financial crises.

Sankin kōtai kept the daimyo coming to Edo to pay homage to the shogun and scheming to enhance their domain's prosperity. Many samurai could not afford the pleasure districts nor did their offices keep them occupied. Rather than concentrate on the public performance of duty, they retreated to the private world of intellectual stimulation and the pursuit of pleasure.

SUGGESTED READING

For the best overview, see C. Totman, *Early Modern Japan* (1993). The most recent book on relations between the shogunate and domains and domainal institutions is M. Ravina, *Land and Lordship in Early Modern Japan* (1999). For foreign relations, see R. P. Toby, *State and Diplomacy in Early Modern Japan: Asia in the Development of the Tokugawa Bakufu* (1984).

For intellectual history, see H. Ooms, *Tokugawa Ideology: Early Constructs, 1570–1680* (1985); T. Najita, *Visions of Virtue in Tokugawa Japan: The Kaitokudō Merchant Academy of Osaka* (1987); P. Nosco, *Remembering Paradise: Nativism and Nostalgia in Eighteenth Century Japan* (1990); and D. L. Keene, *The Japanese Discovery of Europe: Honda Toshiaki and Other Discoverers, 1720–1798* (1954).

For recent work on proto-industrialization, see D. L. Howell, *Capitalism from Within: Economy, Society, and the State in a Japanese Fishery* (1995); T. Morris-Suzuki, *The Technological Transformation of Japan: From the Seventeenth to the Twenty-First Century* (1994); and K. Wigen, *The Making of a Japanese Periphery, 1750–1920* (1995). For transformations in village life, see H. Ooms, *Tokugawa Village Practice: Class, Status, Power, Law* (1996). An excellent summary of demographic issues is by L. L. Cornell, "Infanticide in Early Modern Japan? Demography, Culture, and Population Growth," *Journal of Asian Studies* 55 (Feb. 1996): 22–50. For disease, see A. Jannetta, *Epidemics and Mortality in Early Modern Japan* (1987). The most recent book on social protest is J. W. White, *Ikki: Social Conflict and Political Protest in Early Modern Japan* (1995).

For popular culture, see S. Hanley, *Everyday Things in Premodern Japan: The Hidden Legacy of Material Culture* (1997); M. Nishiyama, *Edo Culture: Daily Life and Diversion in Urban Japan, 1600–1868* (1997); P. F. Kornicki, *The Book in Japan: A Cultural History from the Beginnings to the Nineteenth Century* (1998); and C. N. Vaporis, *Breaking Barriers: Travel and The State in Early Modern Japan* (1994).

For peripheries, see G. Smits, *Visions of Ryukyu: Identity and Ideology in Early Modern Thought and Politics* (1999), and B. L. Walker, *The Conquest of Ainu Lands: Ecology and Culture in Japanese Expansion, 1590–1800* (2001).

For sexuality, see G. M. Pflugfelder, *Cartographies of Desire: Male-Male Sexuality in Japanese Discourse, 1600–1950* (2000), and C. S. Seigle, *Yoshiwara: The Glittering World of the Japanese Courtesan* (1993).

Late Chosŏn Korea (1598–1800)

The end of the Hideyoshi invasion in 1598 was marked by a period of continued difficulty in foreign relations as a result of the challenge to the Chinese Ming Dynasty by the increasing power of the Manchus. After succumbing to the Manchus in 1637, the Chosŏn government made efforts at political, economic, and military recovery. It endured severe fiscal shortages, and agricultural production did not recover to prewar levels until 1700. The local tribute taxes were reformed, and cash entered the economy again.

The poor showing of the army made necessary reorganization of the military, but that ran up against strict Manchu surveillance. Everyone recognized that military weakness had been caused by evasion of military service, and so attention was turned to requiring military duty from slaves. Nevertheless, evasion by the *yangban* persisted, possibly because the powerful Manchu Qing Dynasty protected Korea from invasion and lessened the need for a strong defense.

Political tranquility was achieved after 1728, but it was shaken once again by an act of filicide by King Yŏngjo in 1762 and the introduction of western astronomy and Roman Catholic religious knowledge, which shocked the Confucian literati into a defensive posture. A new intellectual movement arose in the late eighteenth century, challenging conventional economic thinking and prejudiced attitudes toward the Manchu Qing Dynasty.

Women were faced with the reduction of their position and status in society as Confucian principles changed the organization of the family. Confucian thought seemed to get more restrictive in controlling the thought of men as well. Yet the end of the eighteenth century witnessed an outburst of literary activity, culture, and entertainment that appealed to the common people and called into question the repressed position of women and the ordinary peasantry. A potential for radical cultural change was emerging along with the crises in policy and

Landscape of the Diamond Mountains (Kŭmgangsan). This painting, by Chŏng Sŏn (1676–1759), depicts the landscape of the Diamond Mountains (Kŭmgangsan) with a touch of animistic spirits in the swaying mountains. Chosŏn Dynasty. *(Hoam Museum of Fine Arts, Yong'in; Koreana: Korean Cultural Heritage, Volume 1, Fine Arts. Korea Foundation, 1994, p. 56)*

MANCHUS AND FACTIONAL DISPUTES

Korea severed all relations with Japan after Japanese withdrawal from the peninsula in 1598. Hideyoshi's successor, Tokugawa Ieyasu, had no interest in invading Korea, however, and Korea reestablished relations in a 1609 treaty. The treaty restricted trade to Tongnae, near Pusan, where a Japanese office called the *Waegwan* (Japanese Hall) was established behind a palisade fence, and the Japanese were left to administer it. Trade with Japan was regulated through tallies that were issued to the head of the Sō family on Tsushima Island, and then distributed to various daimyo throughout Japan. The trade was limited to a certain number of ships per year. On the continent, however, Korea found itself embroiled in a conflict between a declining Ming Dynasty and the rising Jurchen tribes in Manchuria.

Relations with the Manchus

While the Japanese invasion was going on in the 1590s, the Jurchen tribes in Manchuria, previously divided into a number of independent small units, began to coalesce under Nurhaci, who changed the name of the Jurchen to Manchu. Nurhaci attacked Ming territory and demanded military aid from Chosŏn at the same time that the Ming court demanded Korean reinforcements. Caught in a difficult spot between the two rivals, the Chosŏn king, Kwanghaegun (Lord Kwanghae, who never received a posthumous title because he was deposed in 1623), tried to maintain neutrality, but the vast majority of his own officials opposed him for failing to meet his moral obligation to support the Ming, whose armies had saved Chosŏn from Hideyoshi.

Kwanghaegun also faced domestic opposition to his rule. Kwanghaegun was the son of one of King Sŏnjo's concubines and was elected crown prince by the king during the Imjin War. Once Sŏnjo's second queen gave birth to a son, the

administration. Some of the scholarly issues surrounding this period include the following: Did Chosŏn handle relations with the Manchus well? How successful were the reforms of these two centuries? Why did political factionalism become so bloody after 1659, and was King Yŏngjo able to end it during his reign? Did the Chosŏn economy remain stagnant, or did it progress? How radical were the social changes in the late eighteenth century? How did Korea react to western learning and Christianity?

Great Lord Yŏngch'ang, however, many officials of the small northerner, southerner, and westerner factions wanted to depose Kwanghaegun, as the son of a queen took ritual precedence over the son of a concubine. With the support of the great northern faction, Kwanghaegun had Grand Prince Yŏngch'ang and his younger brother assassinated for plotting against him.

In 1623 the westerner faction led a coup to depose Kwanghaegun and replaced him with King Sŏnjo's grandson, Lord Nŭngnyang, known posthumously as King Injo. All the Northerners who had supported Kwanghaegun were executed or banished, and they remained out of high office for the next two centuries. Upon seizing power, the westerners reversed Kwanghaegun's controversial foreign policy and supported the Ming against the Manchus.

Unfortunately, military defense in the northeast was wrecked when Yi Kwal, one of the coup leaders, rebelled with two-thirds of the seventeen thousand men in the area and occupied the capital in Seoul before the rebellion was put down. Instead of rethinking his anti-Manchu policy, Injo prepared for war but made the error of stationing more soldiers around the capital to guard against potential rebels than on the northern frontier. When the Manchus invaded Korea in 1627 with a force of thirty thousand, they overran the opposition and imposed a peace treaty on King Injo. Fortunately for him, the Manchus withdrew rather than commit troops to occupy Korea.

King Injo stubbornly continued with his anti-Manchu policy. When he refused a demand from the new Manchu Qing Dynasty in 1636 to send anti-Manchu officials to the Qing court for punishment along with a hostage from the Chosŏn royal family, the Qing emperor, Taizong, led a Manchu force of one hundred twenty thousand men in an invasion of Korea in February 1637. The Chosŏn border commander failed to transmit the war beacon signals to the capital on time, causing King Injo to receive word of the invasion in Seoul only two days before Manchu troops arrived. He took refuge in the fort on top of the North Han Mountain (*Pukhansansŏng*) but was surrounded and

forced to submit to the Qing demand that he sever relations with the Ming Dynasty and enroll as a Qing tributary, seven years before the Manchu conquered most of China in 1644.

The Manchus levied heavy tribute demands on Chosŏn, and King Injo turned his anger against those who had favored accommodation with the Manchus. He even suspected his own son, Crown Prince Sohyŏn, of cooperating with the Manchu regent, Prince Dorgon. It was rumored that Injo poisoned his son and then executed Sohyŏn's widow, her family, and two of Sohyŏn's three sons in 1646. He then chose his second son to be crown prince, and he became King Hyojong in 1649.

King Hyojong, who also tried to form an army to avenge Chosŏn's defeat, was frustrated by close Manchu surveillance. By the end of the seventeenth century, Chosŏn kings abandoned that policy, and the Qing court reduced its tribute demands. Most Korean *yangban*, however, still held the Manchus in contempt and remained loyal to the memory of the Wanli Emperor of the Ming for saving Korea from Hideyoshi.

Economic and Institutional Reforms

Once the foreign issue was settled, the Chosŏn government began a program of recovery. Korean kings reformed the system of tribute levies in kind on the villages by legalizing the illegal contracting system by which villagers paid fees to merchants to supply special goods that they no longer produced to the king and government agencies. Under the *taedong* reform, the government replaced local product payments in kind by imposing an extra land tax in grain, which it used to purchase the special goods it needed from the merchants. The new *taedong* tax was adopted gradually, but by 1708 the new system covered the whole country and more than doubled the land tax and the burden on landowners. The law stimulated increased commercial activity, particularly among private, unlicensed merchants.

The government reorganized the army and extended military service to private slaves for the first time. In 1650, the official Kim Yuk returned from a trip to China with large amounts of cash he had purchased with funds saved from his expenses. He received King Hyojong's approval to put it into circulation, and in 1654 persuaded the king to order that the cash be accepted in payment of the *taedong* tax. This marked the first use of cash in about a hundred years.

The devastation of war stimulated some scholars to shift their attention to statecraft and utilitarian problems. Yu Hyŏngwŏn, a reclusive scholar of the northerner faction, spent twenty years between 1650 and 1672 writing a comprehensive analysis of contemporary institutional problems and making recommendations for reform. He derived inspiration for reform from the ancient Chinese classics and the statecraft writings of the Song scholars and active officials. He criticized the hereditary nature of both the *yangban* and the slaves and argued that according to Confucian principles, neither of those two social strata should be determined by birth. He also opposed the examination system because it tested only rote memorization and literary skill. He insisted on eliminating hereditary slavery because passing the sins of the father on to the sons was contrary to Confucian teaching and ancient precedent. Only the enslavement of prisoners of war or criminals was proper. His reforms were rational and radical, but not to the point where he ever questioned the legitimacy and propriety of Confucian values, classical wisdom, and an agricultural economy. Unknown in his own time, his ideas were transmitted through disciples to men like Yi Ik (pen name, Sŏngho) in the early eighteenth century.

The Resumption of Factional Disputes (1659–1730)

Factional disputes subsided after 1623 as officials were consumed primarily with recovery from devastation. In 1659, however, factionalism reemerged when Song Siyŏl of the westerner faction insisted that a member of the royal family should perform a lesser degree of mourning for the deceased King Hyojong because he was the second son of King Injo. The southerner faction, led by Yun Hyu, accused Song Siyŏl and the westerners of impugning the legitimacy of King Hyojong and his heirs. The southerners eventually persuaded King Hyŏnjong to adopt their position and dismiss Song. Westerners led by Yun Ch'ung, who disliked Song's uncompromising and arrogant leadership of the westerner faction, also split to form their own Disciples faction (Soron), leaving Song and his supporters to form their own Patriarchs faction (Noron).

Ostensibly an issue of ritual that should have been resolved without trouble led to a series of major purges and executions. King Sukchong (r. 1674–1720) contributed to the conflict by switching his support almost whimsically back to the Patriarchs and Disciples. He replaced them with southerners in 1689 because they opposed his decision to replace his first queen with a palace concubine and then turned around and purged the southerners in 1694 after he lost interest in her. When the Patriarchs regained power, they excluded the descendants of southerners from office until the late eighteenth century.

The Patriarchs and Disciples factions now turned against each other over the choice between two of King Sukchong's sons for crown prince: the Disciples favored Yi Kyun and the Patriarchs favored Lord Yŏnning. King Sukchong chose the childless and sickly Yi Kyun, but he appointed Lord Yŏnning as crown prince. When Yi Kyun became King Kyŏngjong in 1724, his Disciple supporters persuaded him to execute the four leading Patriarchs for supporting Lord Yŏnning, but Yŏnning remained crown prince. King Kyŏngjong died an early death in 1727, at which time Lord Yŏnning became King Yŏngjo, and his Patriarch supporters exacted revenge on the Disciples (see **Biography: King Yŏngjo**). King Yŏngjo, however, decided that the time had come to put an end to factional strife by announcing his "equal opportunity" policy (*tangp'yŏngch'aek*). In practice, however, King Yŏngjo appointed officials from moderate members of both the Disciples and Patriarchs' factions and excluded not only radical members of those two factions who still

BIOGRAPHY King Yŏngjo

King Yŏngjo (1694–1776, r. 1724–1776) was a complex and strong ruler whose reign lasted a half-century. He came to the throne as part of bloody conflict over the succession and is famed for calling a halt to factionalism. He was a student of Confucianism and began his reign by attending daily the lectures on the Chinese classics by his officials, but he began to challenge their views and to write his own commentaries, contrary to the Confucian admonition to learn from rather than teach his mentors. He sponsored the publication of Confucian texts like *The Five Rituals, Continued* (*Sok Oryeŭi*), the compilation of the first institutional encyclopedia, the *Taedong munhŏnbigo* modeled after the Chinese *Wenxian tongkao,* a new edition of the law code (*Soktaejŏn*), and a manual on classical music (*Akhak kwebŏm*), but did he always live up to those values?

He began his domestic policy with laudable motives, to reinstitute military service for *yangban* and convert some slaves to commoner status, but he backed down in the face of landlord and slave owner opposition. He fought against the expansion of currency because of the traditional fear of the evil effects of inflation, but he finally yielded to entreaties from officials who had a greater understanding of economic matters.

His decision to commit filicide against Crown Prince Sado in 1762 created the basis for continued factional controversy that lasted into the beginning of the next century. As a father, he was aloof and thoughtless, not unusual for many Korean fathers then and now. His incompetent fatherhood was a function of the protocol of the palace, which kept royal children separate from kings and made him dependent on infrequent reports of fact and rumor, all of which was beyond his power to control. Then he chose to kill his son, but only when it was rumored that his son was participating in a conspiracy, not when he murdered a eunuch and his palace paramour in fits of anger. It was theoretically possible for a Confucian gentlemen to pursue filicide in an extreme case, but was that King Yŏngjo's only alternative? Prince Sado's wife, Lady Hyegyŏng, tried to raise these issues long after his death, but she never accused him of a violation of Confucian standards, only laxity in showing care and concern for his son's welfare. Open discussion was, of course, banned lest any aspersions be cast on the reputation of Yŏngjo and his royal line, but to this day he retains a reputation for being one of the greatest kings in the dynasty. Although Yŏngjo could not be expected to appreciate his son's psychosis in a pre-Freudian time, he could have chosen to depose or exile his son instead of starving him to death in a box.

---

sought to take revenge on their opponents but northerners and southerners as well.

The radical Disciples, however, rose up in rebellion under Yi Injwa in 1728 in Ch'ungch'ŏng province. King Yŏngjo put the rebellion down and maintained his coalition cabinet, but the rebellion alerted King Yŏngjo to serious danger in the future if he damaged *yangban* interests.

THE DECLINE OF THE MILITARY SERVICE AND RURAL CREDIT SYSTEMS

By the eighteenth century most *yangban* had succeeded in evading military service, because they regarded it as an embarrassing reduction to com-

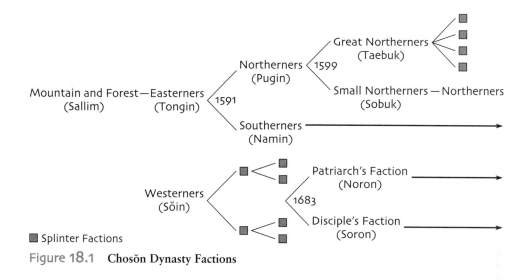

Figure 18.1   **Chosŏn Dynasty Factions**

moner status. Military service now was called commoner service (*yangyŏk*) because *yangban* had escaped military service and regarded it as demeaning, but even commoners were evading it by bribing registration clerks to register them as students. The reduction of eligible commoners to pay the military cloth tax increased the tax burden on registered adult males and weakened the army. The Qing peace was Chosŏn's main defense against foreign invasion.

Since the 1680s, reformers had been proposing the reform of military service by imposing the military cloth support tax on *yangban* households. King Yŏngjo favored the idea, but the resistance to it was so extreme that he refrained from a direct attack against *yangban* interests. When he proclaimed his equal service law (*kyunyŏkpŏp*) of 1750, he abandoned the challenge to the *yangban* and merely reduced the military cloth tax rate on commoners by half.

By the end of the dynasty, the system of rural credit and relief administered by local magistrates also fell apart as corrupt officials robbed the funds or superimposed them on peasants unable to repay loans. Instead of driving impoverished smallholding commoner peasants into bankruptcy, however, local officials chose not to collect payments on principal. Instead they turned the payment of interest on loans into an annual collection that was equivalent to an

additional tax. King Yŏngjo did not address this issue, leaving an unresolved problem that exacerbated peasant resentment against the state.

LATE CHOSŎN SOCIETY: SLAVES AND *YANGBAN*

Between 1750 and 1790 there was a sharp reduction in the slave population: from about 30 percent to less than 10 percent of the population. King Yŏngjo had contributed a little to this reduction by approving the readoption of the matrilineal rule governing the inheritance of slave status by offspring of mixed slave-commoner marriages in 1730. The main cause of the decline, however, was the increase in the number of runaway slaves. Instead of paying the cost of chasing after them, *yangban* and rich landlords took advantage of the recent increase in indebted peasants who had lost their land for failure to repay loans. They simply rented land to the army of landless peasants. Escaped slaves did not necessarily see a rise in income and standards of living because now they had to pay rackrents to landlords, interest on grain loans from the state or private lenders, and payment of the commoner military cloth tax.

Another factor in the decline in the slave population was that the government had begun to replace official slaves with hired commoner labor, further reducing the number of official slaves from three hundred fifty thousand in 1590 to sixty thousand by 1801. King Chŏngjo (r. 1776–1800) entertained several proposals to abolish official slavery, but in the end he failed to take action and paid no attention at all to abolishing private slavery.

The *yangban* preserved their elite position during this period and kept a near monopoly of access to high office. The percentage of successful examination passers from the top two dozen *yangban* families increased as well. While the government had begun to sell rank titles in this period, the purchase of such titles did not confer official posts and did not elevate purchasers into the ranks of *yangban*. Since an average of only thirty men per year passed the examinations, many *yangban* who studied for the examinations were deprived of the chance for office and were left in the countryside to make their way there.

Some were able to form single-family villages and further strengthen their power. In other villages, *yangban* power declined because magistrates unified the variety of taxes previously collected separately in a new single tax called *togyŏl* as a more efficient form of tax collection. In order to alleviate the tax burden, village associations called *tonggye* were formed of all households regardless of status to divide the tax burden equally among all families. Finally, *chung'in*, or middle people, who staffed clerks' posts as well as legal specialists, accountants, and interpreters, gave up any hope of holding regular office and followed their *yangban* superiors to form another hereditary class that excluded ordinary commoners from easy access to their positions.

ECONOMIC DEVELOPMENT IN THE EIGHTEENTH CENTURY

The Chosŏn population grew to 14 million by the year 1810, a 40 percent increase over 1650. Connected to this growth was an increase in agricultural productivity and market activity.

From the late fourteenth century, the use of fertilizer spread throughout the country to provide annual cultivation; it replaced the fallow system, under which land was left alone for a year or two to recover fertility. The conversion of dry to wet, irrigated rice fields also increased, and the adoption of transplantation instead of broadcast seeding improved weeding and achieved higher yields.[1] But by the late seventeenth century transplantation was followed by serious crop failures if weather conditions were bad. By around 1900, average production per acre in Korea was about 15 bushels, about the same as China in 1400 and about one-third less than production in Japan and China around 1880.

The eighteenth century witnessed the development of warehousing and wholesale merchants, and the number of periodic five-day markets increased (see **Material Culture: Five-Day Markets**). The number of commercial towns remained small, however; Seoul was the biggest of these, with only two hundred thousand people. Market growth was slowed when King Sukchong decided to stop minting cash in 1697 because of inflation from excessive minting. That policy continued for thirty-three years and produced deflation. King Yŏngjo reluctantly agreed to mint more cash in 1731, and minting continued for the rest of the dynasty, but no multiple-denomination cash (the equivalent of nickels, dimes, and quarters) was minted until the 1860s because of the fear of inflation. The restriction to penny cash along with the absence of paper money, bills of exchange, or banks was another obstacle to rapid commercial expansion.

Nonetheless, private, unlicensed merchants began to compete with the licensed merchants in the capital. In the 1740s the government capitulated and stopped prosecuting unlicensed merchants trading in certain goods. King Chŏngjong in 1791 adopted a compromise solution, the joint-sales policy, which protected monopoly privileges

---

1. Broadcast seeding is done by throwing out the seed on the field by hand. Transplantation means planting the rice seeds in a small seed bed to make it easier to weed the early sprouts and then transplanting them to the growing field after the rice plants have matured.

MATERIAL CULTURE

Five-Day Markets

The most important material development in this period was the spread of market activity and the use of currency, indicating that Korea was able to move forward economically despite the powerful anticommercial prejudice of Confucian thought in Korea. That development, however, has been exaggerated to the point where it has been perceived as constituting the beginning of capitalism.

One of the best types of evidence to demonstrate that market development was quite sluggish in creating commercial towns with permanent shops was to see what a typical market looked like in the eighteenth century. Rather than a commercial town, it was a five-day market that opened only once every five days. Market development meant that residents of villages were now surrounded by a number of five-day markets that allowed an individual to travel to one of them every day of the ten-day week, a trip that took no more than a day's walk back and forth. Even some of the larger towns, which were more administrative than commercial centers, housed only one of the five-day markets instead of permanent shops, as in Seoul.

Typical Five-Day Market. Chosŏn Dynasty, late nineteenth century. *(Sajinuro ponun Choson sidae: Saenghwal kwa p'ungsok [The Choson period in Pictures: Life and Customs] [Seoul: Somundang, 1986], p. 7)*

only for six shops (*Yug'ŭijon*) in Seoul and allowed private merchants to manufacture or sell all other products. Beyond this, there was no development toward a completely free market system.

POLITICS, IDEOLOGY, AND REFORM AFTER 1762

Despite King Yŏngjo's efforts to end factionalism, he made politics more complicated in 1762 when he decided to lock Crown Prince Sado in a small rice box in the palace courtyard and left

him to starve to death; he died eight days later. King Yŏngjo was an absentee father whose neglect of Sado was compounded by stern expectations of excellence, but the boy had already displayed severe neurotic tendencies. Yŏngjo had given Sado responsibility as prince regent at the age of fifteen in 1749 to take over many of the king's tasks, but Sado was obviously mentally disturbed because of his fear of his father, and his father's ridicule pushed the prince over the edge of sanity. He released his pent-up frustrations in paroxysms of rage in which he murdered ladies of the palace who offended him.

A-Frame Carrier. Chosŏn Dynasty, nineteenth century. *(Sajinuro ponun Choson sidae: Saeghwal kwa p'ungsok [The Choson Period in Pictures: Life and Customs] [Seoul: Somundang, 1986], p. 47)*

King Yŏngjo appears to have decided to commit filicide when it was reported to him that Prince Sado was overheard praying for his own father's death. This action immediately split the bureaucrats into the *pyŏkp'a* (mostly Patriarchs), who agreed with Yŏngjo's decision, and the *sip'a* (mostly Southerners), who sympathized with the deceased crown prince, laying the groundwork for another round of purges. When King Chŏngjo, the son of the deceased Sado, came to the throne in 1776, he ardently desired to find some means to honor his father, restore his reputation, and take out vengeance against the Patriarch and *pyŏkp'a* factions. His grandfather, King Yŏngjo, had explicitly

ordered him not to do so to prevent the reemergence of factional strife, however. Chŏngjo was also beholden to those factions for protecting him against seven assassination plots.

Chŏngjo chastised his officials for their devotion to their own private interests and their failure to master the moral teachings of the Chinese classics. To rectify this problem, he ordered that Chinese classical texts be imported and housed them in a new Kyujanggak Royal Library staffed by his favorite officials. He turned that staff into his own private cabinet for advising him on state affairs. Nevertheless, he banned the free importation of books from China because he disliked the subversive nature of Chinese thought, particularly Wang Yangming's meditational approach to Confucianism, the rising trend of popular genres in literature and art, the writing of sardonic novels, the useless concern with prose and poetry styles, and the influence of Christian theology. He remarked that Korea already possessed more than enough editions of the Chinese classics, a curious position for a king whose reign was marked by a blossoming of popular genres in literature.

Chŏngjo wanted to rule Chosŏn as an active ruler like the ancient Chinese sages, but the Patriarch and *pyŏkp'a* factions believed that a sage king should turn over the administration to men who passed the civil service examinations. They also insisted that their factions represented the morally good men while their opponents were either immoral or amoral, an argument made famous by Ouyang Xiu of the Chinese Song Dynasty. King Chŏngjo told the Patriarchs that he was a better judge than they of good and ethical government and reminded them that the sage kings of ancient China allowed no factions.

Chŏngjo frequently made demonstrations of his ardent devotion to his deceased father. In 1795 he led a procession of six thousand men to Hwasŏng (Suwŏn) with his mother, Princess Hyegyŏng, ostensibly to honor her seventieth birthday, but the underlying goal was to honor his father, who was buried there (see Color Plate 23). He also ordered construction of a new commercial city in his father's honor, but he had to abandon the project because of four crop disasters in the 1790s.

The bad harvests in 1792, 1794, 1797, and 1798 prompted Chŏngjo to put out a call for advice to the nation for reform proposals. The leading private statecraft scholars of that period, including Pak Chiwŏn and Chŏng Yagyong (Tasan), recommended limiting land holdings, but their limits were far too high to be effective because they feared fierce opposition from landlords. King Chŏngjo rejected the idea because land limitation had not been tried in China since the Han Dynasty. Since Chŏngjo also failed to manumit official slaves, his reform project ended in dismal failure. The only policy that apparently did succeed was strengthening central control over district magistrates to clean up corruption, but after his death when corruption resumed, the magistrates had greater power to harass the local population.

NEW MOVEMENTS IN SCHOLARSHIP AND LEARNING

The economic and material devastation caused by the Japanese and Manchu invasions created a crisis that caused some scholars to turn their attention to statecraft problems. Following in the footsteps of Yu Hyŏngwŏn, the Southerner Yi Ik wanted to save the peasants from suffering and poverty, but he opposed the idea of confiscating land from landowners by force lest social order be disrupted. He preferred that limits be placed on the amount of land owned according to the rank and status of the individual. Sŏ Yugu, who wrote in the 1820s, also feared confiscation. He wanted the state to purchase land to establish colonies that would be organized around the well-fields (a large square divided into nine small squares) of the ancient Zhou Dynasty and to recruit skilled managers to increase efficiency.

Northern Learning

In the late eighteenth century a group of reform scholars and officials dubbed the Northern Learning group challenged the conventional prejudice against the Manchus. They urged that

Korea learn from the Qing Dynasty to improve the economy and the material aspects of life. Most came from the minority Southerner or Northerner factions.

Hong Taeyong was attracted to the statecraft writings of Yulgok (Yi I) and Yu Hyŏngwŏn. When he accompanied his uncle on a mission to the Qing capital in 1765, he became interested in western astronomy and mathematics, but he confined his speculations to analogical reasoning rather than astronomical observation. He also rejected the idea that China was either at the center of the earth or the only enlightened country on earth, and he criticized his fellow *yangban* for focusing only on China and neglecting the history and culture of their own country. He criticized the disdain for manual labor by the *yangban* aristocracy and the backwardness and poverty of the economy, but he did not propose any revolutionary social change.

Pak Chiwŏn studied with Hong Taeyong. After accompanying a tribute mission to China in 1780, he left a detailed record of his trip in his *Jehol Diary* (*Yŏlha ilgi*), and was appointed to office in 1786. He attacked the *yangban* monopoly of the examination system and satirized them in stories like *Master Hŏ* (*Hŏsaengjŏn*) and *The Yangban* (*Yangbanjŏn*). He condemned scholars for ignoring practical subjects, and he demanded a ban on discrimination against *nothoi* (sons of concubines), manumission of official slaves, and adoption of a land-limitation scheme.[2] He encouraged everyone to engage in commerce and industry and recommended improving transportation by copying the better carts and boats in Qing China.

Pak Chega was a Southerner who studied with Pak Chiwŏn. In 1786 he proposed that the king invite Christian missionaries from China to Korea to teach western astronomy and mathematics. In 1788 he wrote a book entitled *Northern Learning* (*Puhag'ŭi*) that expanded on

---

2. The Greek term *nothos* (pl., *nothoi*) is very close to the Korean term *sŏŏl*, because they do not convey any notion of illegitimacy to children of concubines. "Secondary sons" has also been used to describe *sŏŏl*, but I prefer the Greek term because it was coined explicitly to fit sons of concubines.

themes introduced by Hong Taeyong and Pak Chiwŏn, and he urged the king to appoint the best merchants to office and expand trade with Qing China.

Northern Learning represented a liberalization of interest and thought among intellectuals in this period, but it had a very limited effect on government policy because anti-Manchu prejudice and the Confucian bias against merchants were too powerful to overcome.

Christianity and Western Learning

After the Jesuit Francis Xavier arrived in Japan in 1549, many Japanese were converted to Christianity. Some Korean captives who were taken to Japan during Hideyoshi's invasions converted, but they had a negligible effect on Korea. Many of Matteo Ricci's works on Catholic theology and western mathematics, astronomy, and geography were brought into Korea from China in the early seventeenth century. The Koreans lumped Christian theology and western science together in a single term, *Western Learning (Sŏhak)*. Koreans were won over to western astronomical ideas and adopted the western calendar in 1653, nine years after the Qing Dynasty had done so.

A few scholars became curious about Christianity in the 1720s. Yi Ik was greatly impressed by "Seven Victories" (*Jige*) by Diego Pontoja (1571–1618) because it praised self-denial, frugality, and other virtues compatible with Confucianism, but otherwise he rejected Christian theology. Yet he urged his disciples to study it. Yi Imyŏng in 1720, however, rejected the Catholic notion of heaven and hell, and Yi Ik's disciple, Sin Hudam, in 1724 condemned Christianity for its resemblance to the selfish aspect of Buddhism (leaving the family to become a mendicant monk in the search for individual salvation) and its concern with life after death. Another disciple, An Chŏngbok, became tutor to King Chŏngjo when he was crown prince and wrote refutations of Catholic dogma.

The Jesuit emphasis on the truth of Catholic dogma as a means of proving the validity of the Christian message in the manner of St. Thomas Aquinas passed over the heads of most of these Confucian scholars, who were interested only in whether Catholic doctrines would aid or hinder adherence to Confucian social morality.[3] Meanwhile, in 1715, the pope's condemnation of Chinese ancestral ceremonial practices as idolatry was followed in 1724 by Emperor Yongzheng's condemnation of Christianity and his ban against Christian proselytization. The papal ban influenced mainstream attitudes in Korea and helped turn the tide later from scholarly criticism to violent repression.

Toleration and Persecution of Christians

King Chŏngjo went much beyond King Yŏngjo in opening opportunities for office to members of the Southerner and Northerner factions, including those who had previously been exiled. This proved to be a risky strategy. One of Yi Ik's disciples, Hong Yuhan, in 1770 began to observe the Sabbath, not to convert to Christianity but to meditate to eliminate selfishness from his mind. In 1779, however, a group of men including some of Yi's disciples participated in a retreat for ten days at the Chuŏ Temple (Chuŏsa) near Kwangju in Kyŏnggi province to explore the available literature on Christianity.

In 1784, Tasan concluded that because virtue could be attained only after a much longer period of arduous practice than even Zhu Xi had imagined, reverence for God was the best way to nourish a feeling of awe and apprehension before the external moral power. Tasan's God (Matteo Ricci's *Sangje*), however, was the Confucian ruler of the universe, not the Christian creator of the universe.

That same year Yi Sŭnghun traveled to Yanjing in China to be baptized, but the Catholic missionaries refused because of his inadequate knowledge of Catholic doctrine. He brought back Christian texts to proselytize among acquain-

---

3. Don Baker, "Confucians Confront Catholicism in Eighteenth-Century Korea," Ph.D. diss., University of Washington, 1983, p. 150.

tances like Tasan and his two brothers and members of the *chung'in* hereditary specialists and clerks. Several dozen men formed the first Christian congregation and worshipped at the home of the *chung'in* Kim Pŏm'u in Seoul in the spring of 1785. When the meetings were discovered, Kim Pŏm'u was beaten and died of his wounds in 1786, becoming Korea's first Christian martyr.

In 1787, however, two students of the National Academy (*Sŏnggyun'gwan*) in Seoul, Yi Sŭnghun and Tasan, were attacked for studying Christian texts, and the next year, two high officials asked the king to ban European books. The southerner Councilor of the Right, Ch'ae Chegong, who was not Christian but a relative of many Catholic southerners, pleaded with King Chŏngjo not to punish the Christians because their knowledge of Confucian doctrine was still insufficient. Chŏngjo agreed, but he also ordered the destruction of all Christian books.

In 1790 Bishop Alexandre de Bouvea in Yanjing sent a letter to the Korean Catholics informing them of the papal ban on the *chesa* ancestral worship ceremony, understood by the pope as idolatry. The ban drove some sympathizers like Tasan from Christianity, but in 1791 two Catholics who were also Southerners from Chŏlla province, Paul Yun Chich'ung and his cousin, James Kwŏn Sangyŏn, burned the ancestral tablets for Yun's mother. When they refused to recant, King Chŏngjo ordered their decapitation, interrogated several others under torture, and forced them to commit apostasy.

In 1794, however, the first Christian missionary to Korea, the Chinese Zhou Wenmo, was discovered. King Chŏngjo executed him and demoted or exiled southerners, and two years later he dismissed Ch'ae Chegong. King Chŏngjo's attempt at toleration had backfired, and he adopted a hard line against southerners and Christians.

THE FAMILY AND WOMEN IN THE CONFUCIAN AGE

By the eighteenth century Confucian ancestor worship had completely replaced Buddhist ceremonies for the deceased, and the Confucian pattern of patriarchal domination of the family reached its zenith. Succession to family headship was restricted where possible to the eldest son, and if there were no sons, adoption was restricted to sons of close relatives in the male line.

At the age of seven, sons and daughters were separated from each other, and daughters were educated in accordance with Confucian manuals to learn the rule of modesty and subordination to men. Their training was confined to female chores, with minimal attention to education unless the child's parents defied convention. Upon marriage, women had to move to their husband's home and lost their right of inheritance to property from their parents. They were subordinated to their mothers-in-law, had to remain silent unless spoken to, and were often treated as little more than household maids. Women were kept in the inner quarters (*nanbang*) of the house for the most part and had to wear a head covering when going out. They had to remain chaste while their husbands were free to chase after women and *kisaeng* (female entertainers), even bringing them into the house as concubines. Wives were subject to expulsion if they failed to produce a male heir or were deemed insubordinate to any member of their husband's household, and they were banned from remarriage after the death of the husband.

A wife who bore a son immediately gained status, but on her husband's death, she had to remain subordinated to her son's decisions. Her only respite came when her son married and she could lord her authority over her daughter-in-law. Since her husband spent his time in study or association with male friends in the *sarangbang*, or outer guest room, she managed the household. She participated in ancestor worship for her husband's parents but not for her own, and she was not allowed to lead the service if there were any male survivors.

At the beginning of the dynasty, women were listed in the family genealogy (*chokpo*) along with their brothers in the order of birth. By the eighteenth century, however, they were all listed after their brothers, and when they married, they were expunged from it and were listed instead in their husband's genealogy as the daughter of their father. Their names were not even recorded.

Female Clothing. Outdoor garb, as depicted in this photo, was required attire for *yangban* women to keep them hidden from the gaze of men. Chosŏn Dynasty, nineteenth century. *(Sajinuro ponun Choson sidae: Saeghwal kwa p'ungsok [The Choson Period in Pictures: Life and Customs] [Seoul: Somundang, 1986], p. 162)*

Marriages among the *yangban* in Chosŏn were the result of an agreement between two families, and they were usually contracted when the partners were quite young. (See Chapter 15.) Commoner women had fewer of these restrictions on them, but *kisaeng* were free to dispense with husbands, choose them, or leave them to find another.

In the home, the woman managed popular religious practices usually frowned on by men. They prayed to mountains, trees, and household gods. They regarded their dreams as predictive of the sex and capacity of a new child, and they had to take care to defend the family against bad omens around the home. A special ceremony might be held for cutting the umbilical cord, and unusual burials were practiced for

women who died in labor or committed suicide to prevent their spirits from plaguing surviving members of the family. Women also attended religious festivals, such as the Tano Festival (see Color Plate 22).

The wife took charge of hiring shamans, usually female ones (*mudang*), to go into a trance and communicate with the angry spirits of her own dead parents and grandparents, who were believed to cause sickness and other problems among family members. For that matter, even kings used shamans. They taxed them, used them for *kut* in the palace to pray for rain or cure illness, and set up an office to control official shamans. Women, as well as many men, continued to believe in Buddhist ideas despite Confucian condemnation, particularly transmigration, karma, and punishment in Buddhist hell, especially in facing illness or impending death.

THE GROWTH OF LITERATURE

In the seventeenth and eighteenth centuries, there was a burgeoning of literary production, including about a hundred tales usually written by men in classical Chinese and women in the *han'gŭl* alphabet. About one-third of them (twenty-five such tales) are about women, and the other two-thirds deal with women at some length. Many of the stories of women portray them defending their womanly virtues, but suffering is usually the main theme. In other tales, *kisaeng* exert their independence despite their low status by demanding or stealing their lovers' money or humiliating them in public.

The most popular of all tales was about Ch'unhyang. It evolved from the troubadour tradition of *p'ansori* singers, which began around 1800 and was written down in several versions. The most complete version includes many references and allusions to Chinese emperors, officials, and poets, obviously to appeal to *yangban* as well as commoners. It was both a didactic tale of the triumph of womanly virtue over evil and a romantic tale between the daughter of a *kisaeng* who chose not to adopt her mother's occupation and the son of a *yangban* official. In defiance of

Shaman Attire. Male (*paksu*) and female (*mudang*) shamans dressed as civil or military officials. Late Chosŏn Dynasty. *(Sajinuro ponun Choson sidae: Saeghwal kwa p'ungsok [The Choson Period in Pictures: Life and Customs] [Seoul: Somundang, 1986], p. 122)*

convention, the two wed secretly at the age of fifteen, but the husband left for Seoul to prepare for the civil service examinations and passed in first place. Meanwhile, a cruel governor arrived in Ch'unhyang's town and demanded that the young woman become his concubine. When she refused, he ordered her beaten unmercifully and threw her in jail to die. The husband then returned as a secret inspector to cashier the governor, and the two lived happily ever after. The story contains many dream sequences, constant reminders of unexpected dangers, and Buddhist awareness of karma, life after death, and resignation to fate. The erotic description of the two lovers affirms the priority of love over stifling convention, undoubtedly the reason that the story has remained so popular.

The *Nine Cloud Dream* was written by Kim Manjung (1637–1692), a high official and member of the Patriarch faction who was dismissed twice, in 1674 and 1689, when the Patriarchs were purged. Despite his deep Confucian training, the story's main message is Buddhist: the glories of a Confucian education, promotion to high office, and unrestricted access to sex with two wives and seven concubines was no more meaningful than a dream. It was better to realize that a humble life devoted to Buddhist devotion was the way to live. In this story, the wives and concubines are all independent, resourceful women who stand out as more vivid characters than the supposed hero.

Two other famous literary works of the period are more political in nature. *The True*

DOCUMENTS

Lady Hyegyŏng's Memoirs

Most outstanding as a literary work was Memoirs of Lady Hyegyŏng (Hanjungnok or Records Written in Silence), *written in* han'gŭl *by the wife of Crown Prince Sado, who was starved to death by his father, King Yŏngjo, in 1762. The book consists of four separate accounts written in 1795, 1801, 1802, and 1805. No other source provides a better introduction to the vicissitudes of palace life, particularly at a time when the slightest slip could mean death. In fact, her uncle and younger brother were executed, in 1776 and 1801, respectively. Probably the most interesting of her narratives was in her Memoir of 1805, in which she relates Sado's psychosis to the deficiencies of King Yŏngjo as a father and a relentless taskmaster.*

His Majesty's [King Yŏngjo] sagacious heart became irritated with small things at the Prince's quarters, mostly imperceptible and of an unspecified nature. Consequently, without really knowing why, he visited his son less frequently. This happened just as the Prince began to grow; that is just when a child, suffering some inattention or relaxation of control, might easily fall under other influences. As the Prince was often left to himself at this stage, he began to get into trouble. . . .

In his study sessions with tutors, however, Prince Sado was a serious and attentive student. . . . Thus it is all the more sad that, in his father's presence, the prince grew inarticulate and hesitant out of fear and nervousness. His Majesty became more

and more exasperated with him during these encounters in which the Prince was hopelessly tongue-tied. He was alternately angry and concerned about his son. Nonetheless, he never sought a closer relationship with his son, never sought to spend more time with him or to teach him himself. He continued to keep the Prince at a distance, hoping that his son would become on his own the heir he dreamed of. How could this not lead to trouble? . . .

Sometime around the *ŭlch'uk* year (1745) [at the age of ten], the Prince's behavior became strange indeed. It was not just the behavior of a child playing excitedly or loudly. Something was definitely wrong with him. The ladies-in-waiting became quite concerned, whispering to each other

History of Queen Inhyŏn (Inhyŏn wanghujŏn), written by an unknown author though presumably a member of the Patriarch faction, was a biased account aimed at justifying the defense of Queen Inhyŏn of the Min family, who was deposed by King Sukchong for Palace Lady Chang in 1689 and then later reinstated. The other was Lady Hyegyŏng's brilliant memoirs, which provide a glimpse into palace life (see **Documents: Lady Hyegyŏng's Memoirs**).

As part of the emergence of popular culture, *p'ansori* was an oral tradition that became part of culture in the countryside in the eighteenth century. It was performed by the singer (*kwangdae*) as a chant, usually in a guttural tone accompanied by a drummer who accelerated or slowed the beat according to the mood of piece as it went through different segments. Famous *kwangdae* had much license in the songs themselves. As time passed, classical Chinese phrases

of their fears. In the ninth month of that year, the Prince fell gravely ill, often losing consciousness. . . .

[In 1749, when Sado was fifteen, King Yŏngjo appointed him Prince-Regent to sit in court and conduct business.] There was nothing that the Prince-Regent did that His Majesty found satisfactory. He was constantly discontented and angry with his son. It reached a point where the occurrence of cold spells, droughts, poor harvests, strange natural omens, or calamities caused His Majesty to denounce "the Prince-Regent's insufficient virtue" and to reproach the Prince most severely. . . .

In the sixth month of *chŏngch'uk* (1757) . . . Prince Sado began to kill. The first person he killed was Kim Hanch'ae, the eunuch who happened to be on duty that day. The Prince came in with the severed head and displayed it to the ladies-in-waiting. The bloody head, the first I ever saw, was simply a horrifying sight. As if he had to kill to release his rage, the Prince harmed many ladies-in-waiting. . . .

In the ninth month of that year, Prince Sado took in Pingae, a lady-in-waiting . . . . Before this, he had been intimate with many ladies-in-waiting. Whoever resisted him in any way he beat until he rent her flesh and consummated the act afterwards. Needless to say, no one welcomed his advances. Despite the many women he had

been intimate with, he neither cared for anyone for long nor showed any particular fondness while it lasted. This was true even of the secondary consort who had borne him children. It was different with Pingae. He was mad about her. . . . His Majesty learned of Pingae. He was highly provoked. He summoned the Prince to question him. "How dare you do that?"

By this time [1761], whenever he was seized by his illness the Prince invariably hurt people. For some time now, Pingae [Prince Sado's concubine who bore him two children] had been the only one to attend the prince when he dressed. Hopelessly in the grip of the disease, he grew oblivious even of his beloved. One day, for one of his outings incognito, he was suddenly overwhelmed by a fit of rage and beat her senseless. No sooner had he left than Pingae drew her last breath there where he left her. How pitiful her end was! . . . Upon his return, Prince Sado heard of what had happened, but he said nothing. He was not in his senses.

———

Source: JaHyon Kim Haboush, trans., *The Memoirs of Lady Hyegyŏng* (Berkeley: University of California Press, 1996), pp. 247, 250–251, 252, 258, 283–285, 301.

were inserted into the songs to appeal to *yangban* as well as commoners, but the tradition remained part of the popular genre. Many of the songs mocked the *yangban*, but rural dances (*talch'um*) and local masked plays (*t'allorum*) were more biting in their sarcasm.

Poetry also remained a favorite pastime of both men (in Chinese) and women (in *han'gŭl*), and the favorite forms in this period were the short *sijo* poems, their longer versions (*sasŏl sijo*), and the still longer lyrical *kasa*.

SUMMARY

The seventeenth and eighteenth centuries began in the aftermath of the destructive Hideyoshi invasions, and the humiliation was compounded by two invasions by the Manchus, in 1627 and 1637. The recovery of agricultural production took a century, but the shock of war acted as a spur to market activity, due to the reintroduction of metal currency and the replacement of the in-kind tribute tax with a land surtax to finance government purchases of goods from the market. After a monetary retrenchment between 1696 and 1729, the state resumed the minting of cash permanently.

In the eighteenth century, technological improvement in agriculture led to a surplus that stimulated market activity and a challenge by private merchants to government-licensed monopoly shops. Those developments nevertheless fell short of the level of commerce and urbanization in either Japan or China.

Internecine political struggle among factions marked both centuries, particularly between 1659 and 1728. That struggle declined between 1728 and 1762, but King Yŏngjo's filicide of Crown Prince Sado reopened factional dispute, and the introduction of Christianity created the basis for more conflict, which was constrained by King Chŏngjo until his death in 1800.

The *yangban* maintained its control over official posts in the capital, but the significant slave population dropped off sharply after 1750, not because the state manumitted them or slaves were buying their freedom, but because they deserted their homes and were replaced by an increase in peasants who had lost their land to creditors.

Intellectual and cultural life flourished in the late eighteenth century because of the Northern Learning school, the introduction of western learning, King Chŏngjo's requests for advice on governance, and the greater use of *han'gŭl* as well as classical Chinese in literature by women as well as men.

There was great promise for greater developments in economy, society, and culture by 1800, but that promise was not fulfilled in the next century.

SUGGESTED READING

For political history and institutional studies, see J. B. Palais, *Confucian Statecraft and Korean Institutions* (1996); J. K. Haboush, *A Heritage of Kings: One Man's Monarchy in the Confucian World* (1988); and M. Deuchler and J. K. Haboush, eds., *Culture and the State in Late Chosŏn Korea* (1999).

For a summary survey of Korean society, see E. W. Wagner, "Social Stratification in Seventeenth Century Korea: Some Observations from a 1663 Seoul Census Register," *Occasional Papers on Korea*, no. 1 (1979): 36–54.

See G. Ledyard, *The Dutch Come to Korea* (1971) for an account of Hendrik Hamel's captivity in the mid-seventeenth century in Korea. Hamel came from Holland and was shipwrecked off the Korean coast.

For Confucian and other modes of thought, see W. T. de Bary and J. Haboush, eds., *The Rise of Neo-Confucianism in Korea* (1985), and M. Kalton et al., *The Four-Seven Debate* (1994).

For studies of women and shamans, see L. Kendall and M. Peterson, eds., *Korean Women: View from the Inner Room* (1983), and L. Kendall, *Shamans, Housewives and Other Restless Spirits* (1985).

For two masterful translations of literature, see J. K. Haboush, *The Memoirs of Lady Hyegyŏng* (1996), and R. Rutt and K. Chong'un, trans. and comm., *Virtuous Women: Three Classic Korean Novels* (1974). For literary analysis, see D. Cho, *Korean Literature in Cultural Context and Comparative Perspective* (1997).

WESTERN IMPERIALISM (1800–1900)

Western Imperialism (1800–1900)

IN CONTRAST TO THE FRAIL WOODEN-hulled sailing ships that carried Europeans to the Pacific Ocean in the sixteenth century, nineteenth-century vessels were increasingly powered by coal-fueled steam engines. The industrial revolution that rescued Europe from the ecological trap of reliance on agrarian products propelled technological innovations in weaponry and an expansion in the state's ability to command men and resources. Following in the wake of trading companies, government officials began to regulate and tax commerce, then administer territories, and finally recruit natives into tightly disciplined, uniformed battalions capable of projecting force thousands of miles from European homelands. No longer mere participants in maritime trade, Europeans transformed their trading posts from India to Indonesia into colonies.

During the eighteenth century, European states had established trading posts throughout the Indian Ocean and the Pacific, the only colony being Spain's in the Philippines. Under Catherine the Great, Russia extended its reach across Siberia to Alaska and sent teams of explorers down the Kamchatka peninsula, along the coast of Sakhalin, and into Hokkaido. Confrontations with Japanese officials led to sporadic efforts to open diplomatic relations. Having defeated French efforts to challenge its forays into India in the middle of the eighteenth century, the British East India Company spearheaded the battle for markets that brought administrators and troops to protect mercantile interests and made Britain the greatest of the European powers. While France was embroiled in revolution, Britain sent an official mission to China in 1793. Headed by Lord George Macartney, its aim was to eliminate what the British saw as frivolous restrictions on trade that limited the number, destination, and schedules for their ships. Since controlling trade helped stabilize the social order, reduced smuggling, and reaffirmed the Qing emperor's superiority over all other monarchs, the mission failed.

The Napoleonic Wars following the French Revolution remade the map of Europe and contributed to a new sense of nationalism. In Asia Britain took over the Dutch colony at Batavia because Napoleon had tried to make his brother king of the Netherlands. The Dutch never told the Japanese that the only place flying the Dutch flag was Dejima in Nagasaki harbor. The Napoleonic Wars had spilled over into European colonial possessions in Latin America. There, wars of liberation starting in 1809 resulted in the establishment of independent nations in the 1820s. The heightened focus on nationhood required a clear demarcation of sovereignty and a clear delineation of boundaries. No longer would small states such as Vietnam, the Ryukyus, and Korea be permitted to claim quasi-autonomy under China's mantle, and every inch of land had to belong to a nation. Regardless of whether peasants saw themselves as Frenchmen, their rulers and the educated classes imagined communities in which everyone spoke the same language, professed similar beliefs, and despised foreigners. The cosmopolitan Enlightenment admiration for Chinese civilization and Confucian rationality gave way to disdain for godless heathens who failed to appreciate the superiority of western technol-

Timeline: Western Advances in Asia

1793: Earl of Macartney travels to Beijing seeking diplomatic recognition; Russians seek same in Japan.

1797: Broughton, a British captain, surveys east coast of Korea.

1804: Russian advances in Siberia and Sea of Okhotsk culminate in emissary to Japan.

1805–1812: Russia builds forts in Alaska and northern California.

1808: British warship enters Nagasaki harbor.

1811: Britain captures Java from the Dutch; returned in 1816.

1816: Anglo-Nepalese War.

1819: Raffles, a British official, occupies Singapore for Britain.

1820: Vietnam bans Christianity and expels missionaries.

1824–1826: First Anglo-Burmese War.

1837: U.S. ship *Morrison* tries and fails to establish relations with Japan.

1839–1840: Opium War and First Anglo-Afghan War.

1842: Treaty of Nanjing.

1846: U.S. Commodore Biddle seeks trade with Japan; refused.

1852: Second Anglo-Burmese War.

1853–1854: U.S. Commodore Perry forces unequal treaty on Japan.

1856–1857: Arrow War between Britain, France, and China.

1858: Treaties of Tianjin; Japan signs commercial treaty with United States.

1857–1858: Great "Indian Mutiny"; British East India Company abolished.

1860: British and French troops occupy Beijing.

1862: Treaty of Saigon: France occupies three provinces in south Vietnam.

1863: France gains protectorate over Cambodia.

1866: France sends punitive expedition to Korea.

1871: United States sends ships to open Korea to foreign trade by force; repulsed.

1874: France acquires control over all of south Vietnam; Japan sends expeditionary force to Taiwan.

1876: Japan signs unequal treaty with Korea.

1877: Queen Victoria proclaimed empress of India.

1882: Korea signs unequal treaties with United States and other Great Powers.

1884–1885: France makes Vietnam a colony.

1885–1886: Third Anglo-Burmese War.

1893: France gains protectorate over Laos.

1894–1895: Sino-Japanese War.

1898: Scramble for concessions in China by European powers.

1898: United States seizes the Philippines from Spain; annexes Hawai'i.

1900: Boxer Rebellion.

ogy. In contrast to older empires that allowed natives the opportunity to participate in running their affairs, new empires discriminated between the white man and everyone else.

By bringing decades of peace to Europe, Napoleon's defeat at Waterloo in 1815 freed nations to concentrate on expanding trade net-works while competing for Great Power status. Great Power status required colonies, and competition with other nations spurred imperialism. France reestablished its preeminence in North Africa, contended with Britain for ports in Burma, and tried to force a commercial treaty on Vietnam. In 1816 Britain was at war with Nepal when it dispatched a second mission to the Qing court. Because the envoy refused to participate in the customary rituals that regulated relations between tribute nations and the Son of Heaven, including the kowtow, the emperor refused to see him. Britain had already established ports on the Malay Peninsula; adding Singapore gave it a harbor to protect and provision British ships sailing between India and China. British ships started appearing off the coast of Japan, sometimes threatening the natives in their quest for food and fuel. Britain and France clashed over Burmese ports while Burmese troops threatened Bengal. The first Anglo-Burmese War ended in victory for Britain, a large indemnity extracted from the Burmese, a British diplomat stationed at the Burmese court, and British hegemony over the Bay of Bengal.

Bengal supplied the opium that Britain used to buy tea. By 1750, Britain was importing well over 2 million pounds of tea from China a year, and demand was rising. Having little that the Chinese found of value, the British at first had to pay for tea with silver, thus leading to a negative trade balance. After 1761, the balance began to shift in Britain's favor. The East India Company allowed the illegal export of Bengali opium into China, bought tea for homeland consumption, and used the silver accruing as a result of the trade surplus to finance its operation and the British administration of Bengal. From the British point of view, that drug addicts multiplied as the price went down and the supply went up, that bribes to allow drug trafficking corrupted local officials, simply demonstrated Chinese racial inferiority.

British merchants remained unhappy with trading conditions in China. Textile manufacturers wanted to sell machine-made cloth, and private traders resented the East India Company monopoly. When the monopoly was abolished in 1834, the government named Lord Napier to be superintendent of trade in Guangzhou. He tried to bypass the Cohong, the merchant guild responsible to the Qing court for managing foreign trade, and negotiate directly with the provincial governor-general, who saw no reason to sully his dignity by dealing with barbarians. Diplomatic incident led to a confrontation between British warships and Chinese defenses. Napier was forced to withdraw. Trade continued, albeit with British merchants calling for more warships to enforce their demands for the elimination of the Cohong monopoly over foreign trade and the opening of ports farther north.

The Opium War tested Chinese morality against British technology. In 1839, Imperial Commissioner Lin Zexu arrived in Guangzhou with orders to suppress the drug trade. He moved swiftly against dealers and users and demanded that opium under foreign control be turned over. When the British merchants proved recalcitrant, he stopped trade altogether. He appealed to Queen Victoria to allow him the same right to regulate trade and suppress drugs that administrators enjoyed in Britain. When the traders reluctantly relinquished their stocks, he allowed them to flee to the Portuguese city of Macao and thence to Hong Kong while he washed twenty thousand chests of opium out to sea. Indignant at the expropriation of their property without compensation, the traders appealed to Parliament. A fleet that included four armed steamships carrying Indian troops under British officers refused to contest the defenses Lin had built upstream to protect Guangzhou. Four ships blockaded the river mouth while the rest of the fleet sailed north to harass Chinese shipping along the coast. By the time it reached Tianjin, the closest port to Beijing, the Qing court realized that it had to negotiate. In the first round of negotiations, China agreed to pay an indemnity to compensate British merchants for their destroyed property and allow expanded trade in Guangzhou, direct access to Qing officials, and British possession of Hong Kong. When these terms proved unsatisfactory to the British home government, another round of fighting forced additional concessions.

China's defeat in the Opium War forced it to open to the West and inaugurated a new era in western imperialism. (See Color Plate 24.) It marked the first time a western power had emerged victorious in battle in East Asia, a debacle that sent shock waves through Japan and Korea. The Treaty of Nanjing opened five ports to British residency and trade, abolished the Cohong, and ceded Hong Kong to Britain. A supplementary treaty signed a year later fixed low tariffs on British imports and included the most-favored-nation clause whereby any privilege granted any western power automatically accrued to Britain. In 1844, Americans signed a treaty with China that gave them the right to build churches and hospitals and to protect American nationals from the Chinese judicial system. "Extraterritoriality" meant that with the exception of opium traders, Americans in China were subject to American laws, judges, courts, and prisons. The British automatically participated in this infringement on Chinese sovereignty, as did the other western powers that signed treaties with China. Historian Akira Iriye has termed this "multilateral imperialism."[1] Because China and its subjects did not enjoy the same privileges abroad, most favored nation and extraterritoriality became the hallmarks of the unequal treaty system.

Following in the British wake, American traders, whalers, and missionaries lured their government into engagement across the Pacific. During the 1840s, swift clipper ships with clouds of sail dominated trade routes. In 1846, an American ship shelled what is now Danang in central Vietnam to win the release of an American missionary who had ignored proscriptions on proselytizing. That same year, Commodore James Biddle tried to open negotiations with Japan, only to suffer a humiliating rejection. The United States completed its westward continental expansion in 1848 when it wrested California from Mexico. (It acquired Alaska by purchase from Russia in 1867.) In developing steamer routes across the Pacific to Shanghai, it saw Japan's coal fields as playing an important role. Whalers too needed access to fuel and fresh water. In 1853, Commodore Matthew Perry sailed four ships, two of them steamers, into Uraga Bay near Edo. He forced shogunal authorities to accept a letter proposing a friendship treaty and promised to return the next year for their response. Despite Japanese efforts to fend him off, Perry obtained the Kanagawa treaty of friendship that opened two small ports to American ships, allowed an American consul to reside on Japanese soil, and provided for most-favored-nation treatment.

The Americans led in imposing modern diplomatic relations on Japan because Britain was busy elsewhere. Angry at what it considered unwarranted obstruction of trade and the exploitation of Burma's magnificent teak forests, Britain launched two more wars against Burma that resulted in Burma's becoming a British colony. Allied with France, Austria, Prussia, and the Ottoman Empire, Britain also fought the Crimean War of 1853–1856 against Russia for control over the mouth of the Danube and the Black Sea. Britain's rule in India suffered a temporary setback with the 1857 revolt, but the result was to strengthen Britain's hand in dealing with the remaining principalities, many of which had to accept British advisers and the protection of British troops.

Determined to open markets, western powers soon imposed fresh demands on China and Japan. After suppressing the 1857 revolt, Britain joined with France to attack Guangzhou and capture its governor-general who had refused to pass their demands on to Beijing. Again the menace of foreign ships at Tianjin compelled the emperor to sign new treaties. Eleven new treaty ports, foreign vessels on the Yangzi, freedom of travel for foreigners in the interior, tolerance for missionaries and their converts, low tariffs, foreign ambassadors resident in Beijing, and the legalization of opium imports accrued to Britain, France, the United States, and Russia. When the Qing court tried to postpone the ambassadors' arrival and had the temerity to fire on British ships from new fortifications at Tianjin, the British and French retaliated by marching twenty thousand troops, many from

---

1. A. Iriye, "Imperialism in East Asia," in *Modern East Asia: Essays in Interpretation,* ed. J. B. Crowley (New York: Harcourt, Brace & World, 1970), p. 129.

A Factory at Guangzhou. Supervised by a merchant, Chinese workers prepare tea and porcelain for export. *(Bridgeman Art Library)*

India, to Beijing, where they destroyed the summer palace outside the city. In 1858, Townsend Harris, the American consul resident in Japan, pointed to what the European powers had achieved with their gunboats in China to convince the shogun's government to sign a commercial treaty with the United States. In addition to setting low tariffs on American goods, it extended the principle of extraterritoriality to westerners in Japan. Angry at the murder of missionaries, a combined French and Spanish fleet attacked Vietnam in 1858. France went on to acquire most of southern Vietnam, a large indemnity, and a commercial treaty.

Western encroachment on East Asia waxed and waned in consort with conflicts elsewhere. In 1861, Russian sailors occupied Tsushima, an island in the strait between Japan and Korea, for six months, in part to forestall a similar action by the British, in part to gain a warm water port. Unable to win official backing for this maneuver, they eventually withdrew. During the American Civil War, 1861–1865, the United States managed only one military initiative: support for reopening the straits of Shimonoseki after the Japanese tried to close them. France, by contrast, made considerable gains. In 1863, it forced the Cambodian king to accept its protection. Two years later, it annexed two more provinces in south Vietnam and attacked Korea in retaliation for the execution of Catholic priests who had entered the country illegally. France's defeat in the Franco-Prussian War in 1871 put a temporary halt to its ambitions in Asia. In the meantime, a small American squadron tried to replicate Perry's success in

Korea. When the Koreans refused to negotiate, it raided Korean forts guarding the entrance to Seoul and withdrew.

Western imperialism demanded new counter-measures from China and Japan. Both nations started sending diplomatic missions abroad in the 1860s, in part to try to revise the unequal treaties or at least mitigate their effects, in part to study their opponents. Korea too sent study missions to China, Japan, and the United States in the early 1880s. Trade increased, especially after the completion of the Suez Canal in 1869 halved travel time. The laying of telegraphic cables made communication between East and West practically instantaneous. To the north, China resolved its boundary disputes with Russia. Chinese laborers migrated to Southeast Asia, the United States, Hawai'i, Cuba, and Peru, where they were brutally exploited because their government was perceived as too weak to protect them.

Japan soon began to mimic the western claim that imperialism was necessary to civilize the savages by acquainting them with the material and spiritual benefits of modern technology and mechanisms of social control. In 1871, it proposed an unequal treaty with China, only to be rejected. Three years later, it dispatched a military expedition to Taiwan to retaliate for the murder of Ryukyuan fishermen. After the Qing court agreed to pay an indemnity, Japan withdrew. A similar plan to invade Korea did not materialize only because Japan's leaders did not think they were ready. Instead, Japan imposed a treaty on Korea that gave it the same privileges of most-favored-nation status and extraterritoriality that westerners enjoyed in Japan. It also solidified its northern boundary by agreeing with Russia that while Sakhalin would become part of Russia, the Kuril Islands belonged to Japan.

Rivalries between the Great Powers brought a fresh wave of western imperialism across Asia and Africa. In 1882, the United States became the first western power to sign a commercial treaty with Korea. Thanks to the most-favored-nation clause, the European powers and Japan immediately gained the same privileges. Follow-ing Vietnam's appeals for help from China, its nominal overlord, the French attacked a new naval base in China. China had to grant that Vietnam existed as a separate country and watch it be combined with Cambodia and, later, Laos into a French colony. Sandwiched between British Burma and French Indochina, Thailand remained independent by acquiescing to a series of unequal treaties. Russia and Britain tried to outbid each other for influence in Korea, while one faction at the Korean court sought American intervention to preserve Korean independence. Following decades of European exploratory trips through Africa, King Leopold II of Belgium in 1876 fostered the founding of the International Association for the Exploration and Civilization of Africa while the British and French took over Egyptian finances to manage that country's debt to its European creditors. Britain performed a similar role in China when it undertook to collect customs duties for the Qing court. Belgium, Germany, Italy, Portugal, and Spain joined Britain and France in carving up Africa into protectorates and colonies notable in varying degrees for the exploitation of natural resources and the brutal treatment of natives. (See Map C6.1.)

Imperialism in Asia entered a new phase when China and Japan fought over Korea in 1894–1895. When the Korean king requested help from China in suppressing rebellion, Japan responded first, lest China gain what it saw as unacceptable influence over the Korean court. After Japan sank a British ship transporting Chinese troops, China and Japan declared war on each other. Japan's victories on land and sea enabled it to claim Taiwan, the Pescadores islands, the Liaodong peninsula in Manchuria, forts on the Shandong peninsula, commercial concessions, and the usual bank-breaking indemnity. Russia opposed the Japanese land grab because of its own designs on Manchuria and Korea. Germany had growing commercial interests in China and wanted to divert Russia away from central Europe. France had an alliance with Russia. The three nations launched the Triple Intervention to make Japan restore

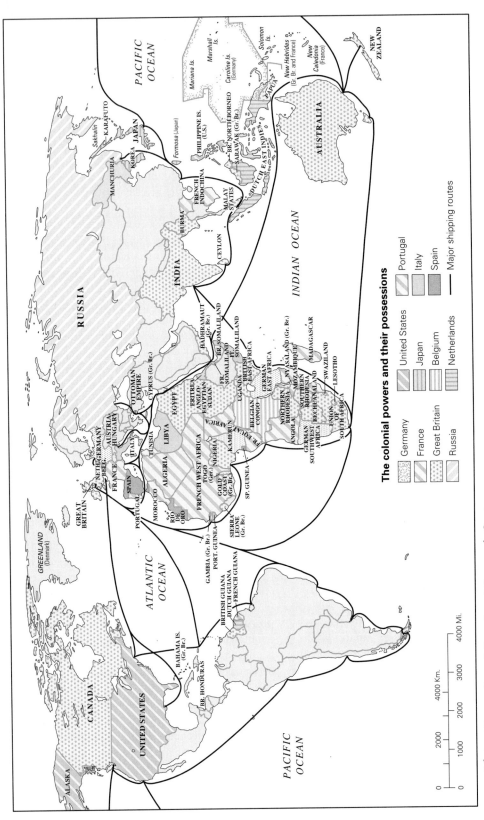

Map C6.1 Western Imperialism, Late Nineteenth Century

The colonial powers and their possessions

Germany	United States
France	Japan
Great Britain	Belgium
Russia	Netherlands
	Portugal
	Italy
	Spain
	—— Major shipping routes

the Liaodong and Shandong peninsulas to China. In a move that the Japanese public saw as blatant hypocrisy, the French then gained concessions in southern China for railroads and mines, and Russia got an eighty-year lease over the Liaodong peninsula from China that was later expanded to include Port Arthur. When the Germans built forts on portions of the Shandong peninsula, Britain took a naval base across from Port Arthur. Competition between the European powers precluded any of them from making China its colony. Instead they scrambled for concessions by carving out spheres of influence dominated by their officials and traders, primarily along the coast and up the Yangzi River. Uneasy at the prospect of being shut out of the market for Chinese goods and souls, American merchants and missionaries called on their government to act. Secretary of State John Hay urged the European powers and Japan to adopt an "open door" policy that would preclude the spheres of influence from excluding Americans. The other powers agreed, albeit with reservations that protected their interests.

Even beyond the spheres of influence, missionaries brought change to northern and eastern China. They built hospitals, schools, and orphanages where none had existed before. They educated women and tried to prevent foot binding. They taught western science and political philosophy, opening a window on the West used to advantage by Chinese reformers. Their letters to parishes back home heightened awareness of and interest in Chinese affairs. The missionaries also proved disruptive. When they forbade the rituals associated with ancestor worship, they seemingly threatened the fabric of family life. Since converts often came from the lower rungs of society, missionary efforts to protect them against the gentry or to rescue them from district magistrates' courts provoked outrage by entrenched local interests. When the missionary presence provoked violence, the western powers dispatched gunboats and troops to intimidate local officials. Worst of all, Christian teachings subverted the Confucian doctrines that fostered loyalty to the state.

Although attacks on missionaries often roiled relations between the western powers and China, none matched the consequences of the so-called Boxer Rebellion. It began in Shandong in 1898 as an antiforeign movement that combined martial arts with rituals promising invulnerability to weapons, somewhat similar to the Ghost Dance that rallied the Sioux against American encroachment in the Dakotas in the late 1880s. Boxers attacked converts and missionaries, sometimes with the quiet approbation of Qing officials. They routed western troops sent to reinforce the defenses for the diplomatic community in Beijing and tore up railroad tracks between Tianjin and the capital. The court ordered the massacre of all foreigners on Chinese soil and declared war on the foreign powers.

Faced with a common threat, the western powers and Japan united against China. Efforts by Chinese generals in central and south China to suppress antiforeign elements in their areas helped Americans to convince the other powers not to expand the scale of conflict beyond an expeditionary force sent to liberate the diplomatic community besieged in Beijing. When it reached the city in August 1900, the Qing court fled to Xi'an. Japanese soldiers watched with amazement as western troops ran amok for three days in an orgy of looting, rape, and murder. Negotiations over the size of the indemnity to be extracted from China and its distribution among the powers dragged on for a year. The indemnity imposed a crushing financial burden on the Chinese government and absorbed funds needed for economic development. Only rivalry among the powers, and particularly distrust of Russia, precluded proposals for China's dismemberment.

The nineteenth century marked the heyday of western imperialism as practice and ideology. Following the spread of Darwin's revolutionary ideas on evolution and the survival of the fittest, Herbert Spencer and others developed the notion of social Darwinism. They thought that not just species but nations stood in danger of extinction unless they emerged victorious in the ceaseless competition between them. States that did not understand this principle or found themselves too weak to resist modern military technology naturally fell prey to conquerors from afar. Social Darwinism provided new justification for the westerners' sense of racial superiority. Some used this notion to justify brutal exploitation of native populations. Others felt it their duty to bring civilization to the heathens. After the American colonization of the Philippines and annexation of Hawai'i, Rudyard Kipling wrote, "Take up the White Man's burden/Send forth the best ye breed/Go bind your sons to exile/To serve your captives' need; . . . /Your new-caught, sullen peoples,/Half-devil and half-child."[2]

Western imperialism in East Asia took a different form than in the rest of the world. Rather than establish colonies (Hong Kong and Macao being the exception), the western powers imposed unequal treaties. Although they sought Asian labor for difficult, dangerous jobs such as building the transcontinental railroad, they issued various discriminatory exclusion laws to prevent first Chinese and then Japanese from residing permanently in their countries or becoming citizens. By dint of a vast westernization project that included the enactment of western-style commercial, civil, and criminal legal codes plus the creation of a modern army, Japan managed to gain abolition of most-favored-nation treatment and extraterritoriality in 1899. Its victory in war with Russia to win control of the Liaodong peninsula in 1904–1905 gave hope to people all over Asia that western dominance might pass.

SUGGESTED READING

For the long view of relations between Asia and the rest of the world, see W. I. Cohen, *Asia at the Center: Four Thousand Years of Engagement with the World* (2000). Studies include P. Chatterjee, *Nationalist Thought and the Colonial World: A Derivative Discourse* (1993), and R. Eskildsen, "Of Civilization and Savages: The Mimetic Imperialism of Japan's 1874 Expedition to Taiwan," *American Historical Review* 107 (2002): 388–418.

---

2. R. Kipling, "The White Man's Burden," *McClure's Magazine* 12:4 (February 1899): 0-004.

China in Decline (1800–1900)

During the early nineteenth century, the Qing Dynasty seemed to be slipping into dynastic decline. Revenues were no longer adequate to cover the costs of administration. Rural poverty was worsening. Then in midcentury, some of the bloodiest rebellions in Chinese history broke out. On top of this, a new enemy had appeared on China's shores, one able to land its ships where it liked and destroy Chinese defenses with its cannons.

Yet the Qing Dynasty did not fall. The generals who suppressed the rebellions did not take to fighting among themselves to see which of them could found the next dynasty, as had happened so many times before in Chinese history. Some credit should go to the Qing elite who in the 1860s and 1870s took on the task of self-strengthening. Yet progress, though real, was never rapid enough, and late in the century China suffered further blows to its pride: first its defeat by Japan in 1894–1895, then in 1900 by the allied occupation of Beijing as a consequence of the Boxer Rebellion.

These internal and external threats and how the Qing responded to them have preoccupied most historians who study nineteenth century China. What made China's encounter with the West so different in the nineteenth century than the eighteenth? How many of China's problems came from within and how many from outside forces? Does putting stress on the new challenges of western imperialism distort understanding of this period, making the West into the actor and China merely a reactor? How did the Chinese elite understand the challenges they faced? Did it matter that China's rulers in this period were Manchu? Could the Qing have fared better if they had adopted different policies? Or were the forces of global capitalism and imperialism so skewed against China at the time that different policies would have made little difference?

ECONOMIC AND FISCAL PROBLEMS

The peace that the Qing Dynasty brought to China allowed the population to grow rapidly. Although scholars have not come to a consensus on the details of China's population growth, there is wide agreement that by the beginning of the nineteenth century, China had a population in the vicinity of 300 million and was continuing to grow, reaching about 400 million by 1850. The traditional Chinese view of population increase was positive: growth was a sign of peace and prosperity. Through the eighteenth century, most still accepted that view. As developed areas became more crowded, farmers tried cultivating more intensively, making more use of irrigation and fertilizer and weeding more regularly, allowing denser population in the richest areas. Others moved to less crowded regions, both at the peripheries of the long-settled areas and the thinly populated southwest, previously occupied largely by minority peoples. The only lands suited to agriculture that were out of bounds were those in Manchuria, which the Qing maintained as a preserve for the Manchus.

China's standard of living fell behind Europe's. From the early nineteenth century on, Britain had benefited from its access to the resources and markets of the New World as well as the first stages of its industrialization. China, in contrast, was feeling the negative effects of its population growth on both its economic productivity and its social fabric. As farms grew smaller and surplus labor depressed wages, the average standard of living suffered. When the best lands were all occupied, conflicts over rights to water or tenancy increased. Hard times also led to increased female infanticide, as families felt they could not afford to raise more than two or three children, but they saw sons as necessities. A shortage of marriageable women resulted, reducing the incentive for young men to stay near home and do as their elders told

them. Many of those who took to the road in hope of finding better opportunities elsewhere never found a permanent home; instead they became part of a floating population of the unemployed, moving around in search of work. They would take seasonal farm work or work as boatmen, charcoal burners, night soil collectors, and the like. In cities they might become sedan chair carriers, beggars, or thieves. Women, even poor ones, had an easier time finding a place in a home because of the demand for maids and concubines. But poverty fed the traffic in women, as poor families sold their daughters for cash, perhaps expecting them to become rich men's concubines, though many ended up as prostitutes. Population growth also added to the burdens placed on local governments. Although the population doubled and tripled, the number of counties and county officials stayed the same. Magistrates often found that they had to turn to the local elite for help, even turning tax collection over to them.

During the Qianlong reign, the government had resources to try to improve the lot of the poor. But in the nineteenth century, even determined emperors like the Daoguang emperor (r. 1821–1850) were chronically short of revenue for crucial public works and relief measures. The Daoguang emperor set an example of frugality at court and encouraged his officials to cut every possible cost, but the fiscal situation steadily worsened. He ordered repairs to the Grand Canal (see **Material Culture: The Grand Canal**), yet the years of neglect meant that more and more tax grain had to be sent by sea, exacerbating unemployment in north China.

Another problem the emperor faced was supporting the hereditary military force, the banners, which in a manner reminiscent of the decline of the Ming hereditary soldiers was no longer effective in war. To suppress the rebellions of the late eighteenth century, the government had had to turn to local militias and the professional (as opposed to hereditary) army of Chinese recruits called the Army of the Green

MATERIAL CULTURE

The Grand Canal

Transport canals were dug in China from ancient times. The first Grand Canal connecting Luoyang to the Yangzi River was completed during the Sui Dynasty. During Song times, the canal extended south to Hangzhou, and in Yuan times, it reached north to Beijing. During the Ming period, the government invested a lot of effort in maintaining the Grand Canal as it carried a large share of the tax grain.

The canal that the Qing inherited was 1,747 kilometers long and crossed five major rivers. It had to rise to 138 feet above sea level to get over the mountains of western Shandong. This necessitated an elaborate system of locks, dams, sluice gates, and slipways. Pulleys driven by animal or human labor pulled boats through sluice gates and skips. Because the canal crossed the Yellow River, maintaining the dikes on the river was crucial to keep floods with their heavy deposits of silt from clogging the canal.

By the early nineteenth century, more than fifty thousand hereditary boatmen and migrant laborers worked moving the tax grain up the canal from the southeast to the capital. In 1824 the grain ships en route to Beijing became mired in silt because the canal had not been properly maintained. Boatmen were put to work making repairs, but more and more grain tax had to be sent by the sea route. By 1850 the canal was largely abandoned. Unemployed boatmen were prominent among those who joined the Nian rebellion in the 1850s.

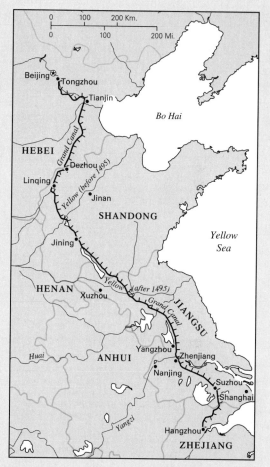

Map 19.1   **Grand Canal During the Ming and Qing Dynasties**

Standard. Because the banners were so tied to Manchu identity and privileges, the emperor could not simply disband them, as the Ming had its hereditary military households. The best the Daoguang emperor could hope for was to keep bannermen from becoming beggars, bandits, opium smugglers, or opium addicts.

MIDCENTURY CRISES

The decline of the Qing military forces was made evident to all in the 1840s and 1850s when the dynasty had to cope with military crises along its coastlines and throughout its interior.

The Opium War

As discussed in Chapter 16, the Qing Dynasty dealt with foreign countries according to a set of rules it had largely taken over from the Ming Dynasty. Europeans were permitted to trade only at the port of Guangzhou and only through licensed Chinese merchants. In the eighteenth century, the balance of trade was in China's favor, as Great Britain and other western nations used silver to pay for steadily increasing purchases of tea. British traders found few buyers when they brought British and Indian goods to Guangzhou to sell. When Macartney asked the Qianlong emperor to alter the way trade was conducted, the emperor saw no reason to approve his request.

As discussed in **Connections: Western Imperialism (1800–1900)**, all this soon changed. By the late eighteenth century, the British had found something the Chinese would buy: opium. Made from poppy plants, opium had been used in China for medicinal purposes for several centuries. Once a way was found to smoke pure opium sap in pipes, opium became a recreational drug, which people took to relieve pain and boredom and to make tedious or taxing work more bearable. The drawback was that it was addictive; those who stopped taking it suffered chills, nausea, and muscle cramps. The Daoguang emperor was outraged when an 1831 investigation showed that members of the imperial clan, high officials, and bannermen were among those addicted to the drug. Once addicted, people would do almost anything to keep up the supply of the drug, even pawning their clothing and selling their children. To fight addiction, the Chinese government banned both the production and the importation of opium in 1800. In 1813 it went further and outlawed the smoking of opium, punishing it with a beating of a hundred blows.

The opium that the British brought to China was grown in India. Following the British acquisition of large parts of India, the East India Company invested heavily in planting and processing opium, over which it had a profitable

Physic Street, Guangzhou. The English photographer who took this picture in the 1860s described the street as one of the finest in the city, not nearly as narrow as others nearby. The shop signs announce the sale of such things as drugs, cushions, seals, and ink. *(Photo by John Thomson/George Eastman House/Getty Images)*

monopoly. Once China made trade in opium illegal, the company did not distribute opium itself; rather, licensed private traders, Americans as well as British, carried the drug to China. Chinese smugglers bought opium from British and American traders anchored off the coast, then distributed it through a series of middlemen, making it difficult for the Qing government to catch the major dealers.

By 1831 there were between one hundred and two hundred Chinese smugglers' boats plying the Guangdong coastal waters. The competition among private traders led to a price war in China that drove the price of opium down and thus spread addiction. Imports increased rapidly, from forty-five hundred chests smuggled into China in 1810 to forty thousand chests in

1838, enough to supply 2 million addicts. By this point, it was China that suffered a drain of silver. The outflow increased from about 2 million ounces of silver per year in the 1820s to about 9 million in the 1830s. This silver drain hurt farmers because their taxes were assessed in silver. A tax obligation of 1 ounce of silver took about 1,500 cash to pay in 1800, but 2,700 cash in 1830.

The Daoguang emperor called for debate on how to deal with this crisis. Some court officials advocated legalizing the sale of opium and taxing it, which would help alleviate the government revenue shortfalls and perhaps make the drug expensive enough to deter some people from trying it. Other officials strongly disagreed, believing that an evil like opium had to be stopped. The governor-general, Lin Zexu, argued that rather than concentrate on the users, the government should go after those who imported or sold the drug. Unless trade in the drug was suppressed, he argued, the Qing would have no soldiers to fight the enemy and no funds to support an army. Lin's impassioned stand and his reputation as incorruptible led the Daoguang emperor in late 1838 to assign him the task of suppressing the opium trade. Once Lin arrived at Guangzhou, he made rapid progress, arresting some seventeen hundred Chinese dealers and seizing seventy thousand opium pipes. He demanded that foreign firms turn over their opium stores as well, offering tea in exchange. When his appeals failed, Lin stopped all trade and placed a siege on the western merchants' enclave. After six weeks the merchants relented and turned over their opium, some 2.6 million pounds. Lin set five hundred laborers to work for twenty-two days to destroy the opium by mixing it with salt and lime and washing it into the sea. He pressured the Portuguese to expel the uncooperative British from Macao, as a consequence of which they settled on the barren island of Hong Kong.

To the British superintendent of trade, Lin's act was an affront to British dignity and cause enough for war. The British saw China as out of step with the modern world in which all "civilized" nations practiced free trade and maintained "normal" international relations through envoys and treaties. With the encouragement of their merchants in China, the British sent from India a small, mobile expeditionary force of forty-two ships, many of them leased from the major opium trader Jardine, Matheson, and Company. Because Lin had strengthened defenses at Guangzhou, the British sailed north and shut down the major ports of Ningbo and Tianjin, forcing the Qing to negotiate (see Map 19.2). A preliminary agreement called for ceding Hong Kong, repaying the British the cost of their expedition, and allowing direct diplomatic intercourse between the new countries.

In both countries, the response was outrage. The Daoguang emperor had withdrawn his support for Lin as soon as the war broke out and had sent him into exile in the far northwest; now the official who negotiated the treaty was also treated like a criminal. The English sent a second, larger force, which attacked Guangzhou, occupied other ports as it proceeded up the coast, including Shanghai, and finally sailed up the Yangzi River to Nanjing. Dozens of Qing officers, both Manchu and Chinese, committed suicide when they saw that they could not repel the British (see **Biography: Manchu Bannerman Guancheng**).

At this point the Qing government had no choice but to capitulate, and its representatives signed a treaty on board a British naval vessel. The 1842 Treaty of Nanjing, which settled the Opium War, was concluded at gunpoint and provided benefits for Britain but not China, making it "unequal." It was soon followed by an amended agreement and treaties with the United States and France. This set of treaties mandated ambassadors in Beijing, opened five ports to international trade, fixed the tariff on imported goods at 5 percent, imposed an indemnity of 21 million silver dollars on China to cover Britain's war costs, and ceded the island of Hong Kong to Britain. Through the clause on extraterritoriality, British subjects in China were answerable only to British law, even in disputes with Chinese. The most-favored-nation clause

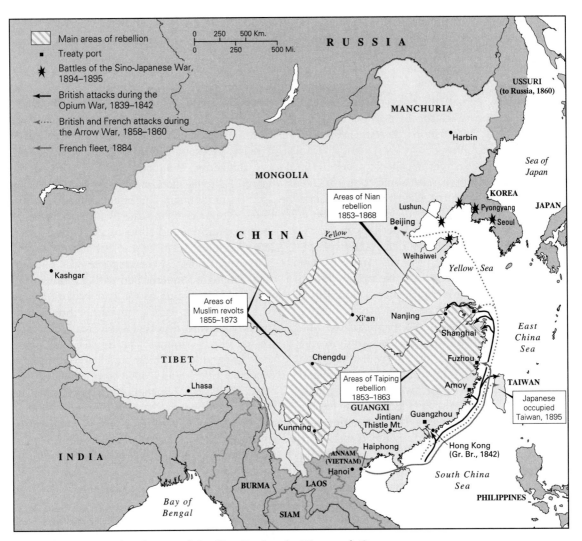

Map **19.2**   **Internal and External Conflicts During the Nineteenth Century**

meant that whenever one nation extracted a new privilege from China, it was extended automatically to Britain. Western imperialism had had its first victory in China.

At the Daoguang court, the aftermath of this debacle was a bitter struggle between war and peace factions, reminiscent of the similar disputes during the Song Dynasty. Those who had favored compromising with the "sea barbarians" to avoid further hostilities included the Manchu chancellor Mujangga; those opposed were mostly Chinese degree holders who had supported Lin Zexu and believed the Qing should have put up stronger resistance. After the Daoguang emperor died in 1850, his successor announced his determination to make no more concessions by dismissing Mujangga and bringing back Lin Zexu. The court kept finding excuses not to accept foreign diplomats at its capital in Beijing, and its compliance with the commercial clauses fell far short of western expectations.

BIOGRAPHY Manchu Bannerman Guancheng

Guancheng (ca. 1790–1843) was born the son of a Manchu bannerman of the Hangzhou garrisons, stationed at the nearby port of Zhapu. Although he would be considered Manchu through descent on the male line, both his mother and his father's mother were daughters of Chinese bannermen in the same garrisons. His father died when he was an infant, and he was raised by his mother and his deceased elder brother's widow. In his youth the banner garrisons were chronically short of funds for bannerman stipends and payments for widows and orphans; therefore, he most likely grew up in straitened circumstances. Still, he attended banner schools, where he studied both Chinese and Manchu. By the age of twenty he was working as a tutor himself, and at age twenty-seven he attained the *juren* degree, availing himself of the special quota for Manchu bannermen. By then he also had a Chinese name, Guan Weitong, which used part of his personal name as a Chinese family name. (In Manchu, his clan name was Gūwalgiya, but Manchu clan names were not used as terms of address.) To supplement his family's income, in this period Guancheng took on some publishing jobs.

In the late 1820s Guancheng traveled to Beijing to take the *jinshi* examinations. Beijing was the great center of Manchu life, home to perhaps one hundred fifty thousand Manchus. Opium addiction had already become a major problem among the underemployed bannermen, something Guancheng would undoubtedly have noticed. But it was also home to Manchu nobles who lived a highly cultivated life. The highest-ranking member of his clan had a mansion in the city and welcomed Guancheng to his social circle. There he met descendants of Qing emperors and heard much lore about Manchu court life. The language in which they discussed these subjects was, however, Chinese.

Although Guancheng did not pass the *jinshi* exam, he was given an honorary degree and in 1833 appointed a probationary magistrate of a county in Sichuan. He took two of his sons, ages nine and eleven, with him to Sichuan but sent his wife and two youngest sons back to Zhapu. At first he was rapidly transferred from one county to another, then from 1834 to 1842 had a long stint as magistrate of Nanchuan county, a tea-producing region 30 miles south of the Yangzi River. Local non-Chinese rebelled during his tenure, adding to hardships caused by locusts. Still, his son remembered the time in Sichuan as a very enjoyable one.

When Guancheng returned to Zhapu in 1842 at age fifty-three, he was something of a celebrity—a local bannerman who had succeeded in the outside world. His home community, meanwhile, had suffered a devastating blow. In 1840, at the start of the Opium War, British ships had shelled the Zhapu ports but had not stayed long. Despite attempts to reinforce the garrisons for a possible return of the British, when they did in fact return in the spring of 1842, Zhapu's defenses proved sorely lacking. Many of those who did not die defending it took their own lives afterward, often first killing their wives and children. On his return, Guancheng, though ill himself, took on the task of writing and printing an account of the heroism of the bannermen in the defense of Zhapu, to be submitted to the court. He wanted help for those who had survived and honor for those who had died. "The officers, soldiers, men and women of our garrison were ill-prepared for this, the corpses having been found piled against buildings and even suspended from the battlements. In mourning our nation's dead, how could we bear to allow these loyal clansmen to be buried without benefit of ceremony?"[1] After Guancheng died in early 1843, his son issued a revised "Record of Martyrs."

---

1. Translated in Pamela Kyle Crossley, *Orphan Warriors: Three Manchu Generations and the End of the Qing World* (Princeton, N.J.: Princeton University Press, 1990), p. 115.

The Opium War exposed the fact that Qing military technology was hopelessly obsolete. The Qing had no navy. Britain had not only large men-of-war but also new shallow-draft steamships that could sail up rivers. Thus, the British could land troops wherever they liked. Troops would pillage, then return to their ships to attack a new target. On a single day in 1841, a British steam-powered warship with long-distance artillery destroyed nine war junks, five forts, two military stations, and a shore battery. Even when Qing forces fought on land, they were no match for the British troops. To fight British soldiers armed with rifles, the Chinese and Manchu soldiers used swords, spears, clubs, and arrows. The minority with firearms had only matchlock muskets that required soldiers to ignite each load of gunpowder by hand.

Taiping Rebellion

Beginning less than a decade after the Opium War, the Qing Dynasty faced some of the most destructive rebellions in world history. The bloodiest was the Taiping Rebellion (1851–1864), in which some 20 to 30 million people lost their lives.

Like many of China's earlier insurrections, this one had its organizational base in an unorthodox religious sect. The founder of this sect was Hong Xiuquan (1814–1864). Hong was a Hakka, a large Han Chinese ethnic group that spoke a distinct dialect and lived predominantly in the far south. Although from humble background, Hong had spent years attempting the civil service examinations. His career as a religious leader began with visions of a golden-bearded old man and a middle-aged man who addressed him as younger brother and told him to annihilate devils. After reading a Christian tract given him by a missionary in Guangzhou, Hong interpreted his visions to mean that he was Jesus's younger brother. He began preaching, calling on people to destroy idols and ancestral temples, give up opium and alcohol, and renounce foot binding and prostitution. Hong spent two months studying with a Christian preacher and adopted the Ten Commandments, monotheism, and the practice of communal prayer and hymns. He called his group the God Worshipping Society and soon attracted many followers, especially among the Hakkas.

Hong was a visionary, not an organizer, and other leaders emerged who learned how to manipulate him. In 1848, while Hong and his closest associate were away from their headquarters, an illiterate charcoal maker and local bully named Yang Xiuqing elevated himself and three others to top posts within the God Worshippers. To claim superiority over Hong, Yang announced that when he spoke, it was the voice of God the Father, putting him above Hong, the mere younger brother.

In 1850 the Taiping leaders told all God Worshippers to leave their homes, pool their money into a common treasury, and move to Thistle Mountain in Guangxi province, a site that soon became a huge military camp. In 1851 Hong declared himself king of the Heavenly Kingdom of Great Peace (Taiping), an act of open insurrection. Men were to abandon the Manchu queue and let their hair grow long. Hong's true believers were brave in battle, maintained strict discipline, and seized large stores of government weapons as they campaigned. Their religious zeal propelled them to destroy local temples, even though this alienated many commoners. They regularly forced those whose villages they captured to join their movement, enrolling men and women into separate work and military teams. Some brigades of women soldiers fought Qing forces.

Once news of the progress of the rebellion reached the court, Qing troops were dispatched to disperse the Taipings and arrest their leaders (see Map 19.2). To the shock of the court, the Qing troops were soundly defeated. A rebel proclamation of 1852 made use of resentment of the Manchus, who, it said, "stole China's empire, appropriated China's food and clothing, and ravished China's sons and daughters."[1] Manchu bannermen and their families were often slaughtered after Taiping forces took a city.

---

1. Franz Michael, *The Taiping Rebellion: History and Documents* (Seattle: University of Washington Press, 1971), 2:145–147.

After making Nanjing their capital, the Taipings announced plans for a utopian society based on the equalization of land holdings and the equality of men and women. Women could take the civil service examinations, which were based on Hong Xiuquan's teachings and translations of the Bible. Christian missionaries at first were excited about the prospect of revolutionaries spreading Christianity, but quickly concluded that the Christian elements in Taiping doctrines were heretical and did nothing to help them. In fact, when the Taipings tried to take Shanghai in 1860 and 1862, the western residents organized counterattacks.

In time the Taipings were weakened by internal dissension. The group of leaders called Kings gave themselves all sorts of privileges, including well-stocked harems, while they made their followers live in sex-segregated housing. Hong and Yang turned on each other. When Yang claimed that God the Father insisted Hong should be beaten for kicking one of Yang's concubines, Hong arranged to have Yang executed. The king entrusted with this task killed not only Yang and his family but twenty thousand followers, leading to another round of revenge killings.

The Chinese elite were horrified by the Taiping movement, with its bizarre foreign gods and women soldiers. In many places local officials and landlords organized their own defense, repairing city walls, gathering food to withstand a siege, and arming and drilling recruits. The Qing government soon realized that it would have to turn to such locally raised armies if it wished to make progress against the Taipings.

The man they turned to, Zeng Guofan (1811–1872), was back at home in Hunan province to mourn his mother. Since passing the *jinshi* exam in 1838, Zeng had risen in the government and had served in Beijing in high positions in the ministries of justice and personnel. Although a man devoted to his family, he was persuaded that his duty to his country superseded his duty as a filial son to mourn his mother.

Zeng knew the failings of the Qing armies and organized his army in a new way. He recruited officers from among the Confucian-educated elite and had them recruit their own soldiers from among farmers in their region. Zeng was given permission to draw on local tax receipts and so could pay the soldiers and officers well. Soldiers were loyal to their officers and the officers to Zeng, creating an essentially private army. After Zeng constructed two hundred forty war junks so that he could attack by river and gathered some modern western weapons such as artillery, he set about recovering Hunan province bit by bit. The Taipings, however, also made advances, and Zeng needed twelve years and one hundred twenty thousand troops before he had fully defeated the Taipings. Generals under him, including close relatives and his protégés Li Hongzhang and Zuo Zongtang, played major roles in the slow stranglehold placed over the Taiping capital at Nanjing. When Nanjing fell, none of the Taipings survived. Elsewhere in south China, the Taipings held out longer, with some armies relocating to Taiwan or Vietnam. In Vietnam, where they were known as the Black Flags, they took an active part in resistance to French colonial expansion.

The devastation wreaked both by the Taipings' campaigns and the Qing campaigns to suppress them was horrendous. One western observer wrote in 1865 that China's plains were "strewn with human skeletons," its rivers "polluted with floating carcasses."[2] Much of the productive power of the lower Yangzi region was ruined for a generation.

Other Rebellions

The Taipings were turned back when they took their campaign into north China, but that region soon found itself torn apart by homegrown insurrections. Along the route of the Grand Canal, poverty and unemployment had driven many villagers into banditry. These groups of the disaffected, called Nian gangs,

2. Cited in R. Keith Schoppa, *Revolution and Its Past: Identities and Change in Modern Chinese History* (Upper Saddle River, N.J.: Prentice Hall, 2002), p. 64.

engaged in a variety of predatory practices. Riding horseback, they would seize villagers' crops, rob traveling merchants, and kidnap the wealthy to hold them for ransom. Severe flooding in 1851 weakened the dikes of the Yellow River, which gave way in 1855, leading to a devastating shift in the Yellow River from south of the Shandong peninsula to north of it. Those made homeless by the floods joined the Nian bands simply to survive. Many of those who joined did so on a seasonal basis, staying home in the summer and winter but raiding and plundering in the autumn and spring. After the Taipings fell in 1864, some of their soldiers joined the Nian rebellion. In 1865, when it was clear that the Qing regular armies had failed to suppress the Nian, Zeng Guofan and Li Hongzhang were assigned the long and difficult task.

With the transfer of armies to the interior to fight the Taipings and Nian rebels, uprisings also got out of hand in the northwest and southwest. These rebellions drew from and also exacerbated ethnic tensions and hatreds. In Yunnan, the large Muslim population had grievances based on Han Chinese settlers moving into their territory and seizing resources such as copper, gold, and silver mines. As tensions escalated, so did feuds and violence. Han Chinese formed militias to kill Muslims, who in retaliation assassinated Chinese officials. Rebels captured the city of Dali and announced the sultanate of Panthay. The remote location of Yunnan and its mountainous topography made it difficult for the Qing to send troops there. The Qing was able to regain control in 1873 only because it learned to play off opposing factions of Muslims.

The Muslim rebellion in the northwest was rooted in the spread of a mystical school of Islam known as Sufism, but much of the violence came from long-standing antagonism between the Han Chinese and the Muslims. By 1867 all of Gansu was in Muslim hands. Preoccupied with its problems elsewhere, the Qing did not send Zuo Zongtang (1812–1885) to retake the region until 1866. Zuo classed Sufis as heterodox, like White Lotus or Taiping sectarians, and ordered their slaughter. The campaign took five years and consisted largely of sieges during which the population slowly starved. Zuo Zongtang marched his troops into Xinjiang, which might well have broken away from Qing control otherwise.

The Second Opium War

While the Qing court was struggling to suppress the Taiping, Nian, and Muslim rebellions, it had to face demands from foreign powers as well. Russia, seeing China's weakness, penetrated the Amur River valley, violating the borders agreed to in 1689. In new treaties of 1858–1860, Russia gained the maritime provinces of eastern Manchuria down to Vladivostok. A large part of the reason the Qing decided to march an army into Xinjiang was fear of Russian expansion there.

Britain and France were pressing China as well. Both sides wanted the trade agreement reached after the Opium War renegotiated, though for different reasons. On the grounds that China had failed to implement all of the provisions agreed to a decade earlier, the British and French decided to make swift, brutal coastal attacks, a repeat of the Opium War. (They called it the Arrow War, from the name of a ship that gave the British a pretext for war.) Guangzhou was easily captured at the end of 1857 and held for three years. By mid-1858 the French and British ships were in the north and took the forts at Tianjin. At this point, the court in Beijing sent senior officials to negotiate. When the British threatened to march on Beijing unless they were allowed permanent diplomatic representation in Beijing, the hard-pressed Manchu negotiator conceded. Also secured in these treaties were the opening of ten new ports; permission for westerners, including missionaries, to travel through China; a fixed transit tariff for foreign goods within China of no more than 2.5 percent; and an indemnity of 4 million ounces of silver for the British and 2 million for the French. Each side was to have its rulers ratify the treaties and return in a year for the signing.

The Qing emperor was strongly opposed to allowing ambassadors to reside in Beijing, viewing them as little better than spies. When the British returned and insisted on taking their ships up the Beihe River toward Beijing instead of going overland, as the Qing wanted them to, Qing forces withstood them. A new expedition was then dispatched with eleven thousand British soldiers and sixty-seven hundred French ones. When Qing authorities did not let them have their way on all matters, they charged into Beijing. The Russian ambassador, already in residence in Beijing, talked the British out of burning the palace in retaliation. The British and French then marched to the summer palace located northwest of the city, a complex of two hundred or so buildings. They looted the buildings of furniture, porcelains, robes, and whatever else attracted them and then torched the entire 10-square-mile complex. The Russian ambassador this time approached the Qing court and talked them into accepting the offered terms, which included having to pay a larger indemnity of 16 million ounces of silver and transfer of the Kowloon peninsula opposite Hong Kong island to Britain.

Because the western powers gained many advantages through these unequal treaties, after 1860 they increasingly saw propping up the faltering Qing Dynasty as in their interest.

SELF-STRENGTHENING

In 1861 the Xianfeng emperor died and was succeeded by a young son. The child's uncle, Prince Gong, and his mother, Empress Dowager Cixi, served as regents. A change in emperor normally meant a change in chancellors and other high officials, making it easier for the court to take new directions. Certainly new policies were needed: much of the most productive parts of the country had been laid waste by the rebellions, none of which was yet suppressed, and the British and French had only recently left Beijing after extracting new concessions.

In that same year a scholar named Feng Guifen (1809–1874) wrote a set of essays presenting the case for wide-ranging reforms. He had taken refuge in Shanghai during the Taiping War and there had seen how the westerners defended the city. In his essays he pointed out that China was a hundred times bigger than France and two hundred times bigger than Great Britain. "Why are western nations small and yet strong? Why are we large and yet weak?" He called for hiring a few "barbarians" to help set up shipyards and arsenals in each major port. To get ambitious men to take on the task of managing these enterprises, he proposed rewarding them with examination degrees if the ships and weapons produced were as good as the foreigners'. He also proposed setting up translation bureaus to translate western books on mathematics and the sciences. Westerners should be hired to teach groups of boys western languages. "China has many brilliant people. There must be some who can learn from the barbarians and surpass them."[3] He pointed out that many westerners had learned the Chinese language and much about the country; surely there should be Chinese people just as capable. To improve the morale of officials, he proposed subjecting high officials to election by lower-ranking officials. Local elites would be given the power to nominate local officials, thus broadening political participation considerably. Undoubtedly influenced by what he had learned of foreign election practices, he specified that the votes were to be counted.

An important minority of officials, including Zeng Guofan and Li Hongzhang, were more and more persuaded by these sorts of arguments. Prince Gong sided with them, and changes were made not only in how soldiers were trained and weapons produced, but also in the conduct of foreign affairs. Arsenals and

---

3. W. Theodore de Bary and Richard Lufrano, *Sources of Chinese Tradition: From 1600 Through the Twentieth Century* (New York: Columbia University Press, 2000), pp. 236, 237.

dockyards were established, schools opened to teach European languages and international law, and a foreign office established to manage diplomatic affairs, with Prince Gong in charge. By 1880 China had embassies in London, Paris, Berlin, Madrid, Washington, Tokyo, and St. Petersburg.

Li Hongzhang's Self-Strengthening Projects, 1862–1893

1862 Created gun factories at Shanghai with British and German instructors

1863 Established a foreign language school in Shanghai

1864 Created a gun factory at Suzhou

1865 Established Jiangnan Arsenal at Shanghai with a translation bureau attached, jointly with Zeng Guofan

1867 Established Nanjing Arsenal

1870 Expanded machine factory in Tianjin

1872 Sent officers to study in Germany. Made request to open coal and iron mines. Jointly with Zeng recommended sending teenagers to study in the U.S. Supported China Merchants' Steam Navigation Company as a "government-supervised merchant enterprise"

1876 Sent seven officers to Germany

1877 Created the Bureau for the Kaiping Coal Mines in Tianjin

1878 Established the Shanghai Cotton Mill

1880 Established a naval academy in Tianjin. Requested permission to build a railroad.

1882 Began construction of a harbor and shipyard at Port Arthur

1884 Sent naval students and apprentices to Europe to learn shipbuilding and navigation

1885 Established a military academy in Tianjin with German teachers

1887 Established a mint at Tianjin. Began gold mining operation in Heilongjiang

1888 Established the Beiyang fleet

1891 Established a paper mill in Shanghai

1893 Set up a general office for mechanized textile manufacturing

---

After Zeng Guofan's death in 1872, Li Hongzhang emerged as the leading Chinese political figure. From 1872 to 1901 he served as the governor-general of Zhili province (modern Hebei) and headed one of the most important of the new armies. As the Chinese learned more about western ways, Li and other modernizers came to recognize that guns and ships were merely the surface manifestation of the western powers' economic strength. To catch up with the West, they argued, China would have to initiate new industries, which in the 1870s and 1880s included railway lines, steam navigation companies, coal mines, telegraph lines, and cotton spinning and weaving factories. By the 1890s, knowledge of the West had improved considerably. Newspapers covering world affairs had begun publication in Shanghai and Hong Kong, and more and more western works were being translated.

For a while China seemed to be taking the same direction as Meiji Japan (see Chapter 21), but in China resistance proved much stronger. Conservatives thought copying western practices compounded defeat. The high official Woren objected to the establishment of an interpreters' college on the grounds that "from ancient down to modern times" there had never been "anyone who could use mathematics to raise a nation from a state of decline or to strengthen it in times of weakness."[4] Even men like Zeng Guofan, who saw the need to modernize the military, had little respect for merchants and profit seeking.

Although to the Qing court new policies were being introduced at a rapid rate, the court never became enthusiastic about the prospect of fundamental change. Most of those in power were apprehensive about the ways changes in education or military organization would undermine inherited values and the existing power structure. Repeated humiliations by foreigners from the 1840s on fostered political rancor and denunciations of men in power. Both the court and much of the population remained opposed to doing anything that smacked of giving in to

---

4. Ssu-yü Teng and John K. Fairbank, *China's Response to the West* (Cambridge: Harvard University Press, 1979), p. 76, modified.

the arrogant and uncouth foreigners. As a consequence, the reforms were never fundamental enough to solve China's problems. Guo Songtao, China's first ambassador to Britain (1877–1879) sent letters from London to Li Hongzhang praising both the British parliamentary government and its industries. On his return he became a persona non grata, and the court ordered that the printing blocks carved to publish his diary be seized and destroyed.

Empress Dowager Cixi

During the self-strengthening period, the most powerful person at court was Empress Dowager Cixi. In 1875, when her son, the Tongzhi emperor, was nineteen, he died of smallpox, barely having had a chance to rule on his own. Cixi chose his cousin to succeed him, who is known as the Guangxu emperor (r. 1875–1908). By selecting a boy of four, Cixi could continue in power as regent for many years to come.

Cixi was a skillful political operator. She recognized the fears of the Manchu establishment that they were being sidelined and presented herself to them as a staunch defender of Manchu privileges. Cixi knew how to use traditional concepts of filial piety and loyalty to control members of the imperial family and officials at her court. She needed modernizers like Li Hongzhang and cajoled them with titles and honors, but she kept them in check by also encouraging their conservative critics.

It was under Cixi's watch that the old tribute system was finally dismantled. Three neighboring countries—Korea, the Ryukyu Islands, and Vietnam—had been regular, loyal tributaries, making them seem to westerners not fully independent countries. Japan forced the Ryukyus away from China in the 1870s. In the 1880s France forced Vietnam away.

Although no part of Vietnam had been under direct Chinese rule since Tang times, Chinese influence there had remained strong. The Vietnamese government was closely modeled on the Chinese, supported Zhu Xi's Confucian teachings, and used examinations to recruit officials.

Empress Dowager Cixi. Cixi spent more than half a century in the palace. She entered in 1852, became Empress Dowager in 1861, and had her nephew the Guangxu emperor put under house arrest in 1898. *(Free Gallery of Art and Arthur M. Sackler Gallery Archives, Smithsonian Institution, Washington, D.C. Purchase. Photographer: Xunling.)*

Chinese was used for official documents and histories. By the mid-nineteenth century, France was eying "Indochina" as the best target for imperialist expansion, given Britain's strength in India. This brought France into conflict with the Qing, which viewed Vietnam as one of its most loyal vassal states, next only to Korea. In 1874 France gained privileges in Vietnam through treaties and in 1882 seized Hanoi. When the Vietnamese ruler requested Chinese help, realists like Prince Gong and Li Hongzhang urged avoiding war, but a shrill group of conservative critics insisted that China had to stop giving in, since appeasement only encouraged the bullying of the powers. Cixi hesitated, called on Li Hongzhang to negotiate, and then scuttled the draft treaty when she was flooded with protests about its terms. When the French issued an ultimatum that China withdraw its forces from Vietnam or they would attack China, Cixi sided with the conservative critics. Skirmishes between the Qing and the French quickly escalated into war. The French sailed their fleet 20 miles up the Min River to Fuzhou, home port of a quarter of the new Chinese navy and the site of the main shipyard. In just 15 minutes on August 23, the French fleet destroyed the shipyard and all but two of the twenty-three Chinese warships. About three thousand Chinese were killed in the action. Cixi had adopted the conservative position and stood firm; the result was not only humiliating but a fiscal disaster. The only consolation, a bittersweet one, was that Li Hongzhang had disobeyed her order to send his northern fleet to Fuzhou to help.

Reparations Imposed on China
(or, the Loser Pays)

1842	21 million ounces of silver to Great Britain at conclusion of the Opium War
1858	4 million ounces of silver to Britain and 2 million to France at conclusion of the Second Opium War
1860	16 million ounces of silver, divided evenly between Britain and France after attack on Beijing
1862–1869	400,000 ounces of silver to compensate for violence against missionaries
1870	490,000 ounces of silver to France after the Tianjin massacre
1873	500,000 ounces of silver to Japan after the Japanese incursion into Taiwan
1881	5 million ounces to Russia for Qing reoccupation of the Ili valley in Xinjiang
1895	200 million ounces of silver to Japan after the Sino-Japanese War
1897	30 million ounces of silver to Japan for its withdrawal of troops from Liaodong
1901	450 million silver dollars to the countries that invaded to relieve the legation quarters

---

Cixi officially retired in 1889 when the Guangxu emperor was nineteen *sui* and she was fifty-five. She insisted, however, on reading all memorials and approving key appointments. Since the court was filled with her supporters, the emperor had little room to go his own way, even after he began to form his own views about reform.

FOREIGNERS IN CHINA

After 1860, the number of westerners in China grew steadily, and a distinct treaty port culture evolved. The foreign concessions at treaty ports were areas carved out of existing Chinese cities. They had foreign police and foreign law courts and collected their own taxes, a situation the Qing accepted with little protest, even though most of the population within the concessions continued to be Chinese. At the treaty ports, the presence of the British and Indians was especially strong, and the habits of the British Empire tended to spill over into these cities. Foreign warships anchored at the docks of the treaty ports, ready to make a show of force when called on. Although missionaries and merchants often had little love for each other, they had similar tendencies to turn to their consuls for support when they got into conflicts with Chinese. When missionaries or their converts were attacked or killed, gunboats were often sent to the nearest port to threaten retaliation, a practice termed *gunboat diplomacy.*

When the disorder of the Taiping Rebellion disrupted tariff collection in Shanghai and Amoy, the British and American consuls there collected the tariffs themselves, a practice later regularized into a permanent Imperial Maritime Customs, staffed at its higher level by westerners. In addition to recording and collecting tariffs, the customs published annual reports on the outlook for trade at each port and undertook projects to improve communications, such as telegraph and postal systems.

By 1900 there were a hundred treaty ports, but only Shanghai, Tianjin, Hankou, Guangzhou, and Dalian (at the southern tip of Manchuria) became major centers of foreign residence. (Hong Kong was counted not as a treaty port but as a colony.) The western-dominated parts of these cities showed Chinese what western "progress" was all about, with their street lights and tall buildings. The Chinese in these cities also felt the disdain of the westerners towards China and the Chinese. To westerners, the Chinese educated class seemed too obtuse to understand progress. Couldn't they see that the world outside China had changed drastically in the last century and that China's response to it was disastrously out-of-date?

Away from the treaty ports, missionaries were the westerners the Chinese were most likely to encounter. Once China agreed in the treaty of 1860 to allow missionaries to travel through China, they came in large numbers. Unlike merchants in the treaty ports, missionaries had no choice but to mix with the local population, and they spent much of their time with ordinary, poor Chinese, finding the best opportunities for conversion among them.

Missionaries often ran orphanages, a "good work" that also helped produce converts, but the Chinese suspected that they were buying babies for nefarious purposes. Widely circulated antimissionary tracts were often filled with inflammatory charges of this sort. The volatility of relations between Chinese and foreign missionaries led to tragedy in Tianjin on a June day in 1870. French troops had been based there from 1860 to 1863, the French had taken over a former palace for their consulate, and they had built a cathedral at the site of a former Chinese temple, all reasons for the local population to resent them. At the cathedral, nuns ran an orphanage. They welcomed (and even paid small sums to receive) sick and dying children, wanting to baptize them before they died. When an epidemic swept through the orphanage in June 1870, so many orphans died that rumors spread that they were being killed for their body parts. Scandalous purposes seemed confirmed when the nuns would not let parents retrieve their children. When a local official came to search the premises, a fight broke out between converts and

onlookers. The official ordered soldiers to put a stop to the disturbance. Meanwhile, the French consul, carrying two pistols, charged into the official's office and shot at him. After the consul was restrained, the official, unhurt, advised him not to go back on the street, where an angry crowd had formed. Claiming he was afraid of no Chinese, the consul went out anyway. On the street, he recognized the city magistrate, whom he shot at, again missing. The crowd then killed the consul and the officer with him, as well as twelve priests and nuns, seven other foreigners, and several dozen Chinese converts. The French victims were mutilated and the cathedral and four American and British churches burned. Although the French consul had incited the violence, it was the Chinese who had to pay reparations, as well as punish members of the mob and send a mission of apology to France.

By 1900 there were 886 Catholic and about 3,000 Protestant missionaries in China, more than half of them women. Although the majority of missionaries devoted themselves to preaching, over the course of the nineteenth century, more and more concentrated on medicine or education, which were better received by the Chinese. By 1905 there were about three hundred fully qualified physicians doing medical missionary work, and the two hundred fifty mission hospitals and dispensaries treated about 2 million patients. Missionary hospitals in Hong Kong also ran a medical school that trained hundreds of Chinese as physicians. At their schools, missionaries helped spread western learning. For their elementary schools, missionaries produced textbooks in Chinese on a full range of subjects. They translated dozens of standard works into Chinese, especially in the natural sciences, mathematics, history, and international law. By 1906 there were nearly sixty thousand students attending twenty-four hundred Christian schools. Most of this activity was supported by contributions sent from the United States and Britain. Missionaries in China had more success in spreading western learning than in gaining converts: by 1900 fewer than 1 million Chinese were Christians.

THE FAILURES OF REFORM

Despite the enormous efforts it put into trying to catch up, the end of the nineteenth century brought China more humiliation. First came the discovery that Japan had so successfully modernized that it posed a threat to China. Japan had not been much of a concern to China since Hideoyoshi's invasion of Korea in the late Ming period. In the 1870s, Japan began making demands on China and in the 1890s seemed to be looking for a pretext for war.

As discussed in Chapter 21, Korea provided the pretext. When an insurrection broke out in Korea in 1894, both China and Japan rushed to send troops. After Japan sank a steamship carrying Chinese troops, both countries declared war. The results proved that the past decade of accelerated efforts to upgrade the military were still not enough. In the climatic naval battle off the Yalu River, four of the twelve Chinese ships involved were sunk, four were seriously damaged, and the others fled. By contrast none of the twelve Japanese ships was seriously damaged. An even worse loss came when the Japanese went overland to take the Chinese port city of Weihaiwei in Shandong province, then turned the Chinese guns on the Chinese fleet in the bay. This was a defeat not of Chinese weapons but of Chinese organization and strategy.

China sued for peace and sent Li Hongzhang to Japan to negotiate a settlement. Besides a huge indemnity, China agreed to cede Taiwan and Liaodong (the southern tip of Manchuria) to Japan and allow Japan to open factories in China. (Liaodong was returned to the Qing for an additional indemnity after pressure from the European powers.) China had to borrow from consortiums of banks in Russia, France, Britain, and Germany to pay the indemnity, securing the loans with future customs revenue. From this point until 1949, China was continually in debt to foreign banks, which made reform all the more difficult.

European imperialism was at a high point in the 1890s, with countries scrambling to get territories in Africa and Southeast Asia. China's helplessness in the face of aggression led to a scramble among the European powers for concessions and protectorates in China. At the high point of this rush in 1898, it appeared that the European powers might divide China among themselves the way they had recently divided Africa. Russia obtained permission to extend the Trans-Siberian railway across Manchuria to Vladivostok and secured a leasehold over the Liaodong Peninsula. Germany seized the port of Qingdao in Shandong province, and the British stepped in to keep them in check by taking a port (Weihaiwei) that lay between Russia's and Germany's concessions. France concentrated on concessions in the south and southwest, near its colonies in Southeast Asia.

The mixture of fear and outrage that many of the educated class felt as China suffered blow after blow began to give rise to attitudes that can be labeled nationalism. The two most important intellectual leaders to give shape to these feelings were Kang Youwei (1858–1927) and Liang Qichao (1873–1929), both from Guangdong province. Kang was a committed Confucian, dedicated to the ideals of personal virtue and service to society. He reinterpreted the classics to justify reform, arguing that Confucius had been a reformer, not a mere transmitter as he had portrayed himself in the *Analects*. Liang, fifteen years younger, was Kang's most brilliant follower and went even further than Kang in advocating political change. Liang contended that self-strengthening efforts had focused too narrowly on technology and ignored the need for cultural and political change. The examination system should be scrapped and a national school system instituted. China needed a stronger sense of national solidarity and a new type of state in which the people participated in rule. Kang, Liang, and like-minded men began setting up study societies in 1895 in several large cities. In Hunan province, for instance, fourteen study societies were founded in 1897 and 1898, the largest with over twelve hundred members. Some of these societies started publishing newspapers (see **Documents: Comparing the Power of China and Western Nations**). Worrisome to the court was that some of these societies expressed anti-Manchu sentiments, seeming to imply that many of China's problems could be solved if only the Chinese were ruling China.

The reformers called for an end to distinctions between Manchus and Han Chinese. Some implied that the bannermen's status as a hereditary military caste should be discontinued, the way the special status of the samurai had been ended in Japan. Others proposed that banner families and Han Chinese families intermarry to break down the separation between the two groups. Many bannermen became alarmed, not seeing how the banner population could survive without government handouts. In Japan, samurai had not only joined the new armies in large numbers as officers, but many had successfully switched to other occupations requiring skill or learning. The hereditary military caste of the Qing did not fare as well. Although banner garrisons had schools for banner children, many were illiterate and unprepared to step forward as the country modernized.

In the spring of 1895, provincial graduates in Beijing for the triennial *jinshi* examinations submitted petitions on how to respond to the crisis caused by the war with Japan. Some twelve hundred signed the "ten-thousand word petition" written by Kang Youwei. Kang called for an assembly elected by the general populace. Such an assembly would solve China's most pressing problems:

> *Above, they are to broaden His Majesty's sage-like understanding, so that he can sit in one hall and know the four seas. Below, they are to bring together the minds and wills of the empire, so that all can share cares and pleasures, forgetting the distinction between public and private. . . . Sovereign and people will be of one body, and China will be as one family. . . . So when funds are to be raised, what sums cannot be raised? When soldiers are to be trained, what numbers cannot be trained? With 400 million minds as one mind: how could the empire be stronger?*[5]

One of the tutors to the Guangxu emperor joined one of these societies in Beijing and introduced its ideas to the emperor. In January 1898, the emperor let Kang Youwei discuss his ideas with the high officials at court. Afterward Kang sent the emperor three memorials on constitutions, national assemblies, and political reform. Kang even implied that the Qing rulers should abandon the queue, noting that in Japan, western dress had been adopted and the Japanese emperor had cut his hair short. In June the emperor gave Kang a five-hour audience. Over the next hundred days, the emperor issued over a hundred decrees on everything from revamping the examination system to setting up national school, banking, postal, and patent systems. He was redesigning the Qing as a constitutional monarchy with modern financial and educational infrastructures.

After three months, Empress Dowager Cixi had had enough and staged a coup with the help of Yuan Shikai's army. She had the Guangxu emperor locked up and executed those of the reformers she could capture. All of the reform edicts were revoked. Kang and Liang, safely out of Beijing at the time, managed to flee to Japan, where each lived for years.

THE BOXER REBELLION

In the summer of 1898, while the Guangxu emperor was issuing reform edicts, Shandong province was suffering from a break in the dikes on the Yellow River, which flooded some two thousand villages and made millions of people refugees. Not only was that year's crop ruined, but in many places the land could not be planted even the next spring. When the government failed to provide effective relief, antigovernment resentment began to stir. Another local grievance concerned the high-handed behavior of Christian missionaries, especially a group of German missionaries who actively interfered in their converts' lawsuits, claiming the privileges of extraterritoriality for their converts. They

---

5. Translated in Philip A. Kuhn, *Origins of the Modern Chinese State* (Stanford, Calif.: Stanford University Press, 2002), p. 123.

DOCUMENTS

Comparing the Power of China and Western Nations

This essay was written in 1898 by Mai Menghua (1874–1915), a twenty-four-year-old follower of Kang Youwei. It responds to conservative critics who saw Kang's program as weakening the ruler's hand. Mai argues that modern western governments are in fact much stronger than the Chinese government.

Nowadays, men of broad learning all say China is weak because the power of the ruler is mighty while the power of the people is slight. Those who like to map out plans for the nation say that the western nations are strong because their way is exactly the opposite of this. Mai Menghua says: This is not so. China's misfortunes arise not because the people have no power but because the ruler has no power. Hence, over all five continents and throughout all past ages, no ruler has had less power than in present-day China, and no rulers have had more power than in present-day European nations. There are far too many points for me to compare them all here, but permit me to say something about a few.

In western countries, the age, birth, and death of every person in every household is reported to the officials, who record and investigate it. An omission in a report is punished as a criminal offense. In China, birth, death, and taking care of oneself are all personal matters, beyond state intervention. In western countries, when property is inherited by descendants, the amount of the property and its location must be reported and registered with the authorities. An inheritance tax must be paid before the property is transmitted to the inheritors. In China, people give and take as they please, and the state is unable to investigate. In western countries, when children reach the age of eight [*sui*], they all go to elementary school. Doting parents who neglect their children's studies are punished. In China, 70 to 80 per cent of the population is indolent, worthless, uncouth and illiterate, and the state can do nothing to encourage them to improve themselves. In western countries, one must go through school to become an official, and unless one does adequately, one cannot make his own way. In China, one can be a slave in the market place in the morning, and bedecked in the robes of high office by evening, and this is beyond the capacity of the state to control. In western countries, the currency system is fixed by the court; one country has the pound, another the ruble, and another the franc, but each cur-

also irritated people by forbidding their converts to contribute to traditional village festivals that involved parading statues of the local gods.

Not surprisingly, this region soon exploded into violence. Small groups began pillaging the property of missionaries and their converts. They were dubbed by foreigners "Boxers" because of their martial arts practices, but these Boxers also practiced spirit possession, which allowed individuals to achieve direct communication with their gods and gain a sense of personal power. The governor of Shandong suppressed them by 1899, but they began drifting into other provinces, even into the capital, where they recruited new members with placards urging the Chinese to kill all foreigners as well as Chinese contaminated by their influence. They blamed the drought on the anger of the gods at the foreign intrusion.

rency is uniform throughout the entire country, and no one dares to differ. In China, each of the 18 provinces has a different currency, and the shape of the money is different. The people are satisfied with what they are accustomed to, and the state is unable to enforce uniformity.

In western countries, only the government may print and distribute paper money within its borders. In China, banks in every province and money changers in every port make and circulate their own money, and the state is unable to audit and prohibit them. In western countries, all new buildings are inspected by officials, who examine the quality of the construction materials as a precaution against collapse causing injuries. Older houses are periodically inspected, and ordered demolished or repaired. In China, one can construct as one pleases. Even if there are cracks and flaws, the state cannot supervise and reprove the builder. In western countries, roads and highways must be broad and spacious, neat and clean. There are legal penalties for discarding trash [on the roads]. Broad roads in Chinese cities are swamped in urine and litter, filled with beggars and corpses, and the state is unable to clean them up. In western countries, all doctors must be graduates of medical schools and be certified before they can practice medicine. In China, those who fail to do well academically switch to the medical profession; quack doctors, who casually kill patients, are everywhere, and the state is

unable to punish them. In western countries, the postal service is controlled by the government. In China, post offices run by private persons are everywhere, and the government is unable to unify them.

In western countries, there is an official for commerce. Inferior goods cannot be sold in the market. New inventions are patented, and other merchants are forbidden to manufacture imitations. In China, dishonest merchants are everywhere, devising illicit means to make imitation products, and everything is of inferior quality, and yet the state has no control. In western countries, wherever railroads pass, homes, temples, huts, or gravestones must be demolished. No one dares obstruct the opening up of new mineral resources in mountains. In China, conservatives raise an outcry and block every major project, and the state is unable to punish them. In western countries, foresters are appointed to superintend mountains and forests, and there are officials to oversee the fishing industry. Trees are felled only at the proper time, and large numbers of fishing nets are not permitted [in order to protect the stock of fish]. In China, no one is master of the woods and waters; the people can despoil them as they please, and the state has no way to know about it.

———
Source: From J. Mason Gentzler, ed., *Changing China: Readings in the History of China from the Opium War to the Present* (New York: Praeger, 1977), pp. 90–91, slightly modified.

The foreign powers demanded that the Qing government suppress the attacks on foreigners. Cixi, apparently hoping that the Chinese people if aroused could solve her foreign problem for her, did little to stop the Boxers. Eight foreign powers announced that they would send troops to protect missionaries. Then, on June 20, 1900, the German minister was shot dead in the street. Cixi, having been told by pro-Boxer Manchus that the European powers wanted her to retire and restore the emperor to the throne, declared war on the eight powers. Although she had repeatedly seen China defeated when it was fighting only one of these powers, she deluded herself into thinking that if the people became sufficiently enraged, they could drive all eight out and solve the foreign problem once and for all. (See Color Plate 25.)

Foreign Troops. Many of the troops brought in by the eight powers to suppress the Boxer Rebellion were native troops in colonial armies, like the ones seen here. *(War Office Records of Military Headquarters, Public Records Office/HIP/The Image Works)*

Foreigners in the capital, including missionaries who had recently moved into the capital for safety, barricaded themselves in the Northern Cathedral and the legation quarter, two miles away. After the Boxers laid siege to the legation quarter, an eight-nation force (including Japan) sent twenty thousand troops to lift the siege. Cixi and the emperor fled by cart hundreds of miles away to Xi'an. By the end of the year, there were forty-five thousand foreign troops in north China. Most of the Boxers tried to disappear into the north China countryside, but the foreign troops spent six months hunting them down, making raids on Chinese towns and villages.

Antiforeign violence also occurred elsewhere in the country, especially in Shanxi, where the governor sided with the Boxers and had missionaries and their converts executed. Most of the governors-general, however, including Li Hongzhang and Yuan Shikai, simply ignored the empress dowager's declaration of war.

In the negotiations that led to the Boxer Protocol, China had to accept a long list of penalties, including canceling the examinations for five years (punishment for gentry collaboration), execution of the officials involved, destruction of forts and railway posts, and a staggering indemnity of 450 million silver dollars.

THE DECLINE OF THE QING EMPIRE IN COMPARATIVE PERSPECTIVE

Late Qing reformers often urged the court to follow in the footsteps of Japan, which had adopted not merely western technology but also western ideas about political organization and even western dress. Ever since, it has been common to compare the fates of Qing China and Tokugawa Japan and ask why Japan was so much more successful at modernizing its government and economy.

The main arguments for lumping together China and Japan are that they were geographically close (both were "the Far East" to Europeans), and some significant features of Japanese culture had been derived from China, such as Confucianism and the use of Chinese characters in writing. The differences, however, should not be minimized. China in the nineteenth century was not an independent country, but part of the multiethnic empire of the Manchus, making it more similar to other large multiethnic empires, like the Mughals in India, the Ottomans in the Middle East, the Romanovs in Russia, and even the Hapsburgs in eastern Europe. Even if only the China proper part of the Qing is considered, it was a much larger country than Japan in both territory and population, with all that that implied in terms of political structure.

Another common way to frame the experiences of China in this period is to compare it to other countries where western imperialism was felt. Those Chinese who urged the court to follow Japan's example also warned of being carved up like Africa or taken over like India. But only small pieces of the Qing Empire were directly ruled by foreign powers in China, giving its history a different trajectory.

Better comparisons for the Qing Dynasty in this period are probably the Ottoman and Russian Empires. All three were multiethnic, land-based Eurasian empires, with long experience with mounted horsemen of the steppe—and in the case of both the Ottomans and the Qing, currently ruled by groups that claimed this tradition themselves. All three knew how to deal with problems of defending long land borders but were not naval powers. During the eighteenth century all had experienced rapid population growth that was reducing the standard of living for much of the population by the mid-nineteenth century. In each place, by then the military pressure put on them both by internal unrest and foreign pressure forced them to spend more on military preparedness at the cost of deficit financing. As the importance of cavalry declined in warfare, each lost its military advantages. In this period western sea powers sought to profit from trade with them, forcing them to accept their terms, but not trying to take over management of their empires. The sea powers gained more by making loans to them that kept them in a type of debt bondage, securing their advantage through treaties without any of the responsibilities of direct rule.

In each of these empires, during the mid- and late nineteenth centuries, the elites were divided between westernizers and traditionalists, each looking for ways to strengthen the government. Urban merchants were usually more willing to see changes made than the imperial elite, who had the most stake in the existing power structure. Even when modernizers won out, improvements were generally too little or too late to make much of a difference when the next confrontation with western powers came. Reform programs could not outpace the destructive effect of economic decline, social turmoil, and the intrusion of the West. Foreign powers did not encourage domestic challenges to the dynastic rulers, perhaps fearing that they would lose the privileges they had gained through treaties. Thus, many of those who sought radical change came to oppose both the foreign powers and the ruling dynasty, giving rise to modern nationalism.

SUMMARY

How different was China in 1900 than it had been in 1800? At the beginning of the nineteenth century, most Chinese had no reason to question the long-held belief that China was the central kingdom: no other country had so many people, Chinese products were in great demand in foreign countries, and the borders had recently been expanded. True, an alien dynasty occupied the throne, but the Manchus administered the country through institutions much like those earlier Chinese dynasties had employed, and even proved generous patrons of strictly Chinese forms of culture, such as publications in Chinese. Chinese civilization thus seemed in no danger. By 1900, this confidence was gone. Besides traditional evidence of dynastic decline—peasant poverty, social unrest, government bankruptcy—new foreign adversaries had emerged. China had been humiliated repeatedly in military encounters with western nations and more recently Japan and was deeply in debt to these countries because of imposed indemnities. Most of the educated class had come to feel that drastic measures needed to be taken. Chinese civilization—not just the Qing Dynasty—was at stake.

SUGGESTED READING

Volumes 10 and 11 of the *Cambridge History of China* cover the nineteenth century. Briefer narrative overviews can be found in the works cited in Chapter 16, plus J. Fairbank, *The Great Chinese Revolution* (1986). Primary sources can be found in W. de Bary and R. Lufrano, eds., *Sources of Chinese Tradition: From 1600 Through the Twentieth Century* (2000), and S. Teng and J. Fairbank, *China's Response to the West: A Documentary Survey* (1971).

On the Daoguang emperor and efforts to strengthen the Qing, see J. Leonard, *Controlling from Afar: The DaoGuang Emperor's Handling of the Grand Canal Crisis, 1824–26* (1996). The relevance of dissatisfaction with the government in this period and later changes in the constitution of the Chinese state are a theme of P. Kuhn, *Origins of the Modern Chinese State* (2002).

On the many nineteenth-century rebellions and their suppression, see J. Chesneaux, *Peasant Revolts in China, 1840–1949* (1973); P. Kuhn, *Rebellion and Its Enemies in Late Imperial China* (1970); E. Perry, *Rebels and Revolutionaries in North China, 1845–1945* (1980); and J. Spence, *God's Chinese Son: The Taiping Heavenly Kingdom of Hong Xiuquan* (1996). On the Boxers, see J. Esherick, *The Origins of the Boxer Uprising* (1987), and P. Cohen, *History in Three Keys* (1997).

On the Opium War, see H. Chang, *Commissioner Lin and the Opium War* (1964); P. Fay, *The Opium War, 1840–1842* (1975); J. Polacheck, *The Inner Opium War* (1992); and A. Waley, *The Opium War Through Chinese Eyes* (1968). For Chinese who went abroad, see D. Arkush and L. Lee, *Land Without Ghosts* (1989). On Christian missionaries, see P. Cohen, *China and Christianity: The Missionary Movement and Growth of Chinese Anti-Foreignism, 1860–1870* (1963), and J. Hunter, *The Gospel of Gentility: American Missionary Women in Turn of the Century China* (1984).

On the Chinese economy as it became more involved in global trade, see S. Mazumdar, *Sugar and Society in China: Peasants, Technology, and the World Market* (1998), and R. Marks, *Tigers, Rice, Silk, and Silt: Environment and Economy in Late Imperial South China* (1998).

On the concerns of intellectuals, see H. Chang, *Chinese Intellectuals in Crisis: Search for Order and Meaning (1890–1911)* (1987); B. Schwartz, *In Search of Wealth and Power: Yen Fu and the West* (1964); and K. Hsiao, *A Modern China and a New World: K'ang Yu-wei, Reformer and Utopian, 1858–1927* (1975). Insight into Chinese society and the culture of the time can be gleaned from D. Cohn, ed., *Vignettes from the Chinese: Lithographs from Shanghai in the Late Nineteenth Century* (1987), and I. Pruitt, *A Daughter of Han: the Autobiography of a Chinese Working Woman* (1967).

Japan in Turmoil (1800–1867)

Many commoners in Japan's cities and villages prospered during the first three decades of the nineteenth century, but the same could not be said for the laboring poor, low-status samurai, or daimyo wrestling with shortfalls in domainal finances. Belying prosperity were problems such as vagrancy, gambling, and prostitution that threatened the social order propped up by administrators and wealthy entrepreneurs. Added to these signs of domestic distress was an increasing fear of threats from abroad. The shogunate's ineffectual and inconsistent attempts to deal with these problems weakened it in the eyes of the military ruling class. Its decision to seek approval for foreign treaties from the monarch opened the door for wide-ranging debate that enabled commoners as well as officials to participate in a new political public realm. Beset on all sides, the shogunate collapsed at the end of 1867, ushering in a regime headed by the newly named emperor.

Historians have long searched the early nineteenth century for clues as to what brought about the Meiji Restoration. Those who emphasize domestic factors point to how the social and political order came unglued in the early nineteenth century. But that begs the question of whether the fall of the Tokugawa shogunate should be seen as a coup d'état or a revolution. Was it primarily the effect of domestic changes or a reaction to foreign pressure?

DOMESTIC SECESSIONS

Early nineteenth-century villages had to deal with internal conflict. Outcasts deemed polluted by their association with dead animals protested discrimination and the indignities they had to suffer. Long accustomed to apportioning the village tax assessment, headmen tended to treat expenses for family business and village administration as one and the same. The walls around their houses had gates; the roofs had eaves that marked their superior status. Complaints against headmen perceived to be unjust in dividing the tax burden, efforts to clarify the costs of village administration, and demands that the headman cease to lord it over his neighbors led to lawsuits that sometimes dragged on for decades. A recalcitrant headman might be subjected to ostracism. Sometimes disputes resulted in the village council's being expanded to include a cultivator's representative to verify the tax assessment. In villages where the position of headman had once been hereditary, it might instead rotate among a group of families. Some villages started a system of having the heads of household elect the headman. When a woman was the house head, she too voted.

In eastern Japan, village leaders agonized over fields gone to waste because of population decline. Worse, gamblers and bandits disrupted the social order. Village officials organized regional leagues, inserting a new level of administration between the village and ruling authority. In the region around Osaka, these leagues launched province-wide appeals beginning in the 1780s to eliminate restrictions on commerce and regulate the price of herring meal fertilizer from Hokkaido. In 1827 the shogunate started sending security patrols through the Edo hinterland, where villages might be fragmented among several domains. Some headmen organized militia; others hired unemployed swordsmen, some running protection rackets, to keep the peace. Longer-term solutions came in the teachings of the peasant sage Ninomiya Sontoku. Sontoku revitalized villages, increasing their population and bringing fields back into production by preaching an ethic of diligence, fortitude, and frugality to repay the bounty of the gods while instituting mutual aid associations to give villagers who had fallen into dire straits access to low-interest loans. His emphasis on rational planning to wring the most from land and labor demanded steady work habits instilled in men and women alike.

Hirata Atsutane and his followers offered a vision of a just social order that largely ignored existing political arrangements. Although they acknowledged shogunal authority and the Confucian principles of social inequality, they sought the wellspring of human virtue in Japan's ancient past and looked to the monarch as a manifest god who linked the divine and human worlds. Atsutane claimed to be a disciple of Motoori Norinaga, thus putting him in the mainstream of nativist thought. Unlike his teacher, he did not envision the afterlife as a filthy, polluted realm but rather as an invisible world that parallels the visible world. From that vantage, the deceased watch over and protect their descendants. Atsutane's teachings placed primacy on agricultural practices that brought people into close communion with the gods and each other. Village officials and rural entrepreneurs were his most numerous disciples because they believed his message to contain the secret for revitalizing the village community without threatening their role either socially or economically (see **Biography: Kitahara Inao**).

Domainal Reforms

Faced with challenges from below, rural entrepreneurs sought new ways to bolster their prestige. Rather than marry within the village, they sought marriage partners of similar background a day's walk or more away. They educated themselves; they also educated their daughters to standards beyond what could be achieved by an ordinary cultivator. They studied Chinese philosophy and classical poetry as well as western science and geography. They took up swordsmanship. In the 1830s and 1840s, their quest for ways to enhance their dignity meshed with the ruling authorities' need for funds. In return for loans, wealthy commoners received permission to wear swords on official business and use a surname, privileges supposedly reserved for the samurai.

The willingness of daimyo to sell markers of prestige to commoners was but one sign that their governments verged on bankruptcy. Owing to rural opposition, tax revenues had long since ceased to cover the expenses of carrying redundant personnel on the books, supporting the

BIOGRAPHY Kitahara Inao

In the early nineteenth century, rural entrepreneurs dominated their villages politically, socially, and economically. A representative figure was Kitahara Inao (1825–1881), who had wide-ranging interests and an abiding concern with national affairs.

Based in the mountains of central Japan, Inao's family claimed warrior connections through an ancestor who died in battle in 1575 and through him to the Minamoto lineage. His father received permission to wear swords and use a surname for his work on water control projects; he also served as one of the village's headmen, managed the family's land, and sold the silk produced by Inao's mother. He educated himself, his children, and his neighbors in western geography and Japanese poetry. When his eldest son wished to learn a musical instrument called the *samisen,* he sent him to Kyoto. The boy was murdered en route. Thus did Inao become his father's heir.

The short-tempered Inao had a short career as village headman. In 1852, cultivators from the village's upper elevations complained that they had to pay for flood control that benefited only their wealthier neighbors on the plain. Four years later, they questioned the way costs had been assessed. A meeting with Inao turned into a shouting match. One man called Inao a liar, and Inao slugged him.

The cultivators announced that to strike one was to strike them all. Inao had to resign his office and concentrate his efforts on teaching village boys and girls.

Inao helped found the Hirata school in the Ina valley by hosting study groups, proselytizing, and publishing Atsutane's works. He used his own capital to publish a chronology composed by Atsutane that traced the monarchy back to the creator gods and raised money to publish Atsutane's magnum opus, the multivolume *Koshiden* (Lectures on Ancient History). In 1867 he helped build a shrine to the four great nativist teachers ending with Atsutane. Through these efforts, his valley acquired the largest population of Hirata disciples outside Edo.

Following the Meiji Restoration, Inao organized a development fund to promote new agricultural products and bring mechanized filatures to the Ina valley. Conditions for loans were so strict and interest rates so high that only landlord families could benefit, to the resentment of poor folk who had contributed to it. Despite his promotion of industrialization, Inao continued to castigate westernizers who did not understand the fundamental principle of respecting Japanese ways and despising the foreign. At the end of his life, he wrote a set of precepts for his descendants that emphasized harmony, diligence, and frugality. He urged them to be modest in dress, eat simple food, and marry plain but intelligent women.

---

daimyo's women and children in the style to which life in Edo had accustomed them, and paying for the trips made by the daimyo and his retinue back and forth to Edo. Daimyo borrowed money from merchants with the promise of repayment out of future tax receipts. In the 1830s, domains across Japan launched administrative and financial reforms. Those that tried to increase exports and restrict imports disrupted markets and created shortages. Some instituted monopolies by strengthening existing controls: Satsuma doubled its profits in sugar. Most domains sought to reduce expenditures by cutting costs. Concerned that luxury-loving commoners both threatened samurai privilege and encouraged samurai extravagance, governments issued sumptuary legislation forbidding socially inferior people to wear silk garments, ornamental hairpins, and other products of the commercial revolution.

The samurai, especially those in the lower ranks, saw themselves beset on all sides. Wealthy commoners in crested kimono carrying swords challenged their sense of status superiority. Educated, capable samurai were frustrated by the system of hereditary ranks that relegated them to dead-end menial tasks. During domainal reforms, low-ranking samurai proposed that men of talent and ability be promoted to decision-making positions. Satsuma heeded this call, allowing Saigō Takamori to rise from rural administrator to the daimyo's adviser in 1854. Efforts to promote men from below often led to factional disputes when upper-status samurai fought to preserve their hereditary privileges. "Borrowing" stipends posed the most ubiquitous threat to samurai welfare. While some domains tried to confine the practice to samurai without regular bureaucratic appointments and pretended that cuts were temporary, others insisted that everyone must make sacrifices. In one case, guards assigned to escort a daimyo to his regular audience with the shogun protested the arrears in their salary by going on strike.

Conditions reached a crisis when poor harvests in the 1830s recalled the famines of the 1780s. Commoners assumed that food shortages owed more to greedy merchants than to crop failures. They turned on village leaders for not offering prompt relief, and they called on the gods of world renewal (*yonaoshi*) for salvation from economic hardship and political ineptitude. Women played an active role, marching with men to protest arbitrary government policies and complaining to rice merchants that hoarding grain threatened the poor with starvation. A retired shogunal policeman named Ōshio Heihachirō decided that government and merchants had become morally bankrupt. Raised in the Confucian tradition that deemed bureaucratic work a service to the people, Ōshio had also studied Wang Yangming, who argued that at time of crisis, a man had to use his intuition, not institutional norms, to guide his behavior. In 1836 Ōshio petitioned the Osaka city magistrate to save the starving. When he

refused, Ōshio sold his books to buy food. In a last desperate effort, he issued a manifesto that charged shogunal officials with corruption and led a rural army against the city. A quarter of Osaka burned before shogunal troops caught up with him, and he committed suicide.

Religion and Play

One secessionist response to economic dislocation and political ineptitude came in the form of new religions. In 1838 a long-suffering rural woman named Nakayama Miki was possessed by a spirit who deemed her to be the "shogun of heaven" and the mouthpiece for the true and original god of salvation. She insisted that her family sell its property, the proceeds of which were used to succor the poor. According to the god's divine wisdom (*tenri*), the shogun and daimyo were far too removed from daily life to aid the people; instead, the people should trust in the god of world renewal and work together, offering mutual assistance in time of need. Like other new religions of the time, Tenri-kyō envisioned a world opposed to the hierarchical and socially stratified system of the past and present. In a renewed world saturated with divine goodness, the poor would receive relief, and everyone, men and women, would be equal.

An alternative to the secessionist impulse found in the new religions came in the form of play. Dominated by the theater, urban culture celebrated bodily pleasures. Townspeople employed the possibilities presented by multiple identities— merchant, poet, sword-wearing samurai—to escape from the rigidities of the status system (see **Documents: Kohei's Lawsuit**). By the 1830s, readers of popular literature had alternatives to didactic tracts that bolstered the official status order. They indulged in novels that depicted the immediate world of human feelings such as Jippensha Ikku's travelogues featuring an irreverent pair, Kita and Yaji, who poked fun at self-important samurai, stole when they could, seduced serving maids, and laughed at farts. Woodblock prints and kabuki, in particular ghost stories staged by Tsuruya Namboku and his successors, portrayed bloodshed and gruesome murders. In 1850 the story of Sakura Sōgorō appeared on stage with scenes of his crucifixion and reincarnation as an angry spirit. Although these dramas went to extraordinary lengths to rivet their audience's attention, they remained linked to social mores. Dramas might be set in the daimyo's domestic quarters, but the subjects of action were commoners who acted according to the logic of everyday life.

Japanese commoners played hard. Festivals in town and country became increasingly elaborate, and laborers demanded ever more of them. Kabuki troupes discovered the money to be made in touring the countryside. In prosperous regions, villages built kabuki stages and competed in presenting plays to their neighbors. City folk flocked to entertainment districts. The shops with female clerks, theaters, and variety shows surrounding Asakusa temple in Edo combined appeals to prayer and play. Play constituted one way to appeal to the gods, and the pursuit of pleasure had a spiritual dimension.

Another sign that the practices of everyday life had escaped governmental control can be seen in prostitution. Unlicensed prostitutes, both men and women, plied their trade in informal entertainment districts that had sprung up across Edo and in castle towns. Post stations employed maids to lure customers to inns and teahouses, where singers, dancers, and servants often doubled as prostitutes. The development of a commercial economy contributed to the spread of prostitution in two ways: it put more money in the pockets of potential customers and stimulated the monetization of female labor. When families' expectations that their women supplement the family income by raising silkworms or working for wages went unmet, prostitution became the logical alternative.

As part of a far-reaching reform effort in 1841, the shogunate tried to curtail what it saw as the excesses of urban culture. It clamped down on unlicensed prostitution by closing teahouses and other venues where women sold their bodies. It forbade women to dress men's hair, teach them music, serve as attendants at archery ranges, or perform onstage in public. It even outlawed men and women sharing public baths in an effort to promote public morality. Gambling, lotteries, and full-body tattoos were forbidden. The shogunate tightened censorship over the publishing industry, refusing to permit romantic novels or erotica, including the serial best-seller, *The False Murasaki and the Rustic Genji,* produced by Ryūtei Tanehiko between 1829 and 1842. Theaters and entertainment districts received undesired attention. The shogunate condemned extravagance and ordered commoners not to dress, eat, or house themselves above their station. It tried to enforce these strictures by making an example of egregious violators in hopes of intimidating the rest. These measures had but a temporary effect.

FOREIGN AFFAIRS

The Russians were the first foreigners to encroach on Japan. During the eighteenth century, they started to trade with the Ainu in the Kuril Islands and Kamchatka. In 1793 Adam Laxman, a delegate to Catherine II, tried to open relations between Russia and Japan. He got as far as Nagasaki, only to be rebuffed by Matsudaira Sadanobu, who insisted that respect for his ancestors required that he not initiate new foreign relations. In 1798 the shogunate sent an expedition to Hokkaido to assess the Russian threat. Based on its report, the shogunate decided to annex Hokkaido and Sakhalin. Its reach exceeded its grasp; it did not have the forces to defend either. Russians again asked for permission to trade at Nagasaki in 1804. When that was not forthcoming, officers attacked trading posts on Sakhalin and the Kurils in 1806 and 1807. In 1811 the Japanese captured Vasilii Golovnin, the captain of a Russian surveying crew, and held him at Hakodate for two years before Russia secured his release. His captivity narrative intrigued readers across Europe.

DOCUMENTS

Kohei's Lawsuit

In a litigious society, people turned to the shogun's court to decide disputes. The summation of a conflict over inheritance that follows, titled "Action by Kohei of Haruki-chō, Hongō, against Heisuke of Sugamo-chō and Kurōbei of Fujimae-chō, Komagome as to the succession and division of personality of Sawamura Gisaburō, Master Carpenter," exposes a particularly complex set of family relations and the permeability of supposedly strict occupational and status boundaries. Note that the people involved in the suit, including the deceased, took different names depending on the occupation of the moment. Why is the conflict over Gisaburō's personality, not simply his possessions?

5th month, 1849, Inquiry by the city magistrate to the engineering magistrates:

Kohei demanded succession and division of personality of Sawamura Gisaburō, master-carpenter, subject to your lordships' authority, producing for evidence Gisaburō's will written by a person other than the testator; the defendants, on the other hand, deny the validity of the will, and the parties are at issue.

Kohei alleges that his sister's husband Sawamura Gisaburō made a will so that his personality may be divided according to the will, and that Gisaburō's adopted son Kosuke may be made to succeed Gisaburō.

Rubric: This Kosuke was one who, calling himself Utazō, tenanted the land of Ichibei in Yanaka, and was engaged in the management of a public bath-house. Four years ago, in 1845, he was adopted by Gisaburō, and in the 11th month of the same year, his petition to be a master-carpenter on probation was granted. It has been found that he is still living in a separate house on Ichibei's land and is working as a master-carpenter on probation.

What Heisuke alleges is as follows: His adoptive father Sawamura Gisaburō was a master carpenter in service of the shogunate.

Gisaburō was formerly called Heisuke and was engaged in the management of a tavern at Sugamo-chō. About that time this person [Heisuke] was adopted by Gisaburō and in 1835 he succeeded to Gisaburō's family name. Gisaburō served as a master-carpenter from 1810, and from 1812 to 1834 he was also registered in the census book of Sugamo-chō under the name of Heisuke. Therefore it seems that he was entered in two different census registers.

Gisaburō bought two years ago in 1846 a piece of land at the market in front of Yushima Tenjin Shrine, and on this occasion Heisuke advanced part of the purchase money. On the deed of sale, the land was entered as the property of Sei, daughter of Saku, Gisaburō's concubine. Gisaburō had a house on this land repaired for Saku to occupy. Lately he himself moved into this concubine's house, and because of old age, he called in one Kosuke, who is more in the relation of a servant to him, to wait on him, and had this Kosuke, by nominally adopting him, serve as a master carpenter on probation. Besides the above piece of land, some other lots in Gisaburō's possession have been nominally the property of Gisaburō's grandson Chōsuke, for whom Heisuke has acted as guardian. The deeds of sale of these lands were kept by Gisaburō, as they were often used, by agreement of Gisaburō and Heisuke, for financing the business when Gisaburō engaged in various contracts, government and otherwise. When in 1847 Gisaburō married Sei, Saku's daughter [by her former husband] to one Mohachi and had Mohachi inherit the family name of Yoshikawa, palanquin-maker for the Shogunate, Heisuke on Gisaburō's request, advanced 500 *ryō* to Gisaburō to cover the expenses. Since Heisuke had advanced Gisaburō great sums of money for the latter's contract business, government, and otherwise, Heisuke should be given the right to decide on the succession and other matters.

Yasuda Chōsuke is son to Hanzaemon and grandson to Gisaburō and was formerly called Toraichirō. He is registered as a houseowner of Fujimae-chō. He has served, under the guardianship of the defendant Heisuke, as purveyor and contractor of commodities and laborers for the Fukiage Garden [in the shogun's palace] and is living with his father.

Nakamura Hanzaemon is adopted husband to Hisa born to Gisaburō by Gin, his former wife, since divorced. He was formerly called Shōgorō, and while tenant of a shop belonging to Kanbei, Fujimae-chō, Komagome, was engaged in dealing in socks. He is said to have become a guard in service of the Banner Magistrates for the Shogunate.

The defendant Kurōbei is nephew to Sawamura Gisaburō and head of Gisaburō's original family. Because of this relationship, Gisaburō, repairing a house on his land, had Kurōbei and his wife Chiyo, whose other name is Shige, live there. Even now Gisaburō's domicile is registered at the office of the Engineering Department as at this house on Kurōbei's land. So it was rumored

that the boxes containing Gisaburō's papers and books etc. are kept in the above Kurōbei's godown [storehouse], including the instruments pertaining to the various money transactions which Gisaburō mentioned in his will.

The plaintiff says that when, during this autumn, he went to negotiate with Heisuke and Kurōbei, Kurōbei together with the ward officers admitted plainly that he had in his care the papers in question. The plaintiff continues that it seems possible, however, that Heisuke, taking advantage of his having access to the household of the Lord of Kaga through his business in contracting for transport horses, may have here done something tricky; that there is no box containing instruments kept now at Kurōbei's house in Fujimae-chō. It is suspected that it has since been taken to Heisuke's house. Heisuke has for several years past been in the habit of advancing loans to the household of the Lord of Kaga out of money belonging to Sawamura Gisaburō.

Instrument of Settlement to be filed: Both parties have agreed that we should petition for Gisaburō's adopted son Sawamura Kosuke to succeed Gisaburō, and should agree that neither party has grounds on which to dispute further about the deposit instruments said to be entrusted by Gisaburō with Heisuke and Kurōbei and about the money which Heisuke claims to have advanced Gisaburō, since the issue utterly lacks proof. Therefore we have come to a compromise, and will never in future resort to action or dispute.

Source: John Henry Wigmore, ed., *Law and Justice in Tokugawa Japan, Pt. VIII-A: Persons: Legal Precedents* (Tokyo: University of Tokyo Press, 1982), pp. 214–242 (modified).

The Closing of Japan

The British posed a more serious threat. In 1808 their warship *Phaeton* barged into Nagasaki bay in search of Dutch ships. Despite orders from the Nagasaki city magistrate to destroy it, the *Phaeton* left with food and supplies. In two separate incidents in 1824, British whaling ships raided villages on the coast north of Edo and southern Kyushu. The first village belonged to the Mito domain, home to one of the shogun's relatives and a leading xenophobe, Tokugawa Nariaki. The second was located in Satsuma, the powerful outside (*tozama*) domain that dominated the Ryukyus. The next year, the shogunate issued new instructions for dealing with westerners. With the exception of the Dutch ships allowed at Nagasaki, all foreign ships, regardless of the circumstances, were to be driven off without hesitation. This order announced that the shogunate was closing the country (*sakoku*) to the West, its first truly isolationist policy.

The decision to close the country came as a result not only of foreign intimidation but also of information gathered by scholars and officials. The head of the shogunate's translation bureau established in 1811 argued that foreigners must be kept away from Japan lest they subvert the credulous masses with Christian teachings. In 1825, an adviser to Tokugawa Nariaki named Aizawa Seishisai wrote his "New Theses" (*Shinron*). Mito scholars believed that loyalty to their lord had to be predicated on his loyalty to the monarch. Although they based their arguments on neo-Confucian principles, their ideas were readily assimilated to the nativist belief that Japan was superior to all other countries, including China, because the monarch was descended from the sun goddess. Aizawa had studied writings about the West, and he interrogated the British sailors who had landed on the Mito coast in 1824. *Shinron* argued that Japan had to beware of foreigners, even if they said they came only to trade. Trade would weaken Japan because Japan would lose precious metals, and the pursuit of novelty and luxury items would erode the people's moral fiber. But traders brought something more pernicious than goods: Christianity. They hoped to beguile the foolish commoners with their religion, turn them against their rightful leaders, and "conquer from within by recruiting the local inhabitants into their ranks." To counter the threat of "barbarian teachings," Aizawa urged his lord to convince the shogunate to launch educational, religious, and military initiatives that would reform the armed forces by allowing daimyo to recruit cultivators as soldiers and educate the masses in Japan's unique spiritual essence (*kokutai*).[1] *Shinron* had a lasting impact on nationalist thought.

Despite domainal penury, the Mito reform movement of the 1830s largely involved strengthening coastal defenses, a policy followed by a handful of other domains. Domains ignored shogunal restrictions on the number of guns permitted each castle. Mito built a reverberatory furnace to cast cannon, and Saga in Kyushu did the same. *Tozama* domains in southwestern Japan—Satsuma, Fukuoka, Kumamoto, and Chōshū—bought mortars, howitzers, and field guns from weapons dealers in Nagasaki and tried to manufacture their own. Fear of foreigners spurred a renewed emphasis on military training. Domains also mobilized militia to man coastal lookout points and serve as a first line of defense. They competed for access to military technology, and they refused to cooperate in developing systems to warn of approaching foreign ships. They saw themselves as defending not an entity known as Japan but rather their own territory. Building coastal fortifications increased their isolation from each other while weakening the shogun's authority in matters of defense.

The shogunate too tried to bolster its military preparedness, spurred by reports of the British victory over China in the Opium War. (See **Connections: Western Imperialism [1800–1900].**) In the 1841–1842 reform, it began to adopt western military technology and trained a small contingent of foot soldiers in the use of guns. It also tried

---

1. Bob Tadashi Wakabayashi, *Anti-Foreignism and Western Learning in Early Modern Japan* (Cambridge, Mass.: Harvard University Press, 1986), p. 211.

to reassert its dominance by ordering an end to domain monopolies that interfered in commerce, seeking to transfer daimyo from one domain to another, and threatening to suppress copper coins and paper money minted in the domains. In 1843 the shogun went to Nikkō to worship at the shrine for his ancestors, escorted by one hundred fifty thousand men provided by the daimyo, who had to serve as his retinue in an affirmation of Tokugawa supremacy. At the same time, the shogunate announced a more conciliatory policy toward foreigners: shipwrecked sailors succored, Japanese castaways allowed to return home, and ships in need to receive supplies before being sent on their way.

Unequal Treaties with the United States

When Commodore Matthew C. Perry sailed four ships into Edo Bay on July 8, 1853, he had been preceded by the 1846 expedition under Commodore James Biddle, and the Dutch had warned of his arrival. Perry treated the shogunate's exclusion order with disdain, and he refused to shift anchorage until he had handed over a letter from President Millard Fillmore addressed to the monarch. He paraded his men, opened his gunports to expose his weaponry, and announced that he would return the next year for a reply. This time he had six ships under his command, having commandeered two more in Hong Kong. Confronted with this display of force, the shogunate reluctantly signed a friendship treaty with the United States. Japan made all the concessions: American ships were to be allowed to call at Shimoda and Hakodate and to obtain coal and other supplies. Shipwrecked sailors were to be treated fairly, and the United States had the right to station a consul at Shimoda.

Perry brought gifts that displayed the wonders of the industrial revolution—a telegraph using Morse code and a quarter-size steam locomotive with carriages and track. Sailors put on a minstrel show in blackface. Men and women flocked to see the strange black ships with their steam stacks and cannon.

Portrait of American Official. This image depicts an American official who landed with Perry at Uraga bay. This woodblock print emphasizes facial features most like those of demons—large nose, red mouth with gaping teeth. (*Peabody Essex Museum, Salem, MA/Bridgeman Art Library*)

The shogunate soon found itself making further concessions. In 1856, Townsend Harris arrived as the first U.S. consul at Shimoda, to the consternation of shogunal officials, who had never expected a barbarian to live on Japan's sacred soil. A failed businessman in the China trade, Harris was determined to sign a commercial treaty with Japan. Realizing Shimoda's isolation, he bullied Japanese officials to allow him to negotiate in Edo. Fearing that delay might bring the same gunboats to Japan that had devastated China's coast, shogunal officials signed the treaty Harris wanted on July 29, 1858. According to its provisions, the two countries were to exchange diplomatic representatives.

Japan was to open six cities—Edo, Osaka, Kanagawa (later Yokohama), Hyōgo (Kōbe), Nagasaki, and Niigata—to foreign residence and trade just as the Chinese treaty ports had earlier been opened. Japan had to accept low tariffs on imported goods, whereas its own exports faced steep tariffs in the United States. Finally, Japan had to allow foreign residents and visitors the privilege of extraterritoriality. Japan soon signed similar treaties with the Netherlands, Britain, France, and Russia.

Debates on the Foreign Threat

Unnerved by the unprecedented responsibility of signing treaties with western powers, the shogunate revoked its two hundred fifty-year-old monopoly over foreign policy. In 1854 it asked leading daimyo for their opinions; in 1858 it asked the monarch Kōmei to endorse the Harris commercial treaty. In neither case was a consensus forthcoming. Worse, Kōmei rejected the treaty, urged the shogun to consult the leading daimyo, and demanded the foreigners' expulsion. When the shogunate signed the treaty against Kōmei's wishes, it was considered treasonous. People from many walks of life began to collect and debate information on political affairs. By ignoring prohibitions on discussion of contemporary events and creating a new public political realm, they helped bring about what hindsight has deemed as the last days of the shogunate.

Some voices supported engagement with the West. Sakuma Shōzan argued for a proactive policy of seeking advanced western military technology in order to strengthen Japan and of fusing western science to Japan's Confucian ethical base. Only by opening Japan to trade could it achieve the knowledge and tools it needed to compete in the emerging world order. His ideas found supporters among advisors to important daimyo such as Yokoi Shōnan, who popularized the slogan *fukoku kyōhei* (rich country, strong army), taken from a line in the Chinese classics. Both Sakuma and Yokoi died at the hands of xenophobic assassins.

The men who opposed signing treaties with the West had a rational basis for their stance. Tokugawa Nariaki believed that allowing trade with the West would weaken Japan both materially, in that Japan would lose precious metals in exchange for fripperies, and spiritually, because it would be infected by Christianity. The only way to revive Japan's martial spirit was to fight, even though it meant certain defeat. Yoshida Shōin had studied military science in Chōshū. In 1854, he opened a small school where he taught public policy under the rubric *sonnō jōi* (revere the monarch and expel the barbarian). By this he meant that the monarch should participate in policy decisions and the foreigners must be driven off. He was furious that by spinelessly signing the treaties, the shogunate had made Japan look weak in the eyes of the world.

The social networks that had previously transmitted information on agricultural innovation and the rice market now disseminated news of current events. Doctors, merchants, and samurai in Edo told friends and relatives in the countryside about Perry's arrival and the shogun's response. Their letters circulated widely, and their recipients copied their contents into diaries to discuss with like-minded neighbors. Proselytizers for the Hirata school and experts in swordsmanship linked people across domainal boundaries. Broadsheets (*kawaraban*) reported gossip on the treaty negotiations. They circulated primarily in urban areas, where they could be easily and anonymously sold, but travelers also took them back to villages. A few commoners presented plans for coastal defense to their daimyo for forwarding to the shogun. They traveled to Edo and Kyoto to see for themselves the changes taking place (see **Material Culture: Foot Traffic**).

POLITICAL TURMOIL

The shogunate found itself stymied by Kōmei's disapproval of the Harris treaty and a dispute over shogunal succession. Prodded by Satsuma,

MATERIAL CULTURE

Foot Traffic

Before the coming of the railroad, feet provided the means of locomotion for most Japanese travelers. Arising at 4:00 A.M. and moving briskly on straw sandals, they generally covered thirty miles a day before seeking an inn for the night. Occasionally a traveler rented a horse for a day's journey, but most horses carried merchandise. Boats plied the Inland Sea and Lake Biwa, carrying travelers as well as goods. Given their reputation for capsizing, many travelers preferred to walk.

The chief alternative to feet was the palanquin. These came in several sizes and styles, depending on their function and the status of the user. Most travelers rode in a wicker basket seated on a cushion, grasping a strap to keep their balance. Rural entrepreneurs transported their brides in enclosed palanquins; in cities these were reserved for the daimyo and high-ranking samurai. Most palanquins were carried by two men, with relays running in front and back.

The rickshaw superseded the palanquin. Invented in 1869 by Izumi Yōsuke, a restaurateur in Tokyo, it substituted human-powered carriages for horse-drawn coaches. Built in various sizes to carry up to four people and various designs depending on whether strength or speed was the object, rickshaws spread from Japan to China and the rest of Asia. They made unmerciful demands on human labor, but they were cheap, simple to make and repair, and nonpolluting. Nothing could beat them for short distances until the taxi arrived in 1912.

Fifty-Three Stations on the Tōkaidō. At Kusatsu, one of the fifty-three stations on the Tōkaidō depicted in woodblock prints by Hiroshige, travelers rest their weary feet. Three types of palanquins are featured in this scene. *(Tokyo National Museum/TNM Image Archives/DNPArchives.com)*

Mito, and other activist daimyo, Kōmei urged shogunal officials to appoint Nariaki's son, Hitotsubashi Yoshinobu, perceived as more capable than the man who had the strongest claim by blood, Tokugawa Iemochi. The senior councilors rejected interference in the decision that was theirs alone to make. They appointed a vassal daimyo, Ii Naosuke, regent for Iemochi and chief senior councilor. Ii purged his daimyo opponents and arrested, exiled, or executed over one hundred men employed as agents by daimyo and court nobles. In 1859, the shogunate executed Yoshida Shōin for plotting to assassinate the shogun's emissary to Kyoto. The daimyo cowed, opponents silenced, Ii asserted that the shogunate had sole responsibility for foreign affairs.

On a snowy morning in the third month of 1860, young samurai from Mito and Satsuma assassinated Ii outside Edo castle. Angry at the execution of men they revered, they believed passionately in the politics of direct action. Their deed galvanized public opinion against Ii by deeming him a traitor for having executed men of high purpose (*shishi*) whose only aim was to serve the monarch. Equally alarming, the assassins had overcome the antipathy that distanced *tozama* domains such as Satsuma from Mito, home to the shogun's relative. The shogunate abandoned its authoritarian stance for a more conciliatory posture. It proposed a union of court and military (*kōbu gattai*) that would give important *tozama* and collateral daimyo advisory positions on foreign affairs and reinstated daimyo purged by Ii. It sealed the deal by having Shogun Iemochi wed Kōmei's younger half-sister, Kazunomiya, in return for a promise to expel the barbarians.

Within this framework of cooperation, a number of self-styled able daimyo called for national reforms to match the military reforms they had carried out at home. They urged the shogunate to employ men of talent and ability, regardless of their domainal affiliation, promote the study of western technology, and strengthen the nation's defenses. To fund these goals, the shogunate agreed to cut its expenses, reduce the daimyo's attendance in Edo to one hundred days every three years, and permit the daimyo to take their families held hostage in Edo to their domains. Women and servants had to abandon the only city they had ever known for life in provincial backwaters.

The *shishi* demanded immediate expulsion of the barbarians in accordance with Kōmei's wishes. Young and reckless, they absconded from their domains to study swordsmanship in Edo and Kyoto and imbibe the ideas of Aizawa Seishisai and Yoshida Shōin. Filled with the Japanese spirit (*Yamato damashii*), they swaggered through the streets, less concerned with personal grooming than with purity of purpose. As soon as Yokohama opened as a treaty port in 1859, they launched a reign of terror against foreign merchants, sailors, and officials. (See Color Plate 26.) Following Kazunomiya's marriage, *shishi* in Kyoto assassinated advisers to the daimyo and nobles they held responsible.

Monarch, shogun, and daimyo feared that the *shishi*'s antics would so weaken the established political order as to invite foreign invasion. Satsuma forced its radicals to return home in disgrace. When *shishi* tried to capture the palace in the eighth month of 1863, planning to place Kōmei at the head of an army to unite western Japan under the slogan of "Restore monarchical rule," Satsuma allied with shogunal forces to drive them from Kyoto. Many fled to Chōshū. The daimyo of Tosa forced *shishi* in his domain to leave or commit suicide. *Shishi*-led uprisings in the foothills of Yamato and at Ikuno near the Japan Sea were brutally suppressed. Conflict between radical expulsionists and conservatives in Mito erupted in civil war. In the seventh month of 1864, Chōshū *shishi* returned to Kyoto with supporters from other domains and rural militia in tow. Once again, the shogunate routed them.

The exploits performed by *shishi* had less impact on policy than on public opinion. They dramatized the monarchy's cause and ruptured the alliance between shogun and court. But how significant was the expansion of a public political sphere based on the discussion and exchange of information given that 60 percent of the population was illiterate? Most commoners remained bystanders because they lacked an organizational structure to mobilize effectively. Historians who claim that commoners remained quiescent during the years leading to the Meiji Restoration and therefore it cannot be deemed a revolution from below overlook a similar inertia in the ruling class. Most daimyo did nothing, either because they sided with the shogun out of loyalty and self-interest, he being the ultimate guarantor of their office, or because opposing factions had gridlocked domainal administration. Most samurai remained embedded in the vertical hierarchy predicated on loyalty and obedience to their lord. They had less to do with the eventual outcome than rural entrepreneurs who provided supplies to traveling *shishi*, enlisted their tenants in rural militia, and supported the monarchical cause or the shogunate with their pocketbooks.

THE FALL OF THE SHOGUNATE

The *shishi's* attacks on foreigners and shogunal forces had unforeseen consequences. The British demanded that the men from Satsuma responsible for killing a British merchant be turned over to them and an indemnity paid. When Satsuma refused, British ships bombarded Kagoshima in the seventh month of 1863. For all its military reforms, Satsuma was still no match for foreign gunboats. In the eleventh month, it signed a peace treaty, acceding to British demands. In compliance with Kōmei's decree that the barbarians be expelled in the fifth month of 1863, Chōshū gunners fired on French and American ships in the straits of Shimonoseki. In the eighth month of 1864, the foreigners retaliated. These salutary lessons were not lost on their victims. Both Satsuma and Chōshū began to rebuild their military along western lines. Just days before foreign ships attacked Chōshū, the shogunate had it branded an enemy of the court for harboring *shishi* and sent a coalition of daimyo troops to its borders. Chōshū backed down. It

apologized for its misdeeds, expelled radical court nobles who had sought refuge there in 1863, and executed three high-ranking officials. The shogunate declared victory and withdrew its forces.

The shogunate had less success controlling the consequences of foreign trade. Beginning in 1859, foreign merchants in the treaty ports at Nagasaki and Yokohama discovered that the silver-to-gold ratio in Japan was one-third what it was in the West, meaning that any man with silver in his pockets could buy gold at ludicrously low prices. The gold rush ended only when the shogunate recoined and devalued gold, silver, and copper. When it granted daimyo permission to mint money, counterfeiters flooded the market, and inflation soared. Foreign merchants bought tea and silk in exchange for weapons, making gunrunning a lucrative enterprise, but also leading to a sudden expansion in cash crops on rice paddies. Weavers lost work because they could not compete with foreigners for silk thread. In the summer of 1866, rising unemployment, crop failures, inflation, and shogunal efforts to tax trade created the conditions for the most widespread riots in Edo history, particularly in the shogun's stronghold of eastern Japan.

The shogunate hoped to use new taxes levied on foreign trade to subsidize its military modernization program. It imported thousands of weapons through Yokohama and drilled its retainer band in rifle companies supplemented by rural recruits. It sent missions abroad. The first in 1860 signed a friendship treaty with the United States; subsequent envoys emphasized the study of foreign technology. In 1861 it opened a naval training school at Hyōgo. In 1865 it started an ironworks at Yokohama and a shipyard at Yokosuka. It also received Kōmei's sanction for signing foreign treaties, and it marginalized the *tozama* daimyo by excluding them from policy making circles.

The shogunate's revitalization campaign destabilized the balance of power with the daimyo. When it announced a second punitive campaign against Chōshū because *shishi* had returned to

Ee ja nai ka. As amulets fall from the sky, men, women, and children, some in costume, dance in thanksgiving, shouting, "ain't it great" (*Ee ja nai ka*). *(National Diet Library, Tokyo, Japan)*

positions of power, it pushed former enemies together. Chōshū and Satsuma formed an alliance in the first month of 1866. Both had launched self-strengthening programs, using emergency funds to buy arms through Nagasaki, sending retainers on fact-finding missions abroad, and organizing western-style armies. Now they argued that the shogunate ought not move against Chōshū when pressing domestic and foreign problems remained to be solved. Few domains responded to the shogun's call, riots in Edo and Osaka tied down garrisons, and the attack on Chōshū ended in ignominious defeat. Iemochi's death at just that juncture provided the shogunate with a face-saving out. But when Kōmei died unexpectedly just five months later, the shogunate lost its strongest supporter at court. Unlike the shogun's opponents who had come to believe that Japan should have but a sin-

gle monarch, Kōmei supported the division of powers that left administrative and foreign affairs in the shogun's hands.

Hitotsubashi Yoshinobu reigned as shogun for less than a year. At first he moved vigorously to reassert shogunal authority and continue military reforms. His efforts stirred up turmoil and strengthened the alliance against him. In the eighth month of 1867, a new popular movement swept the coast from the inland sea to Edo. Claiming that amulets inscribed with the name of the sun goddess that portended a prosperous future had fallen from heaven, men and women danced in the streets chanting, "Ain't it great" (*ee ja nai ka*). When the movement reached eastern Japan, dancers threw stones at foreigners to drive out the barbarian demons and rehearsed a mock funeral for the shogunate. In the tenth month, the court issued a secret decree to Satsuma and Chōshū to overthrow the Tokugawa. Realizing he could no longer fulfill the duties of shogun, Yoshinobu returned his patent of office to the monarch. The restoration of monarchical rule was at hand.

In the name of the Meiji emperor, Kōmei's fifteen-year old son, leaders of the Sat-chō forces abolished the offices of shogun and regent and replaced them with new advisory positions open to daimyo, court nobles, and "men of talent." They declared Yoshinobu a traitor to the emperor, revoked his court rank, and confiscated his family lands. When the shogunate fought back, it was defeated after four days of heavy fighting outside Kyoto in the first days of 1868. The imperial armies moved slowly north, hamstrung for lack of cash, which they tried to ameliorate by demanding loans from wealthy commoners. The long-standing animosity between eastern and western Japan prolonged the fighting until Aizu fell in the ninth month, after suffering heavy casualties of men and women. The last stronghold of shogunal support at Hakodate did not surrender until the middle of 1869, supported to the last by the American envoy. Both official and popular opinion feared that prolonged civil war might give foreign troops an excuse to invade Japan. A better alternative was to unite around the new emperor. Although many retainers died, Yoshinobu and the daimyo of Aizu survived to take their places in the new imperial peerage and join their efforts to the task of strengthening state and economy to compete in the new world order. Hirata disciples and other imperial loyalists rushed to offer their services to the new government; people in Edo watched warily as their old masters were replaced with new.

SUMMARY

Long before the Meiji Restoration, the social and political order crafted in the seventeenth century had ceased to fit everyday practice. The commercial economy, opportunities for travel, and information networks eroded the status and geographical divisions that kept people in their place. Reforms by shogun and daimyo to shore up their authority and fill government coffers could not rectify the gap between reality and their ideal of the proper relations between rulers and commoners. Debates over how to deal with the foreign threat added further strain to the system. When it collapsed in 1867, it left behind a dynamic economy, a large pool of able administrators, and a population well educated for its time.

SUGGESTED READING

Many books have been written on the fall of the shogunate. The most recent include G. M. Wilson, *Patriots and Redeemers in Japan: Motives in the Meiji Restoration* (1992), and A. Walthall, *The Weak Body of a Useless Woman: Matsuo Taseko and the Meiji Restoration* (1998). For a collection of essays focused on the nineteenth century, see M. B. Jansen, ed., *Cambridge History of Japan*, vol. 5 (1989).

For nativism see H. D. Harootunian, *Things Seen and Unseen: Discourse and Ideology in Tokugawa Nativism* (1988). For popular culture, see N.-L. Hur, *Prayer and Play in Late Tokugawa Japan: Asakusa Sensōji and Edo Society* (2000). For Mito, see J. Victor Koschmann, *The Mito Ideology: Discourse, Reform and Insurrection in Late Tokugawa Japan, 1790–1864* (1987), and K. Yamakawa, *Women of the Mito Domain: Recollections of Samurai Family Life,* trans. K. W. Nakai (1992). For an entertaining look at samurai life, see K. Katsu, *Musui's Story: The Autobiography of a Tokugawa Samurai,* trans. T. Craig (1988).

Meiji Transformation (1868–1900)

The restoration of the Meiji emperor as head of state marked the beginning of profound changes in Japanese politics, culture, and society. A small group of self-selected men, who had led the drive to overthrow the shogun, implemented programs to abolish status distinctions that had compartmentalized social groups and to centralize government. Fearful of the West, they acknowledged the necessity of importing western military technology, industry, legal norms, constitutional thought, science, dress, and food. (See **Material Culture: New Food for a New Nation.**) They built railroads, shipyards, and schools. They propounded a new ideology to rally the citizens. They colonized the Ryukyu Islands and Hokkaido. They projected Japan's power abroad in Taiwan and Korea and renegotiated treaties. They faced considerable opposition, often from within their own ranks. Farmers rioted against new state policies that threatened their livelihood; samurai rebelled at the loss of their traditional identity. Local notables promoted democracy. Intellectuals, novelists, and essayists hammered out new identities that refused to fit a single pattern. By the end of the century, modernity had arrived.

To what extent did changes in the latter half of the nineteenth century build on what had gone before? Did the Meiji Restoration herald a revolution in politics and society, or simply a transition? Did modernization mean westernization?

THE MEIJI STATE

The oligarchs who created the institutions for a centralized government had little idea of what they hoped to accomplish and disagreed on what

MATERIAL CULTURE

New Food for a New Nation

Although rice had been grown in Japan since the third century B.C.E., it did not become a staple of the average Japanese diet until imported from Korea and China starting in 1873. Before that, most people ate wheat, barley, and millet. Between 1869 and 1900, the per capita consumption of rice went from 3.5 bushels a year to 5.0 bushels a year. Rice balls became ubiquitous in lunch boxes, and except for the poor, steamed rice replaced rice gruel for breakfast.

The Meiji government officially promoted the eating of meat because it was thought to produce stronger workers and soldiers. In 1869 it established the Tsukiji beef company. In 1871, a butcher shop in Tokyo's Asakusa district became popular selling beef for sukiyaki, a Meiji period invention, as well as milk, cheese, and butter. In the 1880s, butcher shops started selling horse meat. It was cheaper than beef or pork and redder than chicken.

Vegetables, fruits, and breads had a harder sell. Asparagus, cabbage, cauliflower, and tomatoes did not blend easily into Japanese cuisine. Importing apples, peaches, and grapes stimulated the cultivation and spread of indigenous fruits such as persimmon, Satsuma tangerine, and Asian pear. Bread and cakes became popular only after they were modified to suit Japanese taste.

Aguranabe. This flyer advertising Aguranabe, a butcher show, linked eating beef to "civilization and enlightenment." *(Tokyo Metropolitan Foundation for History and Culture/ DNPArchives.com)*

By selectively adapting western foods, Japanese people developed a much more varied diet than they had had in the past. They ate more, and what they ate was more nutritious. An improved diet made them stronger and healthier. It increased life expectancy and childbearing rates. A population of approximately 33 million at midcentury had grown to 45 million by the end of the nineteenth century.

---

to do. An amorphous group of samurai from Satsuma and Chōshū, plus a few activist Kyoto aristocrats and imperial loyalists from other domains, they had diverse interests and goals. Their first pronouncement came in the Oath of 1868, offered by the emperor in the company of court nobles and daimyo to the gods of heaven and earth. In it he promised that everyone was to unite in promoting the nation's well-being, government policy was to be decided through public discussion, all would be allowed to fulfill their

just aspirations, "the uncivilized customs of former times shall be broken through," and "intellect and learning shall be sought throughout the world in order to establish the foundations of the Empire."[1] The Five Injunctions issued to commoners the next day had a different message. It ordered them to practice the Confucian virtues of

---

1. Donald L. Keene, *Emperor of Japan: Meiji and His World, 1852–1912* (New York: Columbia University Press, 2002), p. 139.

loyalty, filial piety, chastity, obedience, and harmony; to desist demonstrations and protests; to abjure Christianity; to conform to international public law; and to stay in Japan. Emigration to the United States began almost immediately.

Ambiguities in the oath speak to the lack of agreement on national goals. The nation's well-being could justify a national land tax and universal military conscription; it could require promoting entrepreneurship and compulsory education. None of the men present envisioned public discussion of national affairs to include anyone but themselves. In the context of the past, in which each daimyo had set policy for his domain, it meant that decisions and power were to be centralized. It did not mean parliamentary democracy, although it was later interpreted that way. The third clause implied that hereditary status distinctions would be abolished and held out the promise of social mobility. Abolishing old customs acknowledged the reality of cultural imperialism inherent in international law and unequal treaties. The purpose of gaining knowledge was to serve the state.

At first, the oligarchs looked to eighth-century models for a new government. The Council of State became the highest deliberative body. It was assisted by a board of 106 advisers, the activists in the Meiji Restoration, who made the real decisions. The Council of Shinto Affairs enjoyed a brief existence equal to the Council of State. This structure was reorganized four times in the next four months. Most daimyo remained in control of their domains, leaving the oligarchs who spoke in the emperor's name only the former shogun's lands. Monetary proof of support for the emperor from daimyo, former shogunal retainers, merchants, and rural entrepreneurs staved off fiscal crisis in the short run. The necessity of finding sufficient tax revenues to fund the government forced the oligarchs to take hesitant steps toward centralization.

Centralization required convincing the daimyo to give up their domains. Some daimyo hoped to play a larger role in national affairs; some concentrated their efforts on self-strengthening. Most stayed aloof from the court and isolated from each other. In 1869, the daimyo of Satsuma and Chōshū agreed to make a formal declaration of returning their land and population registers to the emperor, with the understanding that he would then confirm their holdings as governors. The government put all domainal retainers above the level of foot soldiers into one general category called former samurai (*shizoku*). To eliminate the redundancies of two hundred seventy independent domain administrations and centralize tax collection, the oligarchs in 1871 abolished the domains and established prefectures (see Map 21.1). They started the process of consolidating one hundred seventy thousand towns and villages into larger administrative units with a new hierarchy of local officials and inaugurated a household registration system whereby each household head had to establish a place of legal residence and inform the government of births, deaths, marriages, and divorces in his family.

The daimyo accepted the loss of their hereditary lands with equanimity. The most important became prefectural governors. Since the number of prefectures was seventy-two, later reduced to fifty, the area under their control expanded. All daimyo benefited by no longer having responsibility for their domains' debts and being guaranteed a substantial income for their personal use. They did not have to support standing armies of retainers. In place of their former titles, they received court rank. In return for giving up their already circumscribed autonomy, they received wealth and prestige.

Abolishing domains disinherited roughly 2 million *shizoku*. All they received were small stipends later commuted to government bonds. The oligarchs urged them to find another line of work, in agriculture, forestry, business, and the colonization of Hokkaido. Some succeeded; many did not. Former shogunal bureaucrats staffed the new government offices, but most domain samurai remained in castle towns. Political power had become sufficiently bureaucratized over the course of the Edo period that neither samurai nor daimyo became landed gentry.

Having taken the first steps toward a more centralized state, in 1871 one faction of the oli-

Map 21.1   **Modern Japan**

garchs left for the United States and Europe. Forty-nine officials and fifty-eight students, including five girls, made up the delegation. Headed by Iwakura Tomomi, a former court noble, their goal was to convince the western powers to revise the unequal treaties that infringed on Japanese sovereignty. Informed by President Ulysses S. Grant that western powers would never consent to treaty revision unless Japan reformed its laws and institutions along western lines, the diplomatic mission became a study mission. Wealth and power that the West had created through industrialization and centralized political institutions came as a shock. Officials inspected prisons, schools, factories, and government agencies. They expected their absence to preclude any initiatives by the leaders left behind; in 1873 when Saigō Takamori proposed to invade Korea for having insulted the emperor in the first diplomatic exchange following the restoration, they rushed home to stop him. They opposed not the use of force but its timing. Domestic reform had to precede military engagements abroad.

Reforms and Opposition

The abolition of domains took place in the context of social reforms that did not suit everyone. For many farmers, the emperor's progress from Kyoto to Edo (renamed Tokyo in 1869) in 1868 symbolized the Meiji Restoration. This, they felt, would usher in new prosperity and social justice. Instead, village officials continued to collect taxes, rents remained the same, and moneylenders charged exorbitant interest. Disappointment fueled the rage with which rural and urban people punished what they saw as wrongdoing. When the new government replaced familiar faces in domain administrations with men from foreign parts, this too led to protest, as did the official end to discrimination against outcasts when status distinctions were erased and the outcasts became "new commoners." The first ten years of the Meiji period saw more protest and more violence than at any time during the Edo period.

Bureaucrats initiated reforms and technological innovations to strengthen the state against its domestic and foreign enemies. They hired western experts to transform government, economy, infrastructure, and education. Drawing on western models, they issued civil and criminal codes that replaced different regulations for different statuses with rule by law that considered only the nature of the crime. They built telegraph lines and railroads to improve communications and foster unity. On January 1, 1873, they replaced the lunar calendar that farmers had used as a guide to planting and harvesting with the western calendar. They outlawed traditional hairstyles for men and suppressed village festivals. They issued these laws and directives without warning or explanation. In defense of time-honored custom, farmers rioted.

Religious practices also provoked controversy. In the third month of 1868, the oligarchs ordered the separation of Shinto and Buddhism and the conversion of what had been shrine-temple complexes into shrines by eliminating Buddhist icons, rituals, and priests. In some regions officials infected with Hirata Atsutane's doctrines destroyed Buddhist temples where the farmers' ancestral tablets were kept. The establishment of Yasukuni shrine to the war dead in 1869 used Shinto to promote national goals. The development of State Shinto in the 1870s consolidated local shrines and brought them into a hierarchy with the Ise shrine to the sun goddess at the top. Rather than shrines containing only deities particular to their region, they had to accept deities of national significance in addition. New religions founded in the Edo period received official recognition as Sect Shinto. Meiji period new religions were viewed with suspicion, if not proscribed outright. (See **Biography: Deguchi Nao.**) Farmers protested the destruction of their familiar temples, and Buddhist priests fought back by associating Buddhism with anti-Christian sentiment, recalling ties to the imperial house, and helping immigrants in Hokkaido.

The directives that had immediate effects and aroused the strongest opposition dealt with education, the military, and taxes. In 1872, the government decreed eight years of compulsory education for all children (shortened to four in 1879 and then increased to six in 1907) to fit them for their responsibilities as productive citizens in a modern nation. Communities had to pay for schools themselves. Enraged at the cost, farmers destroyed or damaged nearly two hundred schools between 1873 and 1877. Pre-Meiji teachers continued their unlicensed schools and dissuaded parents from sending their children to new ones. Needing their child's labor or unable to afford tuition, many parents never enrolled daughters or even sons or allowed them to attend only a few months. Over time, compliance increased until it reached 90 percent in the twentieth century.

The slogan of the day was "Rich Country, Strong Army." In January 1873 the government issued the conscription ordinance that summoned all males over the age of twenty to serve three years on active duty in the armed forces,

BIOGRAPHY Deguchi Nao

Women have played a major role in the founding of Japan's new religions; Deguchi Nao (1836–1918), an illiterate commoner, became a prophet.

Nao was born in a castle town near Kyoto to a family in declining circumstances. Her grandfather had the privilege of wearing a sword and using a surname as an official carpenter. Her father squandered his life on drink; he died when she was nine. Nao went to work for a merchant who provided her with room and board. Her earnings went to her mother. Nao helped with the cooking and cleaning; she spun thread and strung coins, thereby gaining a reputation for diligence and hard work. In her third year of service, the domain awarded her a prize for being a filial daughter.

Nao hoped to marry the man she loved, but her widowed aunt Yuri insisted that she accept an arranged marriage and be adopted into the Deguchi family as Yuri herself had done. Yuri drowned herself after Nao repeatedly rejected her offer. A few days later Nao developed a high fever and lost consciousness. Upon her recovery, she attributed her illness to Yuri's vengeful spirit. To placate it and care for the Deguchi ancestral tablets, Nao agreed to marry the man Yuri had selected for her and continue the Deguchi house.

Nao's husband was no better than her father. By 1872 she had borne five children and was living in a rented house in Ayabe. She opened a small restaurant, and when it failed she sold sweet-bean buns. She continued to have children—eleven in all, three of whom died in infancy. When her husband became paralyzed from a fall off a roof in 1885, Nao collected rags to support her family. His death in 1887 freed her to work in a filature as well.

One winter morning in 1892 as she was out collecting rags, Nao became possessed by a god. The experience transformed her personality and her outlook on the world. Instead of being gentle and deferential, she became dignified, filled with divinely inspired authority. She rejected the social order because it rewarded vice and valued money. Since the oligarchs and the emperor were responsible for these conditions, they exemplified absolute evil. They would soon be destroyed and replaced by a divine order of harmony and equality. Under the spell of her god, this formerly illiterate woman wrote hundreds of texts that spelled out what was wrong with the world and what was to come. She also became a faith healer. In 1899, her adopted son Deguchi Onisaburō organized a sect called Ōmoto-kyō based on her revelations. Under his leadership, the group grew rapidly and suffered repeated government persecutions. Nao quarreled with him over his interpretation of her writings and his refusal to reject all that was modern. She died frustrated that she had not been able to reconstruct the world in accordance with her beliefs.

Source: Based on Emily Groszos Ooms, *Women and Millenarian Protest in Meiji Japan: Deguchi Nao and Ōmoto-kyō* (Ithaca, N.Y.: East Asia Program Cornell University, 1993).

followed by four years in the reserves. In accord with the French system, heads and heirs of family farms and businesses received exemptions, and exemptions could be purchased. Its architect was Yamagata Aritomo from Chōshū, who had spent 1869–1870 in Europe studying French and German conscript armies. The conscription ordinance put Japan's defense on the shoulders of the masses. It provided a way to educate conscripts and their families in the goals of government leaders. By revoking the samurai's monopoly of force, it did more than any other reform to eliminate status distinctions and create equality of opportunity.

Both farmers and *shizoku* opposed conscription. The ordinance used the term "blood tax," meaning that all citizens should willingly sacrifice themselves for their country. Farmers who took it literally assumed that the government wanted their blood. Even those who understood the message believed that farmers could best contribute to the nation by growing crops. Commoners opposed to conscription rose up in sixteen localities in the months after the ordinance's promulgation. Samurai opposition took longer to develop but cost more lives. Conservative oligarchs such as Saigō Takamori had already insisted that the national army be composed of the men bred to military service. When Iwakura and his faction outvoted Saigō on whether to invade Korea, he left the government. In 1876, the government ordered *shizoku* to stop wearing the two swords that distinguished them from the rest of the population. Between 1874 and 1877, over thirty rebellions erupted in defense of samurai privilege. The largest and last, in Satsuma, led by Saigō, required the mobilization of sixty-five thousand troops and took eight months to suppress. Saigō committed suicide. In 1878 samurai counterrevolution ended with the assassination of the oligarch Ōkubo Toshimichi, also from Satsuma, because he had opposed invading Korea and arbitrarily initiated reforms.

The Satsuma rebels had had reason to oppose the 1873 tax law. Applied nationwide to agricultural land, its aim was to provide a steady flow of income for the government by replacing the old hodgepodge of domain taxes on fluctuating harvests with a single, uniform property tax. In most regions of Japan, the land surveys that accompanied the new tax simply confirmed de facto proprietary rights farmers already enjoyed. Satsuma domain had allowed *gōshi* (rustic warriors) to assign land to the cultivators and treat them like tenant farmers. Faced with the loss of income as well as hereditary status and privilege, *gōshi* became the shock troops for the Satsuma rebellion.

Even though the Meiji oligarchs tried to promote industry and demanded loans from merchants, they had an agrarian mind-set. Nearly 80 percent of the government's revenues came from tax on agricultural land through the 1880s. Farmers with market access for their products benefited; those who misjudged the market or suffered a crop failure had to sell their land to pay taxes. In some areas, officials imposed the new tax while requiring farmers to continue to pay ancillary taxes it was supposed

Fiscal Year	Land Tax	Liquor Tax	Customs Duties	Income Tax	Corporation Tax	Business Tax	Sugar Excise	Inheritance Tax	Other
				Composition of Tax Revenues, 1872–1940 (%)					
1872	90.1	1.5	3.3	—	—	—	—	—	5.1
1880	72.3	14.9	4.4	—	—	—	—	—	8.4
1890	58.1	22.9	6.9	1.6	—	—	—	—	10.5
1900	34.6	38.0	10.9	4.3	1.2	3.9	1.3	—	5.8
1910	23.8	26.2	15.3	10.0	2.9	7.0	5.1	0.9	8.8
1920	10.2	22.6	11.1	23.5	11.8	6.6	6.8	1.1	6.3
1930	7.9	26.4	15.1	22.1	6.6	6.2	9.6	3.5	2.6
1940	0.9	8.9	2.9	34.0	11.7	2.6	3.2	1.6	33.9

Source: Based on Minami Ryōshin, *The Economic Development of Japan: A Quantitative Study,* trans. Ralph Thompson and Minami with assistance from David Merriman (New York: St. Martin's Press, 1986), p. 340.

to replace. Farmers petitioned for redress; they killed officials suspected of being corrupt. In 1876 widespread, if uncoordinated, opposition to the tax forced the government to reduce it from 3 percent of assessed value to 2.5 percent.

While dealing with opposition from outside the government, oligarchs also quarreled among themselves. They created and abolished ministries to consolidate their power or deny a rival and disputed what kind of government Japan was to have. In the early 1870s, Kido Takayoshi and Ōkubo advocated some measure of popular representation in government lest arbitrary rule generate unrest. Their proposal contained a veiled attack on Itō Hirobumi and Yamagata. Disgruntled at having been shut out of power, Itagaki Taisuke left the government in 1874, joined with disaffected *shizoku* from his home domain of Tosa to form the Patriotic Party, and petitioned the government to establish an elected national assembly. He disbanded the party when he was invited back into the government in 1875 at the Osaka Conference. There, the oligarchs agreed to establish prefectural assemblies (done in 1878) and plan for a national assembly. Four months later, the emperor announced that he would promulgate a constitution after due deliberation.

Constitution and National Assembly

The publicity attracted by the promise of a national assembly and a constitution stimulated responses that coalesced into the Popular Rights Movement. *Shizoku,* village officials, rural entrepreneurs, journalists, intellectuals, and prefectural assemblymen held lengthy meetings and circulated petitions for an immediate national assembly that collected hundreds of thousands of signatures. Radicals and impoverished farmers rioted and planned attacks on the government in the name of human rights. A woman who held property demanded she be allowed to vote in prefectural elections (she was denied). Kishida Toshiko and Fukuda Hideko gave public lectures at which they demanded rights, liberty, education, and equality for women. Baba Tatsui drew on social Darwinism to argue that since democracy based on an egalitarian society was the most advanced form of government, it should be established forthwith. Local notables drafted model constitutions. Activists criticized the oligarchs for blocking communication between emperor and people. They argued that a representative government would harmonize imperial and popular will by providing a forum for the free expression of popular opinion, thereby strengthening the nation. Drawing on the natural rights theories propounded by French and British philosophers, Ueki Emori propounded a theory of popular sovereignty and right of revolution.

The oligarchs responded to the Popular Rights Movement by issuing increasingly draconian peace preservation laws. Press censorship began in 1875; the 1880 Ordinance on Public Meetings stationed policemen at assemblies to ensure that the speakers did not deviate from texts that had been approved beforehand. Excluded from audiences were soldiers, off-duty police, teachers, and students. Demonstrations in Fukushima opposed to a particularly arbitrary governor in 1882, the Chichibu uprising of 1884 that mobilized tenant farmers in demanding debt relief, and other violent incidents met with mass arrests and executions. Having learned the cost of direct action, local notables turned to organizing political parties in anticipation of the first election for the national assembly promised in 1890.

The Meiji Constitution defined institutions established before its promulgation. In 1878 the military General Staff was made directly responsible to the emperor, bypassing the War Ministry run by bureaucrats. A new peerage destined to fill the upper house of the bicameral national assembly known as the Diet was announced in 1884. It included oligarchs, former daimyo, and Kyoto nobility. Over time it expanded to include entrepreneurs and academics. The lower house was to be elected by commoners. The highest policymaking institution, the cabinet, replaced the Council of State in 1885. It was composed of ministers in charge of education, finance, foreign affairs, and other bureaucracies under the prime minister appointed by the emperor.

Itō Hirobumi drafted the constitution in great secrecy. He traveled to Europe in 1882 where he studied nine months in Berlin under the most respected constitutional theorists of his day. Itō and his brain trust then created a document that defined the emperor in terms of his descent from the gods and employed western notions regarding the rights and obligations of citizens. Once they had finished, a new institution, the Privy Council, headed by Itō, met to discuss it. On February 11, 1889, the date chosen to be the anniversary of Jimmu's accession 2,349 years earlier, the Meiji emperor bestowed the constitution on the prime minister. Three days of festivities announced to people across the nation that they were now citizens of a state founded on principles enshrined in a constitution.

The oligarchs wanted a constitution that secured the governing bodies and protected the imperial house through which they exercised power, and they mistrusted the "ignorant" masses. After its promulgation, they designated themselves *genrō*, elder statesmen, charged with picking cabinet ministers for the emperor. The constitution defined the emperor as sovereign and sacred. The emperor:

- exercises executive power through the cabinet
- exercises legislative power with the consent of the Imperial Diet
- has supreme command of the army and navy
- declares war, makes peace, and concludes treaties
- determines the organization of the government
- convokes the Diet and dissolves the lower house

Subjects had these rights and duties:

- present petitions, provided that they observe the proper form of respect

- within limits not prejudicial to peace and order, and not antagonistic to their duties as subjects, enjoy freedom of religious belief
- enjoy freedom of speech, within the limits set by law[2]

Subjects had to serve in the military, a clause that excluded women from the category of subject.

Japan's first experiment with parliamentary democracy nearly did not work. Although Itō and Yamagata had assumed that party politics had no place in an institution directly responsible to the emperor, they had to deal with opposition parties headed by Itagaki and other men who had been ejected from the oligarch's inner circle. Suffrage was limited to men paying at least 15 yen a year in property taxes, a qualification met by only 1.1 percent of the population, most of them in rural areas. Once elected, members discovered that the Diet had more power than the oligarchs had intended. Diet members could criticize the cabinet in memorials to the emperor; they could make speeches, published in newspapers, that outside the Diet might have landed them in jail. They had the power to approve the budget. If they refused, the previous year's budget remained in effect, but it seldom sufficed for the government's needs. When the Diet stood up to the cabinet, the prime minister dissolved it, forcing members into costly reelection campaigns. Campaign finance scandals and vote buying tarnished the reputations of politicians and oligarchs alike. Twenty-five men died during the 1892 election, most at the hands of the police.

Divided by personality, political preference, and self-interest, the oligarchs had to seek political support outside their narrow circle. In so doing, they enlarged the realm of political actors to include bureaucrats, military officers, and politicians. In 1898 Itō had the quasi-oligarchs, Ōkuma Shigenobu, head of the Progressive Party, and Itagaki Taisuke, leader of the Liberal Party,

---

2. Hugh Borton, *Japan's Modern Century* (New York: Ronald Press Co., 1955), pp. 490–507.

Triptych Showing Inauguration of the First Diet. Members of the upper house dressed in uniform are in the foreground; lower house members sit farther back. The emperor is in the box at upper left. *(Museum of Fine Arts, Boston. Jean S. and Frederic A. Sharf Collection, 2000.535)*

participate in a coalition cabinet as prime minister and home minister, respectively. Aghast at this concession to politicians, Yamagata Aritomo sabotaged their cabinet by having the army minister refuse to accept cuts in the military budget. A few months later, Yamagata became prime minister for the second time. To increase military autonomy, he made it a requirement that all army and navy ministers be active-duty officers. To dilute the power of political parties and their resistance to higher taxes, he expanded the suffrage to 2.2 percent of the population and gave more representation to urban districts. In 1900 Itō responded by forming and becoming president of a new political party, the Friends of Government (*Seiyūkai*). His compromise with politicians dramatized the oligarchs' difficulty in controlling the institutions they had created.

Industrialization

The oligarchs promoted economic reform and industrialization. They appropriated the arms-related industries already established by the domains and the shogunate. Some came under state control to supply the military; others were sold at favorable terms to cronies. Iwasaki Yatarō founded Mitsubishi enterprises on the maritime shipping line he acquired from Tosa and expanded it with low-interest government loans. The oligarchs had foreign experts write banking laws; they set up banks and issued paper currency. Their initial investments were in advanced and expensive technologies, the kind needed to build railroads and shipyards. Although building support industries for the military constituted their first priority, they also worried about the effects of unequal treaties on the balance of payments and unemployment. To maintain social stability and to compete with foreign products, they built cotton spinning and weaving factories to make cloth for domestic consumption and imported French silk spinning technology to produce thread for export. They founded a sugar refinery to help growers market their crop and compete with Chinese sugar. By bringing the state's resources to bear on industry, the oligarchs squeezed out private capital.

Agriculture supported industrial growth. Agricultural development groups, seed exchange

Steam Engine. The steam engine epitomized the industrial age. Its use on the railroad that paralleled the Tōkaidō eliminated palanquins and most foot traffic. *(Yokohama Archives of History)*

societies, journals, and lecture circuits taught farmers about new seed varieties, commercial fertilizers, and equipment. Without expanding the amount of arable land, annual agricultural productivity rose between 1.5 and 1.7 percent in the late nineteenth century. Since the land tax remained fixed, the increase put more income into the hands of rural entrepreneurs for use in promoting small-scale industry. Farmers were already accustomed to producing handicrafts; the elimination of internal restrictions on trade made it easier for them to market their goods.

Entrepreneurs and artisans developed intermediate technologies that adapted western machines to Japanese circumstances. They modified the manufacture of new daily necessities such as matches to suit the domestic and Asian markets and undersold western brands. The metric system, the new calendar, and western timepieces brought the standardization and regularization modeled by military organization to ordinary work practices. Local clubs tried to preserve handicrafts in the face of foreign imports and sought national and international markets for specialty products. They pooled capital to upgrade indigenous skills, brought in foreign

technology when it fit their needs, and hosted industrial exhibitions to diffuse technological knowledge and stimulate competition. In the mid-1870s, small water-powered filatures spread throughout the mountain valleys of central Japan, close to the silk-producing regions and a work force of young women. By 1900 silk thread accounted for one-third of the value of Japan's commodity exports and textiles totaled over half.

Another model for private enterprise was Shibusawa Eiichi. The son of a rural entrepreneur, he used his connections with oligarchs to become president of the First National Bank. In that capacity he provided capital for the construction of a privately owned shipyard at the mouth of Tokyo Bay. In 1880 he started the Osaka Spinning Mill and went on to found more than one hundred companies. Thanks to investments like his, Japan's imports by the beginning of the twentieth century were of raw materials; it exported manufactured goods. Other entrepreneurs built equipment for railroads, mines, and factories. Many thrived with the government as their biggest customer. They justified their immense wealth by insisting that they worked for the good of the nation.

In 1880 the government faced financial disaster. It had printed money recklessly during the 1870s to finance its projects, and private banks issued their own notes. It spent heavily suppressing *shizoku* rebellions and other police actions; most of the industries it built operated at a loss. Inflation that doubled the price of rice in Tokyo between 1877 and 1880 reduced the value of property tax revenues, and taxes did not cover expenditures. The negative balance of payments sucked gold and silver out of the country. From an economic point of view, Japan faced the most serious crisis of the Meiji period.

After acrimonious debate, the oligarchs decided on a deflationary policy of retrenchment. Finance Minister Matsukata Masayoshi balanced the budget, reduced government expenditures until they fell within revenues, and established a sound currency backed by gold and silver. Except for railroad, telegraph, and military-related industries, he sold at a loss all industries that the government had tried to develop. He recalled students sent abroad on government scholarships, fired foreign experts, enacted sin taxes on tobacco and sake, and increased old taxes. Between 1881 and 1885, he reduced the quantity of currency by 20 percent and stifled commerce. Farmers who saw the price of rice fall 50 percent while taxes remained the same worked longer hours to increase production. Bad loans bankrupted banks started with samurai capital. Small businesses collapsed. The ranks of tenant farmers and factory workers swelled. By 1886 key industries had become concentrated in the hands of a few wealthy capitalists with excellent government connections. The government had rid itself of drains on its income, the budget was balanced, and prices were stable.

By the 1890s Japan had a substantial work force in light and heavy industry. Filatures employed single farm women who worked eighteen-hour days when demand was high. When they contracted tuberculosis, as many did, they were returned to their families. Spreading of the disease made it modern Japan's most severe epidemic. The women who worked twelve-hour shifts in cotton mills were often married. Factory owners assumed that since women did not maintain households independent of fathers or husbands, they had no need to pay a living wage. The first strike in Japan's industrial history occurred at a filature in Kōfu in 1885 where women protested a proposed increase in hours and decrease in pay. Women unable to find factory work turned to prostitution. Poor women from Kyushu were lured to brothels in Southeast Asia. Money remitted to their families helped Japan's balance of payments.

Male factory workers in heavy industry earned up to five times the wages of women. They worked under bosses called *oyakata* who contracted for specific jobs. Because workers ran the factory floor, they were able to retain a measure of autonomy that gave them pride in their work. They moved at will from one factory to another because they possessed skills in high demand. Despite these advantages, wages barely covered the rent for a shack in the slums and a dismal diet of rice and vegetables. In 1898 railroad workers launched the largest strike of the nineteenth century. They demanded respect, higher status, and an increase in overtime pay.

Conditions for miners were worse. The low wages, dangerous work, and prison-like barracks made it so difficult to attract workers that the owner of the Ashio copper mine contracted for convict labor. By the end of the nineteenth century, the mine's demand for timber had stripped surrounding hills, leading to deadly floods. Effluent from the mine had killed the marine life in the Watarase River, devastated farmland, and caused premature deaths. Responses to environmental damage pitted proponents of "Rich Country, Strong Army" against the well-being of ordinary citizens in a conflict that was to play out repeatedly in Japan's modern history.

Civilization and Enlightenment

The local notables who had responded enthusiastically to the Popular Rights Movement wanted to bring a cultural revolution to their villages. In place of the hidebound customs of the past, they wanted "Civilization and Enlightenment," a slogan promoted by urban intellectuals and by oligarchs bent on modernizing communications, hairstyles, and education. The Meiji 6 Society founded in Tokyo in 1873 published a journal in which the members debated representative government, foreign affairs, modernizing the Japanese language, ethics and religion, and roles for women. That same year, local notable Ida Bunzō bought a copy of Samuel Smiles's *Self Help*. In a local magazine, he explained the virtues of perseverance and frugality, competition and progress, moral responsibility and the national interest. Other local notables used informal discussion groups to promote better hygiene and social improvement through hospitals, new foods, better roads, and technological innovation based on western models. They tried to overcome their neighbors' antipathy to the government-mandated schools that they saw as the best hope for improving conditions for rural people and for raising Japan's standing in the world.

The man who coined the phrase "Civilization and Enlightenment" was Fukuzawa Yukichi, a leading member of the Meiji 6 Society. In 1868 he founded Keiō University for the study of western science and business. His multivolume *Seiyō jijō* (*Western Matters*) described modern institutions—schools, hospitals, newspapers, libraries, and museums and western ideas regarding the importance of entrepreneurship and achievement. In the best-seller *Encouragement of Learning*, he indicted Japan for its backwardness and urged citizens to seek learning for its practical value in the modern world. He also served as adviser to Mitsubishi and Mitsui, destined to become the largest conglomerates in Japan. Although he advocated equality, freedom, and education for women, he kept his daughters ignorant and arranged their marriages.

Civilization and enlightenment also pertained to personal appearance. To use western technology, it was more efficient to wear western-style clothes. Replacing distinctive styles of samurai armor with standardized military uniforms submerged the individual in the ranks. Uniforms distinguished policemen from civilians. Changing appearances might help Japan gain the respect of foreigners who flaunted their cultural superiority. The government issued directives to men to stop shaving their pates and to women to stop blackening their teeth and shaving their eyebrows. Emperor and empress led the way. At his first public performance, the Meiji emperor had dressed in the court robes of his ancestors. He wore cosmetics and powder and had false eyebrows smudged on his forehead. Within two years he had changed to western-style uniforms, cut his hair, and grown a beard. The empress too appeared in western-style clothing and hairstyles.

The new nobility and educated elite followed the imperial family's example. In 1883 the foreign minister built a modern two-story brick building called *Rokumeikan* (Deer-Cry Pavilion) that contained a restaurant, billiard room, and ballroom. Invitations to garden parties, charity balls, and receptions included Japanese and foreigners, husbands and wives, a startling innovation because samurai women had not previously socialized with their husbands. Western-style dance by couples was de rigueur, even at parties far from Tokyo sponsored by prefectural governments. The late 1880s government became known as the "dancing cabinet."

Newspapers, journals, and other mass media exemplified and promoted civilization and enlightenment. Woodblock prints used chemical dyes to depict the marvels of westernization. Prints of horse-drawn carriages, steam locomotives, imposing new schools, and red brick buildings illuminated by gaslight in Tokyo's downtown Ginza district inspired progressive youths to seek modernity. (See Color Plate 27.) Magazines for women urged them to become educated in modern modes of thought to help them fulfill their roles as "good wives and wise mothers" (*ryōsai kenbo*). Fukuchi Gen'ichirō epitomized the professional journalist. He covered Saigō's rebellion in 1877 and later became chief editor of the influential *Tōkyō nichinichi shinbun* (Tokyo Daily Newspaper). It was a so-called big paper written in a style only the highly educated could read, with a focus on politics and serious editorials. Founded in 1874, the *Yomiuri Newspaper* aimed at the barely literate. Like other "small papers," it covered scandals and titillating stories of sex and murder. Hawked on street corners, it exploited the growing market for information and entertainment.

Modern newspapers serialized modern novels. In 1885 the aficionado of kabuki and student of English literature Tsubouchi Shōyō wrote *Essence of the Novel,* which tried to define a new realistic literature. Japan's first modern novel is deemed *Floating Clouds* (1887–1889) by Futabatei Shimei, because it tried to get inside the protagonist's head and used language close to the colloquial. Perhaps the most subtle and gifted writer was Higuchi Ichiyō, who garnered recognition in the male world of letters only at the end of her short life. Dominated at the end of the century by the medical doctor Mori Ōgai who had studied in Germany, and Natsume Sōseki who had studied in Britain, this world embraced modernity while questioning the superiority of western civilization.

CONSERVATIVE RESURGENCE

By the middle of the 1880s, many people thought that aping western customs had gone too far. They tried to retain traditional values while accepting the need for western rationalism in scientific inquiry and western technology. In 1882 Kanō Jigorō began the transformation of martial arts into judo and other forms through the scientific selection of techniques from earlier jujitsu schools. He emphasized that judo built character in a way that complemented developments in the study of ethics by religious figures and western-trained philosophers. By establishing an absolute standard for "the good," they sought to promote community suppression of socially disruptive thought. The head of the Hygiene Bureau, Gotō Shimpei, claimed that the

only way to get people to respond to public health initiatives was to work through established community structures and appeal to community values. Bureaucrats argued the need for the state to promote social welfare and a collectivist ethic through factory laws, tenancy laws, and agricultural cooperatives lest a social revolution undo their efforts to build a strong state. In 1890 the revised Police Security Regulations forbade women to participate in politics. The intent was to eliminate the need for selfish and unpatriotic competition and conflict.

The educational system bore the brunt of the conservative resurgence. In the 1870s, it imparted strictly utilitarian and materialistic knowledge; in the mid-1880s it focused more on Confucian ethics, Shinto mythology, and civic rituals. For the few who could afford to go beyond compulsory schooling, the Educational Code of 1872 had specified that a rigorous examination system would qualify students for middle schools, and the best would then take examinations for university. Founded in 1877, Tokyo University remained the only public institution at that level until 1897. Private universities such as Keiō and missionary schools provided lesser avenues for educational advancement. In 1886 the Ministry of Education established specialized higher schools above the middle schools. The First Higher School funneled students into Tokyo University for positions in the most prestigious ministries. Some higher schools offered degrees in liberal arts for students going to universities and then to careers in the bureaucracy or business world. Others consisted of vocational schools, military schools, teachers' colleges, and women's colleges. Each socialized the students by crafting character suitable to their station in life.

Education prepared citizens to serve the nation; it also provided the opportunity for personal advancement. The oligarchs opened the ranks of government service to men who had demonstrated talent and ability. The way they measured these qualifications was through academic achievement, but only men from families affluent enough to support them through years of schooling had any chance of success. Women were to serve the state as wives and mothers. Class and gender thus placed limits on equality, and the promise of social mobility concealed an economically stratified society.

Education trained citizens in the civic virtues personified by the emperor. In the 1870s and 1880s he toured Japan to unite the people under his gaze. Newspaper reports of his diligent work habits and concern for his subjects' welfare made him into a symbol of national unity and progress. He moved his headquarters to Hiroshima during the Sino-Japanese War (1894–1895), celebrated war victories, and appeared at imperial funerals, weddings, and wedding anniversaries. Hung in every school and public building, his portrait had to be treated with utmost respect. In 1890 he issued the Imperial Rescript on Education. It urged students to practice filial piety, harmony, sincerity, and benevolence; to respect the constitution; to obey the laws; and to be loyal to the *kokutai* (national polity).

The 1898 Civil Code adjusted the norms of western jurisprudence to the conservative concern for civic morality. Unless the primacy of the house and the patriarchal authority of the household head were maintained in law, the legal scholar Hozumi Yatsuka warned, reverence for the ancestors, loyalty, and filial piety would perish. The Civil Code affirmed legal equality, individual choice, and personal ownership of property for all men and single women, regardless of their former social status. Succession was to follow the male line, with all assets to go to the eldest son. A husband had authority to dispose of his wife's real property, though not her personal property (her trousseau); he decided when and whether to register a marriage and their children. Divorce by mutual consent freed both partners for remarriage in a continuation of Edo period practice. The Civil Code thus balanced a concern for social stability and modern, western norms with an understanding of customary mores.

IMPERIALISM AND MODERNITY

When Japan appropriated and adapted western industrial technology, juridical institutions, constitutional theory, and culture, it also imbibed western imperialism. Gaining colonies compensated for the humiliation suffered in accepting unequal treaties, put Japan on the side of the civilized world by exporting enlightenment to the backward peoples of Asia, and demonstrated Great Power status. A sense of national identity that could unite factory owners with factory workers demanded imperialist enterprises to divert attention from their differences. Social Darwinism taught that nations had to conquer or be conquered. Seeing what had happened to China and India, Fukuzawa Yukichi urged Japan to "escape from Asia" lest it too be conquered. (See **Documents: Fukuzawa Yukichi's "Escape from Asia."**)

The connection between modernity and colonization appeared early in the Meiji period. Japan's overtures to China in 1870 included an effort to extract an unequal treaty because having taken steps toward a modern centralized state made it the more civilized. A treaty negotiated in 1871 granted mutual extraterritoriality. In 1874, Japan used the murder of Ryukyuan fishermen by Taiwanese three years earlier as an excuse to send an expeditionary force to Taiwan. The ostensible purpose was to punish the Taiwanese; a covert aim was to bring civilization to the natives by establishing a colony. The war dragged on for five months before a settlement reached in Beijing acknowledged China's claims to Taiwan and Japan's claims to the Ryukyus. The expeditionary force withdrew, though not before Japanese newspapers had celebrated its victory over barbarism.

The Ryukyus and Hokkaido became internal colonies. In 1871 the Ryukyus were incorporated into Kagoshima prefecture. In 1879, the king was invited to reside in Tokyo and become a member of the new Japanese nobility while a Japanese governor took his place. Japanese fishermen and settlers had already spread north as far as Sakhalin and the Kuril Islands, territory that Russia claimed. In 1874 Japan evacuated Sakhalin and negotiated a treaty ceding it to Russia in exchange for Japanese control of the Kurils. It turned Hokkaido into a Japanese prefecture and established a modern definition of property ownership under which it sold off land the Ainu had customarily used for hunting and fishing to Japanese developers. Without material support, Ainu culture lost its meaning.

Japan's relations with Korea illustrate the relationship between modernity and imperialism. The oligarchs sent a diplomatic mission to "open" Korea in 1875–1876 that mimicked Perry's tactics in 1853–1854. The treaty forced on Korea replicated the unequal treaties Japan had been forced to sign in the 1850s. The following years saw successive incidents as factions at the Korean court abetted by Japan and China collided over the country's future course. In Japanese eyes, Korea was a weak, backward nation, easy prey for aggressive western powers. A German military adviser warned that were Korea to be controlled by any other power, it would become a dagger pointing at the heart of Japan. In 1890 Yamagata Aritomo linked parliamentary political participation with a militant international stance by telling the first Diet that for Japan to maintain its independence, it had to protect its territorial boundary, the line of sovereignty, and an outer perimeter of neighboring territory, a line of interest. Korea fell within Japan's line of interest.

The pressure brought by domestic public opinion to revise the unequal treaties affected Japan's diplomatic relations with its Asian neighbors. When negotiations for revision stalled in the face of western intransigence, clamor intensified for an aggressive stance toward China and Korea on the part of patriotic Popular Rights advocates as much as conservatives. In 1886 Britain and Germany proposed the partial abolition of extraterritoriality in exchange for allowing unrestricted travel by foreigners. The strength of domestic opposition to this compromise was so strong that the foreign minister had to resign. Finally, in 1894, western powers promised to abolish extraterritoriality and give Japan tariff autonomy in 1899.

Treaty negotiations took place in the context of the first Sino-Japanese War of 1894–1895. Fought over Korea, it lasted nine months. Japanese troops expelled the Chinese army from Korea, defeated the north Chinese navy, captured Port Arthur and the Liaodong peninsula in south Manchuria, and seized a port on the Shandong peninsula. The Treaty of Shimonoseki in April 1895 gave Japan Taiwan and the Pescadores, Port Arthur and the Liaodong peninsula, an indemnity, and a promise by China to respect Korea's autonomy. Japan's victory took western powers by surprise. In their eyes, it threatened peace and stability in East Asia. A week after the treaty was signed, Russia (with its own designs on Manchuria), France (Russia's ally), and Germany (hoping to steer Russian expansion toward what was now referred to as the Far East) collectively advised Japan to surrender its claim to territories in China. Despite popular outcry at the "Triple Intervention," the government had no choice but to obey. Russia then grabbed control of Port Arthur and the Liaodong peninsula.

SUMMARY

By the end of the nineteenth century, Japan had been transformed from a decentralized, largely agrarian regime into a centralized industrializing nation. Molded by schools and the military, informed by newspapers and journals, the peoples of Japan had become citizens. They had learned to ride on trains, wear western-style clothes, work in factories, and be self-reliant in striving for success. In dealing with the outside world, they had discovered that economic development and national defense required expansion abroad.

DOCUMENTS

Fukuzawa Yukichi's "Escape from Asia"

The most prominent intellectual and promoter of westernization of Meiji Japan, whose views on domestic policy were decidedly liberal, here Fukuzawa takes a hard-line approach to foreign affairs. His ruthless criticism of Korea and China, published on March 16, 1885, can be read as justifying colonialism, while at the same time he urges his readers to reject the civilization they had to offer. In 1895, ten years after writing this call to action, he rejoiced at Japan's victory over China.

Civilization is like an epidemic of measles. The current measles in Tokyo, which has advanced eastwards from Nagasaki in western Japan, seems to have begun to claim more victims with the arrival of springtime. Will we be able now to find a means of checking this epidemic? It is obvious that we have no way to do so. We cannot put up effective resistance, even against an epidemic that carries with it only harm; much less against civilization, which is always accompanied by both harm and good, but by more good than harm.

Though our land of Japan is situated on the Eastern edge of Asia, the spirit of its people has already shaken off the backwardness of Asia to accept the civilization of the West. Unfortunately, however, we have two neighboring countries, one being called China, the other called Korea. The people of these two countries are no different from us Japanese people in having been brought up since olden times in the Asian culture and customs, and yet, whether because they are of another racial origin, or because, while similar in culture and customs, differ from us in the main lines of their traditional education, a comparison of the three countries,

Japan, China, and Korea, reveals that the latter two resemble each other more closely than they do Japan. The people of those two countries do not know how to go about reforming and making progress, whether individually or as a country. It is not that they have not seen or heard of civilized things in the present world of facile communication; yet what their eyes and ears perceive have failed to stimulate their minds, and their emotional attachment to ancient manners and customs has changed little for the past hundreds and thousands of years. In this lively theater of civilization, where things change daily, they still speak of education in terms of Confucianism, cite humanity, justice, civility, and wisdom as their principles of school education, are completely obsessed only with outward appearance, are in reality not only ignorant of truths and principles but so extreme in their cruelty and shamelessness that for them morality is completely non-existent, and yet are as arrogant as if they never gave a thought to self-examination.

In our view, these countries have no likelihood of maintaining their independence in the current tide of civilization's eastward advance. Let there not be the slightest doubt that, unless they are fortunate enough to have motivated men appear in their lands who, as a first step to improve the condition of their countries will plan such a great enterprise of overall reform of their governments as our Restoration was, and succeed in altering their people's minds through political reforms, those countries will meet their doom in but a few years, with their territories divided among the civilized countries of the world. The reason is that China and Korea, confronted by an epidemic of civilization comparable to measles, are impossibly trying to ward it off, despite its inevitability, by shutting themselves up in a room, with the result being that they are cutting off their supply of fresh air and asphyxiating themselves. Though mutual help between neighboring countries has been likened to the relationship between the lips and the teeth, China and Korea of today cannot be of any assistance at all to our country of Japan.

Civilized western man is not without a tendency to regard all three countries as identical because of their geographic proximity and to apply his evaluation of China and Korea to Japan also. For example, when he finds that the governments of China and Korea are old-fashioned autocracies without abiding laws, the western man will suppose Japan too to be a lawless country. When he finds that the gentlemen of China and Korea are too deeply infatuated to know what science is, the western scholar will think that Japan too is a land of Yin-Yang and the Five Elements. When the Chinese display their servility and shamelessness, they obscure the chivalrous spirit of the Japanese. When the Koreans employ cruel means of physical punishment, the Japanese too are surmised to be just as inhuman. Such examples are too numerous to count. This may be compared to the case in which most of those in a string of houses within a village or town are foolish, lawless, cruel, and inhuman; an occasional family that heeds what is just and right will be eclipsed by the other's evil and its virtue will never be noticed. It is indeed not infrequent that something similar happens in our foreign relations and indirectly interferes with them. This should be regarded a great misfortune for our country of Japan.

To plan our course now, therefore, our country cannot afford to wait for the enlightenment of our neighbors and to cooperate in building Asia up. Rather, we should leave their ranks to join the camp of the civilized countries of the West. Even when dealing with China and Korea, we need not have special scruples simply because they are our neighbors, but should behave toward them as the westerners do. One who befriends an evil person cannot avoid being involved in his notoriety. In spirit, then, we break with our evil friends of Eastern Asia.

———
Source: Centre for East Asian Cultural Studies, comp., *Meiji Japan through Contemporary Sources, Vol. 3, 1869–1894* (Tokyo: Centre for East Asian Cultural Studies, 1972), pp. 129–133, modified.

SUGGESTED READING

The transformation of the Meiji state has attracted numerous scholars. Works include J. M. Ramseyer and F. M. Rosenbluth, *The Politics of Oligarchy: Institutional Change in Imperial Japan* (1995); C. Gluck, *Japan's Modern Myths: Ideology in the Late Meiji Period* (1985); and T. Fujitani, *Splendid Monarchy: Power and Pageantry in Modern Japan* (1996).

For contrasting perspectives on foreign affairs, see W. G. Beasley, *Japanese Imperialism, 1894–1945* (1991), and S. Tanaka, *Japan's Orient: Rendering Pasts as History* (1998).

For economic development, see S. J. Ericson, *The Sound of the Whistle: Railroads and the State in Meiji Japan* (1996), and E. D. Westney, *Imitation and Innovation: The Transfer of Western Organizational Patterns to Meiji Japan* (1987).

Two excellent books on education are D. T. Roden, *School Days in Imperial Japan: A Study in Adolescence and Student Culture* (1975), and B. Platt, *Burning and Building: Schooling and State Formation in Japan, 1750–1890* (2004).

For social history, see M. Hane, *Peasants, Rebels, Women and Outcastes: The Underside of Modern Japan* (2003), and H. Fuess, *Divorce in Japan: Family, Gender, and the State, 1600–2000* (2004). For the media, see J. L. Huffman, *Creating a Public: People and Press in Meiji Japan* (1997). For "Civilization and Enlightenment," see D. Irokawa, *The Culture of the Meiji Period* (1985). For disease, see W. Johnston, *The Modern Epidemic: A History of Tuberculosis in Japan* (1995). For religious change, see J. E. Ketelaar, *Of Heretics and Martyrs in Meiji Japan: Buddhism and Its Persecution* (1990), and H. Hardacre, *Shinto and the State, 1868–1988* (1989).

For views from the periphery, see N. L. Waters, *Japan's Local Pragmatists: The Transition from Bakumatsu to Meiji in the Kawasaki Region* (1983), and M. W. Steele, *Alternative Narratives in Modern Japanese History* (2003).

CHAPTER TWENTY-TWO

The Final Years of Chosŏn Korea (1800–1895)

The nineteenth-century decline of Chosŏn Dynasty fortune was marked by three rebellions caused primarily by the failure of government to solve long-standing institutional problems, intermittent persecution of Catholics, domination of the throne and government by consort relatives of mostly minor kings, and the threat to national survival by foreign imperialism. Korea was also faced with demands from foreign powers to open its doors to trade. Despite stubborn resistance, it was forced out of seclusion by Japan in 1876, but attempts to modernize the country were obstructed by conservative Confucian antiforeignism at home. That conflict reached a crisis in 1884, and the conservatives won the day. While reformers retreated abroad, the Chinese asserted themselves in unprecedented ways to block any reforms that would weaken their control over Korea, but domestic rebellion and a strengthened Japan brought Chinese interference to an end in the Sino-Japanese War of 1894–1895 and seemed to open a path for serious reform.

Scholars have concerned themselves with the following questions: What were the reasons behind the rebellions and the resulting obstructions to active response to rebellion and foreign aggression? What influenced the Taewongun's policies, including the anti-Catholic persecution? How should the nature of Chinese and Japanese interference in Korean affairs after 1882 be categorized? What capacity existed for reform and independent action from 1876 to 1895? And finally, what were the causes of the Sino-Japanese War?

THE NATURE OF CONSORT RULE

After the death of King Chŏngjo in 1800, his second queen, the dowager regent, Queen Chŏng-sun of the Kyŏngju Kim family, rose to power. She ruled over the minor king, Sunjo (about eleven years old), until 1804 and died the following year. During that four-year period, the queen elevated the king's father-in-law, Kim Chosun of the Andong Kim clan, to a position of power and influence and chose his daughter for Sunjo's queen. This marked the beginning of consort clan domination of the royal house, which lasted to the end of the century. One important cause of this was that a number of nineteenth-century kings came to the throne as minors under regencies established by the eldest living dowager queen or were selected by such dowager regents when there was no crown prince. The dowager regent remained as such until she resigned voluntarily or the king decided that it was time for him to rule on his own.

The male relatives of the dowager regents and queens benefited the most from this situation because they were appointed to high office. Regencies were established for all four kings of the nineteenth century; everything depended on who the eldest living dowager happened to be. The dominant Andong Kim were challenged by the P'ungyang Cho relatives of King Hŏnjong's queen in 1834. The Andong Kim dowager regent was forced by the P'ungyang Cho to relinquish her regency in 1840, two years after the leader of the Andong Kim died. After King Hŏnjong died in 1849 without a male heir, the Andong Kim dowager queen selected the twenty-year-old King Ch'ŏlchong, declared a regency from 1849 to 1852, chose another Andong Kim for his queen, and replaced many of the top officials with members of the Andong Kim. When King Ch'ŏlchong died without an heir in 1863, however, Queen Sinjŏng of the P'ungyang Cho clan was now the eldest living queen. She selected the twelve-year-old second son of King Ch'ŏlchong's second cousin, Yi Haŭng, as the new king, King Kojong.

The P'ungyang Cho and Yi Haŭng shared something in common: both had been demeaned by the dominant Andong Kim family and hungered for a chance at power. Yi Haŭng was then given the title of Taewongun, or grand prince, a title reserved only for a father of a king who had never been king. He was only the second in the dynasty with that title. The dowager became regent and held the position for only two years, to 1866, but the young King Kojong was oblivious to his right to assert his rule. Instead, the Taewongun continued as de facto regent from 1863 to 1874 even though he had no formal title or position. He then carried out a major reform program.

NEW SOCIAL POLICIES

In 1801, one year after King Sunjo came to the throne, Dowager Regent Chŏngsun manumitted most of the sixty-seven thousand official slaves, while retaining those slaves working in select offices. This constituted an important liberalization of the slave system, but hereditary slavery for several million private slaves remained until 1886, and slavery itself lasted until 1894. The power of the mostly *yangban* slave masters was not broken until the dynasty itself was near its end.

This act of liberalization, however, was followed by a bloody reaction to Catholics and other minority factions. In 1801 Dowager Regent Chŏngsun, supported by the Patriarch and *pyŏkp'a* factions, ordered the institution of a five-family mutual surveillance system (*oga chakt'ong*) to ferret out Christians in the southerner faction. Tasan and his brother, Chŏng Yakchŏn, were among those exiled. The next month, the dowager exiled the Chinese missionary Zhou Wenmo, King Chŏngjo's half-brother, the Ŭnŏn'-gun (Lord Ŭnŏn), his wife, and daughter-in-law.

The situation for Christians took a drastic turn for the worse when officials intercepted a silk letter from the Christian Hong Sayong to the papal court in Rome requesting a military expedition from France to protect Korean Christians from persecution. Outraged by this act of treason, the dowager purged over three hundred Christians that year alone and persecuted members of the southerner and *sip'a* factions. Those factions were kept out of office for another half-century.

The Christian issue would emerge once again in 1839 when the government arrested ten Christian missionaries. Among them was the prominent Korean Christian Kim Taegŏn, who had been proselytizing the faith in secret since the missionaries' arrival in Korea at the beginning of the decade.

FOREIGN INCURSIONS AND REBELLION

In 1842, Korea received news of the defeat of Qing forces by the British in the Opium War (1839–1842) and the imposition of an unequal treaty on China that allowed Britain trading privileges, extraterritoriality, consular jurisdiction, and limitation on import taxes to remove domestic obstacles to imported British goods (see Chapter 19). Two years later, Wei Yuan wrote a book, *An Illustrated Essay of the Maritime Nations* (*Haiguo tuzhi*), which was brought back to Korea in 1845 by a member of a Korean diplomatic mission. The *Haiguo tuzhi* included recommendations for manufacturing advanced western weapons and equipment or hiring foreign technicians to build a better defense, along with descriptions of the western nations. Despite having many admirers, the recommendations made in the book were not followed.

Admiral Perry arrived on the Japanese coast in 1853 with a flotilla of U.S. ships and forced an unequal treaty on Japan the next year. War between China and the British and French occurred after 1856, resulting in the foreign occupation of Beijing and the flight of the emperor to Jehol in 1860. When the British and French imposed another unequal treaty on China, China gave Russia a lease on the Liaodong peninsula and territory east of Manchuria contiguous to Korea for a few miles. News of these events created a crisis atmosphere in Korea.

A major rebellion led by a professional geomancer, Hong Kyŏngnae, broke out in P'yŏng'an province in the northwest in 1812. Part of the cause was the breakdown of the taxation and service systems, but general discontent in that province with the central administration and resentment against blocking promotion to high office among its examination passers were also important factors.

Inside Korea, the failure of the government to solve the problems of maladministration in the land tax, military cloth tax, and grain relief and loan system provided the main cause for a series of rebellions in 1862 throughout the country, but primarily in the three southern provinces. As mentioned before (Chapter 18), taxes due from these three institutions had been combined into a single land tax (*togyŏl*), but corruption by clerks and magistrates more than offset the reductions gained from distributing the taxes equally among all residents.

This rebellion was more massive and widespread than the rebellion of 1812, but it lacked central organization. Despite a few attacks against *yangban* landlords, it was aimed mainly at corrupt clerks and magistrates, not at the overthrow of the dynasty or the overthrow of either the *yangban* or the landlords as a class. The largest uprising occurred in Chinju on the southern coast, and the influence of it spread elsewhere. Although *yangban* participated in the planning of some protests, they usually withdrew when the protests became violent. Commoners provided most of the leadership in the dozens of spontaneous uprisings, but rebellious enthusiasm declined shortly after the release of pent-up animosity in acts of violence against local clerks and magistrates. The government under King Ch'ŏlchong attempted to respond by considering serious reforms, but he died before any action could be taken.

Partly as a result of rebellion, population growth was checked in the nineteenth century. An increase in flood, drought, and disease further reduced the overall population to 12.4 million by 1816. Thereafter, population fluctuated between 12.2 and 12.7 million to 1876, a major contrast with the significant population increase that was taking place in China in the Qing Dynasty.

CH'OE CHEU AND THE TONGHAK RELIGION

Around 1860 Ch'oe Cheu, a member of a déclassé *yangban* family, established a new religion in Korea. Discontented with his own life and the sorry situation of his country, Ch'oe Cheu experienced a vision in which he believed Hanŭnim (the Lord of Heaven) spoke to him and entrusted him with the task of spreading a new faith to the Korean people. He called the faith Tonghak (Eastern Learning, or "Korean National Teaching"). It combined Confucian ethics with Buddhist faith, Taoist naturalism and longevity, geomancy, and the use of talismans, imprecations, and shamanistic appeals to spirits in an amalgam that was supposed to represent Korean thought as a counterpoise to the Western Learning (*Sŏhak*) (see **Biography: Ch'oe Cheu, Founder of the Tonghak Religion,** and **Documents: Tonghak Beliefs**).

Korean Confucians regarded Ch'oe Cheu's teachings as a threat to both the stability of the dynasty and the purity of Confucian belief. Authorities decapitated him even though he was not a participant in that rebellion. The movement went underground and did not remerge (except for one minor rising in 1879) until 1893, but it was a sign that popular discontent with affairs was calling into question the power of Confucian orthodoxy to solve the problems Korea was facing at the time.

THE TAEWONGUN'S DE FACTO REGENCY (1864–1874)

At the beginning of the reign of the Taewongun's second son, King Kojong (r. 1864–1907), the dowager queen of the P'ungyang Cho clan was formal regent from 1863 to 1866. When she retired, a formal declaration was issued in King Kojong's name that he had assumed "personal rule" over the state, but the fourteen-year-old

Taewongun. The Taewongun (Yi Haŭng), father of King Kojong and de facto regent (1864–1873) and rival of the Yŏhŭng Min faction and Queen Myŏngsŏng (the Min family queen). *(B. Cummings, Korea's Place in the Sun, Norton, 1997, p. 74)*

king was kept unaware that he was now in charge. His father, the Taewongun, simply continued his control behind the scenes from 1864 to 1874.

There were several aspects to the Taewongun's policies: an active reform program to address the causes of the 1862 rebellions; palace construction to elevate the prestige and power of the king; abolition of the majority of private academies in the provinces (they had become centers of *yangban* factional interest); persecution of Korean Catholics for suspected treasonous collaboration with foreigners; minting of

BIOGRAPHY   Ch'oe Cheu, Founder of the Tonghak Religion

Ch'oe Cheu (1824–1864) was born to a remarried widow of a *yangban* family; by the age of fifteen, he had lost both parents. He received a Confucian education but was barred from the civil service examinations because his mother had remarried. He became interested in religion through his study of Buddhism, Taoism, and Christianity. Restless in his home village, he took to the road as a peddler but squandered his patrimony, was abandoned by his wife and children, and suffered depression.

He built a thatched hut in the mountains where he meditated, and in 1855 he began to believe that he had superhuman powers to heal the sick. He returned to his home town of Kumi, near Taegu, and changed his given name to Cheu (saving the ignorant). In 1860, Cheu had a revelatory experience in which God (Ch'ŏnju, the Lord of Heaven) spoke to him and entrusted him with the task of saving mankind on earth. He also created a potion for curing illness.

By 1861 he began to preach and developed incantations for his congregation. He left Kumi and moved to Namwŏn in South Chŏlla province to preach, but moved east to Kyŏngju in Kyŏngsang province in 1862, where he created an organization and converted hundreds. His religion became known as Tonghak (Eastern Learning) or Ch'ŏndo (Heavenly Way). It was a syncretic attempt to fuse the religious traditions of Korea as a counterpoise to western learning or Christianity. Cheu's followers were mostly commoners and slaves because the *yangban* regarded his departure from Confucian orthodoxy as unacceptable. Although he was not involved in the many local rebellions that began in the south in 1862, he was arrested by the authorities in 1863 for fomenting rebellion by his heterodox teachings and was executed in March 1864.

the first multiple-denomination coin in Korean history, the 100-cash (*tangbaekchŏn*), to pay for expenses; and total resistance to western and foreign demands for treaties and trade. The reform program resulted in a partial land survey to register land hidden from the tax collectors, the imposition of the military cloth tax on *yangban* households for the first time in three centuries (but in the name of their slaves to save them embarrassment), and the cancellation of past unrecoverable loans in the official grain loan system administered by district magistrates. Indebted peasants no longer had to pay permanent interest on loans they were unable to pay, and the Taewongun shifted the administration of grain loans from corrupt district magistrates and their clerks to local elders.

These reforms were perhaps less radical than they seemed because the land survey was not completed for the whole country, and village *yangban* had already been included among villagers to pay the combined *togyŏl* tax. Nonetheless, imposition of the military cloth tax was particularly galling to *yangban* because it was a direct affront to their status. The abolition of all but forty-seven private academies dedicated to Confucian worthies of the dominant factions was an insult to both hereditary factions and past titans of Confucian scholarship. And government spending and the inflation that resulted from the 100-cash was a violation of conservative Confucian attitudes toward profligacy.

Reaction to the Reforms

The Taewongun's opponents were led by conservative Confucians Yi Hangno and his disciple, Ch'oe Ikhyŏn. Yi opposed institutional tinkering

DOCUMENTS

Tonghak Beliefs

The following sources shed light on some of the fundamental ideas of the Tonghak religion and movement. Ch'oe Cheu illustrates differences between Tonghak and Christianity; the instructions for women of the second patriarch, Ch'oe Sihyŏng, combine Confucian precepts with acceptance of slavery modified with compassion. Kim Ku, a Tonghak and later ardent nationalist, shows how the egalitarian bent of Tonghak attracted him to the religion.

CH'OE CHEU ON THE DIFFERENCE BETWEEN TONGHAK (EASTERN LEARNING) AND SŎHAK (WESTERN LEARNING OR CHRISTIANITY)

Many scholars and gentlemen . . . asked me, "Is it any different from the western way, from Christianity?" I replied, "The [w]estern religion is similar to our religion but also different. They worship a God who is not real. The forms of the truth may be similar, but their doctrines are really different. . . . Our way emphasizes accomplishing things through natural action. . . . But the [w]esterners have no order in their words and no pure concern for God. They pray really for their flesh, and they have no effective God. . . . I was born in the East and received the truth in the East. Therefore, the way is the Heavenly Way and the doctrine is the Eastern Learning (Tonghak).

CH'OE SIHYŎNG (PEN NAME, HAEWŎL) ON TONGHAK PRECEPTS FOR WOMEN (1888), SUGGESTING LIMITATIONS ON TONGHAK SOCIAL EQUALITY

Be a filial daughter to your parents; cherish and respect the head of the house, love your brothers and sisters, cherish your son and daughter-in-law, be cordial to your neigh-bors. Treat your slaves as though they were your offspring, and do not mistreat domestic animals. If you violate these teachings, God will be angry.

KIM KU'S INTRODUCTION TO A TONGHAK MASTER AT THE AGE OF SEVENTEEN (ABOUT 1892)

As I bowed politely to him [O Ŭngsŏn], he bowed in return. Taken aback [by an adult's bow to a mere teenager], I told him my name and clan and protested, "Even if I were a mature man, you as a noble should not bow to me, but since I am only a child of the commoner class, you are treating me [with too much respect]." The noble appeared moved and said, "According to the Master's counsel, there is no distinction between rich and poor, noble and lowborn, and everyone should be treated equally, so there is no need to apologize."

Sources: For Ch'oe Cheu: *Ch'ŏndogyo kyŏngjŏn*, pp. 1–5, trans. Yong Choon Kim in Peter Lee, ed., *Sourcebook of Korean Civilization*, vol. 2 (New York: Columbia University Press, 2000), pp. 316–317. For Ch'oe Sihyŏng: Pak Inho, *Ch'ŏndogyo sŏ* (1921), pp. 86ff., trans. Susan S. Shin, "The Tonghak Movement," *Korean Studies Forum* 6 (1980): 34. For Kim Ku: Kim Ku, *Paekpŏm ilchi* (Seoul: 1947), p. 26, trans. S. Shin, "The Tonghak Movement," p. 33.

and believed that frugality, the reduction of taxes, and the cultivation of Confucian virtue were all that was needed for good government. After Yi died in 1868, Ch'oe Ikhyŏn in 1873 took the lead in impeaching the Taewongun for destroying moral standards throughout the nation.

For their part, almost all Confucian scholars, including Yi and Ch'oe, supported his foreign policy. Their antiforeign slogan was, "Defend

Confucian correctness against foreign perversity" (*wijŏng ch'ŏksa*). The Taewongun rejected all requests from foreigners for treaties because he was determined to avoid imposition of the unequal treaty system imposed on China and Japan by the foreign powers.

In 1866, when some Korean Catholics offered to mediate with the Russians in their demands for trade, the Taewongun suspected collusion to undermine Korean security and ordered a nationwide persecution of Korean Catholics that lasted all the way to 1871 and reduced their ranks from twenty thousand to eight thousand believers. The French landed troops on Kanghwa Island to chastise the Koreans for their refusal to tolerate Christianity, but Korean troops were able to force the small French force to abandon the island.

Military Pressure from the West

In 1866, a ship of U.S. registration, the *General Sherman,* with an English captain and a crew of Malays and Chinese, had run aground in the Taedong River near Pyongyang and demanded trade. The irate local residents attacked the ship, burned it to ashes, and killed all its crew. Pak Kyusu, the governor of P'yŏng'an Province during the *General Sherman* incident, submitted a plan for strengthening coastal defenses by building new forts along the coast, particularly one at the mouth of the Taedong River, recruiting more soldiers skilled in the use of firearms, and instituting a special examination for them. The Taewongun approved this.

About this time, Pak's disciple, Kim Yunsik, submitted a memorial based on Wei Yuan's *Haiguo tuzhi.* Since Wei had written that the secret of western strength was their domination of the seas by a small number of skilled troops with superior cannon, not superior numbers, Kim recommended that Korea concentrate on building advanced cannon and sea mines and distribute them to coastal garrisons. The Taewongun ordered the construction of three new warships and a cannon for laying mines. He even ordered construction of the first steamboat in 1867, although it failed its trial on the water and had to be broken up for scrap metal.

In 1868, the German adventurer Ernst Oppert landed on Korean soil and tried to disinter the bones of the Taewongun's father to hold them as ransom before Korean troops forced his withdrawal. Finally, in 1871, the United States landed marines on Kanghwa Island to teach the Koreans a lesson for their obduracy and to force a treaty of trade and amity (!). They did this by killing dozens of Korean defenders in the process. There is no evidence in either of these two incidents, however, that the new warships, cannon, and mine-laying cannon played any role at all in the fighting. Despite Korean losses from these attacks, the Taewongun declared victories for Korean arms and issued a manifesto that anyone who advocated peace with the foreigner was a traitor to the state.

One of the reasons for the use of violence by the French and Americans was the frustration caused by the ambiguity over who was responsible for the conduct of Korean foreign relations under the tributary system. The foreigners wanted to know whether Korea was a sovereign nation and if its king had the power and right to sign treaties. If not, they would negotiate with China as the suzerain power. Not only did the Taewongun refuse to negotiate with them, but the Qing government also avoided responsibility because it knew that if the Koreans violated any codicil in a treaty with a foreign power, that power would demand reparations from China.

Pressure on Korea from abroad was increased in 1868, when the Japanese overturned their previous system of military rule under the Tokugawa shogunate, restored the Meiji emperor from obscurity to the formal head of a centralized state, and created an oligarchy headed by a few samurai from four domains to change customs and modernize the country. When they sent a note in the Japanese emperor's name to the king of Korea asking for a treaty of trade and amity, the Taewongun refused even to accept the note on the grounds that there was only one legitimate emperor in the world, the emperor of the Qing Dynasty in China. Prior to that, the Korean king had maintained equal relations with a fictitious Japanese "king," a pretense the Japanese were willing to maintain since the emperor had declined to near obscurity. Japanese resentment over what radical samurai perceived to constitute an insult to the restored Japanese emperor almost resulted in a Japanese invasion of Korea in 1873 under Saigō Takamori, the acting prime minister. When Prime Minister Iwakura Tomomi returned from an investigation trip to Europe, he canceled Saigō's invasion plan and decided that Japan could not afford a debilitating and costly war just when it was embarking on a forced march to self-strengthening and industrialization.

KING KOJONG AND THE KANGHWA TREATY OF 1876

In 1874, King Kojong decided that he was old enough to rule on his own, leaving the Tae-wongun no choice but to give up power. King Kojong then adopted the advice of officials who advocated accepting communications from the Japanese emperor on the grounds that existence of the Japanese emperor was a domestic Japanese problem that had no effect on Korea, and that eliminating animosity and restoring friendship with Japan would result merely in a continuation of trade relations and friendship that had prevailed from 1609 to 1868. He adopted the advice but avoided signing a treaty until the Japanese found out about his new attitude toward Japan. The Japanese government created an excuse for hostile action by sending a survey ship off the Korean coast in 1875 in the expectation that Korean shore batteries would fire on it. When the Koreans obliged by doing so, the Japanese landed a battalion of troops on Kanghwa Island and threatened military action unless King Kojong signed the Kanghwa Treaty with Japan in 1876.

With encouragement from Qing authorities to avoid a confrontation with Japan, King Kojong signed the Kanghwa Treaty, which had most of the provisions of the unequal treaty system. He agreed to open up three ports to trade with Japan—two more to be selected in the future in addition to Tongnae near Pusan—and limited Japanese traders under the treaty to a small radius around the three ports. Under the long

tradition of extraterritoriality, the Japanese in the treaty ports were allowed to run their own affairs inside the radius. King Kojong assumed that the situation would return to normal and that the Japanese would be content to trade without invading Korean space elsewhere or making further demands. In fact, he had opened the door not only to trade but to foreign interference and a world of trouble.

FOREIGN INTERFERENCE AND QING CONTROL

The Taewongun had erred in making provision for King Kojong's queen when he chose the niece of his wife from the Yŏhŭng Min clan to become Queen Min (literally, the Min family queen; her formal title was Queen Hyoja). She began to influence her husband, and her male relatives, who began to move into office after the Taewongun was forced into retirement in 1874, remained in power to 1894.

King Kojong had resisted many of the Kanghwa Treaty's provisions at first, including the opening of two new ports and the demands for a Japanese legation in Seoul. However, a recommendation entitled "Strategy for Korea" sent to him in 1880 by Huang Zunxian, the Chinese minister to Tokyo, persuaded him to reconsider his position. Huang argued that Korea should negotiate treaties with all the western powers as a means of self-protection.

Huang Zunxian's recommendation was in line with the policy for Korea of Li Hongzhang, the governor of Zhili province and commissioner for the Five Northern Ports in China and the chief of Qing Dynasty relations with Chosŏn. Li sought to maintain China's suzerainty over Korea by capitalizing on the rivalries among the imperialist powers to check any attempt by Russia and Japan to strip China of its tributary control of Korea. He realized that China was militarily too weak to maintain its control over Korea by military force, but the policy depended on the willingness of foreign powers with little interest in trade with Korea to intervene militarily to check their imperialist rivals. The policy allowed China to maintain control until the Sino-Japanese War of 1894 but only by changing the very nature of the tributary system itself.

By 1881 Korea had agreed to open two additional ports to Japan at Inch'ŏn and Wŏnsan and allow the first Japanese minister to Korea to set up a legation in Seoul. That same year, King Kojong set up a new agency, the T'ongnigimu amun, to handle diplomacy and trade with foreign states, and he welcomed the first Japanese ambassador. He also hired a Japanese officer to train a small unit of troops in the capital in western military tactics and weapons. He dispatched an investigation mission to Japan that year (the *sinsa yuramdan*) to report on developments there, but he did so secretly to avoid conservative opposition. Some of the people on the trip were inspired by Japan's foremost westernizer, Fukuzawa Yukichi, but when they returned to Korea, they found a very inhospitable situation for the kind of reform that Japan had already begun. A conservative protest movement against Huang Zunxian's advice reached its culmination in the fall of 1881, when a plot to overthrow the king and abolish the T'ongnigimu amun was uncovered and the plotters arrested and executed.

King Kojong continued with his reform policy but decided to consult with China on how to make modern weapons and conduct negotiations with the United States and other western powers. In 1881, Li Hongzhang undertook negotiations with Commodore Robert W. Shufeldt of the U.S. Navy to conclude a treaty of amity and trade between the United States and Korea. A draft of the treaty was sent to Korea and signed by King Kojong and Shufeldt in May 1882, a sure sign that the Korean king had by no means ended his inferior status to Chinese suzerainty.

The treaty contained several elements of the unequal treaty system like extraterritoriality and the most-favored-nation clause, which guaranteed the United States any advantages concluded by other foreign powers in future treaties with Korea. During the negotiations Li Hongzhang had tried to insert a clause in the treaty indi-

cating that Korea was a tributary of China. Shufeldt refused to accept it because the United States would never agree to sign a treaty with a dependency, but he finally agreed to compromise by allowing King Kojong to send a letter to President Chester A. Arthur declaring that Korea was both "self-governing" and a Chinese tributary at the same time, a description that fit tributary relations since the Qing regime never interfered with either Korea's domestic problems or its relations with Japan. The U.S. side ignored the contradiction and acted as if Korea was a sovereign state, but the ambiguity was not really resolved because both Korea and China still regarded the tributary relationship as undamaged.

Soon after the signing of treaties with the United States, England, and Germany in 1882, an uprising occurred, led by members of the old capital guard units who were incensed at the favorable treatment afforded the new Japanese-trained unit in the capital and the delay in the payment of their own salaries. Possibly goaded on by the Taewongun, who opposed the treaties with Japan and the United States and hated Queen Min and her relatives in the Yŏhŭng Min clan, the rebel soldiers attacked the Japanese legation and drove the ambassador and his party from Seoul and from Korea. At the same time, they invaded the palace to murder the Yŏhŭng Min officials and the queen as well, but she was able to make her escape. The rebels forced King Kojong to recall his father, the Taewongun, to the capital and appoint him chief of administration.

In China, Kim Yunsik and Ŏ Yunjung warned the Chinese that the Taewongun's hostility to Japan might bring on a Japanese invasion of Korea. The Qing emperor dispatched a few thousand troops on ships, where they landed and pitched camp. They invited the Taewongun to what was supposed to be an amicable meeting, but they hustled him off to one of their ships, transported him to China, and kept him under close surveillance for three years. After the Taewongun's departure, Chinese troops attacked the rebel troops and wiped them out unmercifully.

Although the tributary system with China had involved no written treaties and specifications, the kidnapping of the de facto head of state and father of the king marked a major departure from the long tradition of noninterference in Korean affairs and transformed China's relations with Korea to behavior quite similar to the western imperialists. China negotiated a commercial treaty with Korea for the first time that provided to Chinese merchants trading in Korea privileges denied to other states and instructed King Kojong to pay reparations to Japan to prevent any hostilities. The Chinese restored the king, queen, and her Yŏhŭng Min clan relatives to power and allowed them to repress the Taewongun's supporters.

Late in 1882 King Kojong put out a request to the nation for everyone to submit memorials recommending policy in the current situation. One hundred private memorials were received, of which one-fifth advocated reform, and many of those cited the *Iyan* (*Simple Talk*) by Zheng Guanying. Zheng, a Chinese comprador merchant for a western company, wrote the book in 1862 to alert China to the need to manufacture western-style weapons by hiring western experts. Many Korean reformers traveled to China to meet Zheng, and his book exerted a greater influence in Korea than in China. His main theme was the need to adopt western technology while still maintaining Chinese fundamental Confucian values (*sŏgi tongdo*). Kojong republished the book in *han'gŭl* in 1883 and urged everyone to read it, but this formula was to prove as inadequate for meaningful reform in Korea as it did in China because western culture included more than machines and tools.

The 1884 Coup

King Kojong instituted a number of reforms in 1883 by establishing a modern post office and the Ministry of Culture and allowing publication of the first newspaper, the *Hansŏng sunbo* (Seoul Weekly), supervised by Inoue Kakugorō, a disciple of Fukuzawa Yukichi. Nevertheless,

Koreans who had visited Japan and were eager for more radical reforms began to feel that they were under a serious threat to their lives because of conservative opposition. In 1884, Kim Okkyun with Pak Yŏnghyo, Sŏ Chaep'il, Sŏ Kwangbŏm (Philip Jaisohn), and Yun Ch'iho organized a coup to seize power and carry out the kind of reforms that Japan had undertaken. Most were disciples of Pak Kyusu, who had died in 1877, and Pak's friend, the *chung'in* interpreter Yu Taech'i, had taken over as the intellectual leader of the young reformers.

Because the conspirators had no support inside Korea, Kim Okkyun turned instead to Takezoe Shinichirō, the head of the Japanese legation, to use the Japanese legation guards as the main military force to carry out a coup in 1884 known as the *kapsin* coup. The coup leaders seized the palace, held King Kojong captive as their symbol of legitimacy, and summoned a half-dozen high officials to court, where they decapitated them on the spot. Before they had time to issue any orders, however, Chinese legation guards with some regular Korean troops led by Yuan Shikai (later the first president of the Chinese Republic in 1912) attacked the palace, killed a half-dozen leaders, and drove the rest of the plotters, along with the Japanese ambassador and his entourage, out of the country. Once again, Chinese intervention restored the political situation to the status quo ante and scotched the chance for a significant reversal of policy. Of course, the actions of Kim Okkyun's party had aroused the ire of many conservative Koreans because they had used the hated Japanese as the chief agent of their politics.

China, then bogged down in a dispute with France over Indochina, was powerless to resist Japan. It forced Korea to pay Japan reparations for the murder of Japanese victims and property damage even though the damage was the result of a coup in which the Japanese ambassador, Takezoe, and his troops were part of the plot. Because Takezoe had authorized the use of Japanese troops to aid the plotters without prior authorization from Tokyo, he was tried in the

Kim Okkyun (1851–1894). The leader of the failed reformist coup d'état of 1884. *(Sajinuro ponun tongni undong: Oech 'im kwa t'ujaeng, sang, p. 26)*

Japanese courts but let off for lack of evidence. No further action was taken against him.

The Tianjin Treaty

To settle any potential conflict between Japan and China, the Japanese prime minister, Itō Hirobumi, negotiated the Tianjin Treaty with Li Hongzhang in 1885 by which both sides withdrew their troops and agreed that neither side would supply officers to train Korean soldiers. Furthermore, if either Japan or China should feel it necessary to send troops, it would inform the other side in advance, so that presumably the other side could dispatch an equal number of troops to maintain the military balance between them. Unfortunately, this apparently peaceful settlement had the potential for escalating any conflict that might occur in the future, but the worst did not come to pass until a decade later.

That same year, Li Hongzhang appointed Yuan Shikai resident commissioner for Korea, the first such case of a Chinese foreign overseer on Korean territory since the departure of the Mongols in the mid-fourteenth century. For the next decade, Yuan sat at the side of King Kojong and prevented him from doing anything that might interfere with China's control over Korea and lead to true national independence. Li had also dispatched P. G. von Moellendorff, a German official in the employ of the Chinese Maritime Customs administration in China, to Korea to oversee the Korean customs agency. Von Moellendorff, however, sympathized with the Koreans against Chinese domination, and in 1884 he induced Min Yŏng'ik of the Min clan to negotiate secretly with the Russians for aid and troop instructors. When Li Hongzhang discovered Von Moellendorff's activities, he recalled him.

Yuan Shikai also succeeded in scotching King Kojong's attempt to dispatch an ambassador to the United States and other foreign countries to conduct diplomacy as an independent state. When the British navy temporarily seized Kŏmun Island (Port Hamilton) off the southern coast of Korea in 1885 as a feint to block the Russians from any attempt to obtain a leasehold at Wŏnsan and expand their influence into Korea, the Chinese took no action to force the British to retreat. Russia, which both China and Japan had perceived as a threat to their interests, also decided to accept the continuation of China's traditional relationship with Korea. By mid-1885, the Chinese decided to send the Taewongun back to Korea because King Kojong, Queen Min, and her relatives were defying Qing interests, but the king kept his father under close surveillance.

When a provincial Korean official blocked the export of rice and beans to Japan in 1888 to preserve food stocks during famine conditions after they had been purchased by Japanese merchants, Yuan delayed negotiations but finally pushed Korea to pay. He obstructed Japanese efforts to build a telegraph line from Pusan to Seoul and to reform Korean coinage with Japanese assistance despite the agreement of the Korean court to do so. He also blocked Korean attempts to obtain foreign loans and foreign military advisers. All of Yuan's actions merely demonstrated that Chinese direct intervention in Korea's foreign and domestic affairs had become part of the new relationship. Japan, by contrast, acquiesced in China's domination as long as Korea observed all its treaty obligations to Japan.

WESTERN INFLUENCES

The 1880s brought western influences in education and medicine from Protestant missionaries from the United States. In the 1890s Japanese and other businessmen stimulated interest in trade, modern transportation projects, and the exploitation of natural resources as well. The first streetcar arrived in 1898, demonstrating to the populace its advantage over the hand-carried palanquins for female *yangban*, donkeys and horses for male *yangban*, and ox-drawn carts for commoners. The laying of tracks for streetcars and trains preceded cobblestones or paved streets, overcoming one of the most important obstacles to rapid transportation of goods and people, the unpaved streets and roads that turned to impassable mud in the rainy season (see **Material Culture: Streetcars**).

Protestant Christianity

The first Protestant missionaries arrived in Korea from the United States in 1884. Most were Presbyterians and Methodists who strove to attract reluctant Koreans to the faith by the demonstration of good works, such as the construction of hospitals and schools. The Presbyterian Horace Allen, a twenty-six-year-old

doctor, gained immediate acceptance by King Kojong and Queen Min by saving the life of Min Yŏng'ik during the *kapsin* coup of December 4, 1884. Kojong made him physician to the royal court and allowed him to establish the first western hospital, the Kwanghyewŏn, the next year. Allen later gave up his status as missionary, became a secretary to the Korean legation in Washington, D.C., U.S. minister to Korea and consul-general in 1890, and ambassador plenipotentiary from 1901 to 1905.

Allen was followed in 1885 by the Methodists Horace G. Underwood, Henry G. Appenzeller, and Dr. William B. Scranton and his wife, Mary Fitch Scranton. Scranton founded the first Methodist Hospital, Underwood the *Paejae haktang* (School for Training Men of Talent), and Mary Scranton the first school for women, which Queen Min dubbed the *Ehwa haktang* (Pear Blossom School). The hospital evolved into Severance Hospital, and the two schools became Yonsei and Ehwa universities in the twentieth century. Other important missionaries were educators Homer B. Hulbert and James Gale, who wrote the first histories of Korea in English. Their efforts were not easy because propagating heterodox beliefs was still punishable by death, and the population had strong prejudices against Christians.

Efforts to Modernize

The first efforts to modernize included reorganization of the bureaucracy and the establishment of a western-style post office in 1884. The Protestant missionaries introduced the first western hospitals and medical techniques. Japanese currency and banks and telegraph lines made their appearance. Brick buildings, automobiles, and electricity arrived in the 1890s to power streetcars, and they wended their way through the main streets of Seoul in tandem with oxen and hand-pulled carts.

Most of these developments occurred in Seoul, Pyongyang, and a few border towns, and a small segment of the urban population was

MATERIAL CULTURE

Streetcars

The late nineteenth century was a period of rapid modernization in Korea. The first material signs of western culture came with the modern post office in 1884. By the 1890s, new forms of transportation arose, including streetcars, the first train between Inch'ŏn and Seoul, and a railroad bridge between Seoul and Noryangjin over the Han River in 1900. Pictured here is a streetcar wending its way through Namdaemun (South Gate) in 1904, but the streetcar tracks here and on Chongno (Bell Street) had been laid a decade before.

Streetcars. One of the first streetcars in Seoul, heading toward Namdaemun (Great South Gate), ca. 1900. *(Kim Wonmo and Chong Songgil, Korea 100 Years Ago in Photographs, p. 70, Collection of Chung Sung)*

most affected by education. Housing for the general population did not change much, but modern, public buildings provided models for the future.

THE TONGHAK REBELLION AND THE SINO-JAPANESE WAR (1894–1895)

Peace was finally interrupted by the Tonghak Rebellion, the biggest rebellion in Korean history. Contrary to popular belief that Japan had been planning a war to take over Korea, there is no evidence in the Japanese archives to prove it, but when the Tonghak Rebellion broke out in 1894, the Japanese cabinet seized the opportunity to eliminate the Chinese from Korean affairs. The Tonghak under its second patriarch, Ch'oe Sihyŏng, had been petitioning the govern-

ment repeatedly for an end to persecution by the government and toleration of their religion. It was also fueled by its antiforeign reaction to the presence of Japanese and other foreigners on Korean soil. The Tonghak made a powerful appeal to followers based on their religious declaration of the equality of all people before Hanŭnim (God), its rejection of Christianity, and a powerful organization based on a network of Netrope Coordinating Centers (Chipkangso) to administer captured territory.

In one of his more foolish actions, King Kojong lost confidence in his own army to control or repress the Tonghak rebels and asked the Chinese to dispatch troops to Korea. Even before the Chinese troops arrived, however, the government reached an agreement with the Tonghak military leader, Chŏn Pongjun, to call off the rebellion in return for toleration of their faith and a turnover of administrative responsibility for their captured territory. The Japanese

Chŏn Pongjun (1854–1895). The leader of the Tonghak rebel army after his capture in 1895. *(Sajinuro ponun tongni undong: Oech 'im kwa t'ujaeng, sang, p. 30)*

government took this opportunity to force a war on China by sending more troops than the Chinese had sent and making unacceptable demands. Japan attacked China without bothering to declare war, surrounded the Korean palace, and kept the king and queen under detention while the war continued.

Kabo Cabinet Reforms

Inoue Kaoru, one of the leading Japanese oligarchs, was sent to Seoul to establish a new cabinet. After failed efforts to recruit the Taewongun, Inoue brought Pak Yŏnghyo and Sŏ Kwangbŏm, the leaders of the *kapsin* coup of 1884, back from Japan and placed them in the Kabo cabinet. They were instrumental in drawing up reform decrees to create a more responsible bureaucracy; end the king's control over the exchequer; abolish slavery, concubinage, and child marriage; provide universal medical care and primary education for both sexes; and put an end to the civil service examinations, status distinctions between *yangban* and commoners, economic controls, and the mistreatment of wives.

Alarmed by the Japanese takeover of the Korean government and the return of men they regarded as the traitors of 1884 as cabinet members, the Tonghak under Chŏn Pongjun rose up again to drive the Japanese out of the country. This time, they had to fight a fierce but hopeless struggle against superior Japanese forces with advanced weapons and units of the Korean army. While this struggle was underway in mid-November 1894, King Kojong opposed Japanese control over himself, but Inoue countered that challenge by threatening to withdraw Japanese troops from the battle against the Tonghak rebels. In January 1895 he finally agreed to exclude the queen and her relatives from decisions and consult with ministers before making them. He then declared the end of Korea's tributary relationship with the Qing Dynasty. Inoue thought he had won a victory, but the Min faction proved just as contrary as the Taewongun and intrigued behind the scenes against Japanese interests.

The Japanese reform program called for rationalizing the bureaucracy, abolishing sinecures, establishing a regular budget and a uniform currency, creating a new judicial structure with professional judges and a modern police and military, initiating a modern universal educational system through high school, expanding railroads and telegraph lines, and beginning a modern postal service. The reforms were not carried to completion because they were attempted during war and the central government had weak control over local officials, but the abolition of slavery and the civil service examination system were preserved. Not all slaves were manumitted immediately, and members of the educated *yangban* elite continued to monopolize admission to government office under the new system of examinations run by individual ministries, but the door to upward mobility had been opened to members of lower-status groups, especially the educated *chung'in* clerks and specialists, who began a trek up the bureaucratic ladder despite their low status, which continued into the colonial period after 1910.

Meanwhile, the reform cabinet was being torn apart by Pak Yŏnghyo's ambition to become prime minister. He sealed his fate when a Japanese legation official leaked his proposal to assassinate the queen, and he barely escaped to Japan in July 1895. Inoue was also recalled by his government because of the Triple Intervention in April 1895. Because Russia could not countenance the Japanese takeover of ports and railroad rights in the Liaodong peninsula in

Manchuria as the fruits of victory, it led a three-nation coalition, with France and Germany, to force Japan to give up these territorial gains. Japan also had to retreat from Korea as well.

Assassination of the Queen

In April 1895, the Japanese government replaced Inoue Kaoru with Miura Gorō as minister to Seoul. When Miura was informed that King Kojong was about to appoint Min Yŏng'ik, who had negotiated with Russia in the past, to take charge of the court, he decided that it was essential to assassinate Queen Min without authorization from Tokyo to eliminate the Min family from politics. In October he sent two dozen Japanese police disguised as Korean guards and Japanese thugs (*sōshi*) into the palace, where they killed the queen and two of her palace ladies and then burned her body on the spot. Miura had a Japanese guard escort the Taewongun to the palace to take charge of the government and then appointed Koreans like Ŏ Yunjung and Yu Kilchun, who were willing to serve despite the queen's death, to the Kim Hongjip cabinet. Yu had studied briefly in Japan while living in Fukuzawa Yukichi's house, and then in the United States for four months, returned to Korea in 1887, and while under house arrest wrote his famous account of conditions in western nations, the *Sŏyu kyŏnmun* (What I Saw and Heard in the West), modeled after Fukuzawa Yukichi's *Seiyō jijō* (Conditions in the West). He was a strong advocate of the adoption of western institutions including the English-style constitutional monarchy, but he opposed the radicalism of Kim Okkyun and Pak Yŏnghyo and any idea of republicanism.

Miura tried to evade condemnation by blaming the Taewongun for the queen's assassination, but when eyewitnesses testified about the Japanese assassins, he was recalled to Japan and arrested. His action was so atrocious that it roused the ire of the Korean people and caused deep embarrassment for the Japanese government. In November, a few hundred armed Koreans loyal to the queen attacked the palace to murder members of the cabinet, but were driven off by Japanese guards. The cabinet then added fuel to the fire by having King Kojong issue a decree for all adult men to cut off their top-knots, a traditional Korean rite of passage to adulthood. That type of decree was the same measure adopted in Meiji Japan to mark the rejection of old customs and a commitment to modernity, but Korean men were not ready for the shock, and local guerrillas responded by attacking the authorities.

The Kabo reform cabinets of 1894 and 1895 had carried out major institutional reforms, but those cabinets were protected against conservative forces by the Japanese army. The Triple Intervention of 1895 orchestrated by Russia and Miura's murder of the queen weakened Japan's position in Korea so severely that the reforms and their Korean supporters were placed in dire jeopardy from conservative retaliation.

The reform movement had made some progress but had been blocked by the Chinese. Now that the tributary system was ended, and Japan was forced to withdraw from Korea,

there appeared to be a chance that Korea might be able to push reforms against the conservatives to bolster its independence.

SUMMARY

Faced with internal rebellion and foreign aggression throughout the century, the Taewongun's traditional reform only postponed the inevitable. No sooner had Korea compromised with foreign states by signing trade treaties, when conservative attacks brought China into Korean affairs. The Chinese repressed Kim Okkyun's attempt at modern reform in 1884, and Li Hongzhang imposed Yuan Shikai on King Kojong to prevent any serious liberation from Chinese control. The Tonghak Rebellion sought to drive out foreign influence, but it only sparked Japan's defeat of China and the major Kabo reform, compromised, however, by Japanese sponsorship. The chance for Korean independence was cloudy indeed.

SUGGESTED READING

J. K. Fairbank, ed., *The Chinese World Order* (1968), and M. F. Nelson, *Korea and the Old Orders in Eastern Asia* (1945) provide a theoretical construct of the tributary system. The reign of the Taewongun in the 1860s is covered by C. Y. Choe, *The Rule of the Taewongun, 1864–1873* (1972), and J. B. Palais, *Politics and Policy in Traditional Korea* (1975). The reforms and troubles of the 1880s are covered in M. Deuchler, *Confucian Gentlemen and Barbarian Envoys* (1977); K. Key-Hiuk, *The Last Phase of the East Asian World Order* (1980); and Y.-B. Lee, *Diplomatic Relations Between the United States and Korea: 1866–1887* (1970).

Korea's relations with Japan, Russia, and the powers are covered by H. Conroy, *The Japanese Seizure of Korea, 1868–1910* (1960); P. Duus, *The Abacus and the Sword* (1995); E. Kim and H. Kim, *Korea and the Politics of Imperialism* (1967); and G. A. Lensen, *Balance of Intrigue* (1982). B. Weems, *Reform, Rebellion, and the Heavenly Way* (1964), deals with the Tonghak Rebellion, and V. Chandra, *Imperialism, Resistance, and Reform in Late Nineteenth-Century Korea* (1988), studies the Kabo Reforms of 1894–1895. Chung-shin Park, *Protestantism and Politics in Korea* (2003), concentrates on early Protestantism.

Y. Ch'oe, P. Lee, and W. T. de Bary, eds., *Sources of Korean Tradition*, Vol. 2 (2000), contain primary sources on the period.

PART SIX

EAST ASIA IN THE MODERN WORLD

Remaking China (1900–1927)

The first decade of the twentieth century was a period of rapid change, especially in cities and among the educated. Chinese cities were being paved, lighted, and policed. The Qing court announced plans for gradual transition to a constitutional monarchy. Voluntary reform societies tackled problems like foot binding and opium smoking. Then, in 1911, the Qing Dynasty was overthrown. Although the dynasty handed over its armies to the republican government under Yuan Shikai, military unity was soon lost, and regional armies and warlords competed to secure bases. In the 1920s, the Nationalist Party under Sun Yatsen built a base in Guangdong, and in 1926 launched the Northern Expedition, which reunified the country.

Nationalism was central to much of the cultural activity of this period. Patriots wanted to reconstitute China as a nation of the Chinese people and make it strong enough to stand up to foreign threats. A new type of intellectual emerged: trained at modern universities or abroad, deeply concerned with China's fate, and attracted to western ideas ranging from science and democracy to anarchism and communism. Young people attacked old social norms, especially filial piety and arranged marriages. The encounters between new and old and East and West stimulated a literary and scholarly renaissance.

Understanding these changes has been the central goal of most of the research on this period. Who led the way in the changes to the Chinese economy, education, and political organization? How was resistance to change overcome? What role did foreign countries play? Did the militarization of society slow down or speed up other changes? Which changes were felt even by farmers in the countryside?

THE END OF MONARCHY

As the twentieth century opened, the Qing Dynasty needed to regain the people's confidence after the debacle brought on by its support of the Boxers and the imperialists' subsequent intervention. It faced a fiscal crisis. The Boxer Protocol of 1901 imposed on China a staggering indemnity of 450 million silver dollars, twice as large as the one exacted by Japan a few years earlier and nearly twice the government's annual revenues. It was to be paid from customs revenue in thirty-nine annual installments, with interest. When interest on existing foreign loans was added in, these debts absorbed all of the customs revenue. Little was left for the ordinary operation of the government, much less investment in modernization.

Local Activism

Forced to look after their own interests, local elites increasingly took on modernization projects. They set up new schools and started periodicals, which by one estimate increased tenfold from 1901 to 1910. Interest in western forms of government was growing as people asked how the European powers and Japan had gained wealth and power. Yan Fu, one of the first to study in England, published translations of books such as J. S. Mill's *On Liberty* (1903) and Montesquieu's *The Spirit of Laws* (1909). Yan Fu argued that the western form of government freed the energy of the individual, which could then be channeled toward national goals. As he saw it, the West had achieved wealth and power through a complex package, a key part of which was a very differently conceived nation-state. Yan Fu once commented that only 30 percent of China's troubles were caused by foreigners; the rest were its own fault and could be remedied by its own actions.

Interest in western forms of government did not translate into positive feelings toward the western powers, which were seen as gaining a stranglehold on the Chinese economy. Activists solicited funds to buy back railroads built by foreign firms. Between 1905 and 1907 there were boycotts of the United States for its immigration restriction law and its mistreatment of Chinese at the 1904 World's Fair in Saint Louis. In treaty ports, protests were staged over westerners' extraterritoriality. Some protesters even talked of waging their own opium war after the British refused to stop shipping opium to China on the grounds that opium cultivation in China had not been fully eradicated.

In this period, Japan served as an incubator of Chinese nationalism. By 1906, of the thirteen thousand students studying abroad, ten thousand were in Tokyo. The experience of living in a foreign country, where they felt humiliated by China's weakness and backwardness, aroused nationalistic feelings in the students, who often formed groups to discuss how Japan had modernized so rapidly and what could be done in China. One student newspaper reported, "Japanese schools are as numerous as our opium dens, Japanese students as numerous as our opium addicts."[1] The two best-known reformers, Kang Youwei and Liang Qichao, had settled in Japan. In Chinese magazines published in Japan, Liang promoted the idea that China could become strong through "democracy," which to him meant a government that drew its strength from the people, but not necessarily a representative government or one that defended individual rights. Liang had traveled in the United States for five months in 1903 and found the American form of populist democracy unsatisfactory. He preferred the statist ideas and constitutional monarchies of Japan and Germany. When Japan defeated Russia in 1905 (see Chapter 24), some reformers drew the inference that it was Japan's constitutional form of government that enabled it to best autocratic Russia.

---

1. Cited in Douglas R. Reynolds, *China, 1898–1912: The Xinzheng Revolution and Japan* (Cambridge, Mass.: Harvard University Press, 1993), p. 62.

The Anti-Manchu Revolutionary Movement

Ever since the late nineteenth century, some people had argued that the root of China's problems lay in its subjugation by a different "race"—the Manchus. In 1903 the nineteen-year-old Zou Rong published an inflammatory tract, calling for the creation of a revolutionary army to "wipe out the five million barbarian Manchus, wash away the shame of two hundred and sixty years of cruelty and oppression, and make China clean once again."[2] He described the "sacred Han race, descendants of the Yellow Emperor," as the slaves of the Manchus and in danger of extermination. The language of social Darwinism, with its talk of countries in desperate competition for survival, seemed to many to describe China's plight accurately.

The anti-Manchu revolutionary who would eventually be mythologized as the founding figure of the Chinese republic was Sun Yatsen (Sun Zhongshan, 1866–1925). Like Hong Xiuquan, Kang Youwei, and Liang Qichao before him, Sun came from Guangdong province. Unlike them, he was neither from a literati family nor trained in the Confucian classics. Several of his close relatives had emigrated, and in 1879 he was sent to join a brother in Hawaii. Later he went to Hong Kong to study western medicine, completing his degree in 1892. In Hong Kong, Sun and his friends began discussing the advantages of a republic. The best way to overthrow the Manchus, they concluded, would be to ally with the secret societies so pervasive in south China. Groups like the Triads were anti-Manchu, had large mass followings, and had an organizational base reaching from one province to another, making them an ideal base for an insurrection, they thought.

In 1894 Sun went to Beijing in the hope of seeing Li Hongzhang, but when that failed, he returned to Hawaii, where he founded a chapter of the Revive China Society. The next year he set up a similar group in Hong Kong. The society's efforts to instigate an uprising with secret society members as the muscle never got very far, however. In 1896 Sun cut off his queue and began wearing western clothes. He spent time in England, where he discovered that many westerners saw flaws in their own institutions and were advocating a variety of socialist solutions. Sun began to think China could skip ahead of the West by going directly to a more progressive form of government. He also spent time in Japan, where he found Japanese eager to help in the regeneration and modernization of China. In 1905 some Japanese helped Sun join forces with the more radical of the student revolutionaries to form the Revolutionary Alliance. Despite the difference in social background, the students from educated families were excited by Sun's promise of quick solutions to China's problems. This alliance sponsored seven or eight attempts at uprisings over the next few years. Sun himself continued to spend most of his time traveling in search of funds and foreign backers, especially overseas Chinese.

In these years Sun worked out his theory of the Three People's Principles: nationalism (which opposed both rule by Manchus and domination by foreign powers), democracy (which meant to Sun elections and a constitution), and the "people's livelihood," a vague sort of socialism with equalization of landholdings and curbs on capital. Sun admitted that the Chinese people were unaccustomed to political participation; nevertheless, he believed that they could be guided toward democracy through a period of political tutelage, during which the revolutionaries would promulgate a provisional constitution and people would begin electing local officials.

The Manchu Reform Movement

Amid all this activism and agitation, the Manchu court began to edge in the direction of parliamentary government. Empress Dowager Cixi in 1901 announced the establishment of a

---

2. Cited in Michael Gasster, "The Republican Revolutionary Movement," in *Cambridge History of China*, vol. 11, pt. 2 (Cambridge: Cambridge University Press, 1980), p. 482.

national school system and called for putting questions about foreign government and science on the civil service examinations. In 1905 she took the momentous step of abolishing the civil service examination system altogether, a system that had set the framework for relations between the government and the elite for a millennium. New military academies were set up and new armies formed, trained by German or Japanese instructors. With the death of Li Hongzhang in 1901, Yuan Shikai emerged as the most powerful general, serving as both commander of the Northern Army and head of the Baoding Military Academy.

In 1905 Cixi approved sending a mission abroad to study constitutional forms of government. On its return the next year, the commission recommended the Japanese model, which retained the monarchy and had it bestow the constitution on the country (rather than a constitution that made the people sovereign). In 1907 plans for national and provincial assemblies were announced, with a full constitution to be in place by 1917. The next year, the seventy-three-year-old Cixi died (the thirty-three-year-old Guangxu emperor died suspiciously the day before). She had arranged for a three year old to succeed. His regents did not prove particularly effective leaders and soon dismissed Yuan Shikai. Hope for a Japanese-style constitutional monarchy looked less and less promising.

Still, in 1909 assemblies met in each province and sent representatives to Beijing. Although less than 1 percent of the population had been allowed to vote, the elections generated excitement about participatory government. The provincial assemblies circulated three petitions calling for the immediate convening of the national assembly, the last reportedly signed by 25 million people. In 1910 the provisional national assembly met, with one hundred members elected by the provincial assemblies and one hundred appointed by the court. Anti-Manchu feelings rose, however, when in May 1911 the court announced the formation of a cabinet with eight Manchu, one Mongol, and only four Chinese members.

Cutting Off a Queue. After the success of the 1911 revolution, soldiers often forced men to cut off their queues. *(Roger Viollet)*

The 1911 Revolution

The Manchu court's efforts to institute reform from above satisfied very few, and in October 1911, a plot by revolutionaries finally triggered the collapse of the Qing Dynasty. In the city of Wuchang on the Yangzi River, a bomb accidentally exploded in the headquarters of a revolutionary group. When the police came to investigate, they found lists of the revolutionaries, including many officers of the new army division located there. Once the police set out to arrest those listed, the army officers, facing certain execution, staged a coup. The local officials fled, and the army took over the city in less than a day. The revolutionaries then telegraphed the other provinces asking them to declare their independence. Within six weeks, fifteen provinces had seceded.

The Qing court did not immediately capitulate. In desperation it turned to Yuan Shikai, whom they had dismissed only a few years before, and asked him to mount a military campaign against the revolutionaries. Yuan went back and forth between the court and the revolutionaries, seeing what he could get from each. The biggest fear of the revolutionaries was foreign intervention, and to avoid that they were willing to compromise. In the end, agreement was reached to establish a republic with Yuan as president; the emperor would abdicate, but he and his entourage would be allowed to remain in the Forbidden City, receive generous allowances, and keep much of their property. Thus, unlike the Bourbons in France or the Romanovs in Russia, the Manchu royal family suffered neither executions nor humiliations when it was deposed.

In February 1912, the last Qing emperor abdicated, and in March Yuan Shikai took over as president. As a mark of solidarity with the revolutionaries, men cut off their queues, the symbol of their subordination to the Manchus.

THE PRESIDENCY OF YUAN SHIKAI AND THE EMERGENCE OF THE WARLORDS

Yuan Shikai had strong credentials as a reformer of the old, self-strengthening type. While governor, he had initiated reforms in education, commerce, and industry, and his army not only was equipped with modern weapons but was trained along lines established by German and Japanese advisors. He believed in careful central planning, of the sort Germany and Japan had shown could be effective. He was committed to a strong China but not a republican one. If local or provincial assemblies were empowered to act as they liked, how could China move rapidly toward a modern nation-state?

Yuan did not prevent parliamentary elections from being held in 1913, but when Sun Yatsen's new Nationalist Party won a plurality of the seats, Yuan was unwilling to accept the outcome. The key Nationalist organizer, Song Jiaoren, was soon assassinated, and the shocked public assumed Yuan was responsible. Then Yuan, without consulting the national assembly, negotiated a $100 million loan from a foreign consortium. By summer the Nationalist Party was organizing open revolt against Yuan, and seven provincial governments declared their independence. This second revolution ended in military rout, and Sun Yatsen and other Nationalist leaders once more fled to Japan. Yuan outlawed the Nationalist Party; in 1914, he abolished all assemblies down to the county level, trying to nip in the bud participatory democracy.

Yuan did undertake some progressive projects, extending elementary education, suppressing opium cultivation, and promoting judicial reform. But he was out of touch with the mood of younger people, especially when he announced that Confucianism would be made the state religion. When in August 1915 he announced that he would become emperor, the educated and politically aware elite were outraged, their protests dying down only after Yuan died unexpectedly in June 1916.

During the decade after Yuan Shikai's death, China was politically fragmented. Without a central strongman, commanders in Yuan's old army, governors of provinces, and even gangsters built their own power bases. The outer regions of the Qing Empire, such as Tibet and Mongolia, declared their independence. Tibet soon fell under British sway and Mongolia under Russia's. Manchuria was more and more dominated by Japan. In the far south Sun Yatsen and his allies tried to build a power base for the Nationalist revolutionaries. A government of sorts was maintained in Beijing, under the domination of whichever warlord held the region. It was hardly stable, however, with six different presidents and twenty-five successive cabinets. For a while, the key struggle seemed to be for control of the north, as the strongest warlords waged highly destructive wars across north China.

Warlords, not surprisingly, did little to maintain infrastructure or advance modernization. They disrupted rail lines and allowed the dikes on the Yellow River to deteriorate, leading to some catastrophic floods. They caused havoc in the countryside because the armies lived off the land, looting wherever they moved. One warlord reported, "My men would surround a village before dawn and fire several shots to intimidate the people. We told them to come out and give up. This was the classic way of raiding a village. Sometimes we killed and carried away little pigs. . . . We took corn, rice, potatoes, taro."[3] Because they also needed money to buy weapons, warlords instituted all sorts of new taxes. Foreign countries were more than willing to sell modern arms to the warlords, often backing their own favorite contender. Opium cultivation had been nearly eradicated in many places until the warlords entered the scene and forced peasants to grow it as a revenue source.

TOWARD A MORE MODERN CHINA

Social, cultural, and political change was rapid in the early decades of the twentieth century, some of it flowing directly from the pens of those advocating change of many sorts, some of it the direct or indirect consequence of changes in China's economy and political situation. Even forms of entertainment changed (see **Material Culture: Shanghai's Great World Pleasure Palace**).

The New Culture Movement

Young people who received a modern education felt that they had inherited the obligation of the literati to advise those in power. Their modern education, they believed, uniquely qualified them to "save" China. They had expected much of the 1911 revolution and then had had their hopes dashed.

The newly reorganized Beijing University played a central role in this New Culture movement. Chen Duxiu, the founder of the periodical *New Youth,* was appointed dean of letters. Chen had had a traditional education and taken the civil service examinations before studying in Japan and France. A participant in the 1911 revolution, he became a zealous advocate of individual freedom. In the first issue of *New Youth* in 1915 Chen challenged the long-standing Confucian value of deference toward elders. Youth, he asserted, was worth celebrating: "Youth is like early spring, like the rising sun, like the trees and grass in bud, like a newly sharpened blade." He urged his readers not to waste their "fleeting time in arguing with the older generation on this and that, hoping for them to be reborn and remodeled." They should think for themselves and not let the old contaminate them. In other articles, he wrote that Confucianism had to be rejected before China could attain equality and human rights: "We must be thoroughly aware of the incompatibility between Confucianism and the new belief, the new society, and the new state."[4] To him, "loyalty, filial piety, chastity, and righteousness" were nothing but "a slavish morality."[5] Young people responded enthusiastically to his attack on filial piety and began challenging the authority of their parents to make decisions for them about school, work, and marriage. Conflict between parents and their marriage-age children became extremely common as the young insisted on choosing their own spouses.

Soon leaders of the New Culture movement proposed ending use of the classical literary language that had been the mark of the educated person for two thousand years. The leader of

---

3. Cited in James E. Sheridan, *China in Disintegration* (New York: Free Press, 1975), p. 91.

4. Cited in Chow Tse-tsung, *The May Fourth Movement: Intellectual Revolution in Modern China* (Stanford: Stanford University Press, 1960), p. 482.

5. Ssu-yu Teng and John K. Fairbank, *China's Response to the West: A Documentary Survey* (New York: Atheneum, 1971), p. 241.

MATERIAL CULTURE

Shanghai's Great World Pleasure Palace

Commonplaces of modern life such as malls and window shopping were once new and controversial. In China, they usually appeared first in Shanghai. In 1917 an entrepreneur who had made his fortune in medicine built the Great World, a six-story amusement park touted as the Crystal Palace and Coney Island rolled into one. At the intersection of two major roads in the International District, from the outside it seemed an agglomeration of European building motifs, with columns holding up a decorative tower. Inside, it catered more to Chinese tastes, and its customers were primarily Chinese. On the first floor were gaming tables, slot machines, magicians, acrobats, sing-song girls, and miscellaneous things for sale such as fans, incense, and fireworks. On the next floor were restaurants, as well as acting troupes, midwives, barbers, and earwax extractors. The third floor had photographers, jugglers, ice cream parlors, and girls in high-slit dresses. The fourth floor had masseurs, acupuncturists, and dancers. The fifth floor had storytellers, peep shows, scribes who composed love letters, and a temple. On the top floor were tightrope walkers, places to play mahjong, lottery tickets, and marriage brokers.

Great World Pleasure Palace. The building is seen here in a photo from the 1920s. *(Shanghai Historical Museum)*

the movement to write in the vernacular was Hu Shi, appointed to the faculty of Beijing University by Chen Duxiu after he returned from seven years studying philosophy in the United States at Cornell and Columbia. "A dead language," Hu declared, "can never produce a living literature."[6] Since Chinese civilization had been so closely tied to this language, Hu's assertions came dangerously close to declaring Chinese civilization dead. Hu Shi did recognize that the old written language had allowed speakers of mutually unintelligible dialects to communicate with each other and thus had been a source of unity, but he argued that once a national literature was produced in vernacular Chinese, a standard dialect would establish itself, much as standard vernaculars had gained hold in France and Germany. Chen Duxiu concurred with Hu, and soon *New Youth* was written entirely in vernacular Chinese.

The use of vernacular language had political implications. As Chen Duxiu argued, a modern Chinese nation needed a literate public, and literacy could be achieved more easily when writing reflected speech. The movement to write in the vernacular caught on quickly. In 1921 the Ministry of Education decided that henceforth elementary school textbooks would be written in the vernacular.

One of the first to write well in the vernacular was Lu Xun (1881–1936). In 1902 Lu had gone to Japan to study medicine after traditional doctors had failed to cure his father of tuberculosis. He gave up medicine, however, after watching a newsreel of the Russo-Japanese War that showed a group of Chinese watching apathetically as Japanese in Manchuria executed a Chinese accused of spying for the Russians. From this Lu Xun concluded that it was more important to change the spirit of the Chinese than protect their bodies. He began reading widely in European literature, especially Russian. The May 1918 issue of *New Youth* contained his first vernacular short story, "Diary of a Madman." In it the main character goes mad (or is taken to be mad) after he discovers that what his elders saw as lofty values was nothing more than cannibalism. In his longest story,

"The True Story of Ah Q," the protagonist is a man of low social standing. Always on the lookout for a way to get ahead, he is too cowardly and self-deceiving ever to succeed. No matter how he is humiliated, he claims moral superiority. His ears prick up in 1911 when he hears talk of a revolution, but soon he discovers that the old, classically educated elite and the new, foreign-educated elite are collaborating to take over the revolution for themselves and want him to stay away. In the end, he is executed by representatives of the revolution for a robbery he would have liked to have committed but actually had not managed to pull off. In stories like these, Lu Xun gave voice to those troubled by China's prospects and weary of China's old order but wary of promises of easy solutions. Lu Xun put the blame for China's plight on China's own flaws much more than on foreigners. (See **Documents: Lu Xun's "Sudden Notions."**)

By 1919 *New Youth* had been joined by many other periodicals aimed at young people aspiring for a New China. Magazines were filled with articles on western ideas of all sorts, including socialism, anarchism, democracy, liberalism, Darwinism, pragmatism, and science. The key goals were enlightenment and national survival.

Industrial Development

Despite all of the political and cultural turmoil of the first two decades of the twentieth century, a modern economy began to take off in China. China had opened some modern enterprises as early as 1872, when Li Hongzhang had started the China Merchant Steamship Navigation Company, but those were government-supervised and -supported ventures, not true capitalist ones. In 1895 Japan won the right to open factories in China, and the other imperialist powers leaped at the chance to set up factories as well, since labor costs in China were very low by international standards. By the eve of World War I, China had an emerging bourgeoisie made up of merchants, bankers, industrialists, compradors working for foreign firms,

---

6. Cited in Leo Ou-fan Lee, "Literary Trends I: The Quest for Modernity, 1895–1927," in *Cambridge History of China,* vol. 12, ed. John K. Fairbank (Cambridge: Cambridge University Press, 1983), p. 467.

DOCUMENTS

Lu Xun's "Sudden Notions"

The fiction writer and essayist Lu Xun (1881–1936) disagreed with those who urged preserving China's "national character" or "national essence," as he saw much in China's past and present that could profitably be abandoned. When he considered China's history, he saw the recurrence of undesirable patterns rather than past glories to be remembered with pride. The essay below on these topics was published in February 1925.

I used to believe the statements that the twenty-four dynastic histories were simply "records of mutual slaughter" or "family histories of rulers." Later, when I read them for myself, I realized this was a fallacy.

All these histories portray the soul of China and indicate what the country's future will be, but the truth is buried so deep in flowery phrases and nonsense it is very hard to grasp it; just as, when the moon shines through thick foliage onto moss, only checkered shadows can be seen. If we read unofficial records and anecdotes, though, we can understand more easily, for here at least the writers did not have to put on the airs of official historians.

The Qin and Han Dynasties are too far from us and too different to be worth discussing. Few records were written in the Yuan Dynasty. But most of the annals of the Tang, Song, and Ming Dynasties have come down to us. And if we compare the events recorded during the Five Dynasties period or the Southern Song Dynasty and the end of the Ming Dynasty with modern conditions, it is amazing how alike they are. It seems as if China alone is untouched by the passage of time. The Chinese Republic today is still the China of those earlier ages.

If we compare our era with the end of the Ming Dynasty, our China is not so corrupt, disrupted, cruel or despotic—we have not yet reached the limit.

But neither did the corruption and disruption of the last years of the Ming Dynasty reach the limit, for Li Zicheng and Zhang

and overseas Chinese engaged in import-export. Foreign investment grew rapidly, with big increases especially in Japanese investment. In the first decade of the century, more and more chambers of commerce had been established in cities large and small, giving this bourgeoisie more of a voice in politics. With the deterioration of the national government after 1915, it was often the chambers of commerce that took over running cities, seeing to sanitation, education, and police. Many of those who returned from study abroad took jobs in modern enterprises, where their foreign degrees brought prestige and often higher salaries. (See **Biography: Sophia Chen and H. C. Zen, a Modern Couple.**)

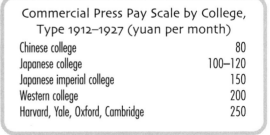

Commercial Press Pay Scale by College, Type 1912–1927 (yuan per month)	
Chinese college	80
Japanese college	100–120
Japanese imperial college	150
Western college	200
Harvard, Yale, Oxford, Cambridge	250

World War I gave China's businesses and industries a chance to flourish. Britain, France, Germany, and Russia were preoccupied with what was happening in Europe and no longer

Xianzhong rebelled. And neither did their cruelty and despotism reach the limit, for the Manchu troops entered China.

Can it be that "national character" is so difficult to change? If so, we can more or less guess what our fate will be. As is so often said, "It will be the same old story."

Some people are really clever: they never argue with the ancients, or query ancient rules. Whatever the ancients have done, we modern man can do. And to defend the ancients is to defend ourselves. Besides, as the "glorious descendants of a divine race," how dare we not follow in our forebears' footsteps?

Luckily no one can say for certain that the national character will never change. And though this uncertainty means that we face the threat of annihilation—something we have never experienced—we can also hope for a national revival, which is equally unprecedented. This may be of some comfort to reformers.

But even this slight comfort may be cancelled by the pens of those who boast of the ancient culture, drowned by the words of those who slander the modern culture, or wiped out by the deeds of those who pose as exponents of the modern culture. For "it will be the same old story."

Actually, all these men belong to one type: they are all clever people, who know that even if China collapses they will not suffer, for they can always adapt themselves to circumstances. If anybody doubts this let him read the essays in praise of the Manchus' military prowess written in the Qing Dynasty by Chinese, and filled with such terms as "our great forces" and "our army." Who could imagine that this was the army that had conquered us? One would be led to suppose that the Chinese had marched to wipe out some corrupt barbarians.

But since such men always come out on top, presumably they will never die out. In China, they are the best fitted to survive; and, so long as they survive, China will never cease having repetitions of her former fate.

"Vast territory, abundant resources, and a great population"—with such excellent material, are we able only to go round and round in circles?

___

Source: From *Lu Xun: Selected Works* (Peking: Foreign Languages Press, 1980), 2:125–127.

had spare goods to export. Imports from the West thus dropped dramatically, giving Chinese manufacturers a chance to sell more profitably. At the same time, the demand for products from China increased, helping China's export industries. The number of Chinese textile mills increased from 22 in 1911 to 109 in 1921. Tonnage of coal produced grew from 13 to 20 million tons between 1913 and 1919. Modern banking took off: between 1912 and 1923, the number of modern banks soared from 7 to 131. Telephone and electric companies were formed not only in major cities, but in county seats and even market towns. New fortunes were made. For instance, the Rong brothers, from a family

of merchants in Wuxi, built a flour mill in 1901 and another in 1913. As opportunities opened up, they built eight new factories between 1914 and 1920, expanding into textiles.

Industrialization had its predictable costs as well. Conditions in China's factories in the 1910s were as bad as they had been a century earlier in Britain, with twelve-hour days, seven-day weeks, and widespread child labor, especially in textile mills. Labor contractors often recruited in the countryside and kept laborers in conditions of debt slavery, providing the most minimal housing and food. That many of the factories were foreign owned (increasingly Japanese owned) added to management–labor friction.

BIOGRAPHY Sophia Chen and H. C. Zen, a Modern Couple

The first generation to return to China from study abroad found many opportunities to put their new skills to work. Although many men returned to marry wives their families had selected for them, others, like Sophia Chen (1890–1976) and H. C. Zen (1886–1961), found their own marriage partners while abroad.

H.C. Zen is the English name taken by Ren Hongjun. He was born into an educated family in Sichuan and in 1904 graduated from a modern middle school. Although he was reading banned publications by the reformer Liang Qichao, he took the first stage of civil service examinations in 1904. After the exam system was abolished, he left China to study at a technical college in Tokyo, where he joined Sun Yatsen's Revolutionary Alliance. When the revolution broke out in 1911, he returned to China and at age twenty-five was made secretary to the president. Disagreeing with Sun's successor, Yuan Shikai, he resigned and went to the United States to study chemistry at Cornell and Columbia (1912–1917), finishing with a master's degree. While there, he became friends with Hu Shi and courted Chen Hengzhe, studying at Vassar. She took the English name Sophia Chen. While still in China, Zen also helped found the Science Society of China, an organization that sponsored scientific monographs and translations, lectures, and exhibitions. He served as its president from 1914 to 1923.

Sophia Chen, from an official family in Jiangsu, had faced more difficulty getting satisfactory schooling in China, either being tutored at home or studying in mediocre schools. In her teens, she convinced her father to withdraw from a marriage arrangement he had made for her so that she could continue her studies. In 1914, at age twenty-four, she was selected to study in the United States in the examinations held for Boxer Indemnity Fund scholarships. She studied history at Vassar, then went on for a master's degree at the University of Chicago in 1920. That year she returned to China, and became the first woman to be offered a professorship at Peking University. That same year, she and H. C. Zen married.

Since he had returned to China in 1917, Zen had held posts at Peking University and the Ministry of Education. When he became editor of the Commercial Press in 1922, the family moved to Shanghai. Two years later, in 1924, they moved to Nanjing, where Zen became vice chancellor of Nanjing University and Chen taught western history. Chen did not continue teaching after 1925, however, deciding to concentrate instead on writing. Her *History of the West* went through many printings. She also edited the *Independent Critic,* a liberal journal that she cofounded and that flourished in the 1930s. Both she and her husband wrote pieces for it. Most of Zen's time, however, was taken up with a series of prominent posts. From 1935 to 1937, he was head of the National Sichuan University.

After the Japanese invasion, the family moved to Kunming, where Zen, as the secretary general of the Academic Sinica and director of its Institute of Chemistry, tried to keep scientific research going in difficult circumstances. After a few years, they moved to Chongqing, where Zen took up other posts.

Both Chen and Zen made return trips to the United States. Chen attended several international conferences and after a meeting in Canada in 1933 traveled in the United States, which she found much changed since the advent of the automobile age. Zen visited the United States after the war, in 1946–1947.

After 1949, both Zen and Chen, nearing retirement age, stayed in China, living in Shanghai. Of their three children, two settled in the United States and one stayed in China.

Demonstrating at the Gate of Heavenly Peace. For months after May 4, 1919, students continued to gather at the Gate of Heavenly Peace to protest. *(The Sidney D. Gamble Foundation for China Studies)*

The May Fourth Incident

In 1914, Japan as an ally of Britain and France seized German territories in China. In 1915, when the European powers were preoccupied with their war, Japan took steps to strengthen its hand in China. It presented Yuan Shikai's government with the Twenty-One Demands, most of which entailed economic privileges in various regions of China. Others confirmed Japan's position in the former German leasehold in Shandong. The fifth group of demands would have made China in effect a protectorate of Japan by requiring that Japanese advisers be attached to key organs of the Chinese government, even the police. When a wave of anti-Japanese protests swept China, Japan dropped the last group but gave Yuan an ultimatum to accept the rest. The day he did, May 7, was in later years called National Humiliation Day.

In 1917 the Republic of China joined the allied war effort, and although China sent no combatants, it did send some one hundred forty thousand laborers to France, where they unloaded cargo ships, dug trenches, and otherwise provided manpower of direct use to the war effort. China was thus expecting some gain from the allies' victory, particularly in the light of the stress placed on national self-determination by the U.S. president, Woodrow Wilson. Unfortunately for China, Japan had reached secret agreements with Britain, France, and Italy to support Japan's claim to German rights in Shandong. Japanese diplomats had also won the consent of the warlord government that held Beijing in 1918. At Versailles the Chinese representatives were not even admitted, while those from Japan were seated at the table with the western powers.

On May 4, 1919, when word arrived that the decision had gone in favor of Japan, there was an explosion of popular protest. Some three thousand Beijing students assembled at Tiananmen Square in front of the old palace, where they shouted patriotic slogans and tried to arouse spectators to action. After some students broke through police lines to beat up a pro-Japanese official and set fire to the home of a cabinet minister, the governor cracked down on the demonstrators and arrested their leaders. These actions set off a wave of protests around the country in support of the students and their cause. Everyone, it seemed, was on the students' side: teachers, workers, the press, the merchants, Sun Yatsen, and the warlords. Japanese goods were boycotted. Soon strikes closed schools in more than two hundred cities. The Beijing warlord government finally arrested 1,150 student protesters, turning parts of Beijing University into a jail, but patriotic sympathy strikes, especially in Shanghai, soon forced the government to release them. The cabinet fell, and China refused to sign the Versailles Treaty. The students were ebullient.

The protesters' moral victory set the tone for cultural politics through the 1920s and into the 1930s. The personal and intellectual goals of the New Culture movement were pursued along with and sometimes in competition with the national power goals of the May Fourth movement. Nationalism, patriotism, progress, science, democracy, and freedom were the goals; imperialism, feudalism, warlordism, autocracy, patriarchy, and blind adherence to tradition were the evils to be opposed. Intellectuals struggled with how to be strong and modern and yet Chinese. Some concentrated on the creation of a new literature in the vernacular, others on the study of western science, philosophy, and social and political thought. Among the prominent intellectuals from the West invited to visit China to lecture were Bertrand Russell (in 1920 and 1921), Albert Einstein (in 1922), and Margaret Sanger (in 1922). When the educational reformer John

Dewey visited between 1919 and 1921, he was impressed. "There seems to be no country in the world," he commented, "where students are so unanimously and eagerly interested in what is modern and new in thought, especially about social and economic matters, nor where the arguments which can be brought in favor of the established order and the status quo have so little weight—indeed are so unuttered."[7]

Not all intellectuals saw salvation in modern western culture. Some who for a while had been attracted to things western came to feel western culture was too materialistic. Fear that China was in danger of losing its "national essence" was raised. Liang Qichao, by now a conservative, saw more to admire in China's humanistic culture than in the West's rationalism and hedonism and worried about the threat to China's national character.

The Women's Movement

All of the major political and intellectual revolutionaries of the early twentieth century, from Kang Youwei and Liang Qichao to Sun Yatsen, Chen Duxiu, Lu Xun, and Mao Zedong, spoke out on the need to change ways of thinking about women and their social roles. Early in the century, the key issues were foot binding and women's education. In a short period of time, women's seclusion and tiny feet went from being a source of pride in Chinese refinement to a source of embarrassment at China's backwardness. Anti–foot binding campaigners depicted the custom as standing in the way of modernization by crippling a large part of the Chinese population. The earliest anti–foot binding societies, founded in the 1890s, were composed of men who would agree both to leave their daughters' feet natural and to marry their sons to women with natural feet. After 1930 it was only in remote areas that young girls still had their feet bound. (Bound feet continued to be seen on the streets into the 1970s or later, as it was dif-

---

7. Cited in Chow Tse-tung, op. cit., p. 183.

Pilgrims at Taishan. Taishan, one of the sacred peaks of China, attracted many pilgrims, like these women, photographed in the 1920s. Notice that some have made it up the mountain despite their bound feet. *(The Sidney D. Gamble Foundation for China Studies)*

ficult and painful to reverse the process once a girl had reached age ten or twelve.)

As women gained access to modern education, first in missionary schools but then also in the new government schools and abroad, they began to participate in politics. Some revolutionaries appeared, most famously Qiu Jin, a woman who became an ardent nationalist after witnessing the Boxer Rebellion and the imperialist occupation of Beijing. Unhappy in her marriage, in 1904 she left her husband and went to Japan, enrolling in a girls' vocational school. Once there, she devoted most of her time to revolutionary politics, even learning to make bombs. She also took up feminist issues. In her speeches and essays she castigated female infanticide, foot binding, arranged marriages, wife beating, and the cult of widow chastity. She told women that they were complicit in their oppres-

sion because they were willing to make pleasing men their goal. In 1906 she returned to Shanghai, where she founded the *Chinese Women's Journal* and taught at a nearby girls' school. In 1907 she died a martyr, executed for her role in an abortive uprising.

Schools for women, like the one Qiu Jin taught at, were becoming more and more common in this period. By 1910, there were over forty thousand girl's schools in the country, with 1.6 million students; by 1919, the figures had reached 134,000 schools and 4.5 million students (though schoolboys still outnumbered schoolgirls seven to one). Schools offered girls much more than literacy: they offered a respectable way for girls to interact with people they were not related to. After 1920, opportunities for higher education also rapidly expanded, leading to a growing number of women working as teachers, nurses, and civil servants in the larger cities. In the countryside, change came much more slowly. A large-scale survey of rural households in the 1930s found that fewer than 2 percent of the women were literate compared to 30 percent of the men.

Young women in middle and high schools became just as avid readers of *New Youth* and other periodicals as their brothers. Lu Xun wrote essays and short stories that targeted old moral standards that constrained women. In an essay on chastity, he noted how a woman who committed suicide to avoid being ravished won great glory, but no man of letters would write a biography of a woman who committed suicide after being forcibly raped. In his short story "The New Year's Sacrifice," a poor widow forced by her parents-in-law to remarry was viewed by herself and others as ill omened after her second husband also died. She ended up surviving by begging, worried that she would have to be split in two after death to serve her two husbands.

Besides attempting to change people's ways of thinking about parental authority and women's proper roles in society, activists fought for changes in women's legal status. Efforts to get the vote were generally unsuccessful. However, in the 1920s, both the Nationalists and Communists organized women's departments and adopted resolutions calling for equal rights for women and freedom of marriage and divorce. Divorce proved the trickiest issue. As Song Qingling, the widow of Sun Yatsen, reported, "If we do not grant the appeals of the women, they lose faith in the union and in the women's freedom we are teaching. But if we grant the divorces, then we have trouble with the peasant's union, since it is very hard for a peasant to get a wife, and he has often paid much for his present unwilling one."[8]

REUNIFICATION BY THE NATIONALISTS

The ease with which Yuan Shikai had pushed the revolutionaries out of power demonstrated to them that they needed their own army. Sun Yatsen in 1917 went to Guangzhou, then controlled by warlords, to try to form a military government there. That year, the Bolshevik Revolution succeeded in Russia, and Sun began to think Russia might offer a better model for political change than Japan. Russia had been a large, backward, despotic monarchy that had fallen behind the West in technology. Both China and Russia were predominantly peasant societies, with only small educated elites. Why shouldn't the sort of revolution that worked in Russia also work in China? The newly established Soviet Union wanted to help build a revolutionary China. In Marxist-Leninist theory, socialist revolution would occur by stages, and since China had not yet gone through a bourgeois, capitalist stage, a victory by the Nationalist revolutionaries who would overthrow the imperialists appeared to be the next stage for China. Besides, a weak China might invite the expansion of Japan, the Soviet Union's main worry to the east.

For help in building a stronger revolutionary party and army, in 1920 Sun turned to the Comintern (short for Communist International, the organization Lenin had founded to promote Communist revolution throughout the world). The Comintern sent advisers to Sun, most notably Michael Borodin, who drafted a constitution for the Nationalist Party, giving it a more hierarchical chain of command. When some party members thought it resembled the Communist model too closely, Sun countered that "the capitalist countries will never be sympathetic to our Party. Sympathy can only be expected from Russia, the oppressed nations, and the oppressed peoples."[9]

By 1925 there were about one thousand Russian military advisers in China helping the Nationalists build a party army. Chinese officers were also sent to the Soviet Union, including Chiang Kaishek, who was sent there for four months' training in 1923. On Chiang's return, Borodin helped him set up the Huangpu (Whampoa) Military Academy, near Guangzhou, and the Soviet Union made a substantial contribution to its costs. The Communist Zhou Enlai, recently returned from France, became deputy head of this academy's political education department. The first class was admitted in 1924 with nearly five hundred cadets ages seventeen to twenty-four. The cadet corps was indoctrinated in Sun's Three Principles of the People and dedicated to the rebuilding of national unity. As they rose within the Nationalist army, the former cadets remained fiercely loyal to Chiang.

At the same time that Comintern advisers were aiding the buildup of the Nationalists' power base, they continued to guide the development of a Chinese Communist Party (discussed in Chapter 26). This party grew slowly, and at no time in the 1920s or 1930s did it have nearly as many members or supporters as the Nationalist Party. In 1922, on Comintern urging, the two parties formed a united front, as a

---

8. Cited in Anna Louise Strong, *China's Millions* (New York: Coward-McCann, 1928), p. 125.

9. Cited in C. Martin Wilbur and Julie Lien-ying How, *Missionaries of Revolution* (Cambridge, Mass.: Harvard University Press, 1989), p. 92.

consequence of which members of the Communist Party joined the Nationalist Party as individuals but continued separate Communist Party activities on the side. Sun Yatsen endorsed this policy, confident that the Nationalist Party would not be threatened by a small number of Communists and eager to tap all possible resources for building a strong state.

Among those the Comintern sent to Guangzhou was Ho Chi Minh, a Vietnamese who had become a Communist in France and gone to Moscow to work at Comintern headquarters. Ho spent much of the next twenty years in China and Hong Kong organizing a Vietnamese Communist movement among Vietnamese patriots in exile in south China.

Nationalism continued to grow during the 1920s, as one incident after another served to remind people of China's subjection to the imperialist powers. On May 30, 1925, police in the foreign-run International Settlement of Shanghai fired on unarmed demonstrators, killing eleven. Three weeks later, a sympathy protest in Guangzhou led foreign troops to open fire, killing fifty-two demonstrators. A fifteen-month boycott of British goods and trade with Hong Kong followed. The time seemed ripe to mobilize patriots across the country to fight the twin evils of warlordism and imperialism.

In 1925, before the planned Northern Expedition to reunify the country could be mounted, Sun Yatsen died of cancer. The recently reorganized Nationalist Party soon suffered strain between the leftists, who shared many of the goals of the Communists, and the rightists, who thought Borodin had too much power and the Communists were acting like a party within the party. Nevertheless, in July 1926, the two-pronged Northern Expedition was finally launched with Chiang Kaishek as military commander and Russian advisers helping with strategy. Communists and members of the left wing of the Nationalist Party formed an advanced guard, organizing peasants and workers along the way to support the revolution. Many warlords joined the cause; others were defeated. By the end of 1926, the Nationalist government was moved from Guangzhou to Wuhan, where the left wing of the party became dominant. By early 1927, the army was ready to attack Shanghai. This would mark the end of the United Front, a topic taken up in Chapter 26.

SUMMARY

How different was China in 1927, compared to 1900? Two thousand years of monarchical government had come to an end. Nationalism had become a powerful force. Political parties had come into existence. Through the spread of modern schools, the outpouring of new publications, and much more extensive study abroad, a much larger proportion of the population knew something of western countries and western ideas. Confucianism was no longer taken to be an obvious good. Radically new ideas such as individualism and democracy were widely discussed and advocated. Young people with modern educations had become important political actors as protesters and agitators. Women had come to play much more public roles in society. An urban proletariat had come into existence with the growth of factories in the major cities.

SUGGESTED READING

An authoritative source for the Republican period is J. Fairbank, ed., *The Cambridge History of China*, vols. 12 and 13 (1983, 1986). Overviews of China in the twentieth century are provided in the texts by Spence, Hsu, Fairbank, and Schoppa, mentioned in earlier chapters. See also J. Sheridan, *China in Disintegration: The Republican Era in Chinese History, 1912–1949*

(1975). A useful reference work is H. Boorman and R. Howard, eds., *Biographical Dictionary of Republican China,* 4 vols. (1967–1977).

The collapse of the monarchical system is treated in M. Wright, ed., *China in Revolution: The First Phase, 1900–1913* (1968); E. Rhoads, *Manchu and Han: Ethnic Relations and Political Power in Late Qing and Early Republican China, 1861–1928* (2000); and H. Schiffrin, *Sun Yat-sen: Reluctant Revolutionary* (1980). For the aftermath of the revolution, see E. McCord, *The Power of the Gun: The Emergence of Modern Chinese Warlordism* (1993).

The intellectual and culture changes of the May Fourth era have attracted many scholars. See T. Chow, *The May Fourth Movement: Intellectual Revolution in Modern China* (1960); L. Lee, *The Romantic Generation of Chinese Writers* (1973); Y. Lin, *The Crisis of Chinese Consciousness: Radical Antitraditionalism in the May Fourth Era* (1979); V. Schwarz, *The Chinese Enlightenment: Intellectuals and the Legacy of the May Fourth Movement of 1919* (1986); W. Yeh, *Provincial Passages* (1996); J. Spence, *The Gate of Heavenly Peace: The Chinese and Their Revolution, 1895–1980* (1981); L. Li, *Student Nationalism in China* (1994); J. Fitzgerald, *Awakening China* (1996);

and M. Goldman and L. Lee, eds., *An Intellectual History of Modern China* (2002).

On women's participation in the movements of the period, see K. Ono, *Chinese Women in a Century of Revolution* (1989); W. Zheng, *Women in the Chinese Enlightenment: Oral and Textual Histories* (1999); and C. Gilmartin, *Engendering the Chinese Revolution: Radical Women, Communist Politics, and Mass Movements in the 1920s* (1995).

Social change is considered in D. Strand, *Rickshaw Beijing: City People and Politics in the 1920s* (1989). The industrial and commercial economy are analyzed in L. Li, *China's Silk Trade: Traditional Industry in the Modern World, 1842–1937* (1981); S. Cochran, *Big Business in China: Sino-Foreign Rivalry in the Cigarette Business, 1890–1930* (1980) and *Encountering Chinese Networks: Western, Japanese, and Chinese Corporations in China, 1880–1937;* and M. Bergere, *The Golden Age of the Chinese Bourgeoisie, 1911–1937* (1990). The lives of urban factory workers are documented in G. Hershatter, *Workers of Tianjin, 1900–1949* (1986), and E. Honig, *Sisters and Strangers: Women in the Shanghai Cotton Mills, 1919–1949* (1986).

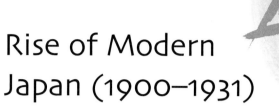

Rise of Modern
Japan (1900–1931)

The early 1900s found Japan ever more deeply entangled in world affairs. Wars on the Asian continent brought it colonies and complicated notions of national identity. Contradictory impulses toward democracy and totalitarianism, modernity and atavism marked the home front. The state impinged more directly than before on the everyday lives of Japanese citizens. The same mechanisms that allowed it to do so—conscription, education, and mass media—provided channels for people to create new organizations at the community level, oppose state policies, and define individual goals. Changes in the economic structure heightened the importance of industrial labor and the fears of social unrest. A new middle class provided a ready market for popular culture. The most visible signs of modern life concentrated in the cities, to the disgust of people who located the preserve of Japanese values in pristine communities of the countryside.

The first decades of the twentieth century are often analyzed to explain what came after. To what extent was Japan's descent into fascism preordained? Why consider countervailing forces, given that they failed? What is this period's legacy for postwar Japan?

A FLUID INTERNATIONAL ORDER

In the 1900s, foreign relations resonated throughout Japan's economy, politics, society, and culture. The imperative to challenge white supremacy by achieving great power status and rising in the hierarchy of nations shaped Japan's national identity. Colonies came to be seen as an economic necessity, both to supply raw materials for Japan's emerging industries and to provide living space for Japan's teeming population.

Japan began the drive for great power status by signing an alliance with Britain in 1902 and going to war against Russia in 1904–1905.

The alliance committed each country to come to the defense of the other should a third party join the enemy in time of war. It functioned as planned against Russia. Russia's leasehold on the Liaodong peninsula and fortification of Port Arthur threatened Japan's interests in Korea. When Russia refused to make concessions, Japan's military launched a surprise attack on Port Arthur. It hoped to win a short war before Russia could mobilize its larger army and bring it to the scene of battle, but the siege dragged on longer than expected. By the time Port Arthur fell, Japan's army was exhausted. U.S. President Theodore Roosevelt offered to negotiate a peace settlement. The Treaty of Portsmouth gave Japan the southern half of Sakhalin, Russia's leasehold on the Liaodong peninsula, the South Manchurian Railway built by the Russians between Port Arthur and Mukden and its associated mining concessions, and Russian acknowledgment of Japan's paramountcy in Korea. In demonstrating that a "yellow race" could beat the "whites," Japan inspired Asians with hopes that they could throw off the colonial yoke.

Japan landed troops in Korea two days before it declared war on Russia. Two weeks later, it forced the Korean king to accept a limited protectorate that made Korea Japan's ally and subject to Japan's lead in administrative matters. The Japanese army then occupied the country. Six months later, Korea had to accept Japanese financial and diplomatic advisers. They reformed the currency and drew up a government budget. They took over the communications system for reasons of national security. The army imposed martial law to prevent sabotage. The Taft-Katsura agreement of 1905 acknowledged Japan's control of Korea in return for Japan's acquiescence in the U.S. colonization of the Philippines. In 1906, Korea became a Japanese protectorate with Itō Hirobumi as resident general. Government offices had to obey Japanese advisers, courts came under the jurisdiction of Japanese judges, the Korean army was disbanded, a Japanese police force maintained order, and Japan took

Cartoon of Amaterasu and Britannia. This cartoon of Amaterasu and Britannia celebrates the 1902 signing of the Anglo-Japanese alliance. The goddesses representing Japan and Great Britain cast their benevolent protection over Korea. *(Saitama Municipal Cartoon Art Museum/DNPArchives.com)*

over Korea's diplomatic relations. When the king complained to the Hague Peace Conference of 1907, Itō forced him to abdicate. In 1909 a Korean nationalist assassinated Itō. In 1910 Japan annexed Korea. At the same time, Japan formalized control over Taiwan. Both remained in the Japanese empire for the next thirty-five years, and Japan had joined the ranks of imperial powers. (See Map 24.1.)

Japan envisioned that its empire would bring not only prestige, but also coal and iron for its factories, food for its people, a market for the export of finished products, and space for its expanding population. Taiwan supplied sugar

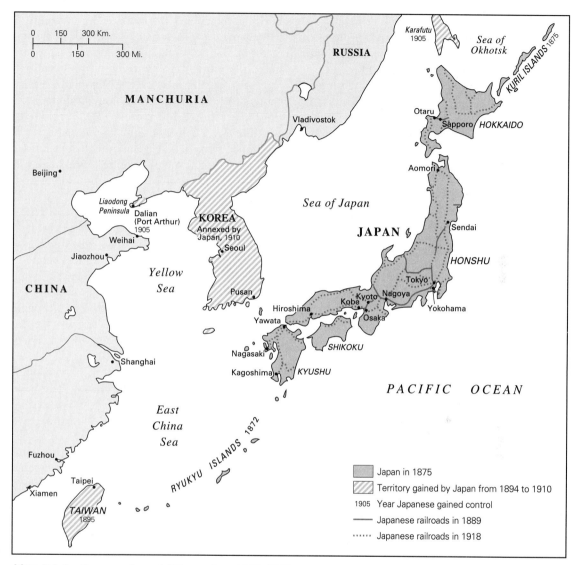

Map 24.1   Japanese Imperial Expansion, 1868–1910

financed by Japanese capital and, after 1920, rice produced on family farms that inadvertently promoted the island's economic development. The Oriental Development Company bought land in Korea to sell to Japanese settlers, channeled capital to Japanese-owned businesses, and participated in the development of Manchurian mines. The military government improved the infrastructure by building roads, railways, and opening schools. It ruthlessly suppressed all dissent.

Japanese who migrated to Korea enjoyed a higher standard of living than Koreans and special privileges in education and employment.

World War I proved advantageous for Japan both economically and diplomatically. Its alliance with Britain allowed it to absorb Germany's leasehold on China's Shandong province and acquire a mandate over German-held islands in the Pacific. In 1918, Japan invaded Siberia along with Allied forces. Japan also tried to impose the infamous Twenty-One Demands on China. Most of them ratified and prolonged Japan's existing privileges in Manchuria and along the China coast. The last set of "requests" would have turned China into a Japanese protectorate. A public outcry in China and abroad forced Japan to back down. The Chinese complained bitterly about the Twenty-One Demands at the Versailles Peace Conference, but to no avail. Despite the open door policy promoted by the United States, no western power was willing to challenge Japan's interests in China.

Following World War I, Japan collaborated with western powers. It joined the League of Nations. In 1921 it participated in the multilateral Washington Conference designed to preserve the status quo in the Pacific and China and prevent a new naval arms race. A delegation of Japanese businessmen sent abroad in 1921–1922 demonstrated Japan's commitment to participation in the developed world's economy. Japan had been unable to get a clause on racial equality in the Versailles Peace Treaty, and in 1924, the United States offended Japan by passing the Oriental Exclusion Act. Despite this insult, Japan signed the Kellogg-Briand Pact of 1928 that outlawed war in the settlement of international disputes. In 1930 civilian diplomats agreed to additional naval limitations in the London Naval Treaty over the navy's objections and without addressing the military's concerns regarding China. When the army acted on its own to take over Manchuria, it ended the era of cooperation with the West.

ECONOMIC DEVELOPMENT

In the early twentieth century, Japanese corporations took advantage of international technological and managerial innovations often called the "second industrial revolution." Japan's electrical technology became second to none. Electric streetcars appeared in Tokyo in 1904. Of Japanese households, 85 percent had electricity in 1935 compared to 68 percent in the United States. Techniques of mass production required both standardized equipment and scientific management or Taylorism, an American theory of rational labor practice that Japan adapted to make the work force more efficient. Localities hoping to attract businesses developed research centers to find foreign technology, channel it to the factory floor, and modify foreign products for domestic consumption. Large enterprises developed new metallurgical and chemical technologies, often at the prompting of the Japanese military, which promoted the automobile and the airplane.

A dual structure characterized Japan's modern economy. Conglomerates linked through holding and trading companies called *zaibatsu* (financial cliques) dominated the most modern sectors of the economy—mining, shipbuilding, machinery, steel, and chemicals—and produced standardized, high-volume products. Although each company within the *zaibatsu* pursued a single enterprise and remained legally distinct, access to the *zaibatsu's* capital through its bank, a central advisory committee that set policy and long-term goals, and interlocking boards of directors tied them together. In some cases *zaibatsu* cooperated in cartels that divided up raw materials and access to markets as in the textile industry and maritime shipping. *Zaibatsu* chairmen enjoyed access to bureaucrats and cabinet ministers, who steered public investment their way and smoothed the regulatory road. Small firms found niches as makers of specialty items and basic consumer goods such as processed food, housing, and clothing. They produced ceramics and toys for export by the *zaibatsu* and functioned as suppliers and subcontractors to the large enterprises.

Japan's industrial sector was well placed to take advantage of World War I. Coal fueled locomotives, factories, and generators. Steel works had capacity to spare. Mitsubishi both built ships and operated a worldwide shipping line in competition with the Sumitomo-backed OSK shipping company. These and other enterprises profited from the Allies' demand for munitions and war-related material. Japanese textiles and consumer goods filled the vacuum

Real National Income Produced, 1878–1936
(million yen at 1928–1932 prices)

Year	Total	Primary Industry	Secondary Industry	Tertiary Industry
1878	1,117	691	95	331
1890	2,308	1,429	224	655
1900	3,640	1,671	818	1,151
1914	5,665	2,127	1,354	2,184
1920	6,316	2,147	1,686	2,483
1925	9,268	2,779	2,216	4,273
1929	10,962	2,740	2,911	5,311
1930	12,715	2,477	3,550	6,688
1931	13,726	2,372	3,716	7,638
1932	13,843	2,594	3,987	7,262
1936	16,133	3,149	5,096	7,888

Primary industry = agriculture, forestry, fisheries. Secondary industry = mining, manufacturing, construction, transportation, communication, and utilities. Tertiary industry = commerce and services. Source: G. C. Allen, *A Short Economic History of Modern Japan* (New York: St. Martin's Press, 1981), p. 284.

left by the departure of British exports from Asia. Business profits soared, and Japan's gross national product jumped by 40 percent between 1914 and 1918. The percentage of real national income contributed by manufacturing passed that of agriculture.

Imbalances between different sectors of the economy and cycles of contraction and expansion characterized the 1920s. Japanese companies assumed that demand would continue after World War I. When Britain took back markets in China and South Asia and European manufacturing replaced Japanese exports, they found themselves overextended financially and forced to lay off workers. They had just pulled out of the postwar recession when the Great Kanto Earthquake of September 1, 1923, leveled factories and workshops between Tokyo and Yokohama: one hundred forty thousand people died, and five hundred seventy thousand structures (70 percent of Tokyo and 60 percent of Yokohama) were destroyed. Aftershocks ruptured gas and water pipes, snapped electrical lines, and halted transportation and communications. Most companies rebuilt using generous credit

provided through the government to banks, which led to a credit crisis in 1927. Trouble came to the domestic market when silk sales slipped and cotton mills in China cut into Japan's biggest Asian market. In contrast to stagnation and decline in the textile industry and agricultural sector, old *zaibatsu* grew by absorbing existing enterprises and diversifying into new areas. Founded in 1908, the Chisso chemical corporation became Japan's third largest manufacturer as a new *zaibatsu* and industrialized northern Korea. When the Great Depression hit at the end of 1929, Japan's economy was already depressed. Japan joined other industrialized nations in imposing steep tariffs on imports, secure in the knowledge that except for oil and scrap iron used in making steel, its colonies had given it the requirements for an autarchic economy.

CONSTITUTIONAL GOVERNMENT

In the public's eyes, the oligarchs' efforts to control the selection of cabinet ministers demonstrated the persistence of clique government dominated by men from Satsuma and Chōshū. To counter Itō Hirobumi's influence in the lower house, Yamagata Aritomo forged a faction of conservative bureaucrats, members of the Privy Council and the upper house, and prefectural governors. In 1907 he made it possible for the military to issue orders in the emperor's name independent of the prime minister. Itō's protégé among elected politicians, Hara Takashi, had experience in the Foreign Ministry and the business world that helped him to arrange compromises between the oligarchs and the Diet and showed him the way to manipulate the bureaucracy. During the Russo-Japanese War, Hara promised Seiyūkai support for the cabinet, and in return, he convinced Yamagata to trust him with the powerful position of home minister.

Hara used his control over the Home Ministry to make the Seiyūkai the dominant party in the Diet. The home ministry appointed prefectural governors and district chiefs. It ran the police, the health bureau, and the public works bureau. Hara worked with bureaucrats in the Tokyo office and built a following for Seiyūkai in prefectural offices. Since prefectural officials supervised elections and influenced the local economy, a prefecture with a bureaucracy that supported the Seiyūkai was likely to elect Seiyūkai politicians to the Diet. Hara also perfected pork barrel politics. Unlike the early parties that simply opposed government spending and tried to cut taxes, the Seiyūkai followed a "positive policy" of government spending for economic development. Railroad lines spidered across the country, linking cities, towns, and centers of Seiyūkai support in remote mountain villages. Roads, schools, bridges, irrigation works, and harbors blessed the districts that voted Seiyūkai.

Even before Hara became prime minister in 1918, Diet members had mastered manipulating the electorate. Businessmen provided political funds in return for favors. They also offered politicians and bureaucrats positions on their companies' boards of directors. In buying votes,

some Diet members relied on election brokers. Others used prefectural assembly members, tainting them as well with the stench of corruption. Playing on Yamagata's fears of a socialist revolution following the Bolshevik takeover in Russia and nationwide rice riots in Japan in 1918, Hara convinced him that party control of an expanded electorate was the safest way to channel popular unrest. The 1919 expansion of the electorate to 5 percent of the population benefited small landlords, not urban workers. In 1921 an unemployed railroad worker assassinated Hara because of what he saw as Hara's disdain for the military.

Between 1924 and 1932, selection of the cabinet shifted back and forth between the two major parties in the lower house. Former bureaucrats and prefectural governors became politicians and ran for the Diet. Although it was not in Seiyūkai's interest to widen the electorate, the pressure of public opinion, maneuvering by other political parties, and the Privy Council's fear of social upheaval led the Diet to pass a bill for universal suffrage for males over age twenty-five in 1925. In the next election three years later, eight proletarian candidates were elected out of four hundred fifty contested seats.

The politics of compromise developed by Hara continued after party cabinets became the rule. The Privy Council, House of Peers, much of the bureaucracy, and the military remained beyond the parties' control. Despite the efforts of the constitutional scholar Minobe Tatsukichi to devise a theoretical legitimization for party cabinets, they rested on neither law nor precedent but on a pragmatic balance of power.

The crises that bedeviled Japan in the late 1920s and early 1930s tested the limits of constitutionally sanctioned parliamentary democracy. Japan had to deal with the Great Depression and fears of Russian or Chinese threats to Manchuria. Right-wing ultranationalists inside the military and outside the government accused the parties of having traitorously weakened Japan by their corrupt pursuit of self-interest. In 1930, one of their number attacked Prime Minister Hamaguchi Osachi for having signed the controversial

London Naval Treaty. He died nine months later. Convinced that the party cabinet was about to sacrifice Japan's interests in Asia, colonels in the army acted unilaterally in taking over Manchuria. The early months of 1932 saw the assassinations of a former finance minister and an industrialist blamed for hardships brought by the depression. Prime Minister Inukai Tsuyoshi also died at the hands of a group of naval cadets, junior army officers, and civilians. The next prime minister was a military man, as were his successors to 1945 with two exceptions, both of whom supported the military. The parties still dominated the lower house, but they received only minor cabinet appointments. Even during the war, the Diet continued to function. The cabinet continued to decide policy, although the military's right of access to the emperor precluded debate over its actions. The constitution remained the law of the land.

Imperial Democracy

According to critics in Japan before World War II, liberalism's focus on the individual contradicted the notion that all Japanese were part of the same body politic, *kokutai,* also translated as "national essence." Democracy was a foreign import, antithetical to indigenous custom based on harmony, consensus, and service to the emperor. Many Japanese people proved them wrong by striving for a more open government and society. In the early twentieth century, the struggle for democracy engaged academic theorists, journalists, feminists, outcasts, and the working men and women who expressed themselves in riots and efforts to organize unions.

For Japanese intellectuals, liberalism meant representative government, constitutionalism, and rule by law. It meant individual rights and freedom from undue governmental interference in the individual's life. It distinguished between the naturalness of society and the artifice of the state. The problem for liberals was that imperial ideology defined the emperor as present at society's inception. The imperial institution was not to be analyzed as though it were an artificial construct because it united state and society. Liberals were patriots. They approved of the government's efforts to promote industrialization and make Japan the equal of the West, and they never questioned the centrality of the emperor.

Intellectuals who professed liberal views jeopardized their careers. Yoshino Sakuzō had to resign his position at Tokyo University because he had argued that the people are the basis of the state and the aim of the state is to promote their well-being. The public interest, that of people as a whole, has to supersede the private, partial interests of oligarchs, bureaucrats, politicians, and businessmen. Minobe Tatsukichi argued that according to the constitution, the Diet, in particular the lower house, was the organ that represented the people. Sovereignty lay not in the emperor but in the state, and the emperor was one of its organs. In 1935 he was accused of disrespect for the emperor, his writings banned, and his membership in the upper house revoked.

Educated women promoted democracy through their organizations and deeds. Teachers, many of them Christian or influenced by missionaries, hoped to improve and reform society. The Woman's Christian Temperance Union found adherents in Japan because men's drinking wrecked the home. In 1886 the Tokyo Women's Reform Society opposed concubinage and prostitution, both deemed trafficking in women. Since the oligarchs kept concubines and the Meiji emperor fathered the crown prince on a concubine, the notion that civilized behavior included sexual fidelity was a hard sell. More acceptable was the Reform Society's work in aiding earthquake victims and providing financial support for former prostitutes. In 1901 members of the Reform Society joined the Greater Japan Women's Patriotic Association. Under its auspices they could speak in public to women, and they received government support for their activities.

The staging of Henrik Ibsen's *A Doll's House* in 1911 and inauguration of the journal *Bluestocking* marked the arrival of the "new woman" in Japan. The play offered a scandalous alternative to the government-sponsored ideology of "good wife and wise mother" when Nora walked out on husband and children. Matsui Sumako who played Nora gained fame as Japan's first western-style actress. Her tumultuous private life dramatized her rejection of domesticity. *Bluestocking* started as a literary magazine, but it soon became a forum for discussing women's roles and expectations. The feminist activist Hiratsuka Raichō and the poet, translator, and social critic Yosano Akiko debated state support for motherhood, Hiratsuka wanting government protection, Yosano arguing that state support would be degrading and would cost women their independence. They agreed that marriage is not sacrosanct, patriarchy need not go unchallenged, and women ought to have equal legal, educational, and social rights.

In the 1920s, feminists advocated family planning and women's suffrage. Katō Shidzue brought Margaret Sanger to Japan in 1924 to promote birth control as a way to deal with the threat to family budgets and women's health posed by too many children. The government refused Sanger permission to land until she promised to make no public speeches. The examples of Britain and the United States that granted women the vote after World War I and the growing numbers of women who followed politics in mass circulation newspapers and magazines convinced some politicians and bureaucrats that political rights for women marked advanced societies. In 1922 the Diet revoked the law that barred women from political meetings. In 1931 a bill for local women's suffrage passed the lower house but foundered on a conservative coalition in the House of Peers. Give women the right to vote, and they will stop having children, predicted one baron. The end to party cabinets stymied proposals for women's political rights.

Mass Movements

Modern mass movements emerged in the context of Japanese imperialism. In 1905, newspapers and speechmakers informed the public that the Russo-Japanese War had concluded without the indemnity that a great power deserved from a defeated foe and with slight territorial gain to justify the sacrifices made by Japanese troops. Riots began at Tokyo's Hibiya Park outside the palace and continued for three days, destroying over 70 percent of police boxes that provided shelter for policemen stationed across the city and fifteen trams. (See Map 24.2.) Smaller riots erupted in Kobe and Yokohama. All but two of the forty-four prefectures reported rallies in cities, towns, and villages. Between 1905 and the rice riots of 1918, Tokyo experienced nine serious riots, many part of larger movements that swept the nation. Although rioters attacked police stations and government offices, they did so in the name of the emperor. By conflating imperial and popular will, they differentiated between evil advisers behind the throne and the throne itself.

The rice riots of 1918 protested high prices, degrading work conditions, and governmental ineptitude. They began with fishermen's wives who organized demonstrations along the Toyama coast and grew to include urban rioters who castigated war profiteers and asserted a right to free speech, tenant farmers who demanded lower rents and decent treatment from landlords, and coal miners who demanded higher wages and respect as human beings. Out of them grew the mass movements of the 1920s for *burakumin* (outcast) liberation and labor organization.

Outcasts found that the Meiji transformation did not improve their lot. Losing the monopoly over leather work and other lucrative, if unpleasant, tasks brought poverty. The household registration system made it well nigh impossible for outcasts to escape their past. Schools refused to admit them, employers to hire them, landlords to rent to them, public baths and barbers to serve them, and other Japanese to marry them. When conscripted into the military, they were assigned menial tasks and never promoted. In the early twentieth century, the central government set up advisory committees to deal with the issue of poverty lest

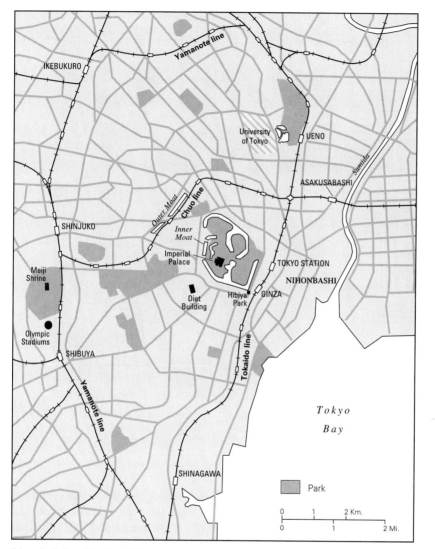

Map **24.2** **Modern Tokyo**

socialism creep into Japan. Since *burakumin* were among the worst off, they became one focus. In 1908 the cabinet encouraged them to emigrate. In 1911 the Home Ministry started to distribute funds for the improvement of *burakumin* communities, and in 1920 it started the Harmony Movement to mobilize the *burakumin* to work for gradual reform. Private organizations lent support. Both assumed that the reason for discrimination lay in *burakumin* filth, ignorance, and immorality. In 1922, a group of

young *burakumin* organized the Leveller's Society (*Suiheisha*) to protest discrimination and promote the equality of all Japanese subjects before the emperor.

The *burakumin* liberation movement of the 1920s blamed the *burakumin*'s problems on prejudice and discrimination. The goal was to change social attitudes, but Leveller's Society members could not agree on tactics. Some believed in educational programs and nonviolent confrontations that aimed at greater democracy. Others wanted

Women Supporters of the Suiheisha. This nation-wide organization tried to end discrimination against burakumin in the 1920s. These women were from the Fukuoka branch in northern Kyushu. *(50 Years of History of Suiheisha by Buraku Liberation Publishing House/DNP Archives.com)*

a social revolution to overthrow capitalism through challenging institutions and individuals known to oppose fair practices. Denunciation campaigns targeted primary schools that permitted students and staff to insult *burakumin* or public officials and individuals who had uttered derogatory remarks. The offenders would have to offer an apology, sometimes publicized in newspapers. In 1926, the first year of the Shōwa emperor's reign, antimilitarism plus anger at the treatment of conscript *burakumin* led to a movement promoting noncompliance with military organizations. Despite police repression, denunciation campaigns continued into the 1930s. Only after the outbreak of the China war in 1937 did the Leveller's Society agree to support national unity and the war effort.

Tenant farmers and industrial workers tried to gain acceptance for their organizations and legitimacy for their grievances. The 1898 Civil Code gave landlords the right to buy, sell, and lease land without any protection for tenants who might have farmed it for generations. Of Japan's farm families, 28 percent owned no land, while another 41 percent owned some and rented the rest. Tenants and tenant-owners organized unions in the 1910s to demand rent reductions and the right of cultivation, especially in the most economically advanced regions in central and western Japan, where landlords had previously been in the forefront of encouraging agricultural improvements. The tenants established a national federation in 1922 that grew to nearly seven hundred branches. In the 1920s, over eighteen thousand disputes between tenants and landlords filled police dockets.

Agricultural conditions in the 1930s began badly. The economic downturn in the 1920s when synthetic fabrics replaced silk and the government allowed the import of rice from Asia reduced the demand for agricultural products and unskilled labor. Real income for farm families declined by 30 percent. Unseasonably cold weather in the agriculturally backward northeast brought crop failures between 1931 and 1933. Landlords tried to repossess tenanted land, refused to reduce rents, or even tried to raise them. Debt-ridden farmers migrated to Japan's overseas colonies or sold their daughters into prostitution. Tenants petitioned the Agriculture Ministry for rural relief. The ministry responded by organizing cooperatives and providing funds for development. In central and western Japan, where absentee landlords no longer performed ceremonial and support functions, tenants lost their former deference. Their habit of looking on the land they cultivated as theirs led to rent refusals and conflict. By the mid-1930s, being a landlord was more trouble that it was worth. With the coming of war in 1937, agricultural conditions improved when the government moved to limit rice imports, and tenant unions disbanded in the drive for national unity.

Industrial development led to labor activism, though not labor solidarity. Heavy industry employed highly skilled and relatively well-paid male workers sufficiently educated to read newspapers and understand socialist theory. Textile mills continued to hire cheaper and, it was hoped, docile women and girls. Even in 1930, they constituted over 50 percent of the factory work force. Urban women found jobs as teachers, journalists, nurses, clerks, ticket sellers, bus conductors, telephone operators, actresses, and café hostesses. Small firms employed male and female workers at low wages to manufacture parts for other sectors of the economy. Below them were rickshaw pullers and delivery boys. At the bottom were the miners.

Worker grievances and the ability to organize varied across industries and within factories. The 1907 riot at the Ashio mine originated with ore diggers, the most highly paid workers, not copper refinery workers whose wages had recently dropped and who feared being laid off. The expansion in heavy industry and the need to raise productivity prompted factory owners to reduce worker autonomy and eliminate the bosses who contracted for specific jobs. Workers countered with demands that they be treated with respect. (See **Documents: Negotiations Between Strike Group Representatives and Company Directors.**) In 1912 they organized the Friendship Society (Yūaikai) to provide mutual aid, self-improvement classes, and improved relations with employers. If workers worked hard and deferred to foremen, then the factory owners ought to treat them with benevolence. To keep skilled workers, employers instituted a seniority system of raises and offered fringe benefits.

In many cases, implementation of paternalistic benefits came only after workers had launched work stoppages and strikes. Over one hundred labor disputes erupted between 1902 and 1917. In 1919 the Hara cabinet interpreted the Public Order and Police Act of 1900 to mean that workers might organize unions and go on strike so long as they remained nonviolent. In 1921 the Yūaikai became the Japan Federation of Labor. Union membership burgeoned in the 1920s, although it never included more than 8 percent of the industrial work force. Hundreds of strikes a year roiled both heavy and textile industries. Although owners resisted unionization, workers bargained collectively for higher wages, severance pay, a minimum wage, better working conditions, shorter workdays, an end to child labor, and improved housing.

Minorities

Although nationalist propaganda assured Japanese people that they were uniquely homogeneous, the pairing of colonialism and modernity created groups perceived as different. The

DOCUMENTS

Negotiations Between Strike Group Representatives and Company Directors

This confrontation between strike group representatives Itō, Iwasa, and Shiga and company directors for the Yokohama Dock Company Tōjō and Miyanaga on September 28, 1921, exposes conflict between workers and management over work conditions and financial issues such as wages and severance pay. The hyperbole on both sides scarcely conceals fundamentally different attitudes regarding company goals, the value of work, and the treatment of workers.

Itō: Today the three of us have come as worker representatives with this petition.

Miyanaga: Does this demand for a 20 percent daily wage increase mean an average wage increase of 20 percent for all the workers?

Iwasa: Our wages average 1 yen 60 sen. Out of 1,000 people, if there is one getting 3 yen, the rest are getting around 1 yen 40 sen. With days off, one month is 25 days and, with a wife and children, we can't make ends meet. This is why we have asked for a pay raise. With the present severance pay, if one of us is fired, he is reduced to poverty.

Miyanaga: We want you to understand the company's situation. As you are well aware, the economy, especially the shipbuilding industry, is facing a severe depression. The question of how to support the workers in this situation is one that troubles us greatly. Because of the shipbuilding depression there have been many layoffs, and aware of your anxiety about this, the other day we announced that we would not carry out any large-scale layoffs. As for ship repairs, which this company has been engaged in since its founding, in good times we were able to charge the shipowners a good price, but today the situation is so bad that, even if we offer a price below cost, they won't take it.

Shipbuilding revived briefly after the war and we were able to make some profit, but now we are making no profit and are taking orders at a loss. In this depression, we are taking on such orders because we do not want to have to lay off you workers. We understand well your plight, but, even at present pay levels, the situation is as I have described, so we would hope to have your understanding regarding the pay raise. You also raised demands regarding severance and retirement pay. As I have already noted, our policy is to avoid layoffs at all costs in the hopes that this will reduce your anxiety, so we would like to gain your understanding on these points also. As for the fourth demand, you use the term "expel." Does that mean you want us to fire them?

All three: That's right.

Miyanaga: You want us to fire the three factory heads. However, the decision to take action against those who break company regulations does rest with these people. Although we hope to avoid such situations, every day two or three people are fired for breaking company rules, and there was nothing exceptional in the case of these three. Thus it would be difficult to take action [and fire the supervisors who had

government defined the Ainu as "formerly indigenous people" and demanded that they assimilate into the Japanese mainstream by renouncing their peripatetic lifestyle and settling

in villages. Officials who supervised their transformation into tenant farmers, laborers, and welfare recipients in the course of selling off their lands and opening Hokkaido to develop-

fired three union members.] As for what the company will do in the future, we feel it would be best to work to harmonize your desires with those of the company and work from a position of mutual understanding. We are presently studying ways to promote your welfare. In due time, we are hoping to implement these plans. Thus we would like to gain your understanding regarding both the company's present position and future plans and have you pass this on to your fellow workers.

Itō: Are you saying you will absolutely not lay off any workers?

Miyanaga: I can't promise "absolutely" but . . .

Miyanaga and Itō (together): Insofar as possible.

Itō: In that case wouldn't it be better to decide on severance pay and relieve our anxieties in that way?

Miyanaga: Our thinking is that is would be even kinder to take the policy of avoiding layoffs rather than getting involved in the severance pay issue.

Itō: So you mean to say that there is no necessity to decide on severance pay? If your policy is not to lay off workers, well, this is a bit of an extreme example, but in that case wouldn't it be just as well to set severance pay at 10 to 20 thousand yen?

Miyanaga: I didn't say that there was no need. We are now considering the issue of severance pay.

Itō: You say "insofar as possible," but does that mean that in the eventuality of a layoff, you will handle it as in the past?

Miyanaga: We are now also considering the possibility of increasing the level in the future.

Iwasa: Isn't what you are saying merely that, if you accept our demands, your profit will be narrowed? For us this is a matter of life and death.

Miyanaga: You say "our profits are narrowed," but in fact, not only are we not expecting any profit, but the company is going so far as to operate at a loss.

Itō: We have already heard at length from Mr. Yamaguchi on this point and understand it well. In any case, we regard the fact that the company will not now announce its intention to change the present severance pay as an indication of the company's total lack of sincerity regarding this entire affair. Let's go back and report this to all the others.

Miyanaga: You say that we are insincere, but as I have already explained the company is striving to promote your welfare and guarantee your security, and we'd like you to report this to the others.

Iwasa: The other day a worker named Tsukui, who was working in one of your manufacturing shops, was fired for going to another shop and talking to a worker there. You said that this was a violation of company rules, so he was fired. But this is something which other workers are constantly doing. If you look for such little matters and fire someone everyday, pretty soon you'll have fired all the workers. Therefore, all your kind words are just the attitude of a man who stands laughing after having strangled seven people. We'll go and report this situation to all the other workers.

Source: Andrew Gordon, *The Evolution of Labor Relations in Japan: Heavy Industry, 1853–1955* (Cambridge, Mass.: Council on East Asian Studies, Harvard University, 1985), pp. 116–119, modified.

ment saw them as a dying race. Many Ainu accepted the necessity of assimilation despite discrimination at the hands of employers, teachers, and non-Ainu neighbors. Others objected to contradictory policies that made them use the Japanese language and forgo tattooing and earrings while setting them up as tourist attractions and anthropological exhibits. During the 1920s,

Ainu scholars recorded Ainu songs, legends, and customs. Ainu activists created self-help programs to cope with alcoholism and violence. Social critics drew on radical thought to counter prejudice and discrimination. Fearful lest Hokkaido go red with the Soviet Union so close to its border, government officials and assimilationist Ainu founded the Ainu Society in 1930 to improve the individual lot through education and to remind Ainu of the gratitude they owed the emperor.

The government's attitude toward the Ryukyus was more complicated. The land tax was not imposed in the Ryukyus until 1903. Ryukyuans had a social hierarchy topped by a monarch and aristocracy that made sense in the eyes of Japanese accustomed to inherent social inequality. Ryukyuan nobles used their status to gain favors from the prefectural governor's office and insisted on their right to speak for the commoners. To be placed on a par with Ainu was, they felt, an insult to their superior culture.

Nearly three hundred thousand Koreans lived in Japan by 1930. The earliest arrivals in the late nineteenth century were students of Japan's resistance to western imperialism. Next came workers forced from their villages by colonial policies that expropriated land and put Japan's dietary needs first. Enticed by labor contractors who promised employment in factories, mines, and construction, workers ended up in low-paying jobs and substandard housing. Excluded from skilled labor except when used to break strikes, they performed dirty and dangerous jobs shunned by Japanese at wages half that of Japanese workers. Although the government made Koreans citizens of Japan and promoted an ideology of racial brotherhood under the emperor, Koreans in Japan were deemed inherently stupid, lazy, bellicose, and vicious. Accused of having set fires and poisoned wells following the Great Kanto Earthquake, thousands died at the hands of Japanese vigilantes.

Koreans who showed intellectual promise earned the mistrust of Japanese officials, who feared, with reason, that they harbored anti-Japanese sentiment. Korean students in Japan suffered arrest, imprisonment, and death for supporting national resistance movements and joining Japanese students who professed universal brotherhood, socialism, and communism. The Osaka Confederation of Korean Laborers earned official enmity when it called for an end to capitalism. Moderate Korean residents feared that opposition to colonialism would only invite repression. They organized mutual aid societies to help Koreans find work, adequate housing, and health care. Government officials promoted assimilation policies to bring Koreans gradually and peacefully into Japanese society, albeit with the proviso that ethnically they could never become Japanese.

Radicals

The government suppressed ideas it deemed dangerous in socialism and other western theories. In 1901 the Socialist Democratic Party enjoyed mere hours of existence before being outlawed. It advocated public ownership of land, capital, and communications; abolition of the military; education funded by the state; workers' rights to unionize; universal suffrage; and abolition of the House of Peers. It did not reject the emperor system, unlike the anarcho-syndicalists Kōtoku Shūsui and Kanno Suga. He opposed capitalists, militarists, aristocrats, and politicians on behalf of workers and farmers. She advocated overthrow of the government and assassination of the emperor. In what is known as the Great Treason Trial of 1911, Kōtoku and Kanno were convicted and sentenced to death, although they were innocent of the charges brought against them. Ōsugi Sakae believed that society consists of two classes: the conquerors and the suppressed. It was up to workers to abolish the state and destroy capitalism. Following the Great Kanto Earthquake, he and his wife, the feminist and anarchist Itō Noe, were strangled by the police. The nihilist Kaneko Fumiko advocated Korean independence. She died in prison. In 1933, the proletarian writer Kobayashi Takiji, who had graphically depicted the brutal conditions of fishermen in *The Cannery Boat* (1929), died at the hands of the police.

During the 1920s, a few socialists enjoyed a brief opportunity to propagate their views. The Red Wave Society founded in 1921 urged women to join the fight against capitalist society that enslaved them inside and outside the home. Sakai Toshihiko organized a study group to discuss socialist ideas in the late 1890s. In 1922 he participated in the secret founding of the Japanese Communist Party. Inuta Shigeru launched a literary movement that advocated self-rule for farmers through land reform. Kawakami Hajime took a torturous path from religious movements and nationalism to Marxism, revolutionary communism, and the study of historical materialism. Between 1927 and 1937, socialists and Communists debated the nature of Japanese capitalism, seeking to find a balance between universal Marxist categories and the Japanese experience that determined the kinds of political action possible in the present. The Peace Preservation Law of 1925 promised punishment for attacks on the emperor system or capitalism. In the early 1930s, the police arrested over ten thousand people a year for propagating ideas disloyal to the emperor and dangerous to the *kokutai*. Their intent was to induce a repudiation of socialist thought and conversion to a belief in Japan's sacred mission. Men and women who refused to confess and convert remained in prison until after World War II.

MODERN URBAN CULTURE

Industrial growth and expansion of the government bureaucracy created a new middle class of salaried white-collar workers. (See **Material Culture: Houses for the Middle Class.**) In contrast to the old middle class of shopkeepers and landlords, these workers got their jobs through educational achievement and enjoyed the security of lifetime employment with fringe benefits such as subsidized housing and medical care. Income depended on seniority as much as proficiency or accomplishment. In his novels *Sanshirō* (1908) and *Kokoro* (1914), Natsume Sōseki depicted socially mobile young men from the countryside. Sanshirō found himself torn between an academic career, the glittering world of business, and a return to his village. *Kokoro* expressed the sense that the era of great expectations passed with the death of the Meiji emperor in 1912. His son, the Taishō emperor, was universally seen as a lesser figure. In the 1920s the opportunities for becoming extremely rich declined, but the new middle class continued to grow.

The Great Kanto Earthquake of 1923 that brought down brick buildings and wooden houses ushered in modern Japanese culture. The new Tokyo had more ferro-concrete. Even before the earthquake, the new middle class had started moving south and west of the city limits. Private railroads and the real estate developers who owned them intensified this trend. With the exception of the publishing industry, light industry moved east of the city; heavy industry moved south to Kawasaki. The space left behind filled with offices, retail shops, and entertainment arcades.

Modern culture incorporated a second wave of westernization driven not by national goals but individual inclinations. Dry goods stores had already transformed themselves into department stores at the turn of the century. After the earthquake, they added theaters, galleries, exhibition halls, and rooftop arcades. In 1926, vending machines started providing refreshment for travelers at Tokyo and Ueno stations. In 1927, the first subway in Asia connected corporate headquarters in Ginza with movie houses and cafés in Asakusa. Mass transit changed urban patterns of work, family life, leisure, and consumption. Unlike the old middle class that lived behind their business and shopped in the neighborhood, the white-collar worker commuted

MATERIAL CULTURE

Houses for the Middle Class

Houses built after the Great Kanto Earthquake for the new middle class were derived from western architectural styles. Rooms had fewer functions but greater privacy than before. They had walls and doors and were further separated from one another by corridors. Guests were received on the first floor at the front of the house in the parlor, decorated with sofa, chairs, antimacassars, and carpet on a hardwood floor beneath a small chandelier. In line with the changing social etiquette of the time, guests were discouraged from making unexpected calls, and the telephone gave them little excuse for doing so. The family living room overlooked the garden. Although located on the dark north side of the house, the kitchen had a floor. Bedrooms were on the second floor. A modern water supply made it possible for each house to have its own bath.

New middle-class furnishings were designed chiefly for entertainment and the convenience of the family, especially the wife, rather than being objects with which to impress guests. The living room ideally contained a phonograph and radio. Appliances included the gas range for cooking, a gas heater with ceramic grill, an electric fan, and an electric rice cooker. For reasons of etiquette and security, old-style houses had required that someone always be home to greet guests and guard the premises. Western-style front doors made it easy for the housewife to lock the door and go shopping, visit friends, or see a movie.

Modern Living Room. This modern living room was photographed for the journal *Homu raifu* (Home Life). Chairs, tables, potted plants, sofa, and cushions provide a western-style backdrop for the woman wearing kimono.

from his suburban home to his work downtown. The entertainment districts that grew up around train terminals enticed him to spend evenings at coffee shops and cafés.

The new middle class consumed a modern culture removed from politics. Mass literacy spurred the development of mass media. Self-help books and magazines taught the rudiments of popular science, how to be modern, how to succeed in business, and how to create the perfect home environment. (See Color Plate 28.) By 1920, eleven hundred newspapers found 6 to 7 million buyers. Registered magazines were ten times that number. Journals for men appealed to the highbrow, the middlebrow, and the vulgar. Women's journals, calibrated according to class, girls' journals, and boys' journals divided the market into ever more discrete segments. Retail bookstores jumped from three thousand in 1914 to over ten thousand in 1927. They sold complete editions of western authors in translation, serious works of idealist philosophy by the Kyoto School, novels by bestselling authors such as Tanizaki Junichirō (male) and Uno Chiyo (female), and illustrated books given to escapist sensationalism. Cinemas showed films from abroad alongside domestically produced animated cartoons and historical dramas. Movie stars became celebrities. Government-operated radio stations started broadcasting in the mid-1920s. Record companies churned out patriotic songs. Popular music celebrated romantic love and the delights of Tokyo, including hanging out in Ginza. A cheap escape from the workaday world was to watch small balls bounce down a pachinko board, the vertical version of the pinball machine.

Modern mass culture promoted a privatizing world of pleasure and self-expression. Women danced in chorus lines and performed in the Takarazuka Girl's Theater. (See **Biography: Kobayashi Ichizō.**) In the novel *Naomi* (1924–1925), Tanizaki depicted the transformation of a café waitress into a *modan gaaru* (modern girl; *moga* for short) who bobbed her hair, wore revealing dresses, and danced the Charleston. The *moga*'s less flamboyant companion was the *mobo* (modern boy). Together they scandalized onlookers by smoking cigarettes and holding hands in public. The late 1920s are often characterized by the words *ero, guro,* and *nansensu*—eroticism, grotesquerie, and nonsense, referring to both the flood of foreign words in urban vocabularies and the perceived decline in public morals. Materialism, individualism, and decadence had apparently replaced the beautiful Japanese virtues of diligence, decorum, and duty.

ALTERNATIVES TO MODERNITY

People repelled by modern culture found solace in folk traditions of rural Japan, high art of ancient Japan, and communities of the devout created by the new religions. Ethnographer Yanagita Kunio sought a cultural authenticity that had been lost in urban areas. He traveled from Tohoku to the Ryukyus, collecting folk tales and documenting what he viewed as pristine customs of the folk. Industrialist and builder of the Mitsui *zaibatsu* Masuda Takashi tried to preserve Japan's artistic patrimony and supported the government's system for designating cultural artifacts as national treasures. First established in 1897, the designation applied foremost to religious objects from the Kyoto area, declared Japan's sovereignty over its past, magnified differences between Japan and the outside world, and demonstrated that Japan possessed the trappings of world-class culture.

The new religions provided alternative visions of modernity that did not please the state. Deguchi Onisaburō, the organizer of Ōmoto-kyō, criticized government policies that disadvantaged the poor. In the 1920s, he proclaimed that as the Maitreya, he would establish a new order on earth, a message that found believers even among government officials and army officers. In the early 1930s, he founded a semimilitaristic youth group to restore the kingdom of God at the Ōmoto-kyō headquarters. Ōmoto-kyō was suppressed in 1921 and again in 1935. New religions

BIOGRAPHY   Kobayashi Ichizō

Entrepreneur, politician, and diplomat, Kobayashi Ichizō (1873–1957) fostered consumer culture by founding a railroad, a department store, a baseball team, and the Takarazuka Girl's Theater.

Kobayashi had wanted to become a writer, but after graduating from Keiō University, he joined the Mitsui Bank in 1893. In 1906 he left the bank to become executive director for a private electrical railroad near Osaka. Through hard work and creative planning in the building of new lines and improving service, he made his company dominant in train travel between Osaka and Kobe. In 1918 he became president of the newly named Hankyū electric railroad. To attract riders he expanded into real estate development by building suburban housing developments for the new middle class.

Kobayashi's interests tended toward popular culture. One of his train lines went to Takarazuka, a fading hot springs resort. To lure customers, he built a zoo and, in 1913, the Takarazuka Girl's Theater. In 1919 he founded the Takarazuka Music Academy to train young women for his productions. The first revue with chorus line and musical spectaculars was *Mon Paris,* staged in 1927. Having watched commuters surge through the Hankyū terminal in Osaka, he opened a market adjacent to the station in 1924. Five years later it became the Hankyū department store with restaurants, an art gallery, and a bookstore. Kobayashi also founded the Tōhō Cinema Company to make and distribute films. He built his movie empire with a mass audience in mind by scheduling show times and setting ticket prices for the benefit of workers. In 1936 he joined other railroad magnates and real estate developers to establish Japan's first professional baseball league to give people another reason to ride trains in search of entertainment. Loyal fans still cheer the Hankyū Braves. In 1940 Kobayashi reached the pinnacle of his career by becoming commerce and industry minister and special ambassador in charge of trade to the Netherlands.

Kobayashi insisted that the performers in the Takarazuka Girl's Theater be of unquestionable virtue; his aim was to provide entertainment for respectable women and to mold his actresses' character so that they could later perform as good wives and wise mothers on their most important stage, the home. The Music Academy provided training in etiquette, ethics, and homemaking as well as singing and dancing. On stage women played male roles; they also played Asians from countries incorporated into the Japanese empire. Lest actresses aspire to make the theater a profession, Kobayashi insisted that they retire at the peak of their popularity while they were still considered young enough to make a good match.

Source: Based on Jennifer E. Robertson, *Takarazuka: Sexual Politics and Popular Culture in Modern Japan* (Berkeley: University of California Press, 1998).

founded after 1905 more commonly based their teachings on Nichiren Buddhism and answered the needs of uprooted, underprivileged masses in the cities. Charismatic leaders preached a gospel of social equality and promised either a pure new world or salvation to come. They emphasized faith healing, deliverance from suffering, and a focus on this world's benefits. For recent urban migrants, the new religions provided self-help groups, a sense of identity, and a community that was neither self-righteously traditional nor alienating modern.

Twentieth-century agrarianism exhibited more virulent antimodernism. It identified agriculture as the ethical foundation of the state when agriculture was no longer the country's main source of wealth. Its adherents professed a farm *bushidō* (way of the warrior) that assimilated the farmers' virtues of diligence, frugality, fortitude, and harmony to loyalty and self-sacrifice on behalf of the state. This agrarianism criticized city life for making people selfish and ambitious; it detested capitalism for increasing the corrupting power of money, destroying the farm family economy, and eroding harmony between city and country. It demanded a spiritual alternative to materialism and a national alternative to universal socialism. Its nostalgic search for a return to a primitive rural society that manifested the *kokutai* frequently turned violent in the 1930s.

SUMMARY

By 1931, modern Japan had parliamentary democracy, an educated citizenry, and an industrialized economy. It also contained conflicting visions of what it meant to be Japanese, who should be incorporated into the nation and how, and what should be Japan's role in the world. The relatively peaceful world of the 1920s allowed space for controversy. When the Great Depression struck in 1930, plural and critical voices within Japan appeared as dangerous as threats from abroad to Japan's economic and national security.

SUGGESTED READING

This period is so well researched by scholars that only a sampling of recent works is listed here. For Japan in Asia, see P. Duus, *The Abacus and the Sword: The Japanese Penetration of Korea, 1895–1910* (1995); P. Duus, R. H. Myers, and M. R. Peattie, eds., *The Japanese Informal Empire in China, 1895–1937* (1989); T. Matsusaka, *The Making of Japanese Manchuria, 1904–1932* (2001); and M. R. Peattie, *Nan'yō: The Rise and Fall of the Japanese in Micronesia, 1885–1945* (1988).

For women, see G. L. Bernstein, ed., *Recreating Japanese Women, 1600–1945* (1991); B. Sato, *The New Japanese Women: Modernity, Media, and Women in Interwar Japan* (2003); and M. Hane, *Reflections on the Way to the Gallows: Rebel Women in Prewar Japan* (1988).

For labor, see A. Gordon, *Labor and Imperial Democracy in Japan* (1991); K. Nimura, *The Ashio Riot of 1907: A Social History of Mining in Japan* (1997); and W. M. Tsutsui, *Manufacturing Ideology: Scientific Management in Twentieth-Century Japan* (1998). For agriculture, see K. Smith, *A Time of Crisis: Japan, the Great Depression, and Rural Revitalization* (2001).

For minorities, see R. Siddle, *Race, Resistance and the Ainu of Japan* (1996); I. Neary, *Political Protest and Social Control in Prewar Japan: The Origins of Buraku Liberation* (1989); and M. Weiner, *Race and Migration in Imperial Japan* (1994). For riots, see M. L. Lewis, *Rioters and Citizens: Mass Protest in Imperial Japan* (1990).

For modern life, see S. A. Hastings, *Neighborhood and Nation in Tokyo, 1905–1937* (1995); S. Garon, *Molding Japanese Minds: The State in Everyday Life* (1997); J. Sand, *House and Home in Modern Japan: Architecture, Domestic Space and Bourgeois Culture, 1880–1930* (2003); and E. K. Tipton and J. Clark, eds., *Being Modern in Japan: Culture and Society from the 1910s to the 1930s* (2000).

CHAPTER TWENTY-FIVE

The Loss of Korean Independence and Colonial Rule (1896–1945)

After the Sino-Japanese War ended in 1895, Korea had an all too brief period to save itself from subjugation to Japan. It failed to do so and lost its independence for thirty-five years. That period was disruptive because it involved major social, economic, cultural, and ideological transformations that entailed both much human suffering and possibilities for development. Liberation from colonial rule as a consequence of the U.S. victory over Japan in 1945 should have resulted in the restoration of a healthy independence for Korea, but the development of nationalism and the introduction of communism created the basis for political division that began soon after 1945 and was caught up in the maelstrom of the Cold War conflict between the United States and the Soviet Union.

There are three major issues of contention among scholars. Should attention be focused mainly on the suffering of the Korean people under Japanese oppression or on the progress made in economic development, modern education, the liberation of women, and the introduction of modern culture? A second is should anti-Japanese guerrilla fighters be given greater credit for their patriotic resistance to Japanese imperialism over cultural nationalists, who acquiesced to Japanese control and sought to educate the masses to higher national consciousness over the long term, and expatriate nationalists in the United States, who sought to persuade western nations to liberate Korea? Finally, were the Communists greater patriots than the non-Communists because they fought against the Japanese in China and Manchuria versus the Korean landlords and businessmen who not

Queen Myŏngsŏng. Queen Myŏngsŏng (a.k.a. Queen Min of the Yŏhŭng Min family), 1851–1895, was assassinated by Japanese thugs and soldiers in the palace in 1895. *(5,000 Years of Korean Art, p. 183)*

only prospered under Japan, but supported Japanese efforts in the late 1930s to eliminate Korean language and culture? Should the landlords and businessmen be absolved of the charge of collaboration because they had no choice but to survive under Japanese rule?

THE TRANSITION TO COLONIAL RULE (1896–1905)

In 1896 King Kojong escaped from his palace, where he was under the watch of Japanese

guards, and fled to the Russian embassy. Once there, he dismissed the reform cabinet. The reform ministers were killed by street mobs, and the new, conservative cabinet reversed the topknot edict and many reforms. The Japanese were forced to withdraw from direct involvement in Korean domestic affairs, and Russia gained the upper hand in Korea. Strapped for funds to pay off indemnities and finance his government, King Kojong began to lease rights to the exploitation of natural resources like lumber to the Russians, gold mines to the Americans, and railroad construction to the Japanese and others in return for loans.

Early Nationalist Movements

Popular reaction against the king's sacrifice of national resources gave rise to the first explicitly nationalist movement, the Independence Club, in 1896. The club demanded the dismissal of corrupt officials and strove to educate people on the need to modernize the country. It organized street meetings and education sessions and established a newspaper, *The Independent* (*Tongnip sinmun*), written in the vernacular language instead of classical Chinese. Membership in the group increased as its leaders made public speeches, established branches in small towns, campaigned for the construction of an Independence Gate as a sign of liberation from subservience to China, held mass meetings and demonstrations in Seoul, and demanded and received a couple of dozen seats on the king's council. Its leaders included men like Sŏ Chaep'il (also called Philip Jaisohn), an American citizen who returned to Korea; Syngman Rhee (Yi Sŭngman), who had attended Paejae Christian missionary school; and Yun Ch'iho, who visited Japan and was educated in the United States. All these men were fired with the zeal to create a truly independent nation, and some talked of forming a constitutional monarchy.

King Kojong decided in 1897 to change the title of his kingdom to "The Great Empire of Korea" (*Taehan'jeguk*) and adopt the title of emperor, but he had no inclination to tolerate a

King Kojong. This photo depicts King Kojong (king of the Chosŏn Dynasty from 1864–1897; emperor of the Great Han Empire, *Taehan'jeguk*, from 1897–1907) as emperor wearing a military uniform in 1897. *(Sajinuro ponun tongnip undong, vol. 1, p. 42)*

to demand the abolition of concubinage. Esther Park, the first woman doctor, began practice at the Women's Hospital (Pogu yŏgwan) in 1900 and taught sanitation in addition to clinical work.

Russian Influences

Russia had acquired a narrow boundary with northeastern Korea in 1860 and constructed a trans-Siberian railway across Siberia to Vladivostok. In 1896, Russia began construction of a second railway, the Chinese Eastern Railway, which stretched across Manchuria to shorten the distance to Vladivostok. The next year Russia obtained a twenty-five-year lease on the Guandong area, Port Arthur, and the commercial port of Dalian on the Liaodong peninsula, which it had taken away from Japan in 1895, and it obtained railroad rights from there to Harbin to connect with the Chinese Eastern Railway. After Germany established the first sphere of influence in China involving exclusive privileges over trade and railways in the Shandong peninsula in 1897, Russia did the same in Manchuria. The Japanese could only watch these events in ever-growing frustration.

In 1896, while King Kojong was residing in the Russian legation, Russia and Japan signed two agreements (the Komura-Weber Memorandum and the Protocol of Moscow) that granted Russia equal rights with Japan to station legation guards and grant loans to the Korean government. Korea also signed the secret Min-Lobanov Agreement in which Russia promised to protect King Kojong and provide military and financial aid.

The Russo-Japanese War (1904–1905)

In 1897, the Russian position in Korea was compromised when the Japanese revealed the terms of a secret agreement with Russia for possible partition of the Korean peninsula. Japan then opened negotiations with Russia in 1898 for resolving the balance of power between them in northeast Asia. The Japanese wanted Russia to recognize Japan's sphere of influence

constitutional monarchy or a republic. He banned the Independence Club suddenly in 1898 and imprisoned its members. Yun Ch'iho went into hiding, and Syngman Rhee was jailed from 1898 to 1904.

The Independence Club had inspired women to debate sexual equality and education. They organized the Ch'anyanghoe (Praise the Lord Society) in 1898 to form a school for women and the Yŏuhoe (Friends of Women) the next year

in Korea in return for Japanese acknowledgment of Russia's sphere in Manchuria. Neither side agreed because neither was willing to sacrifice all interests in Manchuria and Korea. The Nishi-Rosen Agreement between the two powers in April 1898 recognized Korean independence and the right of Japan to pursue commercial and industrial interests in Korea, but it did not solve the fear of future aggression from the other party.

Both countries fought over concessions inside Korea. In 1901 the Japanese made plans to complete the railway between Pusan and Seoul and build a connection from Seoul to Ŭiju while Russia tried to expand its leasehold around the Yalu River and bring soldiers in to defend it. Because of its growing mistrust of Russia, Japan entered into an alliance with Great Britain in 1902. Great Britain would remain neutral if Japan went to war with another country, but if a third country joined in, Great Britain would intervene on Japan's side. This measure prevented both Germany and France from joining with Russia in a repetition of the Triple Intervention of 1895 and opened the possibility of a war by Japan against Russia alone.

Fruitless negotiations continued, and despite a last-ditch appeal by Korea for neutralization of the Korea peninsula, Japanese-Russian relations broke down in February 1904. Japan sent an invasion force to occupy Seoul, thus beginning the Russo-Japanese War. Japanese land forces won the last land battle at Mukden in Manchuria in March 1905, and the Japanese navy under Admiral Tōgō Heihachirō completely destroyed Russia's Baltic fleet in the Tsushima Strait in May. U.S. President Theodore Roosevelt mediated a peace settlement at the Portsmouth Conference that ended the war on September 8, 1905. Russia withdrew from Korea after the Portsmouth Treaty, and Great Britain extended its alliance with Japan and acknowledged its freedom to take any action it saw fit in Korea. That same year, the United States signed the Taft-Katsura Agreement acknowledging Korea as part of the Japanese sphere of interest in return for a Japanese

guarantee of U.S. domination over the Philippines and Guam, which it had captured from Spain in the Spanish-American War of 1898–1900. The United States, which Koreans had hoped would protect them against a foreign predator, betrayed those hopes.

THE INTRODUCTION OF WESTERN TECHNOLOGY AND INFLUENCES

In the last two years of the century, streetcars, electric lights, foreign buildings, a modern hospital, and a bridge over the Han River were introduced to Seoul. The bridge was the first step toward the modern transportation of goods, the reduction of transportation costs, and the expansion of trade.

Women began the fight for equality. After 1900, the royal mint and private textile companies began to hire women workers for the first time. Women's groups were established to pay back the foreign debts incurred by the regime. Others protested administrative corruption, called for independence, and organized participatory groups. Women founded societies in 1906 and 1907 to campaign for women's education, against separation of the sexes, abolition of the shawl to cover women's faces (*ssŭgech'ima*), establishment of a hospital, and publication of new journal, *A Guide for Women* (*Yŏja chinam*). Two of the prominent leaders were Yi Okkyŏng and Helen Kim. Other women, such as Louise Yim, wrote of their struggles to achieve more independence for women (see **Documents: Louise Yim's Writings on Female Independence**).

In 1905, the Tonghak movement changed its name to the Religion of the Heavenly Way (Ch'ŏndogyo). Son Pyŏnghŭi, a Tonghak leader, took a trip to Japan and returned to form the Progressive Party (Chinbohoe), which then linked up with the Unity and Progress Society (Ilchinhoe). Both went a step further than the Independence Club by seeking members from the rural peasants as well as city dwellers. The Unity and Progress Society, under Song

DOCUMENTS

Louise Yim's Writings on Female Independence

Louise Yim (Im Yŏngsin) was a rare patriot who suffered torture for participating in the resistance against Japanese rule. She earned a B.A. and M.A. from the University of Southern California and served in the Republic of Korea National Assembly after the Korean War. She began her career as a protester against Korean conventions, including the restrictions against women's education and independence and early arranged marriage.

On Grammar School

Often I stood outside the boys' school which my father had started and I would listen to the boys repeating the lessons after their teacher. One day after the boys had gone home I went inside the little, square, mud-walled building.

"May I speak?" I asked Cho Tugy, the teacher.

He was so startled that he dropped a pencil. Then he saw me and smiled.

"If I may have the honor to listen," he replied formally.

"Would it be possible for a girl to learn how to read and write?"

He said nothing for a little while. I was afraid he would laugh and send me home. Then he said:

"If the gods have given you the courage to ask, we can hope they have given you the power to learn, little one. Come to school anytime and I will teach you."

By the time I was twelve [1912], there were rumors that Korean girls were going to be forced to marry Japanese. Therefore, all parents were in a hurry to get their daughters married. My sister was to marry soon and my turn was to be next.

One day, two women came to my room. I knew right away who they were. They were matchmakers. I had never hated anybody as much as I did those two women. I felt as though they were trying to imprison me. Instead of answering their questions, I questioned them and I lectured them. They were shocked and sometimes they put their hands to their faces and moaned as I spoke.

I told them it was a crime to force marriage on a girl too young to know what it was all about. This was almost too much for them to bear. A Korean child was not supposed to speak this way to her elders.

When they left, I heard one say to the other, "We will speak to her mother. She will come to no good, that one. Her blood is wild."

On High School, ca. 1916

I knew then that the masculine belief that females did not have a place in the national life of Korea was the belief of men who knew nothing about women and in their ignorance shut them out of the family's life too. It has always been a great mystery to me why men think that women are different from them intellectually. I wish I could go to every man and tell him that besides certain physical differences and the ability of a woman to bear children, a woman thinks of all the things a man does. Just because she allows herself to be exiled in the kitchen a woman does not give up her feelings as an individual.

_____

Source: Louise Yim, *My Forty Year Fight for Korea* (Seoul: Chungang University, 1964), pp. 27, 39, 56.

Pyŏngjun, however, favored Japanese leadership in achieving reform and volunteered to assist Japanese forces during the Russo-Japanese War, a collaborationist act that drove the Progressive Party from its alliance with the society.

During its war with Russia, Japan appointed advisers in all the Korean ministries, and in November 1905, it established a protectorate over Korea. When Emperor Kojong and several of his ministers refused to sign the protectorate treaty, Itō Hirobumi, who was in charge of the negotiations with the Chosŏn court, ignored the king and declared that a majority of ministers had approved it. Min Yonghwan of the Yŏhŭng Min clan and military aide to the emperor committed suicide in protest.

The Japanese government created a new residency general for Korea and appointed Itō to head it. He was directly responsible to the Japanese emperor instead of the Japanese cabinet, which meant that there were no constitutional limits on his arbitrary exercise of power, a precedent carried over after annexation in 1910. Itō's vision was to maintain an "independent" Korean government that would willingly carry out institutional reforms under Japanese guidance. He opposed other Japanese leaders who preferred outright annexation. Nevertheless, Itō used the Japanese police, gendarmerie, and regular army units to maintain order while Emperor Kojong was left on the throne as a figurehead.

Emperor Kojong secretly sent messages to the heads of foreign states in Europe for help in gaining independence, and the American missionary, Homer Hulbert, led a mission to the Hague Conference to present the Korean case, but it was refused admission because they lacked proper credentials. Itō then appointed the opportunist Yi Wanyong to the post of prime minister and Song Pyŏngjun, an advocate of Kojong's abdication, to the cabinet. In 1907 Yi and Song persuaded Kojong to appoint the crown prince as acting monarch, but then immediately declared erroneously that he had abdicated.

Riots broke out in the street during the accession ceremony for the new emperor, Sunjong, but Itō ordered the dissolution of the Korean army. The discharged soldiers began a guerrilla war that lasted for four years before it was crushed by superior Japanese forces, resulting in the loss of thousands of lives. The Home Ministry under Song Pyŏngjun took charge of peace preservation, banned freedom of association, and instituted censorship of the press and book publication.

In 1909 Itō Hirobumi resigned from his position as resident general and agreed to a Japanese cabinet decision to annex Korea. His plan to maintain a facade of Japanese paternalism behind a nominally independent Korea failed in the face of Korean opposition. When Itō made a trip to Harbin to gain Russian acquiescence to the annexation, he was assassinated by An Chunggŭn, a Korean patriot. The new resident general, Terauchi Masatake, clamped down on all criticism of Japanese policy and forced the Koreans to sign the treaty of annexation on August 22, 1910, thus ending Korea's national sovereignty.

JAPANESE COLONIAL RULE (1910–1945)

Japanese colonial rule went through three distinct phases. The first was the period of military rule (*budan seiji*) from 1910 to 1919, during which the Japanese created a police state called the Government-General (GG) of Chōsen. The new regime eliminated all Korean political participation, restricted and banned serious business activity, and invested heavily in the promotion of rice cultivation for the export of rice to Japan. It instituted flogging as punishment for minor offenses even though it had been banished in Japan in 1882. In addition, the GG granted extensive authority to the police to use violence on the spot, levy fines, detain suspects for long periods, and use torture in interrogation.

Despite the draconian nature of the regime, the Korean nationalist movement continued its work underground, mainly through religious groups like the Christians, the religion of the

Heavenly Way (Ch'ŏndogyo), and the Buddhists because the Japanese were reluctant to persecute Christianity and offend western nations. The nationalist movement burst forth right under the noses of the Japanese authorities on March 1, 1919, when thirty-three patriots signed a Declaration of Independence and marched peacefully to the Japanese authorities to petition for liberation. They had been inspired by Woodrow Wilson's call for self-determination for people subject to foreign rule, and they expected support from the United States and other western powers. As opposed to the Independence Club, the participants in the March First movement came from all walks of life and from all over the country, marking a significant spread of national consciousness.

Tragically, the Japanese responded to the non-violent demonstrations with mass arrests and executions. The western powers paid no attention. Nonetheless, the Japanese government in Tokyo under Prime Minister Hara Takashi shifted to a "cultural government" policy (*bunka seiji*) for Korea, which allowed a certain degree of freedom of speech and association and permitted the formation of Korean businesses. That policy marked the second phase of colonial rule and lasted until the Manchurian Incident of 1931, when the Japanese army in Manchuria launched a coup d'état against the Chinese governor and established the puppet state of Manchukuo.

The third phase lasted from the Manchurian Incident to the defeat of Japan by the United States in 1945 (see **Connections: World War II**). During this period Japan invested huge amounts of capital in heavy industry and infrastructure in Korea in support of Japan's expansion into Manchuria in 1931 and China after 1935. Japan initiated the second Sino-Japanese War in 1937, attacked Pearl Harbor before declaring war in 1941, and invaded Singapore, Indochina, and Burma. Japan severely repressed the freedoms of the 1920s in Korea, and after 1937 it instituted military conscription, forced labor, and forced assimilation of Koreans. It forced Koreans to use the Japanese language exclu-

sively, worship the Japanese emperor in Shinto shrines, and adopt Japanese names in an effort to eradicate Korean identity.

Scholars' views of the colonial period in Korea generally fall into two broad categories. The first is a totally negative view of Japanese colonialism, including its cruel and tyrannical behavior, its exploitation of the Korean economy, its reduction of the mass of the population to bare subsistence, its prevention of modern industrial development, and its attempt to obliterate Korean culture without granting equal citizenship rights. The second is a more positive attempt to fit the colonial experience into major trends that lasted to the end of the twentieth century. These trends included abolishing inherited social status as a barrier to advancement; liberating women from male domination; introducing modern mass education for both sexes; creating a modern economy through heavy investment in railroads, bridges, and harbors; establishing a modern financial sector in the 1920s; and industrializing the peninsula in the 1930s. A small middle class of businessmen and shopkeepers was formed, and a half-million peasants were converted to factory wage workers and miners. In retrospect, the most important economic contribution was Japan's use of state-led industrialization involving planning and controls of all kinds in the process of late industrialization to catch up to the advanced economies of the western imperialists. This process, now known as developmentalism, was a far cry from the free-market capitalism of Britain and the United States in the nineteenth century, but it opened the eyes of some Koreans to economic development without liberal democracy.

The Land Survey

Colonial economic policy was based on the expansion of agricultural production in Korea by investment in reclamation, irrigation, chemical fertilizer, and the introduction of new seeds to provide for rice exports to Japan. To create an efficient land tax for raising revenue, the colonial government adopted a land registration program in 1911 to record accurately the owners of all land. Korean nationalists and many scholars have condemned this policy as a sham designed to transfer land from Korean owners to Japanese by force or guile. The Japanese justified it on the grounds that land ownership had not been clearly established in law in the Chosŏn Dynasty. Private landownership had been the economic basis of the Korean elite at least for a thousand years, but the security of tenure was weak because judges in civil cases were district magistrates of *yangban* families who defended landlord interests. Written evidence of land ownership did exist in the form of deeds, inheritance documents, bills of sale, and state registers of land, but not every owner possessed those. Because landowners hoped to avoid registering their land with the state to avoid taxes, the late Chosŏn state lacked the funds to modernize its military and fund development projects.

The Japanese land investigation program did not result in a major transfer of land from Korean to Japanese hands. That took place only because of the world depression of 1929 when indebted smallholding peasants lost their land to creditors. From 1910 to 1925 there was an economic boom in Korea and a rise in the price of rice. The Korean landlords, most of whom were *yangban,* fared far better than the sharecroppers, and the Japanese succeeded in winning *yangban* landlords' compliance to colonial rule by granting them noble titles and guaranteeing their private property rights. As a result, the landlords played very little role in the development of active nationalist resistance to Japanese rule.

The influx of cheap Korean rice into Japan depressed the price of rice there and caused rice riots there in 1918. By 1940 the price of rice dropped continuously to only 39 percent of the 1925 price. Korean peasants who both owned and rented land earned a reasonable living, but pure tenants did not. Rice consumption declined because of exports to Japan, and although the diet was supplemented by millet from Manchuria, Koreans perceived this as a serious deprivation of their favorite staple food.

The Chosŏn Labor-Farmer General Alliance was established in 1924 to address the many tenant disputes of the 1920s and to wage class struggle against the capitalist class. The farmers later split to form their own General Korean Farmer Alliance. Middle peasants, rather than the poorest sharecroppers, led the tenant disputes and demanded sharecropping reduction from 50 to 40 percent or less of the crop. Most tenant disputes ended favorably before 1925, but after 1929 many smallholders went bankrupt. Tenants tried to preserve their sharecropping contracts, but the percentage of tenant households increased from 41 to 50 percent of the farm population in the 1930s, and the number of tenant unions increased from about 30 in 1922 to 1,301 in 1933. When in 1934 the Japanese ended the policy to promote rice production, agricultural production declined continuously to 1945.

Throughout the 1930s sixty-nine radical red peasant unions challenged local officials until the colonial regime banned all such activity. Thereafter, peasants turned to actions of passive resistance like failing to fulfill contracts or hiding crops from the authorities. In 1933 the Japanese government instituted the Tenancy Mediation Law to resolve tenant disputes in the courts, and many were resolved in favor of the tenants. After Pearl Harbor in 1941, however, the GG banned all tenant protest, exacerbating sharecropper resentment.

The Growth of Korean Industry

In the 1920s Korean businesses sprang up overnight on the basis of limited capital resources. Large landlords used their accumulated savings from tenant rents to launch into a number of small-scale enterprises. One of the best examples of this was the Kyŏngbang textile corporation founded by Kim Yŏnsu and Kim Sŏngsu, members of a landlord family with large landholdings in Chŏlla province. The Kim brothers used capital accumulated from tenant rents to establish the company, but when the company was threatened by bankruptcy, they turned to Japanese banks for working capital that saved the company and allowed it to expand. They also received help from Japanese trading companies in marketing products. The GG provided protection by allowing it to carve out a niche in the cheap textile sector for the Korean economy while Japanese textile companies provided more expensive goods. It also summoned the Kims to offer their opinions in economic policy councils.

By 1919 most Korean companies were confined to undercapitalized small-scale operations in dyeing, paper, leather, ceramics, milling, and brewing. Korean-owned breweries grew and supplied half the domestic market demand. The Tong'a Rubber Company was capitalized with 300,000 yen by landlords and rich merchants from Mokp'o in South Chŏlla province, and the Pando Rubber company was founded with 50,000 yen raised by a Korean merchant. By 1930, Korean rubber plants outnumbered Japanese thirty to seventeen. The dominant industry in Korean hands besides cheap textiles was food processing. Most Korean metal factories were no more than blacksmiths' shops, but Japan Steel had a big plant at Kyŏmip'o, and Japan Mining had a smelting plant at Chinnamp'o.

Japanese investment in Korea dwarfed the paid-in capital of Korean firms. Among the major Japanese *zaibatsu,* Mitsui founded the Sansei Mining Company, Mitsubishi the Chōsen Anthracite Company, and Noguchi the Chōsen Nitrogen Company to make fertilizer. Japanese also established chemical, electrical, textile, mining, and railroad companies. The purpose was to provide hydroelectric power, railroad lines from Pusan to Sin'ŭiju on the Manchurian border, and cement, chemicals, and the like for exports to China. Japanese businesses purchased large amounts of forest land and invested in cotton textiles, food processing, brewing, milling, paper, and printing. While some argue that the purpose of Japanese economic interest in Korea was to obtain raw materials and markets for Japanese exports, Japan invested more than it ever received in profits because its strategic and political objectives were more important.

In the 1930s Japan invested heavily to build up both infrastructure and industry to support the Japanese puppet state of Manchukuo and to provide essential equipment to support the military there. By 1941 over 90 percent of the capital invested in Korean industry came from Japan. The railroad system had been constructed on the basis of a south-to-north trunk line into Manchuria that could funnel goods from both Japan and Korea to Manchuria and, after the outbreak of the Sino-Japanese War in 1937, to China. Heavy investment in hydroelectric power plants and power along the Yalu River and elsewhere and power lines throughout the country was accompanied by the establishment of steel, chemical, machinery, metal, chemical, and machine factories to support the war effort elsewhere. Most of the weapons were manufactured in Japan, however, while the Korean machine industry was confined to repairs, vehicles, and shipbuilding. Japan subsidized the Mitsui, Mitsubishi, and Sumitomo *zaibatsu* to mine copper, zinc, manganese, tungsten, molybdenum, and other metals for military purposes. The average annual growth in all industrial production in the 1930s was 15 percent, almost double the rate from 1910 to 1928.

Nevertheless, Koreans were allowed small-scale businesses. They owned about a fifth of metal and machine and tools plants; ceramics, wood and lumber, and chemicals; roughly half of pharmaceutical companies, rice mills, and printing; over 70 percent of beverages; and over 90 percent of textile firms. The large Korean Kyŏngbang textile corporation did not hesitate to take advantage of Japanese expansion by setting up textile plants in Manchuria and buying up a textile plant in Nanjing after the Nanjing massacre there during the second Sino-Japanese War of 1937. When Kyŏngbang had labor problems over wages and working conditions, it summoned the Japanese police to put down strikes. Other Korean businessmen like Min T'aesik, Min Kyusik, and Pak Hŭngsik were also financed by the Japanese Development Bank (Shokusan ginkō). Pak Hŭngsik established the Hwasin Department Store and became one of the wealthiest Korean business-men in the period, and Yi Pyŏngch'ŏl started with a rice mill and then prospered in the liquor business.

Businessmen like Kim Sŏngsu of the Kyŏng-bang Corporation garnered a reputation after liberation in 1945 for being "national capital-ists" because they placed the welfare of the Korean nation above collaboration for profit. He and his brother, Kim Yŏnsu, however, had become a full partner in Japanese imperialism on the continent. Other prosperous Korean businessmen could not have survived unless they collaborated with the Japanese, but recently they have been condemned for collaboration.

Although the Japanese did not aim to improve the welfare of the Korean population, Korea became an industrialized area nonethe-less. The Korean capitalists became the core of a new bourgeoisie, and a miniscule proletariat was expanded in Korea to about five hundred thousand by the time Japan was defeated in 1945, not counting the factory workers, miners, and other forced laborers in Japan and Man-churia during this period. Urbanization was stimulated by the expansion of industry as peas-ants abandoned their homes for higher-paying jobs, and Korea was beginning to take on the lineaments of an advanced industrial economy with most Koreans as the underclass.

Literacy and Education

In the 1920s the colonial government allowed the publication of newspapers, magazines, and books in the Korean language, but it subjected all publications to the sharp eye of the Japanese censors. It expanded primary education beyond what existed in the late Chosŏn Dynasty, but it limited the number of Korean private schools and restricted mass education to a few grades. It founded a single university as part of the impe-rial university system, Keijō (Kyŏngsŏng or Seoul in Korean) Imperial University, but it allowed only a small minority of well-to-do stu-dents to attend it and colleges in Japan.

In the private sector, Kim Sŏngsu, a Korean businessman of the Kyŏngbang Corporation, established the *Tong'a ilbo* (*East Asia Daily*) newspaper and the Posŏng Normal School (later Koryŏ University). Women established educa-tion centers, night schools in churches and rural areas, to educate the illiterate. The Sŏngjukhoe (Pine and Bamboo Society) was founded in 1910 by women to foster national conscious-ness. Helen Kim, a Christian who was later the first person to receive the doctorate in Korean history (from Columbia University in 1929), and other women from the Ewha School took a tour of rural areas to enlighten the public before being shut down by the police. She and Kim Pilye organized the YWCA in 1922, while Bud-dhist women organized the Buddhist Women's Association in 1920. Many women received training in nursing either in Japan or at the Women's Medical College (Pogu yŏgwan) under the missionary nurse Margaret Edmond. The first women's medical school, the Kyŏngsŏng Medical College, was founded in 1928. Women were also hired as workers for the first time by both the Japanese GG and private industry.

The Japanese civil code in 1912 generally con-firmed traditional practices in male succession to family headship, ownership of property, and the sole right of men to initiate divorce. In 1918 women were given the right to petition for divorce, provided they had approval from both their husband and parents. A 1922 ordinance ele-vated the minimal age for marriage for women to fifteen, banned polygamy and concubinage, and allowed a woman to divorce her husband for polygamy or adultery, commission of a crime, insult, and abandonment for three years. Many of the discriminatory practices against women never-theless continued past the end of colonial rule.

In the 1920s two women's journals began publication: Kim Wŏnju's *Sin yŏja* (*The New Woman*) and Na Hyesŏk's *Yŏjagye* (*Women's World*). Socialist women's groups appeared in 1924, and they and the nonsocialists demanded abolition of early marriage, female slavery, licensed prostitution, and wage discrimination.

Korean literature in the vernacular flourished in this period. Yi Kwangsu, whose work was influenced by Tolstoy, published the first modern novel, *Mujŏng* (Heartless) in 1917, followed by *Chaesang* (Rebirth) and *Hŭk* (Earth) by 1933. Hyŏn Chin'gŏn portrayed the suffering of common men and women from traditional customs and colonial rule, but his novel about a Paekche general who resisted Tang armies was banned. Kim Tongin established *Creation* magazine in 1921 and wrote about the denizens of the slums and the life of a shaman. Yi Hyosŏk joined the KAPF (Korean Art Proletarian Federation) literary movement from 1928 to 1932, but he, like almost all other members of KAPF, abandoned socialism to write about itinerant peddlers and the anomie produced by urban life. In 1936 Yi Sang wrote a stream-of-consciousness story, "Wings," about a solipsistic husband who dealt with his wife's prostitution by sealing his mind from the shame of external facts.

Movies first appeared in Korea in the late 1890s, and foreign films were first shown in 1903. After annexation, the Japanese monopolized film production, but the first Korean films appeared: *The Righteous Revenge* (1919) directed by Kim Tosan, and *The Plighted Love under the Moon* (1923), directed by Yun Paengnam. There were close to 9 million moviegoers by 1935. Despite censorship, the movies *Arirang* (1926) and *Searching for Love* (1928), directed by Na Un'gyu, and *Wandering* (1928), by Kim Yuyŏng, produced by the KAPF told stories of oppression of peasants by landlords and the evils of Japanese imperialism. In 1931, however, the Japanese banned Korean films outright.

Radio broadcasting began in 1927 under the Japanese Korean Broadcasting Company. Korean-language programs expanded from one-third to one-half the airtime, and in 1933 the first all-Korean station was allowed. It devoted many programs to Korean history, science, the arts, international affairs, translations of western plays, pop songs with a distinct Korean flavor, and instruction in the use of *han'gŭl* and the standardization of Korean grammar. The Japanese even tolerated Korean language programs after the ban on the use of Korean in 1938. All these programs must have expanded knowledge about Korea and stimulated national consciousness.

The Rise of Communism and Militant Nationalism

The colonial period witnessed the continuing development of nationalism among Koreans. A number of intellectuals looked back on Korea's past and now saw only a sad history of subservience, both political and cultural, to China. Many militant nationalists were attracted to communism after the Russian Revolution of 1917 because Marxist-Leninist theory explained the emergence of western imperialism in economic terms, fit Korea into a universal system of historical development, and promised a chance for modernization and liberation. In addition, the new Soviet state was the only country offering monetary and spiritual support to Koreans for liberation from colonial rule.

Militant nationalists viewed the colonial period in black-and-white terms: one was either a true patriot willing to die for national liberation and independence, or a collaborator who worked with the Japanese and gained riches as a landlord or businessman. Many nationalists expected that a struggle against Japanese rule would kill two birds with one stone by overthrowing the Japanese and Korean capitalists and landlords and achieving Korean independence. They also expected that militancy and struggle were healthy antidotes to Korea's long history of subservience to Chinese power and culture.

Soon after the Russian Revolution of 1917, Yi Tonghwi formed the first Korean Communist Party (KCP) in Siberia. The early Korean Communists were divided geographically by groups in Moscow, Siberia, the Maritime Province of Russia, Manchuria, Shanghai, and Korea proper.

The movement to establish a Korean Provisional Government (KPG) in exile with a provisional national assembly began in April 1919 in Shanghai. The assembly drew up a constitution for a Great Korean People's Republic (Taehan min'guk), and it eventually chose Syngman Rhee (Yi Sŭngman) as president in 1922. Yi Tonghwi, the Communist from Vladivostok and guerrilla commander after 1907, became prime minister. This KPG combined radical left-wing and conservative right-wing elements, but Yi Tonghwi favored military action against Japan while Rhee preferred diplomacy to sway the United States and other powers to intervene on behalf of Korean independence. Yi Tonghwi soon left Shanghai in disdain and returned to Manchuria to resume armed struggle, and Rhee left Shanghai to work in the United States.

Between 1919 and 1924, about fifty Korean anarchists formed a terrorist group, the Ŭiyŏltan (Righteous Heroes), which carried out three hundred acts of violence during the period. After two failed assassination attempts, all three hundred members of the Ŭiyŏltan were exterminated by Japanese police. The patriot and anarchist Sin Ch'aeho founded the Anarchist Black Youth League in 1921, which dissolved in 1924.

Although the colonial government moderated the harsh aspects of the first decade of colonial rule, they increased the number of police and increased surveillance. They also hoped to co-opt potential militants and convert them to the harmless pursuit of educational and cultural projects. Korean nationalists like the author Yi Kwangsu, Yun Ch'iho, and others already believed that the Korean public lacked national consciousness and needed more education to form the basis for a viable nationalist movement. Yi's slogan, *kaejoron* (Reconstruction!), meant just that, but he and the others, known as "cultural nationalists," postponed national independence into the indefinite future.

The Communists and radical non-Communist nationalists, however, claimed that cultural nationalism was tantamount to outright collaboration. This intense nationalism was the product of a new awareness of the long history of Korea's past of supine subordination and subjugation to Chinese dynasties and Chinese culture, particularly to the Confucian ethical justification of tributary relations. Writers like Sin Ch'aeho began a new historiographical tradition of extolling examples of militancy and resistance in the Koguryŏ Dynasty and the leading military heroes of the Korean past. Inside Korea, the Communists supported strikes and succeeded in establishing a Korean Communist Party (KCP) in Korea in 1925, but the Japanese police broke it up, and the Communists abandoned the attempt in 1928.

Korean nationalists were attracted by Marxist theory and Lenin's economic explanation for the rise of imperialism as the product of monopoly capitalism, the last stage of capitalism, in which core capitalist states had saturated their own domestic markets and were seeking colonies around the globe to provide cheap raw materials and markets for their manufactured products. Korean Communists believed that the struggle against Japan would lead simultaneously to the overthrow of capitalism and national liberation. Furthermore, the Soviet Union was the only country in the world willing to offer aid to Koreans and other national liberation movements in European colonies.

The Comintern in Moscow decided that Korea was still in a "feudal" stage of development without a proletariat, and it pushed the Korean Communists to form a united front with the bourgeois nationalists to achieve a bourgeois-democratic revolution. Although the Korean Communists opposed joining their class enemies in a united front, they capitulated to Comintern pressure and joined the united front Singanhoe (New Root Society) in 1927. That took place only a couple of months before Chiang Kaishek, the leader of the Chinese Nationalist Party (Guomindang, or GMD), launched an extermination attack against his Communist allies. In 1927, women organized the Kŭnuhoe (Friends of the Rose of Sharon), which included some socialists and cooperated with the United Front Singanhoe. The Singanhoe helped to organize strikes and tenancy disputes and planned a nationwide protest demonstration after an anti-Japanese student protest movement broke out in Kwangju in Chŏlla province in 1929, but the police arrested the leaders before it could take place. After that, the Singanhoe headquarters turned more moderate and even decided to support the Korean self-government movement and use the legal system to improve conditions, but the Communist members were disaffected by this and called for the dissolution of the Singanhoe in December 1930. The Kŭnuhoe also closed down.

Manchuria

Active Korean resistance against the Japanese began in Manchuria in 1919, but Korean military units were forced to cross the border into the Maritime Province of the Soviet Union by Japanese forces. There they joined Soviet Red Army forces in battles against Japanese armies that had been dispatched to Siberia in 1918 to fight against the new Soviet regime. This action ended when the Soviet Union reached a peace agreement with Japan in 1921, but by 1925 three separate Korean governments were established in Manchuria to handle the affairs of Korean residents in Manchuria.

In 1931 the Japanese "cultural government" policy of limited toleration in Korea came to an end when the Japanese army in Manchuria established the puppet regime of Manchukuo. Northern Jiandao in south Manchuria just north of the Yalu River, where Koreans composed 76 percent of the population, became the center of anti-Japanese activity. Chu Chin, one of four guerrilla commanders in the area, led the nine hundred men of the Second Division of the Northeast People's Revolutionary Army in 1934 and fought hundreds of engagements against the Japanese that year. Kim Il Sung (Kim Ilsŏng), the future leader of the Democratic People's Republic of Korea, organized a small guerrilla unit of eighteen men in Manchuria in 1932.

In 1934, however, the Korean Communist guerrillas were faced with a serious crisis that occurred after the Japanese in Manchuria created the Minsaengdang (People's Welfare Party) to recruit members of the Korean community ostensibly as a defense against "bandits" but actually to infiltrate anti-Japanese Chinese Communist groups. The Chinese Communists

in Manchuria had incorporated Korean Communists in their ranks but insisted that they had to devote themselves entirely to the Chinese struggle against Japan and not dilute the effort by attacking the Japanese in Korea. Now they distrusted their Korean Communist allies for being Minsaengdang spies and began an extermination campaign that killed anywhere from five hundred to two thousand loyal Korean Communists. The Korean patriot Kim San was sent to Manchuria to help smooth relations between the Chinese and Korean Communists but was himself arrested (see **Biography: Kim San**). The persecution continued until March 1935, when the Chinese General Wei Zhengmin called a halt to the persecution. There is circumstantial evidence that Kim Il Sung, who was fluent in Chinese and close friends with Wei, played a crucial role in persuading the Chinese to abandon the persecution.

The Chinese Communists changed their previous policy and offered Kim Il Sung the choice between forming his own unit of several hundred men to operate independently or keeping his unit with Chinese Communist forces. Kim chose to keep his men with a Chinese unit because it afforded a better chance of survival. Some have criticized Kim for subservience to Chinese interests on this occasion, but his decision did enable his guerrilla unit to survive. He then launched the most successful guerrilla raid against the Japanese in the Korean peninsula on June 4, 1937, at Poch'ŏnbo just south of the Yalu River. He occupied it for a day, retreated, defeated a pursuing Japanese police contingent, and a few days later joined another force under Ch'oe Hyŏn to attack the Yokoyama timber camp. Although the attack was followed by a bloody reprisal by the Japanese against the town, Kim earned a reputation for daring heroism.

After Japan initiated a war with China in 1937, it repressed all signs of opposition to Japanese rule among Koreans. The colonial government required all Koreans to attend services at the Japanese shrines (*jinja*) dedicated to the worship of the Japanese emperor, banned the use of the Korean language in the schools and movies, and

BIOGRAPHY Kim San

Kim San (a pseudonym for Chang Chirak; 1905–?) was one of many Korean patriots who became a Communist to fight for Korean national liberation against Japanese imperialism, but he did it by moving to China and joining the Chinese Communist movement because it was easier to fight Japanese imperialism there than by remaining in Korea. In 1937 he was in Mao Zedong's base in Yan'an in northwest China when Helen Foster Snow, journalist Edgar Snow's wife, interviewed him and transcribed his life story into English.

Born to a poor peasant family in 1905 just south of Pyongyang, he was shocked at the age of seven when two Japanese policemen came to his home in 1912 and slapped and bloodied his mother's face because she had delayed reporting for a vaccination. His mother brought him up as a Christian and provided personal warmth, but his father's detachment and harsh discipline turned him away from Confucianism and caused him to run away to live with a married brother nearby.

In grammar school he admired the anti-Japanese guerrillas. He entered a Christian middle school but left it at the age of fourteen to join the March First movement of 1919. Amazed at the passive reaction of praying Christians to the bloody repression of the unarmed civilians by the Japanese, he abandoned Christianity, belief in God, and trust in nonviolence.

He traveled to Tokyo to attend school and was influenced by Japanese anarchists and Marxists. He dropped out of school and moved to Manchuria to attend a Korean Nationalist military school for three months. In 1920 he moved to Shanghai and then in 1921 to Beijing, where he attended the Union Medical College for over three years. He studied Marxist theory and joined the Korean Communist Youth organization, but he left school to join the Chinese Nationalists when the Canton uprising occurred in 1925. After Chiang Kaishek massacred his Communist allies in Shanghai in 1927, he joined the Communists in the Canton Commune. The Nationalists forced him to flee Canton to Peng Pai's Hailufeng Soviet nearby in 1928, and then to escape from Hailufeng through the mountains, where his health was ruined from exposure, malaria, and tuberculosis.

He returned to Beijing to become secretary of the Beijing Communist Party. He was sent to Manchuria in 1932 to smooth relations between the Chinese and Korean Communists there, but he was arrested by the authorities and subjected to water torture for forty days. Released because he refused to confess membership in the Communist Party, he returned to Beijing only to suffer impeachment by fellow Communists for leftist deviation in 1931 and rightist deviation the next year! In 1933 the Chinese Nationalists arrested him briefly. Depressed and near suicide, he recovered and moved to Mao's headquarters in Yan'an in 1937. After that date, neither he nor his two wives and child were heard of again.

He summarized his career as a revolutionary as follows:

My whole life has been a series of failures, and the history of my country has been a history of failure. I have had only one victory—over myself. This one small victory, however, is enough to give me confidence to go on. Fortunately, the tragedy and defeat I have experienced have not broken but strengthened me. I have few illusions left, but I have not lost faith in men and in the ability of men to create history.[1]

---

[1]Nym Wales, *Song of Ariran* (San Francisco: Rampart Press, 1941), p. 315.

Comfort Women. Korean "Comfort women (*wianbu*)," who were abducted by the Japanese to serve as prostitutes for Japanese soldiers on the front, demanding an apology and compensation from Japan, 2000. *(Li Jin-Man/AP/Wide World Photos)*

forced all Koreans to adopt Japanese names. The colonial government requisitioned Koreans for forced labor in Japanese and Manchurian mines and factories (see **Material Culture: Korean Gold Miners**), recruited young men into the Japanese army, and abducted or enticed thousands of Korean women with false promises of jobs and then forced them to become "comfort women"—prostitutes—for Japanese troops in active theaters of operations in China, Manchuria, the South Sea islands, and Southeast Asia.

The Japanese left no wiggle room for Koreans who had prospered under Japanese rule to evade responsibility for leadership in carrying out these programs. Many young Korean men took to the hills to evade forced labor and military conscription, but most were unable to avoid it. There were also those, like Park Chung

Hee (Pak Chunghŭi), the dictator of South Korea from 1961 to 1979, who volunteered and became officers in the Kwantung Army in Manchuria to do battle against opponents of Japanese colonialism, including Korean guerrillas. By contrast, Kim Il Sung fought many battles in Manchuria against the Japanese between 1937 and 1940 until Japanese mopping-up forces eliminated the Chinese Communist armies in Manchuria and forced Kim Il Sung to cross into Russian territory west of Vladivostok by March 1941. Kim's men joined Chinese guerrillas under Zhou Baozhong in a Russian training camp near Vladivostok, and Kim was appointed major in the new 88th Division of the Far Eastern Command of the Soviet army.

Other nationalists struggled for independence outside Manchuria. Korean Communists in China included Kim Wŏnbong, who commanded the Korean Volunteer Corps, and Mu Chŏng, Kim Tubong, and Ch'oe Ch'ang'ik, who commanded Chinese units under Mao Zedong in Yan'an. Non-Communist nationalists like Kim Ku fought with Chinese Nationalist forces. An Ch'angho organized the Hŭngsadan (Corps for Promoting Scholars) in Los Angeles in 1911, joined the KPG in Shanghai, and was arrested in 1932 and sent back to jail in Korea. Syngman Rhee spent two decades in the United States to gain support for Korean liberation. In the end, neither Communists nor non-Communists succeeded in obtaining Korea's independence.

SUMMARY

Japanese colonial rule placed the Korean people under the yoke of a harsh, imperialistic regime that eliminated meaningful participation in the political process. On the other hand, by allowing Korean landlords and businessmen to flourish economically, colonial rule established a few models for successful business operations. By exerting a demonstration effect on the Korean population of successful, rapid, economic development under a powerful, centralized police state, it provided a model to future generations of how to catch up with the West. By breaking down

MATERIAL CULTURE

Korean Gold Miners

In the 1930s the colonial government mobilized Korean laborers to mine alluvial gold in South Chŏlla province. This was part of the Japanese government's mobilization effort after the beginning of the second Sino-Japanese War in 1937. It included forcing Koreans to work in mines in Japan and war materiel factories and to sign up as auxiliaries in the armed forces. Wages were lower than those paid to Japanese, and treatment was so harsh that many Koreans went into hiding or took refuge in the hills to avoid it.

Korean Miners. Korean miners mobilized by the Japanese during the Japanese Colonial Period in the 1930s for mining alluvial gold in South Chŏlla Province. *(Sajinuro ponun Choson sidae: Saenghwal kwa p'ungsok* [The Choson Period in Pictures: Life and Customs] *Seoul: Somundang, 1986, volume on* Independence Movement Through Pictures II, *p. 120)*

hereditary status barriers, it opened opportunities to many people blocked from upward mobility. By introducing a modicum of modern education, it introduced some Koreans to science, foreign languages, and social science—a far cry from the Confucian curriculum of traditional Korea.

Despite the success of the colonial regime in repressing almost all signs of resistance by the

1930s, it created many radical nationalists both Communist and non-Communist who populated the jails or were forced into exile waiting for the chance to return and create some kind of new society. It forced the migration of millions of Koreans from their family farms by removing them from their village communities and subjecting them to the iron discipline of Japanese factories and mines. It created a major contradiction between capitalist industrialists and wealthy landlords versus a new proletariat and a mass of sharecropping tenants. In short, Japanese colonialism had produced both wealth and poverty, contentment and animosity, revolutionary potential and conservative reaction. Whether this mix would lead to peace or disruption depended on whether these contradictions would be resolved peacefully after liberation in 1945.

SUGGESTED READING

For the best work on the period from 1896 to 1910, see E. Kim and H. Kim, *Korea and the Politics of Imperialism* (1967), a political and diplomatic history; Vipin Chandra, *Imperialism, Resistance, and Reform in Late Nineteenth-Century Korea* (1988), a study of the Independence Club; and André Schmid's examination of the reform debate to 1910 in the Korean press in *Korea Between Empires, 1895–1919* (2002). For discussion of Japanese policy in that period, see H. Conroy, *The Japanese Seizure of Korea, 1868–1910* (1960), and P. Duus, *The Abacus and the Sword* (1995). For Russia's relationship with Japan and Korea, see G. Lensen, ed., *Korea and Manchuria Between Russia and Japan 1894–1904* (1966), and A. Malozemoff, *Russian Far Eastern Policy, 1881–1904* (1958).

For the best work on Japanese colonial policy, see Duus, *The Abacus and the Sword*; P. Duus et al., *The Japanese Wartime Empire, 1931–1945* (1996); R. H. Myers and M. R. Peattie, *The Japanese Colonial Empire, 1895–1945* (1984); C. Lee, *Korea, the Politics of Nationalism* (1963); and G. Henderson, *Korea: The Politics of the Vortex* (1968). E. Gragert explored the effects of the Japanese land investigation in *Landownership Under Colonial Rule* (1994).

In economics, C. J. Eckert's *Offspring of Empire* (1991) explored the history of the Kyŏngbang Corporation. S. C. Suh's *Growth and Structural Changes in the Korean Economy* (1978) concentrated on the negative consequences of Japan's economic policy. S. W. Park's *Colonial Industrialization and Labor in Korea* (1999) concentrated on the operations of the Onoda Cement Factory, and G. Shin's *Peasant Protest and Social Change in Colonial Korea* (1996) provides a balanced portrait of tenancy in the 1930s.

The religious history of Protestants is covered by C. Park, *Protestantism and Politics in Korea* (2003), and the political history in K. M. Wells, *New God, New Nation* (1990).

The conflict between cultural nationalists and Communists is handled in M. Robinson's *Cultural Nationalism in Colonial Korea, 1920–1925* (1988), and the best work on Korean communism is found in D. Suh, *The Korean Communist Movement, 1918–1945,* 2 vols. (1981), and *Documents of Korean Communism* (1970); R. Scalapino and C. Lee, *Communism in Korea,* 2 vols. (1972); H. Han, *Wounded Nationalism: The Minsaengdan Incident,* forthcoming; C. Lee, *The Korean Workers' Party: A Short History* (1978); and N. Wales and K. San, *Song of Ariran* (1941).

For a study of comfort women, see G. Hicks, *The Comfort Women* (1994). M. Robinson and G. Shin, eds., *Modernity, Domination, and Identity in Colonial Korea* (1999), contains a variety of articles on the colonial period. B. Cumings includes sharp insights in his general history, *Korea's Place in the Sun* (1997). Translations of literature are found in K. Chong-un and B. Fulton, *A Ready-Made Life* (1998), and P. H. Lee, *Flowers of Fire* (1974).

War and Revolution, China (1927–1949)

During the two decades from 1927 to 1949, China was ruled by the Nationalist Party and its head, Chiang Kaishek. The Nationalist government turned toward the West for help in modernizing the country, but in general was distrustful of intellectuals. In its big cities, above all Shanghai, China took on more of a modern look, with tall buildings, department stores, and western dress. The government had to concentrate most of its energies on military matters, first combating the remaining warlords, then the Communist Party bases, then Japan. The Communist Party attracted a small but highly committed following. Because of the Nationalists' pressure, it was on the run much of the time until a base area was established in Yan'an in 1935, where Mao Zedong emerged as the paramount leader. During the war with Japan (1937–1945), the Communist Party formed itself into a potent revolutionary force, able to mobilize poor peasants into a well-disciplined fighting force. The Civil War of 1947–1949 resulted in the victory of the Communist Party.

The large questions behind much of the scholarly work on this period revolve around the outcome in 1949. Why did May Fourth liberalism decline in significance? Could the economic politics of the Nationalists have brought prosperity to China if Japan had not invaded? How much of a difference did the Comintern's often misguided instructions make to the development of the Communist Party? How crucial was Mao to the way the policies of the party developed? Why did the Nationalist Party and Chiang Kaishek lose the support of the urban middle class?

THE CHINESE COMMUNIST PARTY

With the success of the Bolshevik revolution in Russia in 1917, Chinese intellectuals began to take an interest in Marxism-Leninism, which seemed to provide a blueprint for a world of abundance without exploitation. Communism was scientific, anti-western, anti-imperialist, and successful: it had just proved itself capable of bringing revolution to a backward country. For the May 1919 issue of *New Youth,* Li Dazhao, the librarian at Beijing University, wrote an introduction to Marxist theory, explaining such concepts as class struggle and capitalist exploitation. Soon intellectuals were also looking into the works of Lenin and Trotsky, who predicted an imminent international revolutionary upheaval that would bring an end to imperialism. Although China did not have much of a proletariat to be the vanguard of its revolution, the nation as a whole, Li Dazhao argued, was exploited by the capitalist imperialist countries. In 1920 Li organized a Marxist study group at Beijing University. At much the same time, Chen Duxiu organized one in Shanghai, where he had gone after resigning his university post in Beijing. Another source of knowledge of European Marxism were the thousands of Chinese students, male and female, who had gone to France in 1919 and 1920 to participate in work-study programs. Most worked in factories, where they were introduced to both strikes and Marxism-Leninism.

The early Marxist study groups were offered financial assistance and guidance by the Comintern. In 1920, soon after the Comintern learned of the existence of Marxist study groups in China, agents were sent to help turn the groups into party cells. This entailed teaching "democratic centralism," the secret to party discipline. Each local cell elected delegates to higher levels, up to the national party congress, with its central executive committee and the latter's standing committee. Delegates flowed up, and decisions flowed down. Decisions could be debated within a cell, but once decisions were reached, all were obligated to obey them. This cell structure provided a degree of discipline and centralization beyond anything in the prior repertoire of Chinese organizational behavior.

Following Comintern advice, thirteen delegates met in July 1921 to form the Chinese Communist Party as a secret, exclusive, centralized party. The party broke with the anarchists and guild socialists and asserted the primacy of class struggle. Chen Duxiu was chosen as secretary general. The party agreed to put priority on organizing labor unions and recruiting workers into the party. In Shanghai, the Communist Party oversaw the establishment of a Russian language school, helped organize labor unions, and formed a Socialist Youth Corps.

It was at the insistence of the Comintern, and against the advice of many of the Chinese members, that the decision was made in 1922 to ally with the Nationalists. The United Front between the Nationalist and Communist parties was expedient for both at the time, as they could concentrate on their common foes, the warlords. However, it covered over deep differences. The Nationalist military included many staunch anti-Communists who were appalled by talk of class warfare. One reason the Communists remained in the United Front was that it gave them the opportunity to organize both workers and peasants. Along the route of the Northern Expedition, farmers' associations were established, with membership by the end of 1926 exceeding 1 million people.

The United Front ended in the spring of 1927. On March 21, as the Nationalist army neared Shanghai, the Communist-led General Labor Union called for a general strike. Over six hundred thousand workers responded and seized the city. Flush with victory, they began demanding the return of the foreign concessions. On April 11, the head of the union was invited to the home of the leader of the mafia-like Green Gang, where he was murdered. The next day Green Gang members and soldiers loyal to Chiang attacked union headquarters. Soon soldiers were mowing down civilians with machine guns; an estimated five thousand were killed.

The terror quickly spread to other cities and continued into 1928. The labor union base of the Communist Party was destroyed. Although the party tried to continue working with the left wing of the Nationalist Party in Wuhan, Chiang's show of force carried the day. By July the Soviet advisers had withdrawn from the Nationalist army, and the United Front was over.

That fall, the Communist Party tried to organize uprisings in both cities and the countryside, but none met with much success. A failed uprising in Guangzhou led to the execution of three thousand to four thousand worker revolutionaries. From 1927 through 1930 the hunt was on for Communist organizers all over the country; in some areas, the only evidence that troops needed to conclude that a young woman was a Communist was bobbed hair. What Communist leadership that survived was driven underground and into the countryside. On orders of the Comintern, Chen Duxiu was blamed for these disasters and expelled from the Communist Party. Party membership, which had reached about sixty thousand in April 1927, plummeted to fewer than ten thousand within the year.

Mao Zedong's Emergence as a Party Leader

Through the 1920s, Mao Zedong was just one of hundreds of Communist Party organizers. He ended up playing such an important role in twentieth-century Chinese history that it is useful to begin with his early experiences.

Mao was born in 1893 in a farming village about 30 miles south of Changsha, the capital of Hunan province. He began helping out on his father's 3-acre farm when he was six. At age eight, in 1901, he entered the local primary school, where he studied for six years. Mao then worked full time on the farm for three years, from ages thirteen to sixteen. When he was fourteen years old, he was betrothed to the eighteen-year-old daughter of a neighbor, but she died in 1910, and Mao left the farm to continue his education. One of his teachers was a returned student from Japan, and from him

Mao became fascinated with the writings of Kang Youwei and Liang Qichao. In 1911, at age seventeen, Mao walked the 30 or so miles to Changsha to enter a middle school. Not only was Changsha a large city; the new provincial assembly was then meeting, and all sorts of newspapers were in circulation. Mao joined student demonstrations against the Qing government and cut off his queue. Then, in October, in nearby Wuhan, revolutionary soldiers seized power, and the fall of the Qing Dynasty soon followed. Mao, wanting to be a part of the action, joined the republican army, but after six months of garrison duty in Changsha, he quit to continue his education.

For a year Mao spent his days at the Changsha public library, reading world history and Chinese translations of works by such western writers as Rousseau, Montesquieu, J. S. Mill, Adam Smith, and Charles Darwin. Only when his father refused to support him any longer unless he enrolled in a school that gave degrees did he enter the Hunan Provincial Fourth Normal School, where he studied for five years (1913–1918). The teacher there who had the greatest impact on him was Yang Changji, a social science teacher deeply interested in philosophy, which he had studied during his decade abroad in Japan, Great Britain, and Germany. Mao came to share Yang's dissatisfaction with the physical fitness of Chinese intellectuals, and he wrote an article on physical education that was published in *New Youth* in 1917.

Mao was twenty-four years old when he graduated. When Yang moved to Beijing to take up an appointment at Beijing University, Mao followed him there. Yang helped him get a job as a clerk in the library, which made him a subordinate of Li Dazhao, only four years his senior but already well known in intellectual circles, having studied law for six years in Japan and been offered a position on the editorial board of *New Youth*. That year Li Dazhao wrote about Marxism and the Russian Revolution for *New Youth*.

Before he had been in Beijing a year, Mao had to return home because his mother was ill, but he stopped to visit Shanghai for a couple of weeks on the way. Mao thus missed the excitement of Beijing University during the May Fourth incident. Back in Changsha Mao took a teaching job and started his own magazine, producing four issues with articles on topics such as democracy, unions, and fighting oppression. Mao also turned his hand to organizing, forming the Hunan United Students Association and organizing a strike of thirteen thousand middle school students against the local warlord.

After his mother died, Mao returned to Beijing to find Professor Yang desperately ill. At the beginning of 1920, both Yang and Mao's fathers died. When Mao returned to Hunan a few months later, he was appointed principal of a primary school. That seems to have left him some time, as he also organized a cooperative bookstore that proved a commercial success. Professor Yang's daughter Yang Kaihui also returned to Hunan, and by the end of 1920 she and Mao were living together. Two years later, their first son was born, and they spoke of themselves as married.

It was not until 1920 that Mao showed particular interest in Marxism. Part of this new interest came from letters he received from fellow students who had gone to France. When the first meeting of the Communist Party was held in Shanghai in July 1921, Mao was one of the two delegates from Hunan. He was sent back to Hunan with instructions to build up the party there and develop ties to labor unions. Mao recruited former classmates, his two younger brothers, and others to help him organize unions and strikes. In early 1923, conforming to party policy, Mao joined the Nationalist Party. That June he went to Guangzhou for the third congress of the Chinese Communist Party. In December he sent in a pessimistic report on the situation in Hunan, where peasant organizations had been crushed and many factories had closed.

During much of 1924, Mao was away from home, in Guangzhou or Shanghai, doing United Front work. In 1925 he did the opposite, returning to his home village to work with peasants,

out of the reach of the party authorities. In October 1925 he returned to Guangzhou and took up work for the Nationalist Party's propaganda department, becoming the director of the Peasant Training Institute in 1926. During the Northern Expedition, Mao and those he had trained organized peasants in advance of the army. In February 1927 Mao submitted a highly positive report to the Communist Party on the revolution among the peasants in Hunan who had seized power from landlords and felt the joy of righting ancient wrongs.

In April 1927, when Chiang Kaishek unleashed the terror in Shanghai, Mao was in Hunan. Following party instructions, he tried to ignite peasant insurrection, but found that the terror had crushed the movement that only recently had looked so promising to him. Mao now wrote a report that emphasized the need to back political ideas with military force, contending, in his oft-quoted phrase, that "political power is obtained from the barrel of the gun." In October 1927 he led his remaining peasant followers into a mountain lair used by secret society members on the border between Hunan and Jiangxi, called Jinggangshan. Mao lost contact with Yang Kaihui, who had just given birth to their third son. He also was out of touch with the party hierarchy. He began to draw in other Communists, among whom was nineteen-year-old He Zizhen, from a nearby landlord family, who had joined the party during the Northern Expedition. She and Mao, then thirty-four years old, became lovers and had a child in 1929.

In the mountain area that Mao's forces controlled, he pushed through an extreme form of land reform, redistributing all the land of the rich and requiring all the physically able to work. His troops suffered, however, with little in the way of arms or ammunition, clothes, or medicine.

In January 1929 Mao decided to look for a better-supplied base area that would be less vulnerable to Nationalist attacks. His choice was a border region between Jiangxi and Fujian, where he set up what came to be called the Jiangxi Soviet. The party leadership, which could reach him there, quickly condemned him for his views on rural revolution and the role of military force. Mao fell ill and managed to avoid responding to the party's order that he go to Shanghai. Mao did, however, in 1929–1930 conduct an exhaustive study of rural life in one county in the Jiangxi Soviet, Xunwu County, to learn more about how a party could be built on a peasant base. In his analysis of land ownership, he classified the population into landlords (those who lived off the rents of their lands, subdivided into large, medium, and small landlords), rich peasants (those who rented out some land or made loans but worked the rest themselves), middle peasants (those who worked their own land without borrowing or hiring help), poor peasants (tenants and owners of plots too small to support them), and others, including hired hands, loafers, and those who did such manual labor as boatmen and porters. The vast majority of the population fell into the category of poor peasant or lower. When land was redistributed many more would receive land than would lose it. In his study of Xunwu, Mao also recorded literacy rates, postal service, shops and services, and even the number of prostitutes.

The Communist Party leadership was still trying to ignite urban uprisings and in October 1930 assaulted Changsha. Not only did the attack fail, but the Nationalists arrested Yang Kaihui and had her shot. The three young boys were sent by friends to Shanghai. The youngest died, and Mao did not see the other two until 1946.

THE NATIONALIST GOVERNMENT IN NANJING

The decision of the Nationalist Party to purge itself of Communists did not delay the military unification of the country, and in 1928 the Nationalists gained the allegiance of three key warlords to reunite the country. It established its capital at Nanjing, not used as a capital since the early Ming Dynasty. International recognition quickly followed, and western observers were more optimistic about the prospects for China than they had been for decades. Men who had studied in western countries were appointed to many key government posts, and progressive policies were adopted, such as a new land law limiting rents and a new marriage law outlawing concubinage and allowing women to initiate divorce. (See **Biography: Yuetsim, Servant Girl**). Over the next several years, most of the foreign powers consented to reductions in their special privileges. Tariff autonomy was recovered, as well as control over the Maritime Customs, Salt Administration, and Post Office. Foreign concessions were reduced from thirty-three to thirteen, and extraterritoriality was eliminated for some more minor countries.

From 1928 on, Chiang Kaishek was the leader of the Nationalists. From a landlord-merchant family near Ningbo, Chiang had aspired to take the civil service examinations, but when they were abolished he went to Japan to study military science, joining the precursor of the Nationalist Party while there. His appointment to head the Huangpu Academy in 1924 was a crucial one in his rise because it allowed him to form strong personal ties to young officers in the party's army. Once Chiang, a skillful politician, became fully enmeshed in party and government matters, he proved able to balance different cliques and build personal ties to key power holders. In 1927 he married Soong Meiling, the daughter of a wealthy merchant family and the sister of Sun Yatsen's widow.

To modernize his army, Chiang turned to Germany, attracted by the success the Nazis were having in mobilizing and militarizing Germany. Indeed, Chiang once argued, "Can fascism save China? We answer: yes. Fascism is now what China most needs."[1] German advisers helped Chiang train an elite corps, plan the campaigns

---

1. Cited in Lloyd Eastman, *Abortive Revolution* (Cambridge, Mass.: Harvard University Press, 1974), p. 40.

BIOGRAPHY Yuetsim, Servant Girl

Yuetsim, born around 1910, knew nothing about her natal family. All she knew was that she had been kidnapped when she was about three years old and sold, through intermediaries, as a "slave girl." She thought disbanded soldiers, then roaming the countryside, might have been the ones who kidnapped her.

A Hong Kong family, the Yeos, purchased Yuetsim. Her master's father had been a successful merchant and had three concubines besides his wife. Her master, Mr. Yeo, was the son of the first concubine, and he held a modest government position as a clerk. When his wife had no children, he purchased a prostitute as a concubine, and she gave birth to four children. The wife, with bound feet, rarely left her room. To help the concubine with the housework and care of the children, the family bought little Yuetsim. It is difficult to imagine that a three year old could be of much use to anyone, but by four or five she could at least fetch and carry. Naturally she never learned to read or write.

Since Yuetsim knew no other life, she put up with the way she was treated. Her mistress, the concubine, was often harsh and contemptuous. In this period Hong Kong newspapers were filled with agitation against the custom of selling girls into bondage. Yuetsim, however, never heard anything of the movement or the 1923 law that took the first steps toward outlawing selling girls into service. In December 1929, a further strengthening of the laws against child slavery required owners of slave girls to register them with the government, pay them wages, and free them at age eighteen. Since Mr. Yeo worked for the government and was known to have had a slave girl for years, he had to take some action. He might have married her off, as many masters did, but his concubine was so angry at losing Yuetsim's services that she simply ordered Yuetsim out of the house.

In 1930 one of the officials in charge of the registration of slave girls found a place for Yuetsim in a home for women and girls in need of protection, and she stayed there several years. Finally she went back to the Yeos as a maid, knowing no other place to go. Soon after her return, both the wife and the concubine died. Yuetsim continued to take care of the master and his children.

After the death of his wife and concubine, Mr. Yeo wanted to make Yuetsim his concubine. His children, however, were adamantly opposed and threatened to cut off contact with him if he went through with the marriage. They, after all, had known her all their lives as a humble servant. Although their own mother had been a prostitute before becoming their father's concubine, they thought marriage to a former slave girl would disgrace the family. Mr. Yeo gave in to them.

Yuetsim stayed on anyway. In retirement, Mr. Yeo's fortunes declined, but she nursed him in his illnesses and shopped and cooked for him. She was still living with him when she told her story in 1978.

Source: Based on Maria Jaschok, *Concubines and Bondservants: The Social History of a Chinese Custom* (London: Zed Books, 1988), pp. 69–77.

against the communist base in Jiangxi, and import German arms. Young officers became members of the Blue Shirts, an organization devoted to the nation and against such New Culture ideas as individualism. Chiang entrusted political training in the army and schools to the Blue Shirts, who also took on secret service work.

Chiang Kaishek and Soong Meiling. In 1927 Chiang Kaishek married Soong Meiling, the younger sister of Sun Yatsen's widow. Soong came from a wealthy family, had been educated in the United States, and after the Japanese invasion worked hard to gain American support for China. *(Popperfoto/Retrofile)*

Chiang was not a political progressive. He made no attempt at elective democracy, as this was to be a period of "political tutelage." The press was heavily censored, and dissenters and suspected Communists were arrested and often executed. To combat the intellectual appeal of the Communists and build support for his government, Chiang in 1934 launched an ideological indoctrination program, the New Life Movement. Its goal, he claimed, was to "militarize the life of the people of the entire nation" and to nourish in them "a capacity to endure hardship and especially a habit and instinct for unified behavior," to make them "willing to sacrifice for the nation at all times."[2]

Chiang was a patriot, however, and wanted a strong and modern China. Much progress was made in economic modernization. Life in the major cities took on a more modern look. Conveniences like electricity were gradually changing how all major cities functioned. A professional class was gaining influence, composed of scientists, engineers, architects, economists, physicians, and others with technical expertise, often acquired through study abroad.

The primary failing of the Nationalists' modernizing programs was their failure to bring improvements to the countryside (see **Documents: The Peasant Exodus from Western Shandong**). The government and private philanthropic organizations sponsored rural reconstruction projects that tried to raise the level of rural education, create facilities for credit, encourage modern enterprises, and form peasant associations, but gains were usually limited to small areas and short periods. Most peasants had seen no improvement in their standard of living since Qing times. Continued population growth to over 500 million by 1930 relentlessly increased the pressure on available land. The advantages brought by modernization—cheaper transportation by railroads and cheaper manufactured consumer goods—were yet to have a positive impact on the rural economy. China's exports were struggling, silk and tea having lost ground to Japanese and Indian competition, then all exports facing decreased demand due to the worldwide depression of the 1930s. The Nationalist government did little to disturb the local power structure in the countryside. Getting the new land or marriage laws observed in rural areas was never given much priority. The Northern Expedition had succeeded by accepting virtually anyone willing to throw in his lot with the Nationalists, and thus all sorts of local power holders had been incorporated. Villagers thus suffered from local bullies and local elites who put their own survival first.

---

2. Cited in Jonathan Spence, *The Search for Modern China* (New York: Norton, 1990), p. 415.

DOCUMENTS

The Peasant Exodus from Western Shandong

In the 1930s, those with modern educations were well aware of the problems facing Chinese farmers and discussed at length what could be done to solve them. The article below was published in the magazine Minjian (Among the People) *in 1937. The author, Hao Pensui, describes what he learned by visiting villages and talking to peasants.*

Toward the northwest of Jinan, in western Shandong, is the district of Yuecheng. . . . Deforestation, dumping, and lack of any river conservancy have prevailed for so many years that the main river bed is narrower than either of its branches. Whereas the Dengjin river is now 32 feet wide and the Zhaonui 48 feet wide, the joint stream is only 28 feet wide. No wonder then that since 1930, five out of the seven years have witnessed floods.

The peasants were able to maintain themselves with what little grain store and money savings they had for the first two flood years, but when the fourth and fifth floods came they had absolutely nothing to fall back on. Usurers in the city and at the railway station who were more resourceful than the village usurers, naturally refused to loan at this time, realizing that they had very little chance of being repaid. In such cases the peasants were unable to borrow even at the very high interest rates of four or five per cent per month, and indeed the higher the interest rate the more hesitant was the usurer to loan. . . .

In the winter of 1935 the peasants of Chengnan were reduced to eating the bark from trees and the roots of herbs. . . . Destitute peasants from this large area had no alternative but to rove from one place to another. This further agitated the peasants of Chengnan, who organized themselves to petition the magistrate for relief. The magistrate immediately ordered the shutting of the city gate in order to prevent the entry of over 3,000 peasants into the city. Only a few peasant delegates were permitted to talk to him, resulting in the usual way with the magistrate promising to petition the provincial government for relief from the public granary.

Unending delays and bureaucratic red tape proved once again complete indifference to the acute suffering of the hungry masses. A year's delay meant a year of hunger and it was not until the spring of 1936 that the peasants received from the public granary 6 kg of unhusked rice per person. . . .

The investigations in one village by the writer of the present article may be taken as a typical example. The village in Chengnan that he investigated is named Zhaozhuang and it had a population of 530 people in 76 families. In the winter of 1935, 25 entire families left the village, and from each of 39

Shanghai

During the Nanjing Decade, Shanghai emerged as one of the major cities of the world. Since 1910 it had been China's most populous city, and by the 1930s it had about 4 million residents. It attracted Chinese entrepreneurs, especially ones willing to collaborate with foreigners. It had China's largest port and was the commercial center of China. In the 1920s and 1930s it had half of China's modern industry.

Shanghai attracted more foreigners than any other of the treaty ports, a high of over thirty-six thousand. The largest number were British

families one to three persons left, leaving only 12 families intact. In all, 230 people left the village that winter. . . .

The almost annual flood created great confusion among the peasants who were quite unable to effect any organized control. Whatever feeble attempts they did make to turn back the water, such as the building of small mud banks, proved useless in nine cases out of ten. The flood meant the loss of a year's crop, for when the water receded the fields were left in very bad condition, covered with a thick layer of black silt which dried and cracked in a hard crust. Having lost their seed and probably their animals, the peasants had no hope of starting afresh, so after every flood a procession of peasants could be seen from nearly every village abandoning their homes and setting out in search of food. Creaking wheel-barrows, piled high with quilts, clothing and household utensils, were pushed by able-bodied men along narrow paths, each being followed by a group of women and children. Behind them they would leave some houses with the doors sealed with mud, or others with one or two people too old to travel, left to scrape a living as best they could. . . .

The writer himself was in the village of Zhaozhuang in 1936 just two months after the wheat harvest and his own investigation brought to light the fact that out of the total of 76 families, only nine, at that time, had as much as three months food, 11 only had two months, 19 only one month and as many as 37 families had already exhausted their supplies. These figures are all the more significant because it was a year in which there was no flood and a good harvest.

Once the writer met a peasant of sorrowful appearance who said,

> This year our family harvested about 600 kg of wheat out of which 72 kg were paid for rent, 150 for the repayment of loans in kind, about 108 for taxes, about 60 for the purchase of a working animal, and about 60 to repay recent credit purchases. Thus only about 150 kg remained, and of these 108 had already been consumed by the family. How we are to manage to live with less than 50 kg in hand until the next harvest is hard to conceive. Furthermore, there are still some outstanding debts from credit purchases, some $12 worth of things in the pawnshop to be redeemed and school fees for the boys to be met.

Such a budget reveals the almost hopeless condition of the peasantry in this area, for it not only allows of no leeway to meet such emergencies as flood, drought and locusts, but it also shows that even in normal years a moderately well-to-do peasant family is being rapidly reduced in its economic status. This explains why the peasant exodus is more or less continuous, regardless of the harvest or the presence of natural calamities.

Source: From *Agrarian China: Selected Source Materials from Chinese Authors* (London: George Allen and Unwin, 1939), pp. 247–251, modified.

---

or Japanese, as they owned the most foreign companies. Some of Shanghai's foreigners had come in the nineteenth century and stayed; others were there for only a few years. Among the merchant families who amassed huge fortunes were the Sassoons, from a family of Jewish traders active in Baghdad and Bombay. David Sassoon began by trading cotton from Bombay to China in the 1870s, his son Elias Sassoon bought warehouses in Shanghai later in the nineteenth century, and his grandson Victor Sassoon turned to real estate, in the 1930s owning a reported nineteen hundred buildings in Shanghai, including what are now the Peace

The Shanghai Bund. The European character of Shanghai was nowhere more striking than on its main boulevard, the "Bund" along the river, seen here in the 1910s. The domed building in the center is the Hong Kong & Shanghai Bank. *(Ivan D. Yeaton Collection)*

and Cypress hotels. Some of the early employees of the Sassoons also made fortunes, including Silas Hardoon and Elly Kadoorie. Hardoon started as a night watchman in the 1870s. Kadoorie's mansion is now the Shanghai Children's Palace.

Because the international districts admitted anyone, no matter what their passport or visa status, Shanghai became a magnet for international refugees. After the Russian Revolution many of the Russian bourgeoisie fled east via the trans-Siberian railroad. Later they made their way south through Manchuria, many eventually settling in Shanghai, often to find only menial jobs. In the 1930s, thousands of Jews fleeing the Nazis also found refuge in Shanghai, where they were aided by the wealthy Jewish families already there, such as the Sassoons, Hardoons, and Kadoories.

The foreign presence in Shanghai was visible to all in its western-style roads and buildings. Along the river an embankment was built called the bund and made into a park where signs were posted that read, "No dogs" and "No Chinese."

With its gambling parlors and brothels, Shanghai had the reputation as a sin city. Reportedly about fifty thousand women worked in Shanghai as prostitutes in the 1930s. Young women were also drawn into Shanghai to work in textile mills or as servants. In 1930 over one hundred seventy thousand women worked in industry, about half in cotton mills. The typical prostitute or mill hand was a young, unmarried, illiterate woman recruited in the countryside by labor contractors. The contractor would supply a small advance payment, often to the girl's parents, and would make arrangements in the city for employment, housing, and food. The women were often kept in conditions of debt servitude. Some factory workers joined unions and engaged in strikes; others put their hopes on getting married and returning to the country. Women in Shanghai, from factory girls and prostitutes to office workers and the wealthy, commonly wore dresses called *qipao,* a compromise between western and Chinese styles. (See **Material Culture: Qipao.**)

Shanghai also attracted Chinese intellectuals, especially as Nationalist censorship got more severe. If they worked from the International District or French Concession, they were usually safe from the Chinese police. Dissidents, radicals, and revolutionaries chose Shanghai for much the same reasons.

Relocating the Communist Revolution

The Central Committee of the Communist Party in 1932 gave up trying to foment urban insurrections and joined Mao in the Jiangxi Soviet. Mao was the chairman of the soviet, but after their arrival, he was on the sidelines, his recommendations often overruled. In the fall of 1934, with the German-planned fifth "extermination campaign" of the Nationalists encircling them with a million-man force, the Communist Party leadership, without consulting Mao, decided to give up the Jiangxi Soviet. In October, about eighty-six thousand Communist soldiers, cadres, porters, and followers broke out of the encirclement, the start of the much mythologized year-long Long March in search of a new place to set up a base. Most wives and children had to be left behind (only thirty-five women joined the march). To protect them and the thousand or so sick or wounded soldiers left behind, about fifteen thousand troops remained in Jiangxi. Mao's wife, He Zizhen, was allowed to come, although pregnant, but they had to leave their two-year-old child behind with Mao's younger brother. When Mao's brother, like many of those left behind, was killed in 1935, Mao lost track of the child.

Month after month the Red Army kept retreating, often just a step or two ahead of the pursuing Nationalist troops. Casualties were enormous. The farther west they went, the more rugged the terrain; as they skirted Tibet, they also had to deal with bitter cold. By the time they found an area in Shaanxi where they could establish a new base, they had marched almost ten thousand kilometers. Only about eight thousand of those who began the march made it the whole way, though some new recruits and communists from other base areas had joined en route, to bring the total to nearly twenty thousand. (See Map 26.1.)

To the Nationalists in Nanjing, the Long March must have seemed a huge victory. The Communist Party's urban activists had been crushed in 1927–1928, and now the rural activists had suffered just as devastating a blow, their numbers greatly diminished and the survivors driven into remote and poverty-stricken regions. Those who made the Long March, however, saw it as a victory. That they had overcome such daunting odds reinforced their belief that they were men of destiny with a near-sacred mission to remake China.

It was during the Long March that Mao Zedong reached the top ranks of party leadership. When the marchers reached Zunyi in Guizhou province in early 1935, they paused to hold an enlarged meeting of the Politburo and assess their strategy. Seventeen veteran party leaders were present, including Mao, the Comintern representative Otto Braun, and thirty-year old Deng Xiaoping to take notes. Blame was placed on Braun and others who had urged positional warfare to defend against the Nationalist attack. Mao was named to the Standing Committee of the Politburo and given new responsibility for military affairs.

From 1936 to 1946 the Communist Party made its base at Yan'an, a market town in central Shaanxi where homes were often built by cutting caves into the loess soil cliffs. When the American journalist Edgar Snow visited Yan'an in 1936, the survivors of the Long March appeared to him to be an earthy group of committed patriots and egalitarian social reformers, full of optimism and purpose. They lived in

MATERIAL CULTURE

Qipao

In the first decades of the twentieth century, as educated young people came to look on the West as the source of everything modern, they turned to western styles of dress, especially those who had worn this style while studying abroad. Some people adopted full western-style dress, but others tried to develop a style that would be both Chinese and modern at the same time. The so-called Mao suit, first popularized in China by Sun Yatsen, is an example of this sort of hybrid style for men. For women in the early twentieth century the garment that most successfully modernized Chinese dress was the *qipao*.

The *qipao* is a one-piece dress characterized by an upright ("mandarin") collar, an opening from the neck to under the right arm, and a fairly narrow cut, often with a slit, especially if the skirt reached below midcalf. The *qipao* was much more form fitting than anything worn in the nineteenth century, but reflected traditional styles in its collar, its slanted opening, and sometimes its fastenings. It could be made in silk, cotton, or synthetics, for everyday wear or elegant occasions.

Well-Dressed Young Women. These three young women wear *qipao* with short sleeves and high slits. Notice also their high-heel shoes and curled hair. *(Hulton Archive/Getty Images)*

caves, ate simple food, and showed no disdain for the peasants whom they were mobilizing to fight against the Japanese. During the war, too, outside observers were impressed with the commitment to group goals of the Yan'an forces. All through Mao's lifetime the official media promoted this image of the leaders of the Yan'an Soviet as a cohesive group of idealistic revolutionaries.

Mao's standing in Yan'an was high, but he still had rivals. A group of Communists who had gone to Russia for training arrived in late 1935 and provoked debate on the errors that had cost the lives of so many party members.

Mao realized that he would have to improve his grasp of Communist dialectic and began systematic study. His new secretary, Chen Boda, who had studied in Moscow for several years in the late 1920s, began writing of Mao as a theorist. Mao was becoming more set against the claims of the well educated, even if their education was in Marxism. To contrast himself from the urban intellectuals, Mao would act like a peasant, opening his clothes to look for lice with guests present.

Mao was victorious over the Soviet returnees in part because he was the better politician but also because he seems to have become truly con-

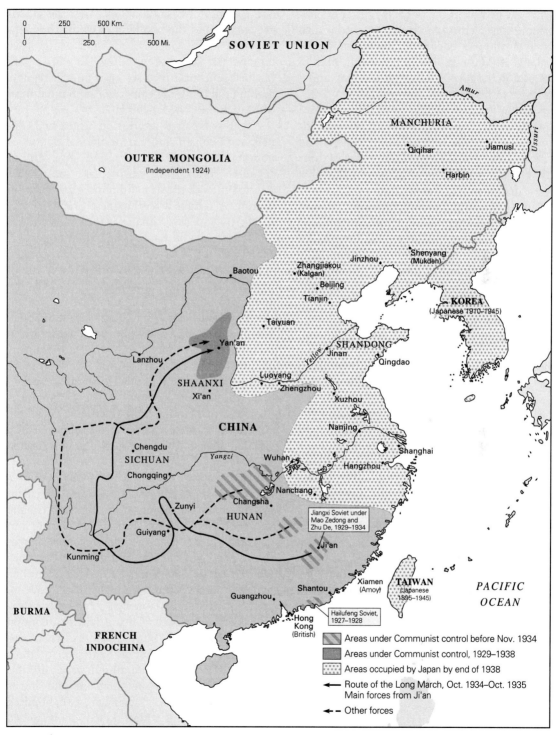

Map **26.1** China in 1938

fident that he was in the right. He began spending more time lecturing party members. He also started to allow or encourage the beginnings of the cult of Mao: in 1937 a portrait of him appeared in the revolutionary newspaper, and a collection of his writings was printed.

It was in this period that Mao took up with Jiang Qing. He Zizhen and Mao's surviving children had gone to the Soviet Union for safety and medical treatment. Jiang Qing, twenty-four years old, had worked as an actress in Shanghai and made her way to Yan'an after the Japanese invasion. Some of the other Communist leaders resented her liaison with Mao, having liked and admired He Zizhen. Mao and Jiang Qing had a daughter in 1940, the last of his four surviving children (six were lost or died).

THE JAPANESE INVASION AND THE RETREAT TO CHONGQING

From the time of the May Fourth protests in 1919, Chinese patriots saw Japan as the gravest threat to China's sovereignty. In 1895 Japan had won Taiwan. In 1905, after an impressive victory over Russia, it gained a dominant position in southern Manchuria. In 1915, by applying pressure on Yuan Shikai, Japan had secured a broad range of economic privileges. The Japanese Army in Manchuria, ostensibly there to protect Japan's railroads and other economic interests, was full of militarists who kept pushing Japanese civil authorities to let the army occupy the entire area. In 1928, Japanese officers assassinated the warlord of Manchuria, Zhang Zuolin, hoping for a crisis that would allow Japan to extend its power base. In 1931 Japanese soldiers set a bomb on the Southern Manchurian Railroad to give themselves an excuse to occupy Shenyang "in self-defense." China did not attempt to resist militarily but did appeal to the League of Nations, which recognized China as being in the right but imposed no real sanctions on Japan. Then in January 1932, Japan attacked Shanghai to retaliate against anti-Japanese protests. Shanghai was by that point such an international city that the Japanese assault and the bombing of civilian residential areas was widely condemned. After four months, the Japanese withdrew from Shanghai, but in Manchuria they set up a puppet regime, making the last Qing emperor the nominal head of Manchukuo ("Manchu land").

Anger at Japanese aggression heightened Chinese nationalism and led to the formation of national salvation leagues and boycotts of Japanese goods. Still, Chiang, like most other military men of the day, did not see any point in putting up a fight when Japanese firepower was so clearly superior. Chiang was convinced that all Chinese would have to be united under one leader before China could hope to thwart Japan.

In 1936 troops that had been driven out of Manchuria by the Japanese were ordered by Chiang to blockade the Communists in Yan'an. When Chiang came to Xi'an, they kidnapped him and refused to release him until he agreed to form a united front with the Communists against Japan. These troops did not want to be fighting other Chinese when the Japanese had occupied their home towns. The Communists played no part in the kidnapping but joined the negotiations when Stalin urged them to keep Chiang alive and create a nationwide united front against Japan.

The next year, 1937, Chiang did put up a fight when the Japanese staged another incident as an excuse for taking more territory. Chiang was probably hoping to inflict a quick defeat to convince Japan that the Nanjing government was a power to be reckoned with, so that they would negotiate with him rather than continue to move into China as though it was unoccupied. Japan instead launched a full-scale offensive, sweeping south. Chiang had to abandon Beijing and Tianjin, but he used his best troops to hold off the Japanese at Shanghai for three months. He asked for an all-out stand, and his troops courageously persisted despite heavy shelling and bombing, absorbing two hundred fifty thousand casualties, killed or wounded (compared to forty thousand Japanese casualties). When Shanghai fell, the Nationalist troops streamed toward the Nationalist capital, Nanjing. After the Japanese easily took Nanjing in December 1937, they went on a rampage, massacring somewhere between forty thousand and three hundred thousand civilians and fugitive soldiers, raping perhaps twenty thousand women, and laying the city waste. The seven weeks of mayhem was widely reported in the foreign press, where it was labeled the Rape of Nanking. If this violence was intended to speed a Chinese surrender, it did not achieve its goal.

During the course of 1938, the Japanese secured control of the entire eastern seaboard and set up puppet regimes headed by Chinese collaborators (see Map 26.1). Terror tactics continued, including biological and chemical warfare in Zhejiang in 1940, where bubonic plague was spread and poison gas released. Civilian casualties were also inflicted by the Nationalist government. When the Chinese had to retreat from Kaifeng, Chiang ordered his engineers to blow up the dikes on the Yellow River, creating a gigantic flood that engulfed more than four thousand villages, drowned some three hundred thousand people, and left 2 million homeless. It held up the Japanese for only three months.

Japan had assumed that once they captured the capital at Nanjing and inflicted an overwhelming defeat on the Nationalist army, Chiang Kaishek would come to terms. When he refused and moved inland, the war bogged down. Rather than persuading the Chinese to surrender, Japanese terror tactics instead intensified popular hatred for the Japanese. China's great distances spread Japanese forces. In north China, Japan concentrated on holding rail lines, and Chinese guerrilla forces concentrated on blowing them up. Guerrilla soldiers depended on local peasants to feed them and inform them of enemy concentrations and movements. They acquired weapons and ammunition by capturing them from the Japanese. Many resistance fighters worked in the fields during the day and at night acted as guides or scouts to help blow up bridges, rail lines, and roads. Peasant cooperation with the guerrillas provoked savage Japan-

ese reprisals, including killing everyone in villages suspected of harboring resistance fighters, which the Japanese called their "kill all, burn all, loot all" policy. Chinese resistance forced Japan to keep about 40 percent of its troops in China even after the Pacific War had begun in late 1941 (see **Connections: World War II**).

The Nationalists' capital was moved inland first to Wuhan, then to Chongqing, deep in Sichuan. Free China, as it was called in the western press, started with the odds heavily against it. The capital, Chongqing, suffered repeated air raids and faced not only shortages of almost everything, but runaway inflation, as high as 10 percent a month, leading to widespread corruption as government workers' salaries fell to a pittance. The army was in worse shape. China had lost most of the army Chiang had spent a decade training in preparation for war with Japan. From 1939 on, the bulk of China's 5 million soldiers were ill-trained peasant conscripts. Press gangs would enter villages and seize the able-bodied. As many as a third of the conscripts died on the forced marches to their bases because they were not given enough to eat or medical care. Desertion, not surprisingly, was a huge problem. Another serious disability for Free China was the lack of an industrial base inland. Chinese engineers made heroic efforts to build a new industrial base, but constant Japanese bombing, the end of Soviet aid in 1939, and the closing of the route through Burma in 1942 frustrated their efforts. From 1942 on, American advisers and American aid flown over the mountains from Burma enabled Chiang to build a number of modern divisions, but not an army able to drive the Japanese out of China.

During World War II, international alignments began to shift. After Britain proved unable to defend Hong Kong, Singapore, or Burma from Japanese invasions in 1941–1942, it lost its standing in Chinese eyes as the preeminent western power. Its place was taken by the United States, which ended up doing most of the fighting against Japan. The American-educated wife of Chiang, Soong Meiling, was popular with the American press and lobbied effectively for China. President Franklin D. Roosevelt, looking ahead, wished to see China become the dominant power in East Asia after the defeat of Japan, and convinced his allies to include Chiang in major meetings of the allies at Cairo and Yalta (though Churchill referred to making China one of the Big Four as an absolute farce). It was as a result of this sort of geopolitics that China, so long scorned as weak and backward, became one of the five permanent members of the UN's Security Council after the war.

THE CHINESE COMMUNIST PARTY DURING THE WAR

During the first few years of the war, there was some genuine cooperation between the Communists and Nationalists. This largely ended, however, when the Communist divisions of the New Fourth Army were attacked by the Nationalists in January 1941 on the grounds that they had not complied rapidly enough with an order to retreat north of the Yangzi. Not only were around three thousand troops killed in battle, but many were shot after arrest or sent to prison camps. From this point on, the Nationalists imposed an economic blockade on the Communist base area.

Some one hundred thousand people made their way to Yan'an during the war, about half students, teachers, and writers. Party membership swelled from forty thousand in 1937 to about eight hundred thousand in 1940. The fight against Japan helped the Communists build a base of popular support. In areas of north China where the Japanese armies had penetrated, peasants were ready to join forces against the Japanese.

Resistance forces were not exclusively Communist. Patriotic urban students fled to these relatively uncontested rural areas where they helped both Nationalist and Communist resistance forces. The Communists, however, were more successful in gaining control of the social, political, and economic life in villages because they gave peasants what they wanted: an army of friendly troops who not only did not steal their crops but

helped them bring in the harvest and implemented popular but gradual economic reforms.

Class struggle was not emphasized during the war against Japan, nor was there much confiscation of land. Still, considerable redistribution was accomplished by imposing graduated taxes that led larger landholders to sell land that was no longer profitable. Landlords were more than welcome to help with forming and supplying militia forces, and educated youth from better-off families were recruited as party members. Party propagandists did their best to stoke patriotic passions, glorify the Soviet Union, and convey the message that the Communist Party could build a better, more egalitarian future. They called so many meetings that rural folk in Hebei quipped, "Under the Nationalists, too many taxes; under the Communists, too many meetings."[3]

The Japanese did not penetrate as far west as Yan'an, and during the war Mao could concentrate on ideological issues. As the party grew rapidly, Mao sought ways to instill a uniform vision. He began giving lectures to party members in which he spelled out his version of Chinese history, the party's history, and Marxist theory. Neither Marx nor Lenin had seen much revolutionary potential in peasants, viewing them as petty capitalist in mentality, and in Russia the party had seized power in an urban setting. Since the Communists in China had failed in the cities, Mao reinterpreted Marxist theory in such a way that the peasants could be seen as the vanguard of the revolution. Indeed Mao came more and more to glorify the peasants as the true masses and elaborate the theory of the mass line: party cadres had to go among and learn from the peasant masses before they could become their teachers. Marx was a materialist who rejected idealist interpretations of history. Ideas did not make history; rather, they reflected the economic base, the mode of production, and the relations of production. Mao's vision of rev-

3. Edward Friedman, Paul G. Pickowics, and Mark Selden, *Chinese Village, Socialist State* (New Haven, Conn.: Yale University Press, 1991), p. 41.

The Communist Leadership. Zhou Enlai, Mao Zedong, and Zhu De (left to right) were photographed in the winter of 1944, by which time the Communist Party had gained a foothold behind Japanese lines all across north China. *(Popperfoto/Retrofile)*

olution, by contrast, was voluntaristic: it emphasized the potential for people, once mobilized, to transform both themselves and the world through the power of their wills.

This "Thought of Mao Zedong" did not win out in a free competition of ideas among the survivors of the Long March, but in a power struggle in which Mao proved a master tactician, able to eliminate his rivals one after the other and get the Central Committee to label them deviationists of the right or left. To reform the thinking of both old cadres who had deviated from the correct line and new recruits from bourgeois families, in 1942 Mao launched the first of many rectification campaigns. Cadres had to study documents Mao selected in small groups, analyze their own shortcomings in Maoist terms, listen to criticism of themselves at mass struggle sessions, and confess their errors. Everyone watched the dramatic public humiliations of the principal targets, including

the party theorist Wang Ming and the writer Wang Shiwei. People learned to interpret any deviation from Mao's line as defects in their thinking due to their subjectivism and liberalism, characteristics of their petty bourgeois background. One man, for instance, who confessed to being bothered by the party elite's special privileges (such as getting to ride on horseback while others walked) was taught that liberal ideas elevating the individual over the collective lay behind his feelings. Those who balked were punished; some even died. Many of those invited to overcome their errors truly developed a new collective consciousness that greatly increased their usefulness to the party. Others simply learned to be more circumspect when they talked.

In May 1943 Mao received a new title, chairman of the Central Committee, and began to be treated as the party's paramount leader. The people of China were urged to arm themselves with Mao Zedong's thought. The Seventh Party Congress, the first to be held since the 1920s, was held at Yan'an in the spring of 1945. The preamble of the new constitution recognized Mao's new role as sage of the party: "The Chinese Communist Party takes Mao Zedong's thought—the thought that unites Marxist-Leninist theory and the practices of the Chinese revolution—as the guide for all its work, and opposes all dogmatic or empiricist deviations."[4]

THE CIVIL WAR AND THE COMMUNIST VICTORY

The end of the war with Japan set the stage for the final confrontation between the Nationalists and the Communists. When Japan surrendered in August 1945, there were over 1 million Japanese troops in China proper and nearly another 1 million in Manchuria, as well as about 1.75 million Japanese civilians. Disarming and repatriating them took months, as the

---

4. Cited in Jonathan Spence, *Mao Zedong* (New York: Viking, 1999), p. 101.

Nationalists, the Communists, the Americans, the Russians, and even some warlords jockeyed for position. The United States airlifted one hundred ten thousand Nationalist troops to key coastal cities like Shanghai and Guangzhou, and fifty-three thousand U.S. Marines were sent to help secure Beijing and Tianjin. The Russians had entered Manchuria in early August in fulfillment of their secret promise to the United States and Britain to join the eastern front three months after victory in Europe. They saw to it that large stores of Japanese weapons got into the hands of the Red Army—some seven hundred forty thousand rifles, eighteen thousand machine guns, and four thousand artillery pieces—giving them about as much Japanese equipment as the Nationalists got.

From August 1945 until January 1947, the United States made efforts to avert civil war by trying to convince Chiang to establish a government in which opposition parties could participate. The American ambassador brought Mao and Chiang together for several weeks of meetings in Chongqing, but the agreements reached on cooperation led nowhere. Full-scale civil war ensued.

The civil war itself lasted only about two years. The Red Army (now called the People's Liberation Army, or PLA) began to isolate the cities, starting in Manchuria and working south. It lost battles but built support through moderate land reform. When Nationalist soldiers defected, they took their equipment with them, and the PLA incorporated them into its armies. Within a year the Nationalist forces in Manchuria were routed and the PLA was moving into China proper. In 1948, a two-month battle near the railway center of Xuzhou pitted six hundred thousand of Chiang's troops against an equal number of Communist ones. Although Chiang had air support, his army was smashed and he lost almost half a million men. Thus, although the Nationalists had started with much more in the way of modern armaments and several times the number of troops, they fared poorly on the battlefield. In early 1949 Chiang Kaishek and much of his army and government retreated to Taiwan and reestablished their government there.

The unpopularity of the Nationalists had many roots. Prices in July 1948 were 3 million times higher than they had been in July 1937, and inflation did not let up then. People had to resort to barter, and a tenth of the population became refugees. Nationalist army officers and soldiers were widely seen as seizing whatever they could for themselves rather than working for the common good. Student protests were often put down by violence. When liberals demanded that Chiang widen participation in his government, he had his secret police assassinate them. No amount of American support could make the Chinese want to continue with this government in power.

SUMMARY

What changed between 1927 and 1949? How different was China? More than half a century of struggle against a Japan intent on imperialist expansion was over: Japan had been thoroughly defeated and had turned against war. The Nationalist Party had been defeated by the Communist Party and had withdrawn from the mainland. The Communist Party itself had changed dramatically. The party had broken free from Comintern control and tied itself intimately to the peasantry. Mao had risen to the top position in the party and established his version of Marxism as the correct ideology of the party. The party had grown enormously and acquired extensive experience in redistribution of land, mobilizing peasants, and keeping intellectuals on a tight rein.

SUGGESTED READING

Most of the general works mentioned in Chapter 23 also cover this period. In addition, see D. Klein and A. Clark, eds., *Biographic Dictionary of Chinese Communism, 1921–1965*, 2 vols. (1971). On the first United Front between the Nationalists and the Communists, see H. Issacs, *The Tragedy of the Chinese Revolution*, rev. ed. (1951), and D. Jacobs, *Borodin: Stalin's Man in China* (1981).

On the Nationalists, see L. Eastman, *The Abortive Revolution: China Under Nationalist Rule, 1927–1937*, rev. ed. (1990) and *Seeds of Destruction: Nationalist China in War and Revolution, 1937–1949* (1984); F. Wakeman, *Policing Shanghai, 1927–1937* (1995); and B. Martin, *The Shanghai Green Gang: Politics and Organized Crime, 1919–1937* (1996). On the Chinese economy in this period, see P. Coble, *The Shanghai Capitalists and the Nationalist Government, 1927–1937* (1986), and T. Rawski, *Economic Growth in Prewar China* (1989).

The lively literature of the 1920s and 1930s is treated in C. T. Hsia, *A History of Modern Chinese Fiction* (1971); O. Lee, ed., *Lu Xun and His Legacy* (1985); and O. Lang, *Pa Chin and His Writings: Chinese Youth Between the Two Revolutions* (1967). For translations, see *The Selected Stories of Lu Hsun* (1972); Pa Chin, *Family*, trans. S. Shapiro (1972); and Lao She's *Rickshaw*, trans. J. James (1979). On Shanghai in the culture of the period, see H. Lu, *Beyond the Neon Lights: Everyday Shanghai in the Early Twentieth Century* (1999), and L. Lee, *Shanghai Modern: The Flowering of a New Urban Culture in China, 1930–1945* (1999).

On the war against Japan, see J. Hsiung and S. Levine, *China's Bitter Victory: The War with Japan, 1937–1945* (1992), and J. Fogel, ed., *The Nanjing Massacre in History and Historiography* (2000).

On the Communist victory, see O. Wou, *Mobilizing the Masses: Building Revolution in Henan* (1994); J. Yick, *Making Urban Revolution* (1995); A. Dirlik, *The Origins of Chinese Communism* (1989); M. Selden, *The Yenan Way in Revolutionary China* (1971); and S. Pepper, *Civil War in China: The Political Struggle, 1945–1949* (1978). Early firsthand accounts still of value are E. Snow, *Red Star over China* (1938); J. Belden, *China Shakes the World* (1970); and W. Hinton, *Fanshen: A Documentary of Revolution in a Chinese Village* (1966). For a brief biography of Mao, see J. Spence, *Mao Zedong* (1999); for a long one, see either R. Terrill, *Mao: A Biography* (1999), or R. Short, *Mao: A Life* (2000).

World War II

In both the western and eastern theaters, World War II was characterized by indiscriminate bombing of civilian populations and death tolls in the millions. The aggressors were the Axis: Japan, Germany, and to a lesser extent, Italy. Allied against them were the British Commonwealth (including officially India and Australia), the United States, and the Soviet Union, along with the Chinese government under Chiang Kai-shek. What is known as the fifteen-year war began with Japan's takeover of Manchuria in 1931. In 1937 Japan launched all-out war against China. The war in Europe began in 1939 when Hitler provoked a declaration of war from Britain and France by invading Poland. The United States got involved when Japan bombed Pearl Harbor on December 7, 1941, and Hitler declared war on the United States.

Timeline: The Greater East Asia War

1931–1932	Japan's Kwantung army takes over Manchuria
1932	January 28: Japan bombs Shanghai
1933	May 27: Japan withdraws from the League of Nations
1935	November 24: Puppet government established in Beijing
1936	January 25: United Front against Japan
1937	July 7: Marco Polo Bridge Incident; Japan invades China
	November 20: Chinese capital established at Chongqing
	December 13: Rape of Nanjing begins
1938	United States embargoes war materiel to Japan
1939	May through August: Japanese and Soviet troops fight at Nomonhan
1940	Spring: U.S. Pacific Fleet moves to Pearl Harbor in Hawai'i
	September 26: Japan invades North Vietnam
	September 27: Japan, Italy, and Germany sign Tripartite Mutual Defense Pact
	October 15: United States embargoes scrap iron and steel to Japan
1941	April 13: Japan signs neutrality pact with Soviet Union
	July 26: Britain and United States cut off trade with Japan
	December 7: Japan attacks Pearl Harbor
	December 8: Japan attacks the Philippines, Wake, Guam, Hong Kong, and Malaya
	December 23: Japan bombs Rangoon, Burma
1942	January 23: Japan takes Rabaul north of New Guinea
	January 26: Japan lands on Solomon Islands
	February 15: Japan captures Singapore
	February 27–March 1: Battle of Java Sea
	March 9: Japan conquers Java

	April 9: U.S. Army on Bataan peninsula in the Philippines surrenders
	May 2: Japan captures Mandalay in Burma
	May 7: Battle of Coral Sea
	June 4–7: Battle of Midway
	June 12: Japan occupies Attu in Aleutian Islands
	July 9: Chinese Nationalist forces win a major battle in Jiangxi province
	July 21: Japan captures Buna, New Guinea; drives toward Port Moresby
1943	February 9: Japan retreats from Guadalcanal in Solomons
	July 1: Allied offensive in South Pacific
	July 29: United States drives Japan from Aleutian Islands
	November 22: U.S. troops land on Tarawa in Gilbert Islands
1944	February 2: Invasion of Marshall Islands
	February 17: Battle of Truk lagoon
	June 15–July 7: U.S. forces take Saipan
	August 11: U.S. forces take Guam
	August: Britain retakes Burma
	October 23–25: Battle of Leyte Gulf
1945	March 10: Firebombing of Tokyo
	March 17: United States captures Iwo Jima
	April 1: Invasion of Okinawa begins
	June 22: Okinawa falls
	July 26: Potsdam Declaration
	August 6: Atomic bomb dropped on Hiroshima
	August 8: Soviet Union declares war on Japan
	August 9: Plutonium bomb dropped on Nagasaki
	August 15: Japan surrenders

The belligerents each had reasons for fighting. Still angry at the punitive terms that included a loss of territory imposed on it by the armistice that ended World War I, Germany insisted that it needed living space for its growing population. Hitler's Nazi Party believed Aryans were superior to all other races and destined to rule the world. Many people in Japan believed it was superior to the rest of Asia. Junior officers agreed with the Nazis and the Fascists in Italy that social dislocations in the early twentieth century had resulted from individualistic liberalism expressed in hedonistic urban culture and the compromises and corruption of politicians. They opposed capitalism and the capitalist powers—England, France, and the United States—that dominated the world economically and militarily. They also feared universal socialism emanating from the Bolshevik revolution that threatened the national polity. Japan's government and many of its citizens believed that Japan needed colonies for its national security. Fear that Soviet expansion threatened Japan's interests in Asia led it to take over Manchuria. It fought in China to protect its interests in Manchuria; once in that quagmire, it was sucked inextricably into conflict with the Allied powers.

Officers in the Japanese army took control of Manchuria to protect Japanese railroads and mines built after victory in the Russo-Japanese War. The army installed a puppet government in what it called Manchukuo headed by Puyi, the last Qing emperor. Treating Manchukuo as a new frontier, it encouraged settlers to displace indigenous people in farming what then became wide-open spaces. By 1945, Manchuria had absorbed approximately two hundred seventy thousand Japanese immigrants.

Japan's conquest of Manchuria sparked a wave of anti-Japanese demonstrations and a boycott of Japanese goods in China's major cities. The Japanese navy retaliated by bombarding civilian quarters in Shanghai before the eyes of the largest international community in China. An explosion of outrage filled foreign newspapers, but foreign governments did little. The League of Nations sent a fact-finding team to China, and when the League Assembly accepted the team's report that castigated Japan's aggression in Manchuria, Japan withdrew from the League.

Japan's attempts to establish a buffer zone in north China fed the growing anti-Japanese nationalist sentiment among Chinese people. A national salvation movement led by student demonstrations demanding national unity and resistance to Japan erupted in Beijing and spread to other cities. The Communists in Yan'an issued a call for all to resist Japanese imperialism. Even warlords in southwest China joined the clamor, though their patriotic fervor was tinged with a self-interested desire to obstruct Chiang Kaishek's nationalist government in Nanjing. The United Front of 1936 allied Communists and Nationalists against Japan. The development of anti-Japanese organizations meant that when the Japanese army invaded north China in July 1937 to protect its interests in Manchuria and seize attractive resources, it met fierce opposition.

The war in China was marked by the first atrocities of World War II committed against civilian populations. Japan did not expect the level of resistance offered by Chinese troops that attacked Japanese forces in and around Shanghai in retaliation for Japan's capture of Beijing and Tianjin. Not until December did the Japanese army capture Nanjing. When the city surrendered, Japanese army spokesmen contended that Chinese troops had taken off their uniforms

Crying Baby. This photograph of a crying baby that appeared in *Life* magazine following the Nanjing Massacre garnered America's sympathy for China in its struggle against Japan. *(Getty Images)*

to mingle with the civilian population, thereby justifying the murder of thousands of Chinese civilians. Frustrated that five months of warfare had not resulted in decisive victory, Japanese officers encouraged their men to loot stores and rape women. The number killed is disputed even today. This horror was dubbed the "Rape of Nanking" by the foreign press. Although this was the worst, it was by no means the last of the atrocities committed by Japanese troops.

Shocked at the international outcry and disturbed by the troops' behavior that they had encouraged, Japanese officers decided that indiscriminate rape threatened Japan's international reputation and military discipline. To provide for what was deemed the soldiers' physical needs and to combat venereal disease, the army developed a system of "comfort stations," already inaugurated in Shanghai in 1932. Japanese prostitutes were primarily reserved for officers in the rear. To find women for soldiers on the front lines, the military turned to its colonies and then to territories conquered after 1940. Koreans composed 80 percent of the "comfort women" who serviced troops as far away as Burma and island Southeast Asia. In some areas they had to service up to fifty men a day for a modest fee per soldier. Only the end of the war brought release from sexual slavery.

The China war demonstrated the importance and limitations of air power. Having few planes of its own, the Chinese nationalist army had to use natural defenses to hold off Japanese troops and delay their advance. When Chiang moved his government to Chongqing in the mountains of Sichuan, nearly perpetual fog protected the city from Japanese bombers. The narrow Yangzi gorges precluded an overland attack. Instead, Japanese troops fanned out along the eastern seaboard and along railroad lines in the interior. By the end of 1938, they occupied cities and major towns from Manchuria to Guangdong. In the days before helicopters, their superior air power had less effect in the countryside.

Although Chinese living under Japanese occupation tried to remain inconspicuous, many had to make a choice between collaboration and resistance. Collaborators set up a provisional government in Beijing in 1937 to administer north China. In 1940, Japan created the Reorganized Government of the Republic of China under Wang Jingwei, a member of Chiang Kaishek's Nationalist Party who hoped to win peace with Japan in the name of Greater East Asianism. In 1943 Japan allowed him to declare war on the United States and Great Britain. In the countryside, persistent guerrilla warfare led Japanese army units to launch indiscriminate punitive missions against villages thought to be harboring Communists. These "rural pacification" campaigns proved ineffective. Although 1 million Japanese troops occupied China's richest regions for eight years, they could not subdue the people or find an exit strategy from a war neither side could win.

Japan expected more than collaboration from its Korean subjects in its war with China. It expanded cotton and wool production at the expense of cereals; it developed hydroelectric power in the north. In 1936, it declared a new policy of forced assimilation: all Korean were to be taught that they too were children of the emperor. Later it banned the use of the Korean language in classrooms and ordered Koreans to adopt Japanese names. Japanese became the only language allowed in public offices and in record keeping by businesses and banks. Koreans had to worship at Shinto shrines and pray for the emperor's good health. Over six hundred thousand Korean men were drafted to work in Japanese and Manchurian mines, harbors, and factories. Although Japan taught that Korea and Japan were one, it did not trust the Koreans to fight its battles. By 1944 upwards of 4 million Koreans worked outside Korea, some as policemen and guards as far away as New Guinea, where they died in battles that made no distinction between combatants and noncombatants.

Japan's aggression in China provoked a response similar to what greeted Italy's conquest of Ethiopia in 1936. Both the League of Nations and the United States (which had not joined the League) officially deplored Japan's action. Neither tried to stop it, even though Japanese forces destroyed American property, sank an American warship, and killed American civilians. Fearful of Japan's intentions north of Manchuria, only the Soviet Union provided significant aid to China. It shipped munitions and airplanes to both Communist and Nationalist forces along with military advisers. Over two hundred Soviet pilots died in China's defense. In May 1939 the Japanese army in western Manchuria confronted Soviet forces at Nomonhan. The fight cost Japan eighteen thousand men and exposed critical weaknesses in the army's tactics and equipment. Japan sued for peace following the Russo-German Non-Aggression Pact signed in August. In 1941 Japan and the Soviet Union signed a neutrality pact. After Germany invaded the Soviet Union at the end of June, the Japanese army both kept alive the possibility of war with the Soviet Union and tried to honor the neutrality pact. Soviet aid to China came to an end with the outbreak of the war in Europe.

The United States relied on sanctions and threats to try to force Japan out of China and check Japan's expansion in Indochina. It placed a series of increasingly stringent embargos on goods to Japan and helped Chiang Kaishek by extending credit with which to buy American arms. When President Roosevelt had the Pacific Fleet move to Pearl Harbor to protect U.S. shipping lanes and intimidate Japan, Japan's navy took it as a threat to its interests in Micronesia and the South Pacific. In September 1940, Japan invaded North Vietnam to secure raw materials for its war machine and cut supply lines running to Chiang Kaishek. When the United States, Britain, and the Netherlands, which controlled the oil fields of Indonesia, cut off trade unless Japan pulled out of China and North Vietnam, Japan felt it had to fight or accept humiliation.

Neither the Allies nor Japan understood the other's motives, and they underestimated their opponents. Japan claimed to be liberating Asia from colonial powers. In 1940 it promoted, though it did not practice, the notion of a Greater East Asia Co-Prosperity Sphere, an economic regional power bloc similar to that envisioned in the western hemisphere under the Monroe Doctrine. In Japan's eyes, the United States and Soviet Union had everything they needed for an autonomous defense, but without colonies, Japan did not. Japanese soldiers saw themselves as spiritually superior to the materialistic West; they were hard and high-minded, whereas British and Americans were soft. Public opinion in the United States saw China as a victim of Japanese totalitarian aggression. Madame Chiang Kaishek gave an impassioned speech before the U.S. Congress in which she contrasted China striving for democracy and Japanese warmongers. Henry Luce, son of missionaries in China and owner of *Time-Life*, flooded his magazines with heart-rending pictures from war-torn China. Editorial cartoons drew on racial stereotypes to mock Japanese for their physical and mental inferiority and portrayed them as vermin to be exterminated.

Japan's desperation to find a solution to its war with China pushed it to open one battlefront after another, many over 3,000 miles from the home islands. To break through what it called the ABCD encirclement (American, British, Chinese, Dutch) and secure the oil crucial for its China campaign, it struck south. It bombed Pearl Harbor in hopes of forcing the United States to negotiate a settlement. Ten hours later, it launched an invasion of the Philippines, a U.S. colony. Britain had expected attack on Singapore to come from the sea; Japanese troops advanced through the jungle to capture the city. (The same month that saw the fall of Singapore also saw President Roosevelt sign Executive Order 9066 to place one hundred ten thousand Japanese Americans, over half of them U.S. citizens, behind the barbed wire of relocation camps in the western United States.) Within months Japan captured Indonesia, the Philippines, Guam, Wake, and the Solomon Islands. The Japanese army took over the rest of Vietnam, forced an alliance on Thailand, chased Britain out of Burma, closed the Burma Road that had carried to supplies to Chongqing, and threatened India and Australia. Combined with the islands taken from Germany in World War I, this gave the Japanese a vast empire, albeit mostly over water. (See Map C7.1.)

Beset with enemies from within and without, Japan's new empire lasted a scant two years. In some cases, men who were later to lead independence movements against western imperialism began by collaborating with Japan, as did General Aung San of Burma. When British soldiers beat a hasty retreat to India, units left behind formed the Indian National Army to fight for Indian independence. These instances serve as reminders that South and Southeast Asia welcomed Japan's message of liberation from colonial rule, but not the way it was delivered. Japan's arrogant sense of racial superiority soon made it enemies. Resistance to Japanese occupation from China to Indonesia to the Philippines contributed significantly to the Allies' counterattack. The British led Indian troops to reconquer Burma, Australians pushed Japan out of New Guinea, Chiang Kaishek's forces inflicted a major defeat on troops in China, the U.S. Army under General Douglas MacArthur advanced through the South Pacific before returning to the Philippines, and the U.S. Navy island-hopped across the Central Pacific.

Much of the fighting in the Pacific and Southeast Asia took place in jungles hated by both

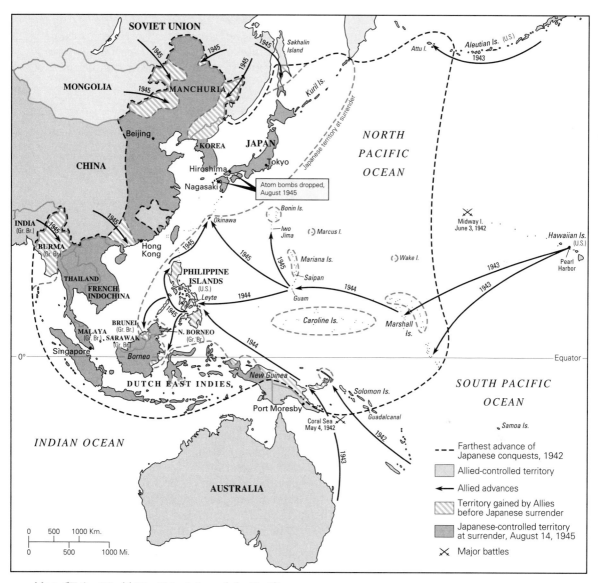

Map C7.1   **World War II in Asia and the Pacific**

sides. After four months on the Bataan peninsula in the Philippines, one-third of the U.S.
troops were in rain-dampened field hospitals
suffering from festering wounds, dysentery, and
malaria. Although the Japanese army used the
jungle to advantage in taking Singapore, its
troops too fell victim to disease in Burma and
Malaya. Japanese troops tried to cross the spine
of New Guinea from Buna to Port Moresby

over steep mountain passes covered with rain
forest. Thrown back by Australian forces, both
sides struggled through knee-deep mud to
engage an enemy seen only sporadically. Communications with headquarters broke down,
and fighting erupted haphazardly when individual units ran afoul the enemy.

Fighting on so many fronts meant that Japan
lacked the ability to provide its troops with

adequate supplies. Troops dispatched to far-flung islands and atolls were expected to live off the land. When U.S. submarines sank supply ships, they starved. Because the United States had signed a disarmament pact before the war that abjured submarine warfare as inhumane, Japan did not anticipate attacks on tankers and freighters sailing the western Pacific behind its defensive perimeter. In 1942, Japan received 40 percent of Indonesia's oil. Owing to the war of attrition, it received only 5 percent in 1944, and it received none in 1945. Taxis in Tokyo ran on wood-burning engines, and the air force adulterated scarce fuel with sap from pine roots.

Lacking adequate resources meant that the Japanese army and navy had to rely on men over machines. When Japan built runways on Pacific islands, it used human labor—natives, Koreans, Okinawans, prisoners of war. The Allies used bulldozers. At war's beginning, Japan had well-trained pilots flying the Zero, the most advanced fighter of its day. When those pilots were gone, their barely trained replacements had to fly against American pilots in planes constantly improved through new technology. Japan lost so many planes trying to defend Truk in Micronesia that American pilots called the battle "a turkey shoot." After the Japanese fleet lost six aircraft carriers at the battle of Leyte Gulf, the navy asked its pilots to crash their planes into enemy ships. Designated the Divine Wind Special Attack Corps to recall the typhoon credited with repelling Mongol invaders almost seven hundred years earlier, *kamikaze* pilots struck fear and loathing into Allied hearts. Nearly five thousand young men sacrificed their lives in a futile effort to stem the Allied tide sweeping toward Japan.

Air power made the decisive difference in the major battles on sea and land. From the battle of the Coral Sea, to Midway, to Leyte Gulf, although enemy ships saw each other's planes, the ships themselves never fought. Even before the attack on Pearl Harbor, the Allies had broken Japanese codes, and at the decisive battle of Midway, the United States used its knowledge of Japan's positions and intentions to sink three

of Japan's aircraft carriers and severely damage a fourth. The battle of the Coral Sea ended with Japan thinking it had lost, even though it sank more ships than the Allies. Throughout the war, Japan's admirals sought the decisive sea battle fought with battleships that would turn the tide of war just as Admiral Tōgō's stunning defeat of the Russian navy in 1905 had brought victory then. Little did they realize that aircraft carriers had made battleships irrelevant.

When Japan destroyed U.S. planes on the ground in the Philippines, it left U.S. troops defenseless against aerial attack. Later in the war, Japan's troops, and later cities, suffered the same experience once its air force had been decimated. The fall of Saipan in Micronesia after the navy lost over four hundred planes and every Japanese soldier had died in its defense put Japan's main islands within range of U.S. heavy bombers. The first raids, carried out at high altitudes, did little but psychological damage. Once General Curtis E. LeMay arrived from Europe, pilots in the Pacific perfected the art of carpet bombing, that is, dropping incendiary bombs at low attitudes that decimated Japan's wooden cities. In the largest air offensive in history, U.S. planes destroyed the remnants of the Japanese navy, shattered Japanese industry, and dropped forty thousand tons of bombs on population centers. Approximately ninety thousand civilians died in the firestorm that engulfed Tokyo. The plane that carried the atomic bomb to Hiroshima took off from Tinian, just north of Saipan. Its flight was virtually unimpeded.

Even before the fall of Okinawa that sacrificed one-quarter of the island's population to the defense of the homeland, cabinet members began to call for an end to the war. The army rebuffed them. With 5.5 million men relatively unscathed in China and Manchuria, it demanded that all Japanese prepare to make the ultimate sacrifice, to die like "shattered jewels" in protecting the emperor-centered national polity. Recalling President Theodore Roosevelt's mediation of an end to the Russo-Japanese War in 1905 and hoping to keep the Soviet Union neutral, the army finally agreed to let the Japan-

Suicide Bomber. A Japanese bomber makes a suicide dive on the *U.S.S. Hornet* on October 26, 1942, off Santa Cruz in the Solomon Islands. *(Bettmann/Corbis)*

ese ambassador to Moscow ask Foreign Minister Molotov for help. Busy with preparations for the Potsdam Conference, Molotov repeatedly put him off. On July 26, Churchill and Truman issued the Potsdam Declaration (Stalin did not sign it) demanding that Japan submit to unconditional surrender. Japan was to agree to allow occupation by foreign troops and to renounce all claims to territory on the Asian mainland and Taiwan. Its leaders and soldiers were to be tried for war crimes, and the Japanese people were to choose the form of government they wanted. The alternative was "prompt and utter destruction."

The Potsdam Declaration was both extremely specific and maddeningly vague. Japanese leaders had no way of knowing that destruction was to come via a bomb first tested ten days before.

To the distress of his loyal subjects, the declaration made no mention of the emperor. The cabinet decided to sit tight and hope for mediation by the Soviet Union. For three days in early August, the atomic bomb, the Soviet Union's declaration of war, and the plutonium bomb sent shock waves through the cabinet. At a climatic meeting on August 14, the emperor instructed the cabinet to surrender. Later, he made a recording to tell the Japanese people that they must bear the unbearable. Despite a plot by junior army officers to steal it, it was broadcast at noon on August 15. World War II was over.

After the war, Japanese military personnel were prosecuted for war crimes. In Indonesia, the Dutch convicted Japanese who had forced European women to service Japanese troops; they ignored cases involving Indonesian women. Other war crimes trials made no mention of comfort women. Nor did they include men from Unit 731 who had turned over their data on bestial experiments performed on Chinese in Manchuria to test bacteriological weapons. Instead the trials focused on crimes against humanity broadly defined as the decision to wage war; atrocities such as the Bataan death march in which thousands of American and Filipino soldiers died; the indiscriminate bayoneting of British doctors, nurses, and patients in Singapore; the machine-gunning, decapitation, and drowning of civilians in Southeast Asia; and the massacre of Filipinos in Manila at the end of the war. Japan's treatment of prisoners of war merited special condemnation; soldiers who survived surrender were starved, tortured, and forced to labor for the Japanese war machine in contravention of the Geneva Convention. The war crimes tribunals ignored atrocities committed by Allied forces.

Following World War II, the world split into two camps: the free world dominated by the United States and the Communist bloc led by the Soviet Union. An iron curtain came down in Europe. Forgetting that Japan's early victories had exposed their vulnerabilities, some western powers assumed that their former colonies in South and Southeast Asia would welcome them as liberators. The United States freed the Philippines in 1946. Britain pulled out of Burma and India in 1947. Two years later, the Dutch grudgingly granted independence to Indonesia. France refused to leave Vietnam until defeated in 1954. Civil war in China ended with the establishment of the People's Republic of China and the Nationalist Party's flight to Taiwan. Soviet troops began to enter Korea in August 1945. Hoping to prevent the whole country from falling into their hands, the United States got the Soviet Union to agree to a dividing line just north of Seoul at the 38th parallel. The two nations then sponsored the creation of two separate states on the Korean peninsula. Japan escaped that fate. Under U.S. occupation, it became a bulwark against communism.

SUGGESTED READING

There is a vast array of books on World War II. Some of the most recent include: E. Bergerud, *Touched with Fire: The Land War in the Pacific* (1996); N. Tarling, *A Sudden Rampage: The Japanese Occupation of Southeast Asia* (2001); and J. C. Hsiung and S. I. Levine, *China's Bitter Victory: The War with Japan, 1937–1945* (1992). The classic is J. W. Dower, *War Without Mercy: Race and Power in the Pacific War* (1986). On related topics, see K. Honda, *The Nanjing Massacre: A Japanese Journalist Confronts Japan's National Shame* (1999); Y. Tanaka, *Japan's Comfort Women: Sexual Slavery and Prostitution During World War II and the US Occupation* (2002); and S. H. Harris, *Factories of Death: Japanese Biological Warfare, 1932–1945 and the American Cover-up* (2002).

27

War and Aftermath in Japan (1931–1964)

Japan's war in Asia and the Pacific expanded in response to military imperatives and domestic problems. It spurred institutional and economic development; it caused devastation and loss of life. After surrender, the United States occupied Japan and instituted reforms designed to transform it into a demilitarized democracy. Those that had lasting impact built on trends apparent during the war; others, including Japan's diplomatic relations with the United States, sparked controversy. The despondency of defeat turned into a determination to rebuild. High-speed economic growth began in the 1950s. When the economy reached prewar levels of production in 1956, the government declared the postwar period to be officially over. In 1960 it announced the Income Doubling Plan. The 1964 Tokyo Olympics marked Japan's return to the world order and restored its self-confidence as a nation.

The further World War II recedes into the past, the more historians emphasize continuities across its divide. Although the impact of the war on individual lives is undeniable, its long-term consequences on the economy and society are more problematic. Other questions to consider are: Who was responsible for the war? What kind of impact did the Occupation have on Japan? What enabled the postwar recovery?

ROAD TO WAR

Military actions exacerbated by rural crises dominated politics in the 1930s. The army demanded support for its takeover of Manchuria in 1931; the navy criticized the limitations imposed by the London Naval Treaty. The armed forces transformed Japan into a militaristic state by forcing the Diet to curtail freedom of speech and approve its war budgets. Anger at capitalist *zaibatsu* for sucking the farmers' blood and at corrupt politicians who put their interests ahead of the nation erupted in abortive coups d'état that exposed factions within the military. Mass organizations drew the farmers' support to the military; farmers also participated in self-improvement drives sponsored by bureaucrats and civilian reformers. Only a few intellectuals dared criticize imperialist policies. For the majority of citizens, being Japanese meant taking pride in the slogan, "Asia for the Asiatics," which obfuscated Japan's colonizing project.

Junior Officers and the Citizenry

Radical junior officers drew inspiration from diverse sources. They heard their men's stories of sisters being sold into prostitution to save the family farm from moneylenders. They read in the newspapers of how the *zaibatsu* profited from currency speculation when Japan went off the gold standard in 1931. They studied Kita Ikki's *A Plan for the Reorganization of Japan*. Kita proposed that the "people's emperor" suspend the constitution and have the government confiscate surplus wealth, manage the economy, and provide social welfare and "world knowledge based on the Japanese spirit." When these goals had been accomplished, Japan would liberate Asia and "the Sun Flag of the Land of the Rising Sun will light the darkness of the entire world."[1] Officers modeled their plans for revolution on the Meiji Restoration. Like men of high purpose (*shishi*), they had to act to remove evil advisers who prevented the emperor from making his will known to the people. They credited violence with purifying the state and mistrusted old men who might tarnish their youthful idealism.

The junior officers responded to and exacerbated factions in the military. Their hero, General Araki Sadao, promoted spiritual training to inculcate devotion to the emperor and martial virtues of loyalty and self-sacrifice. The Japanese spirit (*Yamatodamashii*) sufficed to overcome mere material obstacles. His Imperial Way faction opposed the Control faction's arguments that battles could be won only by rational planning using the latest military technology and sophisticated weaponry. In 1935, an Araki supporter assassinated the Control faction's General Nagata Tetsuzan and electrified the nation with his diatribe against military men and their civilian toadies who had corrupted army and *kokutai*. On February 26, 1936, junior officers armed with the slogan, "Revere the Emperor, Destroy Traitors," led fourteen hundred troops to seize the Diet building and army headquarters, kill cabinet ministers, and call on the emperor to announce a Shōwa Restoration. Horrified at the threat of insurrection, the emperor summoned the army to suppress the rebellion. After a four-day standoff, the junior officers surrendered. They were executed along with their mentor Kita Ikki in a victory for the Control faction.

A symbiotic relationship developed between the military and the old middle class of shopkeepers and factory owners as well as teachers, low-ranking officials, and farmers. The army founded the Imperial Military Reserve Association in 1910, the Greater Japan Youth Association in 1915, and the Greater Japan National Defense Women's Association in 1932. Organized at the hamlet, not the amalgamated village level, the Reserve Association took over community functions such as firefighting, police, road and canal repairs, shrine and temple maintenance, emergency relief, and entertainment. It promoted drill practice, "nation-building" group calisthenics, and bayonet competitions. It hosted lectures by military-approved speakers, and it corresponded with battalion adjutants regarding the welfare and conduct of conscripts. The women's association sank roots in urban as well as rural areas. These associations identified the

---

1. George M. Wilson, *Radical Nationalist in Japan: Kita Ikki 1883–1937* (Cambridge, Mass.: Harvard University Press, 1969), pp. 75, 81.

individual with the community, the community with the army, and the army with the emperor.

Social Reform

In the 1930s, bureaucrats and social reformers focused on devastation resulting from crop failures in northeastern Japan. When students dispatched by Hani Motoko, journalist and founder of the magazine *Woman's Friend* (*Fujin no tomo*), reported that farmers knew nothing of modern hygiene and sanitation, spent money foolishly on ceremonies, lazed about, and drank, Hani established settlement houses that taught poor women sewing, cleanliness, etiquette, nutrition, and thrift. The Agriculture Ministry supported similar plans that promoted social education, agricultural cooperatives, economic planning, and moral betterment. The emphasis on thrift and frugality paralleled the nationwide effort by the Home Ministry, social reformers, educators, and women's leaders to increase Japan's savings rate, both to help individuals plan for emergencies and to fund national projects.

WARTIME MOBILIZATION

During eight years of war between 1937 and 1945 (see **Connections: World War II**), government ministries were often poorly informed, disorganized, and overextended. Faced with unexpected challenges, they cobbled together ad hoc measures and made mistakes in prosecuting the war overseas and on the home front. Just as the army and navy competed for resources, the former emphasizing the threat from the Soviet Union while the latter focused on the United States, so did civilian ministries duplicate each other's efforts and fight for control of domestic policy. Like the Germans, the Japanese at first refused to mobilize women, a policy that limited the war effort.

Civilian commitment to the war varied. Businessmen supported military goals so long as they did not threaten survival of their firms. Under pressure to conform, citizens greeted news of the first victories with exultation. Dwindling food supplies, higher taxes, and a black market led to forbearance and despair. Malnutrition increased the incidence of tuberculosis (one hundred sixty thousand deaths in 1942), rickets, and eye disease. First children and then adults fled cities for the countryside. When the flower of Japan's youth was called to make the supreme sacrifice in the Special Attack Forces (*kamikaze*), many did so gladly; others did not. (See **Documents: Excerpts from the Diary of Hayashi Toshimasa**.)

Unlike other belligerents in World War II, Japan's wartime leadership changed repeatedly. Seven prime ministers served between the outbreak of war with China on July 7, 1937, and surrender on August 15, 1945. Executed as a war criminal for having declared war against the United States, General Tōjō Hideki served concurrently as prime minister (1941–1944), army minister, home minister, and munitions minister and filled other posts as he perceived the need. He never directed naval operations nor did the navy inform him when it fought. Even the army general staff challenged his authority. Civilian bureaucrats, especially in the Justice Ministry, maintained their constitutional autonomy. Only the Shōwa emperor received complete information on military policy and operations, including plans for surprise attacks on American, Dutch, and British bases in 1941. For fear of jeopardizing the throne, he sanctioned military decisions as his ancestors had done for centuries.

Government planning of the economy began in 1931 when the Diet passed the Major Industries Control Law. It promoted cartels and required industries to tell the government their plans. In 1937 came the New Economic Order to make the Japanese Empire self-sufficient. Bureaucrats allocated funds to critical industries, nationalized electrical plants, supervised banks, and spun a web of regulation. The National Mobilization law of 1938 focused research on chemicals and machine technology. Large companies had to introduce on-the-job

DOCUMENTS

Excerpts from the Diary of Hayashi Toshimasa

Why do soldiers fight? What do they think about as they wait to die? This diary, written by Hayashi Toshimasa, a graduate of Keiō University who was killed in action on August 9, 1945, affords one answer to these questions and provides glimpses of the camaraderie and resentments that supported members of the Special Attack Forces in their final days.

April 13, 1945

First Lieutenant Kuniyasu was killed in action, as was Second Sub-lieutenant Tanigawa Takao. Everyone is dying away. The lives of plane pilots are short indeed. I just heard today that Second Sub-lieutenant Yatsunami also died the day before yesterday; he dove straight into the sea while participating in night-training, and his dead body was washed ashore yesterday onto the white beach of Kujūkuri-hama. Dear Yatsunami! I enjoyed getting together with him again here—the last time was in Mie. Dressed in his nightclothes, he came to my room rather late on the evening of the day before the accident, and we drank beer together. I wonder whether or not it was some kind of premonition. He was very gentle and quiet. When I said, "What a splendid nightwear," he just chuckled and said that it had been made by his wife, whom he just married in January. His wife too suffered the misfortune on this earth of a typical pilot's wife. How is she going to spend the long life that stretches ahead of her?

Tanigawa has a fiancée too, in Kobe. Those who were left behind may be unlucky, but their sacrifice is an offering for Japan's ultimate victory. So I would ask to please continue to live with strength and pride, and in such a way as not to bring shame to the brave men who courageously and willingly died for their country.

April 23

Nighttime flying began. After our flying operation we drank beer at a welcome party for Kamiōseko. I got a little high. Second Sub-lieutenant Kamiōseko and I were enraged at the current situation. It was all about our position as reserve officers in the Imperial Navy. Now I declare! I will not fight, at least not for the Imperial Navy. I live and die for my fatherland, and, I would go so far as to say that it is for my own pride. I have nothing but a strong antipathy for the Imperial Navy—absolutely no positive feelings at all. From now on I can say in and to my heart, "I can die for my own pride, but I would not die—absolutely not—for the Imperial Navy." How terribly we, the 13th class of pilots to come out of the "students mobilized for war" program, have been oppressed by the Imperial Navy! Who exactly is fighting this war now anyway? A full half of my classmates of the 13th class who were bomber pilots on carriers, and my friends, are now already dead.

I will live and die for my fatherland, my comrades of the 13th class, all those senior fighting men who are members of the "students mobilized for war" program, and, lastly, for my own pride. I shall do so cursing all the while the Imperial Navy, which to me merely means a certain group of officers who graduated from the Etajima Naval Academy.

training for workers. Labor was rationed according to production needs. Military requirements prompted the rise of new industries in fields such as optics, determined techniques used in existing industries such as steel, and stimulated technological innovation. Wartime priori-

June 30

It was raining when I woke up this morning, and I was so glad I could sleep some more that I pulled a blanket over me again. I got up a little after seven, took a late breakfast, and at a barracks I went over some slides designed to help us recognize the different types of enemy ships. Now I have finished with the slides. I returned to my own room, and am writing this and playing a record. Next door, on a blanket spread over the floor, Kamiōseko, Yamabe, Tejima, and Nasu are having fun playing bridge. No change outside—the steady rain continues.

I cannot begin to do anything about everything.

Simply because I shall have to leave this world in the very near future.

I should thank the Navy's traditional spirit, or rather their cliquishness, which drove Eguchi to say: "I want to go to the front soon—I want to die soon," and even drove me into that sort of psychological state. It even drove all the rest of us, university students transformed into pilots, into that same state of mind.

July 31

Today is a sortie day. It is the day for the eight planes of our Ryūsei (Falling Star) squad to carry out a special attack. The fog was extremely thick when I got up. It turned into water that dripped from the leaves and treetops on the mountain.

When I arrived at the airport, the items that were to be carried onto our planes were neatly set out in rows.

Last night, I completely changed everything that I was wearing. I also wound tightly around my waist the thousand-stitch cloth my mother sent me. Then there was the brand-new muffler my aunt in Yudate gave me.—In other words, I put on the very best things I had.

I am all alone and, expecting the sortie command to come along at any moment, I am writing this in an air-raid shelter.

Farewell dear Father, Mother, Brothers and Sisters, and other relatives and friends.

Please continue to live on enjoying very good health.

This time I am going right into Han Christian Andersen's fairyland, and I will become its prince.

And I shall be chatting with little birds, flowers, and trees.

I pray for the eternal prosperity of the great Japanese Empire.

August 9 A clear day

Once again the enemy's mechanized divisions are approaching the home islands.

In one hour and a half I shall leave here for the sortie, as a member of the special attack force. The skies are a breathtakingly deep blue, and there is a sharp touch of autumn.

August 9th!

Today I shall fly one of the very latest in war planes, a Ryūsei, and will slam it into an enemy carrier.

Source: *Listen to the Voices from the Sea: Writings of the Fallen Japanese Students*, comp. Nihon Senbotsu Gakusei Kinen-Kai, trans. Midori Yamanouchi and Joseph L. Quinn (Scranton, Pa.: University of Scranton Press, 2000), pp. 247–250, modified.

ties transformed Japan's industrial structure. Textile industries declined; heavy and chemical industries expanded.

The Home Ministry bent social mores and popular culture to the war effort. Foreign words being considered symptomatic of foreign sympathies, "baseball" became *yakyū*. Martial music replaced jazz. Hair permanents were criticized because they were western and wasted resources. Women had to dress in baggy pants called *monpe*. The Communications Ministry founded the Dōmei News Agency in 1936 to channel national and international news to newspapers. It already controlled radio broadcasts through the national public radio station, NHK. To extend its reach, the ministry distributed free radios to rural villages.

The Education Ministry suppressed academic freedom and promoted patriotism. Professors critical of the war in China and military dominance over politics had to resign. School children performed physical exercises to build bodies for the emperor; after 1940 they volunteered for community service projects. Starting in 1941 they took paramilitary training to identify enemy aircraft and practiced charging with bamboo spears. Published in 1937, the textbook *Cardinal Principles of the National Polity* (*Kokutai no hongi*) taught students that the emperor was the divine head of state and benevolent father to the Japanese people. The Japanese were superior because of their racial homogeneity. They possessed a distinctive culture and history infused by the radiant presence of the imperial house. No sacrifice was too great to protect this unique heritage.

In the name of national unity, the government suppressed all pacifist new religions under the Religious Organizations Law of 1939. Social reformers and feminist activists joined the Greater Japan Women's Society that sent soldiers off to war and disseminated ways to practice frugality. Patriotic Associations united tenant farmers and landlords, workers and businessmen. The ideology of "dedicated work" valorized labor as a public activity in service to the nation. Neighborhood associations organized air raid drills and kept watch for dangerous thought. In 1944 the Home Ministry folded them all into the Imperial Rule Assistance Association.

A dedicated citizenry and long-range planning could not overcome growing shortages. The government struggled to shore up the collapsing economy. Lacking imported technology, compa-nies developed new techniques that took military needs and scarce resources into account. The Zero fighter was crafted with extreme precision and used minimal amounts of steel regardless of the pilot's safety. In addition to the lack of fuel because of disruptions to shipping, the destruction of factories meant fewer manufactured goods such as fertilizer. Food production dropped.

Military conscription created labor shortages in industry and mining. The first to fill the gap were Koreans. In 1943, the government allowed women to volunteer for work in ordnance and aircraft industries. It drafted prisoners of war to work in steel plants and mines. The military ended educational deferments and drafted university students. In 1944 middle school boys started factory work.

The last months of the war brought widespread hardship. Evacuees to the countryside put an extra burden on scarce resources. Nutritional levels declined following the meager harvest of 1944. A few people criticized their leaders in anonymous graffiti and letters to the editor. Worker absenteeism rose, product quality slipped, and work stoppages spread. Although signs of disaffection were slight, they were enough to make politicians and bureaucrats worry about the threat of social revolution. By the time most factions in the government were willing to admit defeat, approximately 3 million Japanese had died. Despite the evidence of destruction, the emperor's announcement on August 15 that the war had been lost came as a shock.

OCCUPATION

Defeat did not bring an end to hardship. The suburban middle class was spared the fate of poor and working-class urban residents who lost everything in the firestorms, but everyone was short of food. Farmers were better off, although stunned by defeat that called into question cherished ideals of loyalty, patriotism, and service to the emperor. Occupation by a

labor camps. Soviet soldiers raped and killed women and children. Of Japanese settlers in Manchuria, 50 percent died at the end of the war, many at the hands of Chinese. Japanese settlers in Korea made their way across hostile territory to refugee camps and then on crowded ships to Japan. Seventy thousand Japanese in the Philippines had to wait until the end of 1946 before seeing Japan; the British and Dutch did not return their prisoners of war until 1947. On Pacific islands, pockets of Japanese soldiers resorted to cannibalism or starved. The last soldiers came home in the 1970s.

Repatriated soldiers and civilians met a cold welcome in war-devastated Japan. War widows, homeless orphans, and maimed veterans became social rejects. Most shunned were the victims from Hiroshima and Nagasaki, subject to radiation sickness that turned them into pariahs. With the economy at a standstill, there was little work even for the able-bodied. Competition for jobs depressed already low wages. The winter of 1945–1946 was worse than the winters of wartime. Rationed supplies of coal and food were not enough to stave off freezing and starvation. Urban women traveled to the countryside to trade heirlooms for food and patronized the black market.

For some, defeat meant liberation. If life had no meaning, why not drink, take drugs, and steal? In his 1947 novel *The Setting Sun*, Dazai Osamu mourned the loss of prewar values and presented the only choice left: to live for oneself alone. People who celebrated the end to restrictions on freedom of thought and behavior had an easier time coping with material shortages. Defeat vindicated the beliefs of prewar Marxists and socialists who hoped to build a just society out of the rubble of failed capitalist fortunes. The black market flourished at every train terminal, organized and patrolled by gangsters. Small factory owners made pots instead of helmets, and former soldiers became businessmen. Prostitutes called pan-pan girls who serviced GIs dressed in rayon dresses and nylon hose, curled their hair, and painted their faces in an orgy of self-expression not seen since the 1920s. The

Japanese Women Working in an Ordnance Factory. With able-bodied men drafted for the war effort, women had to take their place in industry. *(AKG, London)*

military dictatorship under General Douglas MacArthur began on August 30, 1945. At first the mood was to punish Japan, perhaps by returning it to an agrarian economy. After the beginning of the Cold War with the Soviet Union and the 1949 Communist takeover of China, the emphasis shifted to making Japan a bulwark against communism.

Despair and Liberation

The war left 6.6 million Japanese soldiers and civilians stranded in enemy territory from Manchuria to Southeast Asia. The Soviet Union sent five hundred seventy-five thousand military personnel and adult male civilians to Siberian

dominant themes in popular culture were titillation and sex; the carnal body replaced the *kokutai,* the body politic.

Occupation Goals

As Supreme Commander of the Allied Powers (SCAP—also shorthand for the Occupation bureaucracy), MacArthur intended to demilitarize Japan and work through existing governmental institutions to install democracy. The United States kept the Allies out of Japan by putting them on the Far East Commission (FEC) that oversaw SCAP policy. It met in Washington, D.C. The United States bought off the Soviet Union by handing over islands north of Hokkaido. Only judges for the Tokyo war crimes trials represented countries that had suffered under the Japanese war machine. One SCAP faction wanted to restrict Japan's international trade and dispatch the fruits of industrialization to Japan's victims as war reparations. The other consisted of economists and lawyers primed to practice social engineering. By instituting land reform, revising education, promoting labor unions, emancipating women, limiting police powers, and rewriting the constitution, they planned to make Japan fit to rejoin the community of nations.

What was to be done with the Shōwa emperor? He did not sign the instrument of surrender on September 2, 1945; that humiliation was left to a general and a diplomat. Instead, he, the cabinet, and his staff tried to distance him from responsibility for the war, taking a stance of plausible deniability on all decisions save the last that ended it. MacArthur dissuaded him from admitting even moral responsibility. Although the British wanted to try him as a war criminal, MacArthur believed that once the military was gone, the emperor was needed as a bulwark against communism. By refusing to accept responsibility for the war in which so many had died in his name, the emperor also alienated far right militarists. The issue of his responsibility for the war has continued to rankle at home and with Japan's neighbors. On January 1, 1946, the emperor announced that he was a human being, not a manifest god. Defined by the new constitution as symbol of the state, he continues to embody a national identity predicated on ethnic homogeneity.

Occupation Reforms

On October 13, 1945, the prime minister appointed a committee at SCAP's urging to consider constitutional revision. Political parties, progressive and socialist groups, scholars, and think tanks drafted constitutions ignored by the prime minister's committee. Its recommendations were so minor that in February 1946, MacArthur ordered his Government Section to take over the task lest a grass-roots movement for a constitutional convention lead to too much democracy and an attack on the emperor. His people hid their work from the United States and Japanese governments, the FEC, and other branches of SCAP. After conferences between SCAP officials and cabinet representatives to debate the draft, it was published in early March 1946. SCAP intervened repeatedly in Diet deliberations to limit discussion and prevent substantial revision. The new constitution replaced the Meiji constitution, to which it was offered as an amendment, when the Upper House approved it in October. The emperor promulgated it on November 3, 1946.

Articles in the constitution define the rights to life, liberty, and the pursuit of happiness as the rights to education, health care, police protection, work, and a minimum standard of living. Women received the right to vote. People detained by the police had the right to legal counsel. Freedoms included freedom from arbitrary arrest and unauthorized search and seizure plus freedom of assembly, speech, and religion. The judiciary became separate and independent. The Privy Council was dissolved in accordance with the principle of popular sovereignty. The Diet acquired the sole authority to make laws. Its vote of no confidence sufficed to dissolve the cabinet. Within the Diet, the Lower House of Representatives took precedence over the Upper House of Councilors, which became an elected body.

The new constitution had clauses that MacArthur would have deplored in the U.S. Constitution. Workers obtained the right to organize unions and bargain collectively, professors had the right to academic freedom, and women were guaranteed equal rights with men. Most controversial was Article 9: "The Japanese people forever renounce war as a sovereign right of the nation . . . land, sea, and air forces will never be maintained."[2] This wording was later interpreted to mean that armed forces could be created for self-defense. When the FEC insisted on a clause that limited the cabinet to civilians, this too was interpreted as implying the existence of a military. In 1950, SCAP wanted Japan to create an army to fight in Korea. Prime Minister Yoshida Shigeru refused. He created a Police Reserve, soon transformed into the Self-Defense Force.

Once the constitution had been promulgated, the Justice Ministry reformed the civil code. The new code emphasized the equality of the sexes and the dignity of the individual. It abolished patriarchal authority in the household, reiterated the freedom of marriage promised in the constitution, and required that all children share the family estate. This was not a burden for middle-class families whose assets consisted of their children's education. For shopkeepers, restauranteurs, or farmers, an equal division of property plus heavy inheritance taxes all too often meant selling off the patrimony.

SCAP quickly imposed additional reforms. The most radical forced landlords to sell their holdings to the government for resale to tenants, a measure met with approval by the Agriculture and Forestry Ministry that wanted a class of independent farmers even before the war. Absentee landlords had to relinquish all their land; resident landlords were allowed to keep only land they farmed themselves plus an additional five or so acres depending on the region. Although collecting tenant fees had already

proved so onerous that many landlords welcomed the chance to sell out, they lamented the loss of their ancestral way of life. By 1950, farmer-owners cultivated 90 percent of Japan's agricultural land.

SCAP also intervened in educational reform. With American schools as the model, a new single-track system of primary school, middle school, and high school replaced the specialized higher schools. Compulsory education was extended to nine years. Teachers embraced the new curriculum that stressed the civic virtues of democracy and individual responsibility. Locally elected school boards selected texts, although in later years they did so from a list vetted by the Education Ministry. The Parent-Teacher Association involved mothers in school activities. New junior colleges, colleges, and universities made higher education available to a wider segment of the population than before. None rivaled Tokyo University, and all required that students pass entrance examinations.

SCAP kept itself above the law. Despite the separation of church and state, MacArthur allowed Christian missionaries to use U.S. government equipment and encouraged the emperor and empress to take instruction in Christianity. Censorship of printed materials and movies continued. Left-wing publications that criticized capitalism faced prepublication scrutiny. In movies, sword fighting and criticism of the emperor were out. Instead, SCAP encouraged movie makers to depict romance between men and women. The first mouth-to-mouth kiss made headlines.

Economic Developments

Economic reform took many turns. Trustbusters took aim at the *zaibatsu* because they had contributed to Japan's war effort (Mitsubishi made the Zero fighter) and because their economic dominance appeared inherently undemocratic. SCAP ordered the holding companies for the ten largest *zaibatsu* dissolved, broke up the Mitsui and Mitsubishi trading companies, forced

---

2. Dale M. Hellegers, *We, the Japanese People: World War II and the Origins of the Japanese Constitution,* 2 vols. (Stanford: Stanford University Press, 2002), p. 576.

family members to sell their stock and resign from boards, and purged fifteen hundred executives accused of aiding the war machine. Japanese bureaucrats allowed government assets, including construction materials and machinery, to disappear into the black market or the hands of business cronies. To cover the deficit and the run on savings deposits at war's end, the Finance Ministry printed reams of money. Official prices soared 539 percent in the first year of the Occupation, with black market prices ranging from fourteen to thirty-four times higher. Fearing the destabilizing effects of inflation, at the end of 1948, Washington dispatched a banker from Detroit named Joseph Dodge. At Dodge's command, the government collected more in taxes than it paid out. It eliminated government subsidies to manufacturers. Public works, welfare, and education suffered cuts. Dodge curbed domestic consumption and promoted exports. He got the United States to agree to an exchange rate of 360 yen to the dollar. Deflation and economic contraction forced small businesses into bankruptcy.

The Korean War rescued Japan from the brink of depression and laid the foundation for future economic growth. The industrial sector gorged on procurement orders for vehicles, uniforms, sandbags, medicines, electrical goods, construction materials, liquor, paper, and food. Despite the prohibition on the manufacture of war materiel, Japanese companies made munitions. Their mechanics repaired tanks and aircraft. Businesses plowed profits into upgrading equipment and buying advanced technology from the United States through licensing agreements and the purchase of patent rights. Industries that looked beyond the war for a way to compete in the expanding world economy incorporated the quality control method that the statistician W. Edwards Deming had introduced to Japan in 1949. By the end of the Korean War, the increase in wages and economic growth had brought food consumption back to pre–World War II levels. Consumers were able to buy household amenities and still put money into savings accounts.

Labor and the Reverse Course

To promote democracy, SCAP had the Trade Union Law issued in December 1945, and workers seized the opportunity to organize. Free to participate in politics, the Japanese Communist Party (JCP) and the Japanese Socialist Party (JSP) fostered trade unions. By the middle of 1948, unions enrolled over half of the nonagricultural work force, including white-collar workers, especially in the public sector. Other workers organized production control movements to take over businesses, factories, and mines that owners were accused of deliberately sabotaging in revenge for democratization. Like unionized workers, they wanted to get back to work and make a living wage.

Labor union activism led to the "reverse course." Workers united around issues including adequate food, support for working mothers, equal pay for equal work, and democratic elections. Before the postwar election of April 10, 1946, in which women voted for the first time, a rally in Tokyo brought together workers, farmers, Koreans, and ordinary citizens to listen to speeches by Communists, Socialists, and liberals demanding a people's constitution and criticizing the cabinet for obstructing democratic reform. On May 1, International Workers' Day, cities nationwide witnessed demonstrations in support of worker unity and democracy. On May 19, women joined demonstrations demanding that the emperor force the government to deliver food. Students held demonstrations a week later to demand self-government at their institutions. Socialist- and Communist-led labor unions formed in August organized strikes in October. In January 1947, the prime minister warned that striking government workers would be fired. A coalition of labor unions announced plans for a general strike on February 1. MacArthur called it off. In 1948 SCAP had the Japanese government issue regulations forbidding public employees to strike.

The reverse course had additional dimensions. The Cold War led the United States to view its erstwhile enemy as an ally against com-

Color Plate 25
Boxer Print. The Boxers spread word of their invincibility through woodblock prints like this one, which shows their attack on the treaty port city of Tianjin.

(British Library)

Color Plate 26
People of the Five Nations: A Sunday. This woodblock triptych published in 1861 showed Japan how westerners dressed and entertained themselves in the foreign settlement at Yokohama.

(Arthur M. Sackler Gallery, Smithsonian Institution, Washington, DC: Gift of Ambassador and Mrs. William Leonhart, S1998.96a–c)

Color Plate 27
Gas Lights. Gas lights illuminating the streets of Tokyo became
a favorite subject for modern woodblock print artists.
(Edo Tokyo Museum/Tokyo Metropolitan Foundation for History and Culture Image
Archives/DNP Archives.com)

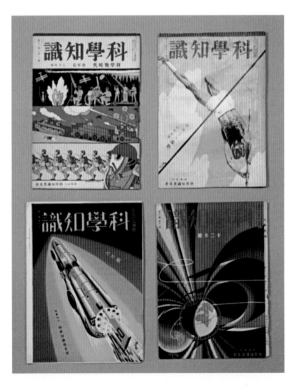

Color Plate 28
Magazine covers for *Kagaku chishiki* (Scientific
Knowledge) by Sugiura Hisui from 1931–1935
illustrated the wonders of science and technology
for young readers.

(The National Museum of Modern Art, Tokyo)

Color Plate 29
Raising Mao Zedong's Thought. This 1967 poster is titled "Revolutionary Proletarian Right to Rebel Troops, Unite!" The books they hold are the selected works of Mao Zedong. The woman's armband reads "Red Guard."

(David King Collection, London, UK)

Color Plate 30
Goddess of Democracy. During the 1989 demonstrations in Tiananmen Square, art students provocatively placed a 37-foot tall statue labeled the Goddess of Democracy facing the portrait of Mao Zedong.

(Jeff Widener/AP Wide World Photos)

Color Plate 31
The Takenoko Zoku (Bamboo Tribe). Young people gather each Sunday on the bridge between trendy Harajuku and the Yoyogi stadiums built for the 1964 Tokyo Olympics to dance and show off.

(Lonely Planet Images)

Color Plate 32
Industrial Plants. This photo depicts industrial plants stretching along Japan's Pacific coast, transforming what had once been scenic views of mountains and water into a modern landscape.

(Corbis)

munism. SCAP compiled lists of "reds" to purge first the public sector and later, during the Korean War, the private sector. Approximately twenty-two thousand workers lost their jobs, and most of the JCP leadership went underground. Previously purged politicians, bureaucrats, and business leaders were rehabilitated. In 1948, plans to dismantle the *zaibatsu* came to a halt. The Diet gave the bureaucracy greater control over trade and investment than it had during the war. The Ministry of International Trade and Industry (MITI) had the Japan Development Bank lend money from the government's postal savings system to private companies. MITI also advised the Bank of Japan on its loans to private banks. It approved the transfer of foreign technology to industries it deemed worthy and provided them with administrative guidance. The Finance Ministry regulated currency transactions by restricting the amounts of money individuals and corporations could take or send out of the country.

Before ending the occupation, the U.S. Senate had Japan sign a peace treaty with the Nationalist Chinese on Taiwan that precluded recognition of and trade with the People's Republic of China. The peace treaty and security treaty signed with the United States plus associated agreements signed in 1951 continued the Occupation under a different name. After SCAP was dismantled in 1952, one hundred thousand American personnel plus dependents stayed on at military bases that dotted the islands. The right of extraterritoriality protected them from the Japanese judicial system and removed the bases from oversight by the Japanese government. Okinawa remained under U.S. military jurisdiction until 1972. Under the U.S. security umbrella, Japan was free to pursue economic development, although it had to follow the U.S. lead in international relations. On Bloody May Day 1952, four hundred thousand workers, students, and housewives denounced the Security Treaty, Japanese rearmament, the status of Okinawa, and government plans to pass an "antisubversive" bill that threatened academic freedom. Political positions divided between left-wing support for neutrality, democratization, and demilitarization and the conservative affirmation of alliance with the United States.

POLITICAL SETTLEMENT AND ECONOMIC RECOVERY

A host of political parties contended for Diet seats in the first postwar election of 1946. Yoshida Shigeru pulled together a coalition of conservative parties willing to make him prime minister, but he had to resign when elections the following year gave a significant share of the votes to the JSP. Taking advantage of the JSP's inability to deal with economic crises, Yoshida regained the prime ministership in 1948 and held it until 1954. He recruited former bureaucrats into his party whose administrative experience and skill at in-fighting gave them an edge in faction building. The JSP split over whether to support the U.S.-Japan Peace Treaty; it reunited in October 1955. The next month, the two conservative parties formed the Liberal Democratic Party (LDP). It dominated Diet and cabinet until 1993. During this period of one-party rule, heads of factions within the LDP selected the prime minister, who rewarded his supporters with powerful and lucrative ministerial appointments.

The LDP promoted economic growth as the nation's highest goal, less to enhance state power than to wean workers from socialism by offering them a better life. Starting in the late 1950s, the LDP spread the benefits of the growing economy across all sectors of society through higher wages and a higher standard of living. In 1958, it inaugurated national health insurance. It helped farmers increase productivity by mechanizing production and spreading chemical fertilizers and pesticides. The government paid villages to reorganize land holdings into fewer, bigger plots and individuals to diversify crops. It encouraged companies to locate factories in rural areas and hire farmers. It built roads and sewer systems. It restricted the import of rice and subsidized rice production. Through these programs and the outright purchase of votes, the LDP acquired a lock on rural electoral districts. The appeal of conservative policies to small businessmen and shopkeepers gave it urban votes as well.

The LDP also maintained power by aligning itself with bureaucrats and businessmen. Advisory groups composed of businessmen and bankers, consumers and union officials, consulted with cabinet ministers on policy and proposed legislation. Ex-bureaucrats either ran for office or joined corporations whose fortunes they had helped guide. Undergirding the web of personal connections was a flow of cash from businessmen to politicians to voters.

Political and Social Protest

Opposition parties in the Diet so little impeded the LDP juggernaut that citizens with grievances sought other forms of protest. Demonstrations against American bases and nuclear testing erupted periodically during the 1950s. The Japan Teachers' Union resisted the centralization of educational policy and personnel practices instituted by the Education Ministry in 1955. The General Council of Japanese Trade Unions (Sōhyō) opposed the Japan Productivity Center set up by Japanese businessmen with U.S. assistance because the unions feared it would exploit workers. When the government decided to switch Japan's chief energy source from coal to oil, the Mitsui Mining Company called for the voluntary early retirement of six thousand workers at its Miike mine in Kyushu. The union responded with a strike marked by violence and death that lasted 113 days. Workers learned that radical calls for class struggle undercut job security, and corporate managers learned that it was cheaper to transfer redundant workers to other operations than to fire them.

The largest political demonstrations in Japanese history erupted from late 1959 to June 1960 over revision and extension of the U.S.-Japan Security Treaty. Negotiations removed the clause that permitted the use of U.S. troops to quell internal disturbances, but bases remained off-limits to Japanese scrutiny. Indicted as a war criminal and former minister in Manchuria, Prime Minister Kishi Nobusuke rammed the revised treaty through the lower house with the help of police who evicted the JCP and JSP opposition. Outraged at Kishi's high-handed tactics, masses of demonstrators gathered outside the Diet. Sōhyō had already coordinated strikes and mobilized workers against the treaty. The All Japan Federation of Student Self-government Associations (Zengakuren) organized weeks of agitation. Some 134 groups and organizations including farmers and housewives joined the protest. Kishi had planned to celebrate the revised security treaty by welcoming U.S. President Dwight D. Eisenhower to Japan, but Eisenhower canceled the trip. Daily demonstrations continued at the Diet and in cities across Japan. On June 18, several hundred thousand people surrounded the Diet, but they could not prevent the treaty's automatic ratification at midnight. Kishi resigned five days later. In 1965 Japan signed a peace treaty with South Korea, to the outrage of the left wing, which demonstrated against the exclusion of North Korea and the People's Republic of China. The ideological divide between conservatives and progressives sparked political unrest throughout the 1960s.

The constitution's guarantee of social equality and the Civil Code's emphasis on human dignity spurred the *burakumin* to renew their struggle for equal rights. Founded in 1955, the Buraku Liberation League (BLL) allied itself with the JCP and JSP to publicize unfair treatment by individuals and institutions. It participated in demonstrations against the renewal of the U.S.-Japan Security Treaty that gained it widespread support. Later protest marches focused nationwide attention on the *burakumin*'s plight. A government commission report in 1965 blamed *burakumin* problems on unwarranted social and economic discrimination. The Diet responded in 1969 by passing the Special Measures Law for Assimilation Projects that decried discrimination without instituting measures to stop it. To ameliorate this defect, the BLL resorted to denunciation campaigns sometimes escalating to violence and threats that silenced public discussion of *burakumin* problems.

Women's organizations in the 1950s worked to protect children and encourage respect for

Demonstrations Opposing the U.S.–Japan Security Treaty. During demonstrations opposing the U.S.–Japan Security Treaty, men and women marched on the American Embassy demanding cancellation of President Eisenhower's visit, the prime minister's resignation, and dissolution of the Diet. *(Bettmann/Corbis)*

mothers. Women joined movements to prohibit nuclear testing and to promote world peace for the sake of their children. They demanded clean elections. They elected women to the Diet who pushed for sexual equality and human rights. Women had campaigned for the abolition of state-sanctioned prostitution before the war; their goal became a reality in 1956 when the Diet passed the Prostitution Prevention Law that took effect two years later. While it abolished legal protection for prostitutes, it did not eliminate sex work. Women justified political activism on two grounds: their responsibility for their families and their constitutional rights.

Post-Occupation Economic Development

International and domestic factors promoted economic growth. Under the Potsdam Declara-

tion, Japan was guaranteed access to raw materials it had previously extracted from its colonies. Exchange rates remained stable until 1971. The world market was relatively open. Economic expansion across the free market world stimulated a growing demand for manufactured goods. Japan still had infrastructure developed before and during World War II. The most important prewar legacies were human resources—trained engineers, accountants, and workers—and the commitment to achievement through education. The first postwar generation of workers went into factories on graduation from high school, received on-the-job training, and worked long hours for the sake of their companies. Enterprise unions held demonstrations during the yearly spring offensive but interfered as little as possible in production. Management upped basic wages, promised lifetime employment, and distributed raises based on seniority. Workers came to live middle-class lives.

Heavy industries developed in wartime, and new companies that fashioned products for domestic consumption and export saw the greatest expansion. Steel producers, ship builders, manufacturers of synthetic fibers, and electronics and household appliance makers invested heavily in technologies imported from the United States and in labor-saving mass-production facilities. The government provided low-cost financing that made Japan the largest shipbuilder in the world in the 1950s. MITI protected car and truck manufacturers by forbidding foreign investment in the auto industry and imposing tariffs of up to 40 percent on imported cars. Companies that enjoyed less help from MITI were Matsushita, maker of household appliances, and the electronics innovator Sony. (See **Material Culture: The Transistor.**) Supporting corporate growth were subcontractors that produced quality components for finished products. Between 1947 and 1952, the economy grew at an average annual rate of 11.5 percent. From 1954 to 1971, it grew at over 10 percent a year, to rank second to the United States among free market economies.

Increases in domestic consumption stimulated high-speed economic growth. During the Occupation, SCAP broadcast images of American prosperity in the comic strip *Blondie* and other media to promote American values. Department store exhibitions and magazine advertisements illustrated the material life of the conqueror. Once the quality of food had improved, people wanted fashionable clothes. Every household wanted labor-saving devices such as a washing machine, refrigerator, and vacuum cleaner. Television broadcasts began in 1953 because the owner of the *Yomiuri* newspaper and key bureaucrats believed that national pride required Japan to have the latest technology. The wedding of Crown Prince Akihito to the industrialist's daughter Shōda Michiko in 1959 swept televisions from retailers' shelves as viewers reveled in the democratic dream of a love marriage. Beginning in 1955, a massive exodus from farms to cities fueled a housing boom of high density apartment buildings in suburbs. In these years, 90 percent of Japan's production went into the domestic market.

Postwar Culture

The consumption of mass culture stimulated growth in the entertainment industries, publishing, and film. Commercial television stations demanded an endless supply of programming. The government-owned NHK had two channels: one devoted to news analysis, dramas, and *sumo* wrestling, the other specializing in education. Magazine and book publishers continued prewar trends without the fear of censorship that had kept them from sensitive political topics. Kurosawa Akira directed *Ikiru* (To Live), which criticized bureaucratic arrogance. His 1951 film *Rashomon,* which questioned the possibility of knowing the truth, brought international recognition to Japanese cinema when it won the grand prize at the Venice Film Festival. A series with wider appeal was *Godzilla,* started in 1954, which drew on Japan's sense of victimhood by depicting a monster roused from the deep by nuclear explosion. Misora Hibari captured hearts with her songs of parting and loss. They spoke to the will to survive that had carried women through the hardships of war and Occupation. Public intellectuals and writers such as Maruyama Masao and Mishima Yukio questioned the ingredients of Japan's national identity. What did it mean to be Japanese if the nation's only goal was economic success? Wherein laid responsibility for wartime aggression?

New religions provided one answer to these questions. Founded in 1930 and suppressed during the war, Sōka Gakkai (value-creating society) was Japan's largest new religion in the 1960s. Its political arm, the Clean Government Party (Kōmeitō), founded in 1964, became Japan's third largest political party. Today its leaders serve as town councilors and school board officers. It owns land, businesses, and shops. It provides a sense of family and community, help in finding marriage partners, jobs, loans, and

MATERIAL CULTURE

The Transistor

Every electronic product today relies on transistors, symbol and product of the technological age. Invented by Bell Laboratories in 1948, the early transistors were too unreliable and delicate for consumer applications, and they could not handle high frequencies for the human voice. It took Sony researchers months of experimentation to find a useable combination of materials.

Sony introduced a transistor radio in January 1955, only to discover that it disintegrated in summer heat. The second version placed on the market in August had poor sound quality, but it sold domestically owing to its battery's long life. Sony could not compete with American transistor radios until 1957 when it started selling a tiny "pocketable" radio. More important than the radio's size was the technological breakthrough based on the high-performance alloy germanium. In 1960 transistor radios became Japan's second biggest earner on the export market after ships. Teenagers loved carrying them to parks, mountains, and beaches to listen to rock and roll.

Sony introduced the world's first all-transistor television in 1960 and successfully miniaturized it two years later. In 1964 Sony displayed a prototype of a transistorized calculator at New York's World Fair. Three years later it introduced a desktop calculator.

The transistors in the early radios, televisions, and calculators were huge compared to the silicon transistors in integrated circuits today that work liquid display calculators and watches. People typically buy electronic goods on impulse, indulging in a plethora of gadgetry that fills purses, pockets, and homes.

The TR-63. Sony's first successful transistor radio, the TR-63, could be called 'pocketable' only because Sony salesmen wore shirts with extra large breast pockets. *(Sony Corporation)*

higher education. The *zadankai*, a type of group therapy, helps followers solve personal problems and gain self-confidence. Sōka Gakkai teaches that the purpose of life is the pursuit of happi-ness; the three virtues of beauty, gain, and goodness bring happiness; following the teachings of Nichiren and having faith in the *Lotus Sutra* bring virtue. The constitutional guarantee of

BIOGRAPHY Daimatsu Hirobumi

Soldier, prisoner of war, women's volleyball coach, and Diet member, Daimatsu Hirobumi (1921–1978) gained worldwide fame for his draconian coaching methods when his team won the gold medal at the 1964 Tokyo Olympics.

Hirobumi's wartime experience marked him for life. Conscripted into the army after the attack on Pearl Harbor, he attended an officers' preparatory school in China and fought in China and Southeast Asia. The last months of the war found him in Burma with only raw bamboo shoots for food. Many soldiers died; sheer willpower kept him alive. He ended up at a prisoner of war camp run by the British in Rangoon. In revenge for the atrocities that the Japanese army had inflicted on British POWs and the humiliating surrender of Hong Kong and Singapore, British officers subjected Japanese POWs to shameful indignities. Hirobumi later recounted how he cleaned the latrines for British and Indian soldiers with his bare hands. Worse, he had to clean the female officers' rooms and wash the underwear that they removed before his eyes in a gesture calculated to be emasculating.

Repatriated to Japan after twenty-two months as a POW, Hirobumi found work coaching a women's volleyball team at the Nichibō textile factory in Kaizuka. At that time volleyball was a popular sport among factory workers because it could be played with just a ball in whatever space was available. In 1954 Nichibō organized a company team with Hirobumi in charge. In 1958, the team won all of Japan's major titles; in 1962 it won the world championship.

Hirobumi's training methods were brutal. He hurled balls at the players until they collapsed from pain and exhaustion. He insisted that they play regardless of injuries. He allowed them only three and one-half hours of sleep a night before the Olympics and had them practice for four hours the day of the final match. He also emphasized the incremental improvement of technique, relying on methods similar to quality control circles. His players once complained to the factory management that he was an enemy of women because he worked them unmercifully. He expected them to sacrifice everything for the chance to win, first for the company, then for Japan, just as he had sacrificed himself in wartime.

Eight-five percent of Japan's television sets were tuned to the Olympics the night the Japanese team defeated the Soviet Union in three sets. The women's unprecedented success made volleyball a national obsession. Hirobumi's fame swept him to a seat in the Diet's upper house in 1968. He lost his bid for a second term.

Source: Based on Yoshikuni Igarashi, *Bodies of Memory: Narratives of War in Postwar Japan* (Princeton, N.J.: Princeton University Press, 2000).

---

religious freedom and the population shift from country to town led to an explosion in the numbers of new religions and their membership. Although they criticize the excesses of popular culture and consumerism, part of their appeal lies in their promise of material benefits.

The Tokyo Olympics of 1964 marked the climax of high-speed economic growth and a turning point in Japan's postwar history. (See **Biography: Daimatsu Hirobumi.**) The national and Tokyo metropolitan governments cleaned up and paved city streets; rebuilt stores, schools, and government offices; constructed stadiums at Yoyogi Park; dug new subway lines; laid new roads; and renovated Haneda Airport and connected it to the city by monorail. New hotels became Japan's first postwar high rises. The centerpiece of this vast public works project was the Shinkansen (bullet train), which covered the distance between Tokyo and Osaka in three hours and ten minutes. It was the fastest, most reliable, and safest train in the world.

Japan had been allowed to join the United Nations in 1956, and the Olympics marked the culmination of its reentry into the global community. Worldwide coverage of the games focused attention on Japan as a peaceful modern state. When Kawabata Yasunari received the Nobel Prize in Literature in 1968, the international accolade testified to Japan's acceptance by world opinion.

SUMMARY

Between 1931 and 1945, Japan passed through the dark valley of wartime aggression and deprivation. It recovered thanks to the changing international climate of the late 1940s and early 1950s, the reforms initiated by the U.S. Occupation, the protection provided by the security agreement with the United States, and the U.S. recognition that democracy required economic stability. It must not be forgotten that recovery also built on the educational and industrial foundation laid before the war.

SUGGESTED READING

For general coverage of this period, see H. P. Bix, *Hirohito and the Making of Modern Japan* (2000), and T. Nakamura, *A History of Shōwa Japan, 1926–1989* (1998). For prewar Japan, see M. Barnhart, *Japan Prepares for Total War: The Search for Economic Security, 1919–1941* (1987), and S. Vlastos, ed., *Mirror of Modernity: Invented Traditions of Modern Japan* (1998). For wartime, see S. Ienaga, *The Pacific War, 1931–1945* (1978); B. Shillony, *Politics and Culture in Wartime Japan* (1981); and L. Young, *Japan's Total Empire: Manchuria and the Culture of Wartime Imperialism* (1998). For the Occupation, see K. Hirano, *Mr. Smith Goes to Tokyo: Japanese Cinema Under the American Occupation, 1945–1952* (1992), and J. W. Dower, *Embracing Defeat: Japan in the Wake of World War II* (1999).

For the postwar era, see A. Gorden, ed., *Postwar Japan as History* (1993); A. Gordon, *The Wages of Affluence: Labor and Management in Postwar Japan* (1998); L. F. Hein, *Fueling Growth: The Energy Revolution and Economic Policy in Postwar Japan* (1990); J. V. Koschmann, *Revolution and Subjectivity in Postwar Japan* (1996); W. Sasaki-Uemura, *Organizing the Spontaneous: Citizen Protest in Postwar Japan* (2001); and B. Johnstone, *We Were Burning: Japanese Entrepreneurs and the Forging of the Electronics Age* (2000).

China Under
Mao (1949–1976)

By the end of 1949, the Communist Party had gained control of almost the entire country, and Mao Zedong had pronounced the establishment of the People's Republic of China (PRC). The party quickly set about restructuring China. People were mobilized to tackle such tasks as redistributing land, promoting heavy industry, reforming marriage practices, and unmasking counterrevolutionaries. Wealth and power were redistributed on a vast scale. Massive modernization projects created new factories, railroads, schools, hospitals, and reservoirs. Ordinary people were subject to increased political control as the central government set policies that determined what farmers would produce, where and how their children would be educated, what they might read in books and newspapers, where they could live or travel. The most radical phase was during the Cultural Revolution, especially 1966 to 1969, when the party itself was attacked by students and workers mobilized to make permanent revolution.

Until the late 1970s, western scholars had limited access to the PRC and had to rely heavily on analyzing official pronouncements and interviewing refugees. Scholars studied the structure of the government, its policies, its top figures, and their factional struggles. As China has become more open in the past two decades and new sources have become available, research has revealed much more complex pictures of how China fared during the Mao years. Not only can the human dramas be examined with more nuance, but variation from one place to the next can be assessed. Mao still fascinates. Can the excesses of the Great Leap and the Cultural Revolution be fully blamed on Mao's inadequate grasp of reality? How could one person make such a difference? The party is also a subject of renewed interest. How did policies set at the center play out at the local level? What means did local cadres (party functionaries) use to get compliance with policies? What were the consequences of vilifying intellectuals? How did day-to-day life change for ordinary people in villages or towns?

THE PARTY IN POWER

From 1950 on, the Communist Party, under the leadership of Mao Zedong (to use the phrase of the time), set about to fashion a new China, one that would empower peasants and workers and limit the influence of landlords, capitalists, intellectuals, and foreigners. New values were heralded: people were taught that struggle, revolution, and change were to be celebrated; compromise, deference, and tradition were weaknesses. People throughout the country were filled with hope that great things could be achieved.

In terms of formal political organization, the Soviet Union's model was adopted with modifications. Rather than a dictatorship of the proletariat, as the Soviet Union called itself, China was to be a "people's democratic dictatorship," with "the people" including workers, both poor and rich peasants, and the national bourgeoisie, but excluding landlords and certain classes of capitalists. The people so defined were represented by a hierarchy of irregularly scheduled People's Representative Congresses.

Real power, however, lay with the Communist Party. The People's Liberation Army (PLA) was not subordinated to the government but rather to the party, through its Military Affairs Commission. By the end of the 1950s, there were more than 1 million branch party committees in villages, factories, schools, army units, and other organizations. Each committee sent delegates up to higher units, including county and province committees, leading up to the three top tiers: the Central Committee with a few dozen members, the Politburo with around a dozen members, and its Standing Committee, which in 1949 consisted of Mao Zedong, Liu Shaoqi, Zhou Enlai, Zhu De, and Chen Yun and later was expanded to include Deng Xiaoping. Mao Zedong was recognized as the paramount leader and treated almost as though he was an emperor. In 1953, when he was sixty years old, Mao was chairman of the party, chairman of the Military Affairs Commission, and chairman of the PRC. The central government had dozens of ministries, and Mao needed an array of secretaries to handle all of the paperwork he had to process. Expert organizers like Zhou Enlai and Liu Shaoqi, both of whom had been active in the party since the early 1920s, coordinated foreign and economic policy, respectively.

The Communist Party faced enormous challenges. After forty years of fighting in one part of the country or another, the economy was in shambles. Inflation was rampant. Railroad tracks had been torn up and bridges destroyed. Harbors were clogged with sunken ships. People displaced by war numbered in the millions. Many of those manning essential services had been either Japanese collaborators or Nationalist appointees and did not inspire trust. Chiang Kaishek had transferred much of his army to Taiwan and had not given up claim to be the legitimate ruler of China.

In December 1949, Mao went to Moscow to confer with Joseph Stalin. He stayed nine weeks—his first trip abroad—and arranged an agreement on Soviet loans and technical assistance. Soon more than twenty thousand Chinese trainees went to the Soviet Union, and some ten thousand Russian technicians came to China to help set up 156 Soviet-designed heavy industrial plants. To pay for these projects, agriculture was heavily taxed, again on the Soviet model. According to the First Five Year Plan put into effect for the years 1953 to 1957, output of steel was to be quadrupled, power and cement doubled. Consumer goods, however, were to be increased by much smaller increments—cotton piece goods by less than half, grain by less than a fifth.

But China could not create everything from scratch. Ways had to be found to maintain the infrastructure of modern urban life, the factories, railroads, universities, newspapers, law courts, and tax-collecting stations, even as the party took them over. When the Red Army entered cities, its peasant soldiers put an end to looting and rounded up beggars, prostitutes, opium addicts, and petty criminals. They set up street committees, which were told to rid the cities of flashy clothes, provocative hairstyles, and other signs of decadence. But illiterate soldiers were not qualified to run all urban enterprises themselves.

Some enterprises the new state took over outright. By taking over the banks, the government brought inflation under control within a year. The new government took control of key industries, such as the railroads and foreign trade. In other cases, capitalists and managers were left in place but forced to follow party directives. A large-scale campaign was launched in 1951–1952 to weed out the least cooperative of the capitalists still controlling private enterprises. City residents were mobilized to accuse merchants and manufacturers of bribery, tax evasion, theft of state assets, cheating in labor or materials, or stealing state economic secrets. In the single month of April 1952, seventy thousand Shanghai businessmen were investigated and criticized. The targets often felt betrayed when their family members and friends joined in attacking them. Once businessmen confessed, they had to pay restitution, which often meant giving shares of their enterprises to the government, turning them into joint government-private ventures. To keep enterprises running, the former owners were often kept on as government-paid managers, but they had been discredited in the eyes of their former subordinates. Smaller manufacturing plants, stores, and restaurants were gradually dominated by the government through its control of supplies and labor.

As the party took control, it brought the advantages of modern life, such as schools and health care, to wider and wider circles of the urban and rural poor. During the 1950s rapid progress was made in cutting illiteracy and raising life expectancy. Employment was found for all, and housing of some sort was provided for everyone.

Ideology and Social Control

China's new leaders called their victory in the civil war "the liberation." As they saw it, the Chinese people had been freed from the yoke of the past and now could rebuild China as a socialist, egalitarian, forward-looking nation. China would regain its stature as a great nation and demonstrate to the world the potential of socialism to lift the masses out of poverty. Achieving these goals required adherence to correct ideology, identified as "Mao Zedong Thought." Since Mao's ideas changed over time and put emphasis on practice over theory, even those who had studied Mao's writings could never be totally sure they knew how he would view a particular issue. As long as Mao lived, he was the interpreter of his own ideas, the one to rule on what deviated from ideological correctness.

Spreading these ideas was the mission of propaganda departments and teams, which quickly took over the publishing industry. Schools and colleges were also put under party supervision, with a Soviet-style Ministry of Education issuing directives. Numerous mass organizations were set up, including street committees in cities, the Youth League, Women's Federation, and Labor Union Federation. Party workers who organized meetings of these groups were simultaneously to learn from the masses, keep an eye on them, and get them behind new policies. Meeting halls and other buildings were festooned with banners and posters proclaiming party slogans. (See **Material Culture: Political Posters.**)

The pervasive attack on the old led to the condemnation of many features of traditional culture. Traditional religion was labeled feudal superstition. In 1950 the Marriage Reform Law granted young people the right to choose their marriage partners, wives the right to initiate divorce, and wives and daughters rights to property. The provisions of these laws did not go much further than the Nationalists' Civil Code of 1930, but they had a considerably greater impact because campaigns were launched to publicize them and to assure women of party support if they refused a marriage arranged by their parents or left an unbearable husband or mother-in-law. During the first five years of the new law, several million marriages were dissolved, most at the request of the wife. This campaign should not, of course, get full credit for changes in the Chinese family system, as many other forces contributed to undermining patriarchal authority, such as the drastic shrinkage of family property as a result of collectivization of land and appropriation of business assets, the entry of more children into schools and mass organizations like the Youth League,

MATERIAL CULTURE

Political Posters

Under Mao, political posters, reproduced from paintings, woodcuts, and other media, were displayed prominently in classrooms, offices, and homes. The artists who produced these works had to follow the guidelines set by Mao Zedong at the 1942 Yan'an Forum for Literature and Art. Art was to serve politics and further the revolutionary cause. Toward that end, it had to be appealing and accessible to the masses. "Cultural workers" were sent out to villages and factories to study folk art and learn from real life. In addition, workers and peasants were encouraged to attend art schools and create artwork of their own. During the Cultural Revolution, Jiang Qing, Mao's wife, dominated cultural productions during this period, and art showed a new militancy. (See Color Plate 29.)

Mao Among Happy Peasants. The caption for this poster reads "All Living Things Depend on the Sun." Viewers would have understood that Mao is China's sun. *(David King Collection, London, UK)*

the mobilization of women in large numbers into the work force, and the public appearance of more women in positions of authority, ranging from street committees to university faculties and the upper echelons of the party.

Art and architecture were deployed to spread new ideas. The old city of Beijing was given a new look to match its status as capital of New China. The huge walls around Beijing were torn down as outmoded obstacles to traffic. The area south of the old imperial palace was cleared of buildings to create Tiananmen ("Gate of Heavenly Peace") Square. On either side of this square, two huge Soviet-style buildings were erected: the Great Hall of the People and the Museum of Chinese History. In the center was placed a hundred-foot-tall stone Monument to the People's Heroes, with friezes depicting heroic revolutionaries of the past century in the new international socialist realist art style. When huge May Day and National Day rallies were held, China was visually linked to Communist countries all around the world.

The Communist Party developed an effective means of social and ideological control through the *danwei* (work unit). Most people's *danwei* was their place of work; for students it was their school; for the retired or unemployed, their neighborhood. Each *danwei* assigned housing, supplied ration coupons (for grain, other foodstuffs, cloth, and anything else in short supply), managed birth control programs, and organized mass campaigns. One needed permission of one's *danwei* even to get married or divorced.

The Korean War and the United States as the Chief Enemy

The new government did not have even a year to get its structures and policies in place before it was embroiled in war in Korea. After World War II, with the ensuing Cold War between the United States and the Soviet Union, Korea had ended up with the Soviet Union dominant above the 38th parallel and the United States below it (see Chapter 30). Mao knew that China's development plans hinged on respite from war. Stalin, however, approved North Korea's plan to invade South Korea, which occurred in June 1950. In October U.S. forces, fighting under the United Nations flag in support of the South, crossed the 38th parallel and headed toward the Yalu River, the border between North Korea and China. Later that month, Chinese "volunteers," under the command of Peng Dehuai, began to cross the Yalu secretly, using no lights or radios. In late November they surprised the Americans and soon forced them to retreat south of Seoul. Altogether, more than 2.5 million Chinese troops were sent to Korea, as well as all of China's tanks and over half its artillery and aircraft. A stalemate followed, and peace talks dragged on until 1953, largely because China wanted all prisoners repatriated but fourteen thousand begged not to be sent back.

This war gave the Communist Party legitimacy in China: China had "stood up" and beaten back the imperialists. But the costs were huge. Not only did China suffer an estimated three hundred sixty thousand casualties, but the war eliminated many chances for gradual reconciliation, internal and external. The United States, now viewing China as its enemy, sent the Seventh Fleet to patrol the waters between China and Taiwan and increased aid to Chiang Kaishek on Taiwan. China began to vilify the United States as its prime enemy.

With Taiwan occupying the China seat on the UN Security Council, the United States pushed through the UN a total embargo on trade with China and enforced it by a blockade of China's coast. Of necessity, self-reliance became a chief virtue of the revolution in China. When the United States helped supply the French in their war to regain control of Vietnam, China supplied Ho Chi Minh and the Vietminh. China became more afraid of spies and enemy agents and expelled most of the remaining western missionaries and businessmen. A worse fate awaited those who had served in the Nationalist government or army. A campaign of 1951 against such "counterrevolutionaries" resulted in the execution of tens or hundreds of thousands, with similar numbers sent to harsh labor reform camps. This campaign was also used to disarm the population; over five hundred thousand rifles were collected in Guangdong alone.

Collectivizing Agriculture

The lives of hundreds of millions of China's farmers were radically altered in the 1950s by the progressive collectivization of land and the creation of a new local elite of rural cadres. Ever since the 1930s, when the Communist Party took control of new areas, it taught peasants a new way to look on the old order: social and economic inequalities were not natural but a perversion caused by the institution of private property; the old literati elite were not exemplars of Confucian virtues but the cruelest of exploiters who pressured their tenants to the point where they had to sell their children. That antiquated "feudal" order needed to be replaced with a communal order where all would work together unselfishly for common goals.

The first step was to redistribute land. Typically, the party would send in a small team of cadres and students to a village to cultivate relations with the poor, organize a peasant association, identify potential leaders from among the poorest peasants, compile lists of grievances, and organize struggles against those most resented. Eventually the team would supervise the classification of the inhabitants as landlords, rich peasants, middle peasants, poor peasants, and hired hands. The analysis of class was supposed to be scientific, but moral judgments tended to intrude. How should one classify elderly widows who rented out their meager holdings because they were incapable of working them themselves? Somewhat better-off families of veterans?

Families that had bought land only recently from money earned in urban factories? Or families newly impoverished because the household head was a decadent wastrel or opium addict?

These uncertainties allowed land reform activists to help friends and get back at enemies. In some villages, there was not much of a surplus to redistribute. In others, violence flared, especially when villagers tried to get those labeled landlords or rich peasants to reveal where they had buried their gold. Landlords and rich peasants faced not only loss of their land but also punishment for past offenses; a not insignificant number were executed. Another result of the class struggle stage of land reform was the creation of a caste-like system in the countryside. The descendants of those labeled landlords were excluded from leadership positions while the descendants of former poor and lower-middle peasants gained preference.

Redistribution of land gained peasant support but did not improve productivity. Toward that end, progressive collectivization was promoted. First, farmers were encouraged to join mutual aid teams, sometime later to set up cooperatives. Cooperatives pooled resources but returned compensation based on inputs of land, tools, animals, and labor. In the "old liberated areas" in north China, this was accomplished in the early 1940s; in south China, these measures were extended during the period 1950–1953. From 1954 to 1956 a third stage was pushed: higher-level collectives that amalgamated cooperatives and did away with compensation for anything other than labor. Most of these higher-level cooperatives were old villages or parts of large villages. Once higher-level cooperatives were in place, economic inequality within villages was all but eliminated.

In 1953, the Chinese state took over control of the grain market. After taking 5 to 10 percent of each collective's harvest as a tax, the government allowed the unit to retain a meager subsistence ration per person; then it purchased a share of the "surplus" at prices it set, a hidden form of taxation. Interregional commerce was redefined as criminal speculation, an extreme form of capitalist exploitation. Trade was taken over by the state, and rural markets ceased to function. Many peasants lost crucial sideline income, especially peasants in poorer areas who had previously made ends meet by operating such small enterprises as oil presses, paper mills, or rope factories. Carpenters and craftsmen who used to travel far and wide became chained to the land, unable to practice their trades except in their own localities.

Rural cadres became the new elite in the countryside. How policy shifts were experienced by ordinary people depended on the personal qualities of the lowest level of party functionaries. In some villages, literate middle peasants who knew a lot about farming rose to leadership positions. In other villages, toughs from the poorest families rose because of their zeal in denouncing landlord exploitation. To get ahead, a team leader had to produce a substantial surplus to serve the needs of the revolution without letting too much be taken away and thus losing his team's confidence. As units were urged to consolidate and enlarge, rural cadres had to spend much of their time motivating members and settling squabbles among them. For those with the requisite talents, serving as a rural cadre offered farmers possibilities for social mobility way beyond anything that had existed in imperial China, since local team leaders could rise in the party hierarchy.

Much was accomplished during collectivization to improve the lot of farmers in China. Schools were opened in rural areas, and children everywhere enrolled for at least a few years, cutting the illiteracy rate dramatically. Basic health care was brought to the countryside via clinics and "barefoot doctors," peasants with only a few months of training who could at least give vaccinations and provide antibiotics and other medicines. Collectives took on responsibility for the welfare of widows and orphans with no one to care for them.

Minorities and Autonomous Regions

The new China proclaimed itself to be a multinational state. Officially the old view of China as the civilizing center, gradually attracting, acculturating, and absorbing non-Chinese along its frontiers, was replaced by a vision of distinct ethnic groups joined in a collaborative state. "Han" was promoted as the correct term for the most advanced ethnic group; "Chinese" was stretched to encompass all ethnic groups in the People's Republic.

The policy of multinationality was copied from that of the Soviet Union, which had devised it as the best way to justify retaining all the lands acquired by the czar in the eighteenth and nineteenth centuries. For China the model similarly provided a way to justify reasserting dominion over Tibet and Xinjiang, both acquired by the Qing but independent after 1911. (Mongolia had fallen away as well, but under the domination of the Soviet Union it had established a Communist government in the 1920s, so China did not challenge its independence.)

Identifying and labeling China's minority nationalities became a major state project in the 1950s. Stalin had enunciated a nationalities policy with four criteria for establishing a group as a "nationality": common language, common territory, a common economic life, and a common psychological makeup manifested in common cultural traits. Using these criteria, Chinese linguists and social scientists investigated more than four hundred groups. After classifying most as local subbranches of larger ethnic groups, they ended up with fifty-five recognized minority nationalities making up about 7 percent of the population. Some of these nationalities were clear cases, like the Tibetans and Uighurs, who spoke distinct languages and lived in distinct territories. Others seemed matters of degree, like the Hui, Chinese-speaking Muslims scattered throughout the country, and the Zhuang of Guangxi, who had long been quite sinified. In cases where a particular minority dominated a county or province, the unit would be recognized as autonomous, giving it the prerogative to use its own language in schools and government offices. Tibet, Xinjiang, Ningxia, and Inner Mongolia were all made autonomous provinces, and large parts of Sichuan, Yunnan, and Guizhou were declared autonomous regions of the Zhuang, Miao, Yi, and other minorities. (See Map 28.1.) By 1957, four hundred thousand members of minority groups had been recruited as party members.

Despite the protections given minorities in their autonomous regions, many of them became progressively more Han through migration (see **Biography: Jin Shuyu, Telephone Minder**). Inner Mongolia soon became 90 percent Han Chinese, and the traditional Mongol nomadic culture largely disappeared as ranch-style stock raising replaced moving the herds with the seasons. In Xinjiang too, in-migration of Han Chinese changed the ethnic makeup, especially in the cities. Manchuria, now called the Northeast, had for nearly a century been the destination of millions of Han Chinese, a process that continued as the Communists built on the heavy industry base left by the Japanese.

Tibet was a special case. It had not come under rule of any sort from Beijing until the eighteenth century, and the Manchu rulers had interfered relatively little with the power of the Lamaist Buddhist monasteries. From the 1890s on, Tibet fell more under the sway of the British, but Britain left India in 1947, ending its interest in Tibet. In 1950, when Lhasa would not agree to "peaceful liberation," the PLA invaded. Tibetan appeals to the UN were not considered, on the recommendation of India. Tibet had no choice but to negotiate an agreement with the Chinese Communist Party. Tibet recognized China's sovereignty and in exchange was allowed to maintain its traditional political system, including the Dalai Lama. From 1951 to 1959, this system worked fairly well. By 1959, however, ethnic Tibetans from neighboring provinces were streaming into Tibet, unhappy with agricultural collectivization. When massive protests broke out in Lhasa, the army opened fire. The Dalai Lama and thousands of his followers fled to India, which welcomed them. The aftermath included more pressure on Tibet to conform to the rest of the People's Republic and the sense among Tibetans that theirs was an occupied land.

Intellectuals and the Hundred Flowers Campaign

In the 1920s and 1930s some of the most enthusiastic supporters of socialism were members of the educated elite (now usually called intellectuals). Professors like Chen Duxiu and Li Dazhao

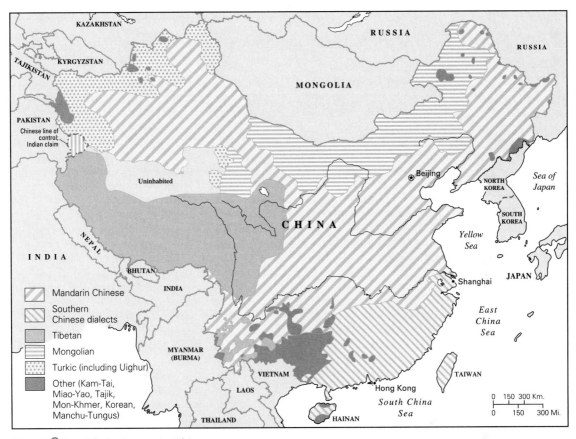

Map **28.1** Ethnic Groups in China

Legend:

- Mandarin Chinese
- Southern Chinese dialects
- Tibetan
- Mongolian
- Turkic (including Uighur)
- Other (Kam-Tai, Miao-Yao, Tajik, Mon-Khmer, Korean, Manchu-Tungus)

and writers like Lu Xun and Ding Ling saw socialism as a way to rid China of poverty and injustice. Many intellectuals made their way to Yan'an, where they soon learned that their job was to serve the party, not stand at a critical distance from it (see Chapter 26).

After 1949 the party had to find ways to make use of intellectuals who had not publicly sided with it, but rather had stayed in the eastern cities, working as teachers, journalists, engineers, or government officials. Most members of this small, urban, educated elite were ready and eager to serve the new government, happy that China finally had a government able to drive out imperialists, control inflation, banish unemployment, end corruption, and clean up the streets. Thousands who were studying abroad in 1949 hurried home to see how they could help. China needed

expertise for its modernization projects, and most of the educated were kept in their jobs, whatever their class background.

Mao, however, distrusted intellectuals and since Yan'an days had been devising ways to subordinate them to the party. In the early 1950s the educated men and women who staffed schools, universities, publishing houses, research institutes, and other organizations were "reeducated." This "thought reform" generally entailed confessing one's subservience to capitalists and imperialists or other bourgeois habits of thought and one's gratitude to Chairman Mao for having helped one realize these errors. For some going through it, thought reform was like a conversion experience; they saw themselves in an entirely new way and wanted to dedicate themselves to the socialist cause. For others, it was devastating.

BIOGRAPHY   Jin Shuyu, Telephone Minder

Jin Shuyu was born in 1917 to an ethnic Korean family in southern Manchuria near the border with Korea. Her father was a doctor, but when she finished middle school in the early 1930s, Japan had taken over Manchuria, and she, like many of her classmates, ran away into the hills to join the anti-Japanese resistance. They engaged primarily in guerrilla action, trying to blow up storehouses or convoy trucks and the like. To support themselves, they would kidnap rich people and hold them for ransom. Their group accepted advice from Communist organizers but was not a Communist group. Finally, they were hard hit by the Japanese and had to scatter. Her family could not hide her because the Japanese knew she was a "bandit." She therefore decided to try to slip into Korea. She worked first as a servant near the border. After she was able to get forged papers, she went to Seoul, where she got a job teaching middle school. In Seoul she married a Han Chinese eleven years her senior who owned a Chinese restaurant and soon had children. At the end of the war in 1945, the Japanese ransacked their restaurant. Added to that, they lost all their savings when the banks failed. Yet they were able to borrow enough money to start another restaurant.

In 1949, when the Communists won in China, Jin was thirty-two and wanted to return to China, but her husband was against it. Then the Korean War started. Their restaurant did well, as Seoul was swollen with foreign soldiers who liked Chinese food, but she wanted to return home. Her husband said she could go; he would stay behind until she had sized up the situation. In 1953 she took their children with her across the 38th parallel, then made her way through North Korea and back into China. Her husband never followed. They wrote to each other through a cousin in

Japan, and in 1983 they were both able to go to Japan to see each other, the first time in thirty years. Her son tried to convince his father to return with them to China, but he said he still wanted to wait to see how things turned out. She thought he kept on putting off joining them because he was too influenced by the anticommunist propaganda of South Korea, or perhaps because he had taken a new wife and never told them.

Jin's life in China was relatively uneventful. In 1958 she was given a job by her street committee to mind the community telephone. Those who wanted to make a call would pay her the fee and she would let them use it. She also would go get people when a call came in for them. Her salary was very low, but she got half of the fees people paid to make calls. Moreover, as she told her interviewer in 1984, she enjoyed listening to people talk on the phone, especially young people who often grinned through their calls or bowed and scraped when seeking a favor from someone.

During the Cultural Revolution, people accused Jin of having a bad class background. She had to locate some of her old comrades to speak up for her, and they said she had distinguished herself in an unofficial anti-Japanese force and should be getting money from the government. After that things were easier because she was classified as an "Anti-Japanese Alliance Veteran" and a repatriated overseas Chinese. She also had some minor privileges as an ethnic minority. However, she told her interviewer, "I'm no more Korean than you are. I became Han Chinese long ago."[1]

Her son did well, not only graduating from college but becoming a college professor, and by the early 1980s Jin lived comfortably. Her only complaint was that her daughter-in-law thought too highly of herself.

---

1. Zhang Xinxin and Sang Ye, *Chinese Lives: An Oral History of Contemporary China* (New York: Pantheon Books, 1987), p. 20.

Independence on the part of intellectuals was also undermined by curtailing alternative sources of income. There were no more rents or dividends, no more independent presses or private colleges.

In response to de-Stalinization in the Soviet Union, in 1956 Mao called on intellectuals to help him identify problems within the party, such as party members who had lost touch with the people or behaved like tyrants. "Let a hundred flowers bloom" in the field of culture and a "hundred schools of thought contend" in science. As long as criticism was not "antagonistic" or "counterrevolutionary," it would help strengthen the party, he explained. The first to come forward with criticisms were scientists and engineers who wanted party members to interfere less with their work. To encourage more people to come forward, Mao praised those who spoke up. Soon critics lost their inhibitions. By May 1957 college students were putting up wall posters, sometimes with highly inflammatory charges. One poster at Qinghua University in Beijing even dared attack Mao Zedong by name: "When he wants to kill you, he doesn't have to do it himself. He can mobilize your wife and children to denounce you and then kill you with their own hands! Is this a rational society? This is class struggle, Mao Zedong style!"[1]

Did Mao plan this campaign to ferret out dissidents? Or was he shocked by the outpouring of criticism? Whatever the truth of the matter, in June 1957, the party announced a campaign against rightists, orchestrated by the newly appointed secretary general of the party, Deng Xiaoping. In this massive campaign, units were pressed to identify 5 percent of their staff as rightists. Altogether almost 3 million people were labeled rightists, which meant that they would no longer have any real influence at work, even if allowed to keep their jobs. Half a million suffered worse fates, sent to labor in the countryside. Some of those labeled rightists had exposed party weaknesses, like the thirty reporters who had reported on secret shops where officials could buy goods

not available to ordinary people. But other "rightists" had hardly said anything, like the railroad engineer relegated to menial labor for twenty years because someone reported hearing him say "how bold" when he read a critique of the party.

By the end of the campaign, the western-influenced elite created in the 1930s was destroyed, condemned as "poisonous weeds." Old China had been dominated, culturally at least, by an elite defined by lengthy education. Mao made sure the educated would know their place in the New China: they were employees of the state, hired to instruct the children of the laboring people or provide technical assistance. They were not to have ideas of their own separate from those of the party or a cultural life distinct from the masses. Most of those labeled rightists in 1957 had to wait until 1979 to be rehabilitated (that is, to have their rightist label removed and their civil rights restored).

DEPARTING FROM THE SOVIET MODEL

By 1957, China had made progress on many fronts. The standard of living was improving, support for the government was strong, and people were optimistic about the future. Still, Mao was not satisfied. Growth was too slow and too dependent on technical experts and capital. As he had found from the Hundred Flowers campaign, people's ways of thinking had not been as quickly transformed as he had hoped. Mao was ready to try more radical measures.

The Great Leap Forward

Why couldn't China find a way to use what it was rich in—labor power—to modernize more rapidly? In 1956 Mao began talking of a Great Leap Forward. Through the coordinated hard work of hundreds of millions of people, China would transform itself from a poor nation into a mighty one. With the latent creative capacity of the Chinese masses unleashed, China would surpass Great Britain in industrial output within fifteen years.

---

1. Gregor Benton and Alan Hunter, eds., *Wild Lily, Prairie Fire* (Princeton, N.J.: Princeton University Press, 1995), pp. 100–101.

These visions of accelerated industrialization were coupled with a higher level of collectivization in the countryside. In 1958, in a matter of months, agricultural collectives all over the country were amalgamated into gigantic communes. Private garden plots were banned. Peasants were organized into quasi-military production brigades and referred to as fighters on the agricultural front. Peasant men were marched in military style to work on public works projects, while the women took over much of the fieldwork. Those between ages sixteen and thirty were drafted into the militia and spent long hours drilling.

Both party cadres and ordinary working people got caught up in a wave of utopian enthusiasm. During the late summer and fall of 1958, communes, factories, schools, and other units set up "backyard steel furnaces" in order to double steel production. As workers were mobilized to put in long hours on these projects, they had little time at home to cook or eat. Units were encouraged to set up mess halls where food was free, a measure commentators hailed as a step toward communism. Counties claimed 1,000 and even 10,000 percent increases in agriculture production. The Central Committee announced with great fanfare that production had nearly doubled in a single year.

Some Great Leap projects proved of long-term value; bridges, railroads, canals, reservoirs, power stations, mines, and irrigation works were constructed all over the country. All too often, however, projects were undertaken with such haste and with so little technical knowledge that they did more harm than good. With economists and engineers downgraded or removed in the antirightist campaigns of the year before, plans were formulated not by experts but by local cadres eager to show their political zeal. Fields plowed deep were sometimes ruined because the soil became salinized. The quality of most of the steel made in backyard furnaces was too poor to be used. Instead it filled railroad cars and clogged train yards all over the country, disrupting transportation.

It was not just the legacy of the Hundred Flowers campaign that kept cadres from reporting failures. The minister of defense and hero of the Korean War, Peng Dehuai, tried to bring up problems in a private letter he gave to Mao at a party conference in July 1959. In the letter Peng began by saying that the Great Leap was an indisputable success, but pointed to the tendency to exaggerate at all levels, which made it difficult for the leadership to know the real situation. He also noted that people began to think that the food problem was solved and that they could give free meals to all. Peng's language was temperate, but Mao's reaction was not. Mao distributed copies of the letter to the delegates and denounced Peng for "right opportunism." He made the senior cadres choose between him and Peng, and none had the courage to side with Peng, who was soon dismissed from his post. Problems with the Great Leap were now blamed on all those like Peng who lacked faith in its premises.

Mao's faulty economics, coupled with droughts and floods, ended up creating one of the worst famines in world history. The size of the 1958 harvest was wildly exaggerated, and no one attempted to validate reports. Tax grain was removed from the countryside on the basis of the reported harvests, leaving little for local consumption. No one wanted to report what was actually happening in his locality for fear of being labeled a rightist. Grain production dropped from 200 million tons in 1958 to 170 million in 1959 and 144 million in 1960. By 1960 in many places people were left with less than half of what they needed to survive. Rationing was practiced almost everywhere, and soup kitchens serving weak gruel were set up in an attempt to stave off starvation. But peasants in places where grain was exhausted were not allowed to hit the roads, as people had always done in the past during famines. From later census reconstructions, it appears that during the Three Hard Years (1959–1962) there were on the order of 30 million "excess" deaths attributable to the dearth of food. Yet neither Mao nor the Communist Party fell from power.

Producing Steel in Henan Province. During the Great Leap Forward, inexperienced workers labored for long hours to produce steel in makeshift "backyard" furnaces. *(Xinhua News Agency, Beijing/Sovfoto)*

Death Rates in Hard-Hit Provinces, 1957 and 1960			
Province	1957	1960	Change
Anhui	c. 250,000	2,200,000	780%
Gansu	142,041	538,479	279
Guangxi	261,785	644,700	146
Henan	572,000	1,908,000	233
Hunan	370,059	1,068,118	189

Source: Based on Roderick MacFarquar, *The Origins of the Cultural Revolution, vol. 3: The Coming of the Cataclysm, 1961–1966* (New York: Columbia University Press, 1997), pp. 2–3.

The Great Leap destroyed people's faith in their local cadres, who in the crisis put themselves and their families first. Another blow to peasants was new curbs on their mobility. Beginning in 1955 a system of population registration bound rural people to the villages of their birth, or in the case of married women, their husbands' villages. When the hasty expansion of the nation's industrial plant was reversed, millions of unemployed workers were sent back to the countryside. To keep them from returning, or other peasants from sneaking into the cities, a system of urban household registration was introduced. Only those with permission to reside in a city could get the ration coupons needed to purchase grain there. These residence policies had the unintended effect of locking rural communities with unfavorable man-land ratios into dismal poverty.

It is not surprising that the rural poor would want to move to the cities. Those who got jobs in state-run factories had low-cost housing, pensions, and health care, not to mention a reliable supply of subsidized food. Children in the cities could stay in school through middle school, and the brightest could go further. In the countryside, only a tiny proportion of exceptionally wealthy communities could come at all close to providing such benefits. In the poorest regions, farmers, forced by the government to concentrate on growing grain, could do little to improve their situations other than invest more labor by weeding more frequently, leveling and terracing fields, expanding irrigation systems, and so on. Such investment often brought little return, and agricultural productivity (the return for each hour of labor) fell across the country.

The Sino-Soviet Split

In the 1920s and 1930s Stalin, through the Comintern, had done as much to hinder the success of the Chinese Communist Party as to aid it. Still, in 1949, Mao viewed the Soviet Union as China's natural ally and went to Moscow to see Stalin. Mao never had the same respect for Stalin's successor, Khrushchev. The Great Leap Forward put further strain on relations between China and the Soviet Union. China intensified its bellicose anti-imperialist rhetoric and began shelling the islands off the coast of Fujian still held by the Nationalists on Taiwan, and the Russians began to fear that China would drag them into a war with the United States. In 1958 and 1959, Khrushchev visited Beijing and concluded that Mao was a romantic deviationist, particularly wrongheaded in his decision to create communes. All of the assistance the Soviet Union had given to China's industrialization seemed to have been wasted as Mao put his trust in backyard furnaces.

When Mao made light of nuclear weapons— saying that if using them could destroy capitalism, it would not matter that much if China lost half its population—Khrushchev went back on his earlier promise to give China nuclear weapons. There was also friction over India and its support for the Dalai Lama and other refugees from Tibet. Russia wanted India as an ally and would not side with China in its border disputes with India, infuriating Mao. In April 1960 Chinese leaders celebrated the ninetieth anniversary of Lenin's birth by lambasting Soviet foreign policy. In July 1960, just as famine was hitting China, Khrushchev ordered the Soviet experts to return and take their blueprints and spare parts with them. By 1963 Mao was publicly denouncing Khrushchev as a revisionist and capitalist roader and challenging the Soviet Union's leadership of the international Communist movement. Communist parties throughout the world soon divided into pro-Soviet and pro-China factions. As the rhetoric escalated, both sides increased their troops along their long border, which provoked border clashes. China built air raid shelters on a massive scale and devoted enormous resources to constructing a defense establishment in mountainous inland areas far from both the sea and the Soviet border. As the war in Vietnam escalated after 1963, China stayed on the sidelines, not even helping the Soviet Union supply North Vietnam. Meanwhile, China developed its own atomic weapons program, exploding its first nuclear device in 1964.

THE CULTURAL REVOLUTION

After the failure of the Great Leap Forward, Mao, nearly seventy years old, withdrew from active decision making. Liu Shaoqi replaced Mao as head of state in 1959, and he along with Chen Yun, Zhou Enlai, Deng Xiaoping, and other organization men set about reviving the economy. Mao grew more and more isolated. Surrounded by bodyguards, he lived in luxurious guest houses far removed from ordinary folk.

Senior colleagues had not forgotten the fate of Peng Dehuai, and honest debate of party policy was no longer attempted in front of Mao. Any resistance to his ideas had to be done in secret.

By the early 1960s Mao was afraid that revisionism was destroying the party—that Marxism was being undermined by contamination by capitalist methods and ideas. In 1962 he initiated the Socialist Education campaign to try to get rural cadres to focus again on class struggle. When Liu Shaoqi and Deng Xiaoping rewrote the directives to deemphasize class struggle, Mao concluded that the revisionists were taking over the struggle for control of the party.

After gathering allies, Mao set out to recapture revolutionary fervor and avoid slipping in the inegalitarian direction of the Soviet Union by initiating a Great Revolution to Create a Proletarian Culture—or Cultural Revolution for short—a movement that came close to destroying the party he had led for three decades.

Phase 1: 1966–1968

The Cultural Revolution began in the spring of 1966 with a denunciation of the mayor of Beijing for allowing the staging of a play that could be construed as critical of Mao. Mao's wife, Jiang Qing, formed a Cultural Revolution Small Group to look into ways to revolutionize culture. Jiang Qing had not played much of a part in politics before and was widely seen as a stand-in for Mao. Soon radical students at Beijing University were agitating against party officials' "taking the capitalist road." When Liu Shaoqi tried to control what was going on at Beijing University, Mao intervened, had him demoted by a rump session of the Central Committee, and sanctioned the organization of students into Red Guards.

The Cultural Revolution quickly escalated beyond the ability of Mao, Jiang Qing, or anyone else to control or direct. Young people who had grown up in New China responded enthusiastically to calls to help Mao oust revisionists. In June 1966 middle schools and universities throughout the country were closed as students devoted their full time to Red Guard activities.

Millions rode free on railroads to carry the message to the countryside or to make the pilgrimage to Beijing, where they might catch a glimpse of Mao, their "Great Helmsman," at the massive Red Guard rallies held in Tiananmen Square. (See **Documents: Big Character Poster.**)

At these rallies, Mao appeared in military uniform and told the students that "to rebel is justified" and that it was good "to bombard the headquarters." The Red Guards in response waved their little red books, *Quotations from Chairman Mao*, compiled a few years earlier by Lin Biao to indoctrinate soldiers. The cult of Mao became more and more dominant, with his pictures displayed in every household, bus, train, even pedicabs, and his sayings broadcast by loudspeaker at every intersection. From early 1967 on, the *People's Daily* regularly printed on its front page a boxed statement of Mao.

In cities large and small, Red Guards roamed the streets in their battle against things foreign or old. They invaded the homes of those with bad class backgrounds, "bourgeois tendencies," or connections to foreigners. Under the slogan of "destroy the four old things [old customs, habits, culture, and thinking]," they ransacked homes, libraries, and museums to find books and artwork to set on fire. The tensions and antagonisms that had been suppressed by nearly two decades of tight social control broke into the open as Red Guards found opportunities to get back at people. At the countless denunciation meetings they organized, cadres, teachers, or writers were forced to stand with their heads down and their arms raised behind them in the "airplane" position and listen to former friends and colleagues jeer and curse them. Many victims took their own lives; others died of beatings or mistreatment.

Liu Shaoqi, the head of state but now labeled the "chief capitalist roader," became a victim of the Red Guards. In the summer of 1967 Red Guards stormed Zhongnanhai, the well-guarded quarters where the party hierarchy lived, and seized Liu. Then they taunted and beat him before huge crowds. Liu died alone two years later from the abuse he received. His family suffered as well. Liu's wife ended up spending ten years in solitary

DOCUMENTS

Big Character Poster

Red Guards used "big character posters" to declare their political values and revolutionary zeal. The poster below was selected by the journal Red Flag *in November 1966 as exemplary because it used the "invincible thought of Mao Zedong" to launch an offensive against the old ideas and habits of the exploiting classes. It was written by a group of Red Guards at a high school in Beijing.*

Revolution is rebellion, and rebellion is the soul of Mao Zedong's thought. Daring to think, to speak, to act, to break through, and to make revolution—in a word, daring to rebel—is the most fundamental and most precious quality of proletarian revolutionaries; it is fundamental to the Party spirit of the Party of the proletariat! Not to rebel is revisionism, pure and simple! Revisionism has been in control of our school for seventeen years. If today we do not rise up in rebellion, when will we?

Now some of the people who were boldly opposing our rebellion have suddenly turned shy and coy, and have taken to incessant murmuring and nagging that we are too one-sided, too arrogant, too crude and that we are going too far. All this is utter nonsense! If you are against us, please say so. Why be shy about it? Since we are bent on rebelling, the matter is no longer in your hand! Indeed we shall make the air thick with the pungent smell of gunpowder. All this talk about being "humane" and "all-sided" —let's have an end to it.

You say we are too one-sided? What kind of allsideness is it that suits you? It looks to us like a "two combining into one" all-sidedness, or eclecticism. You say we are too arrogant? "Arrogant" is just what we want to be. Chairman Mao says, "And those in high positions we counted as no more than the dust." We are bent on striking down not only the reactionaries in our school, but the reactionaries all over the world. Revolutionaries take it as their task to transform the world. How can we not be "arrogant"?

You say we are too crude? Crude is just what we want to be. How can we be soft and clinging towards revisionism or go in for great moderation? To be moderate toward the enemy is to be cruel to the revolution! You say we are going too far? Frankly, your "don't go too far" is reformism, it is "peaceful transition." And this is what your daydreams are about! Well, we are going to strike you down to the earth and keep you down!

There are some others who are scared to death of revolution, scared to death of rebellion. You sticklers for convention, you toadies are all curled up inside your revisionist shells. At the first whiff of rebellion, you become scared and nervous. A revolutionary is a "monkey king" whose golden rod is might, whose supernatural powers are far-reaching and whose magic is omnipotent precisely because he has the great and invincible thought of Mao Zedong. We are wielding our "golden rods," "displaying our supernatural powers" and using our "magic" in order to turn the old world upside down, smash it to pieces, create chaos, and make a tremendous mess—and the bigger the better! We must do this to the present revisionist middle school attached to Tsinghua University. Create a big rebellion, rebel to the end! We are bent on creating a tremendous proletarian uproar, and on carving out a new proletarian world!

Long live the revolutionary rebel spirit of the proletariat!

Source: From Patricia Buckley Ebrey, ed., *Chinese Civilization: A Sourcebook*, rev. ed. (New York: Simon and Schuster, 1993), p. 450.

Red Guards. In September 1966 a teenage girl Red Guard humiliates the governor Li Fanwu by forcing him to bow, making him wear a placard saying he is a member of the Black Gang, and clipping his hair. *(Li Zhensheng/Asia-Network.co.jp)*

confinement. Four other members of his family also died either of beatings or mistreatment in prison where interrogators made every effort to get them to reveal evidence that Liu or his wife was a spy. Deng Xiaoping, another target of Mao, fared better, sent off to labor in a factory in Jiangxi after being humiliated at struggle sessions.

By the end of 1966 workers were also being mobilized to participate in the Cultural Revolution. Rebel students went to factories to "learn from the workers" but actually to instigate opposition to party superiors. When party leaders tried to appease discontented workers by raising wages and handing out bonuses, Mao labeled their actions "economism" and instructed students and workers to seize power from such revisionist party leaders. Confusing power struggles ensued. As soon as one group gained the upper hand, another would challenge its takeover as a "sham power seizure" and attempt "counterpower seizure."

As armed conflict spread, Mao turned to the People's Liberation Army to restore order. Told to ensure that industrial and agricultural production continued, the army tended to support conservative mass organizations and disband the rebel organizations as "counterrevolutionary." Radical Red Guard leaders tried to counterattack, accusing the army of supporting the wrong side. In Wuhan in July 1967, when radicals seized trains loaded with weapons en route to Vietnam, the army supplied their opponents. Then a conservative faction in Wuhan kidnapped two of the radical leaders from Beijing, and the Cultural Revolution Small Group responded by calling on the Red Guards to arm themselves and seize military power from the "capitalist roaders" in the army. Thus began the most violent stage of the Cultural Revolution, during which different factions of Red Guards and worker organizations took up armed struggle against each other and

Big Character Posters. Soldiers of the PLA and peasants of the model commune at Dazhai are shown here putting up big character posters in 1970. *(Sovfoto)*

against regional and national military forces. Rebels seized the Foreign Ministry in Beijing for two weeks, and others seized and burned the British diplomatic compound. With communication and transportation at a standstill, consumer goods became scarce in urban areas.

In the first, violent phase of the Cultural Revolution, some 3 million Party and government officials were removed from their jobs, and as many as half a million people were killed or committed suicide.

Phase 2: 1968–1976

By the summer of 1968, Mao had no choice but to moderate the Cultural Revolution in order to prevent full-scale civil war. In July he disbanded the Red Guards and sent them off to work in the countryside. Revolutionary Committees were set up to take the place of the old party structure. Each committee had representatives from

the mass organizations, from revolutionary cadres, and from the army; in most places the army quickly became the dominant force. Culture remained tightly controlled. Foreign music, art, literature, and books (other than works on Marxism, Leninism, and Stalinism) disappeared from stores. Revolutionary works were offered in their place, such as the eight model revolutionary operas Jiang Qing had sponsored. The official line was that it was better to be red than expert, and professionals were hounded out of many fields. High school graduates were sent into the countryside, as the Red Guards had been before them, some 17 million altogether. Although the stated reason for sending them to the countryside was to let them learn from the peasants and give the peasants the advantage of their education, this transfer also saved the government the trouble and expense of putting the graduates on the payroll of urban enterprises or finding them housing when they married.

The dominance of the military declined after the downfall in 1971 of Lin Biao. To the public, Lin Biao was Mao's most devoted disciple, regularly photographed standing next to him. Yet according to the official account, Lin became afraid that Mao had turned against him and decided to assassinate him. When Lin's daughter exposed his plot, Lin decided to flee to the Soviet Union. His plane, however, ran out of fuel and crashed over Mongolia. Whatever the truth of this bizarre story, news of his plot was kept out of the press for a year, the leadership apparently unsure how to tell the people that Lin Biao turned out to be another Liu Shaoqi, a secret traitor who had managed to reach the second highest position in the political hierarchy.

By this point Mao's health was in decline, and he played less and less of a role in day-to-day management. The leading contenders for power were the more radical faction led by Jiang Qing and the more moderate faction led by Zhou Enlai. In this rather fluid situation China softened its antagonistic stance toward the outside world and in 1972 welcomed U.S. president Richard Nixon to visit and pursue improving relations. In 1973 many disgraced leaders, including Deng Xiaoping, were reinstated to important posts.

The Cultural Revolution's massive assault on entrenched ideas and the established order left many victims. Nearly 3 million people were officially rehabilitated after 1978. Urban young people who had been exhilarated when Mao called on them to topple those in power soon found themselves at the bottom of the heap, sent down to the countryside where hostile peasants could make life miserable. Their younger siblings received inferior educations, out of school for long periods, then taught a watered-down curriculum. The cadres, teachers, and intellectuals who were the principal targets of the Cultural Revolution lost much of their trust in others. When they had to continue working with people who had beaten, humiliated, or imprisoned them, the wounds were left to fester for years. Even those who agreed that elitist values and bureaucratic habits were pervasive problems in the party hierarchy found little positive in the outcome of the Cultural Revolution.

THE DEATH OF MAO

Those who in 1976 still believed in portents from heaven would have sensed that heaven was sending warnings. First, Zhou Enlai died in January after a long struggle with cancer. Next, an outpouring of grief for him in April was violently suppressed. Then in July, north China was rocked by a huge earthquake that killed hundreds of thousands. In September Mao Zedong died.

As long as Mao was alive, no one would openly challenge him, but as his health failed, those near the top tried to position themselves for the inevitable. The main struggle, it seems with hindsight, was between the radicals, Jiang Qing and her allies, later labeled the Gang of Four, and the pragmatists, Deng Xiaoping and his allies. In March 1976 a newspaper controlled by the radicals implied that Zhou Enlai was a capitalist roader. In response, on April 4, the traditional day for honoring the dead, an estimated 2 million people flocked to Tiananmen Square to lay wreaths in honor of Zhou. The radicals saw this as an act of opposition to themselves, had it labeled a counterrevolutionary incident, and called the militia out. Yet the pragmatists won out in the end. After a month of national mourning for Mao, Jiang Qing and the rest of the Gang of Four were arrested.

Assessing Mao's role in modern Chinese history is ongoing. In 1981 when the party rendered its judgment on Mao, it still gave him high marks for his military leadership and his intellectual contributions to Marxist theory, but assigned him much of the blame for everything that went wrong from 1956 on. Since then, Mao's standing has further eroded as doubts are raised about the impact of his leadership style in the 1940s and early 1950s. Some critics go so far as to portray Mao as a megalomaniac, so absorbed in his project of remaking China to match his vision that he was totally indifferent to others' suffering. Some Chinese intellectuals, however, worry that making Mao a monster relieves everyone else of responsibility and undermines the argument that structural changes are needed to prevent comparable tragedies from recurring.

Mao Zedong has often been compared to Zhu Yuanzhang, the founder of the Ming Dynasty. Both grew up in farming households, though Mao never experienced the desperate poverty of Zhu's childhood. Both were formed by the many years of warfare that preceded gaining military supremacy. Both brooked no opposition and had few scruples when it came to executing perceived opponents. Both tended toward the paranoid, suspecting traitorous intentions others did not perceive. But Zhu Yuanzhang cast a shadow over the rest of the Ming Dynasty. As will be seen in the next chapter, within a short period of Mao's death, much of what he had instituted was undone.

SUMMARY

How different was China in 1976 compared to 1949? Although the Cultural Revolution had brought enormous strain and confusion, China was by many measures better off. It was not dominated by any other countries and held itself up as a model to developing nations. The proportion of the population in school more than doubled between 1950 and 1978. Life expectancy reached age sixty-seven for men and age sixty-nine for women, due in large part to better survival of infants and more accessible health care. Unemployment was no longer a problem, and housing was provided for all. Inflation had been banished.

But life was also much more regimented and controlled. There was no longer anything resembling a free press and not many choices people could make about where they would live or what work they would do. Peasants could not leave their native villages (or in women's cases, the villages of their husbands). Graduates of high schools or universities were given little choice in job assignments. From the experience of repeated campaigns to uncover counterrevolutionaries, people had learned to distrust each other, never sure who might turn on them. Material security, in other words, had been secured at a high cost.

SUGGESTED READING

The first four decades of the PRC are covered in vols. 14 and 15 of *The Cambridge History of China,* ed. R. MacFarquhar and J. K. Fairbank (1987, 1991). For briefer overviews, see C. Dietrich, *People's China* (1994), and M. Meisner, *Mao's China and After* (1986).

After the death of Mao and the opening of China, quite a few Chinese who went abroad wrote revealing memoirs of their time in China. Among the better ones are J. Chang, *Wild Swans* (1991); H. Liang and J. Shapiro, *Son of the Revolution* (1984); N. Cheng, *Life and Death in Shanghai* (1987); X. Zhu, *Thirty Years in a Red House: A Memoir of Childhood and Youth in Communist China* (1999); B. Liu, *A Higher Kind of Loyalty: A Memoir by China's Foremost Journalist* (1990); J. Yang, *Six Chapters from My Life "Downunder"* (1983); and D. Chen, *China's Son: Growing Up in the Cultural Revolution* (2001). Fiction can also be very revealing of ordinary life. Much of the fiction of the 1980s depicts life during Mao's time. See, for instance, J. Zhang, *Love Must Not Be Forgotten* (1986) and *Heavy Wings* (1989); H. Yu, *To Live* (2003) and *The Past and the Punishments: Eight Stories* (1996); H. Bai, *The Remote Country of Women* (1994); H. Siu and Z. Stern, eds., *Mao's Harvest: Voices from China's New Generation* (1983); and P. Link, ed., *Stubborn Weeds: Popular and Controversial Chinese Literature After the Cultural Revolution* (1983).

The social science literature on China under Mao is enormous. On the government, see K. Lieberthal, *Governing China* (1995); R. MacFarquhar, *The Origins of the Cultural Revolution,* 3 vols. (1974, 1983, 1997); and H. Wu, *Laogai: The Chinese Gulag* (1992). On changes in the family and on women's lives, see K. Johnson, *Women, the Family, and Peasant Revolution in China* (1983); M. Wolf, *Revolution Postponed: Women in Contemporary China* (1985); and N. Diamant, *Revolutionizing the Family: Politics, Love, and Divorce, 1949–1968* (2000). On life at the village level, see J. Jing, *The Temple of Memories: History, Power, and Morality in a Chinese Village* (1998); P. Seybolt, *Throwing the Emperor from His Horse: Portrait of a Village Leader in China, 1923–1995* (1996); H. Siu, *Agents and Victims in South China* (1989); and A. Chan, R. Madsen, and J. Unger, *Chen Village Under Mao and Deng* (1992).

On the Cultural Revolution, see E. Perry and X. Li, *Proletarian Power: Shanghai in the Cultural Revolution* (1997), and A. Thurston, *Enemies of the People: The Ordeal of Intellectuals in China's Great Cultural Revolution* (1988). On Mao, besides the biographies of Mao listed in Chapter 26, see Z. Li, *The Private Life of Chairman Mao* (1994).

On literature and the arts, see J. Andrews, *Painters and Politics in the People's Republic of China, 1949–1979* (1994), and P. Link, *The Uses of Literature: Life in the Socialist Chinese Literary System* (2000).

China Since Mao (1976 to the Present)

After the death of Mao in 1976, the Chinese Communist Party turned away from class struggle and made economic growth a top priority. Gradually the intrusion of the government into daily life abated, leaving people more leeway to get on with their lives in their own ways. Not only did the government permit increased market activity and private enterprise, but it began courting foreign investment and sending students abroad. The infiltration of western popular culture and political ideas troubled authorities, but with the spread of technologies like telephones, shortwave radios, satellite television, telephones, fax machines, and the Internet, it became nearly impossible for the government to cordon China off from global cultural trends.

The aggregate figures for China's economic growth in the 1980s and 1990s are very impressive, but not everyone has benefited equally. In broad terms, those in cities have gained more than those in the countryside, those in the coastal provinces more than those in the interior, and those entering the job market during these decades more than their parents and grandparents.

Every facet of China's rapid changes since 1976 has intrigued scholars and journalists who have been able to live in China and observe development firsthand. With the collapse of communism in Russia and eastern Europe, many have speculated on the hold of the Communist Party in China. Can it maintain tight control over political expression when communications with the rest of the world have become so much more open? Can it dampen the unrest that results from unemployment, unpaid pensions, and political corruption? Will the disparities between the rich and the poor in China continue to widen? Is China becoming, as it claims, a country that follows the rule of law? Will China accept the pressure to conform to international standards that comes with its increased participation in international organizations? Is a return to Maoist policies possible any longer?

THE COMMUNIST PARTY AFTER MAO

The pace of change in the quarter-century after the death of Mao was extraordinary. Much of what had been instituted in the 1950s was abolished outright or slowly transformed. The Communist Party, however, maintained its large membership and its political power.

In the immediate aftermath of Mao's death, Hua Guofeng took over as head of the Communist Party. He was a relatively obscure party veteran singled out by Mao only months before his death. Soon after Mao's funeral, Hua sided with the pragmatists and arranged for the arrest of Mao's wife, Jiang Qing, and three of her closest associates. This "Gang of Four" was blamed for all the excesses of the Cultural Revolution. In 1977 Deng Xiaoping was reappointed to his old posts, and in December 1978 he supplanted Hua as the top official.

Like Mao, Deng had an impressive revolutionary pedigree, going back to the early 1920s when he was active with Zhou Enlai in France, and continuing through the Shanghai underground, the Long March, and guerrilla warfare against Japan. In 1956, at age fifty-two, he became a member of the Standing Committee of the Politburo and secretary general of the party. Twice ousted from power during the Cultural Revolution, he labeled absurd the Cultural Revolution slogan that it was "better to be poor under socialism than rich under capitalism," insisting that "poverty is not socialism."

A pragmatist, Deng Xiaoping took as his catchword "the Four Modernizations" (of agriculture, industry, science and technology, and defense). He openly admitted that China was poor and backward and saw no reason not to adopt foreign technology if it would improve the lives of the masses. Thousands of people who had been sent to the countryside were allowed to go home. People everywhere were eager to make up for what they saw as the "wasted years."

Party membership stood at 39 million when Mao died. Deng quickly set about weeding out the leftists recruited during the Cultural Revolution and rehabilitating those who had been persecuted. Deng knew that party members qualified to manage and direct the modernization projects were in short supply. Only 14 percent of party members had finished the equivalent of high school, and only 4 percent had college educations. Moreover, many of those who had gone to high school or college did so during the 1970s when admission was on the basis of political fervor and the curriculum was watered down to conform to the anti-elitist and anti-intellectual ideology of the period. About 15 million party members were sent back to school to learn to read and write. Retirement ages were imposed to reduce the number of elderly party members. Party recruitment was stepped up to bring in younger people with better educations.

Asserting that the influence of the Gang of Four had created "an entire generation of mental cripples," Deng pushed for reform of universities. Intellectuals responded to the more open atmosphere with a spate of new magazines and a new frankness in literature. In 1978 the Democracy Wall in Beijing attracted a wide variety of self-expression until it was shut down the following spring.

Television coverage was extensive in 1979 when Deng Xiaoping visited the United States and discussed deepening commercial and cultural ties between the United States and China. The need to modernize was also brought home that year when the People's Liberation Army did poorly in its invasion of Vietnam (in retaliation for Vietnam's invasion of Cambodia). In 1980, with Deng Xiaoping's sponsorship, the first Special Economic Zone was created at Shenzhen, just across the border from Hong Kong. By the early

1980s China was crowded with foreign visitors. Thousands of western teachers were brought to China especially to teach English and other foreign languages. Christian churches reopened, as did Buddhist and Daoist temples. People began wearing more varied colors, giving the streets a very different look from China in the 1960s.

Economic restructuring placed many party cadres in positions where corruption was easy and tempting—they were the ones to supervise distribution or sale of state and collective assets. Between 1983 and 1986 some forty thousand party members were expelled for corruption, and in 1987 the number reached one hundred nine thousand.

Not everyone in the party was happy with the rapid changes or the new interest young people were taking in the West. In 1983 the party launched a campaign against "spiritual pollution" to warn against overenthusiasm for things western. After political unrest at several universities in 1986, the party revived a campaign from the early 1960s to "learn from Lei Feng," a model of the selfless party member devoted to advancing China's development. Still, an even bigger political protest movement occurred in 1989, with huge demonstrations at Beijing's Tiananmen Square (see Color Plate 30). After its bloody suppression, the 48 million party members had to submit self-evaluations in order to weed out sympathizers. About 1 million were sent to the countryside to learn from the masses.

By the early 1990s, the collapse of communism in eastern Europe and the Soviet Union added to Deng Xiaoping's determination to persist in economic reform. In Deng's view, the Soviet Union broke up because central planning had not produced prosperity. To show his support for market reforms in 1992 Deng went south to visit the Special Economic Zones. He told people not to worry if policies were capitalist or socialist, only whether they would make China more prosperous. Soon the party constitution was rewritten to describe China as a "socialist market economy" and to declare "the essential nature of socialism" to be "to liberate and develop productive forces." Joint ventures grew more and more common in the 1990s, with businessmen from Hong Kong, Taiwan, and South Korea especially active. Local elections that allowed people to elect some of their leaders were changing the nature of political participation.

By the time Deng died in 1997, it was clear that China's rapid economic growth was not a simple success story. In many places, plans had been too ambitious, and new buildings stood vacant. The efforts to privatize the huge state-owned factories had led to massive layoffs and rarely turned the enterprises profitable. Many levels of government were out of money and failed to pay their workers for months. In rural areas, cadres often supported themselves by levying taxes and fees, sparking protests by farmers.

By the year 2000, there were some 63 million party members, about 83 percent of whom were male, half high school graduates or better, and about 6 percent members of minorities. Corruption remained a major problem. In 1998 alone, twenty-two thousand seven hundred cases of abuse of power were brought before the courts. The scale was sometimes staggering. In 2000 fourteen corrupt officials embezzled about $60 million in the funds for resettling those displaced by the Three Gorges Dam. That same year nearly two hundred officials accepted bribes to help a Fujian magnate escape tariffs of nearly $10 billion.

RESTRUCTURING THE ECONOMY

Deng Xiaoping's economic policies set in motion an economic boom that led to the quadrupling of average incomes by 2000. Overall poverty declined sharply. According to the World Bank's statistics, the proportion of the rural population below the poverty line fell from 33 percent in 1976 to 6.5 percent in 1995 (or from 262 million to 65 million). Life expectancy has continued to rise (to sixty-eight for men and seventy-one for women in 2000), as has the average height of Chinese, both reflecting improvements in nutrition.

Encouraging Capitalist Tendencies

In the countryside the most important reform was the dismantling of collective agriculture. In the early 1980s Deng Xiaoping instituted a "responsibility system," under which rural households bid for land and other assets that they could treat as their own (though legally held on leases of up to fifty years). In turn they agreed to provide the team with specified crops in exchange for use of particular fields; whatever the household produced above what it owed the team was its to keep or sell. Sideline enterprises like growing vegetables and raising pigs or chickens were encouraged, as were small businesses of all sorts, ranging from fish farming and equipment repair to small factories producing consumer goods for export. Rural industry boomed. By 1995 township and village enterprises employed 125 million workers. Especially in the coastal provinces, where commercial opportunities were greatest, the income of farmers rapidly increased.

Deng Xiaoping abandoned Mao's insistence on self-sufficiency and began courting foreign investors. Special Economic Zones were created—the best known were Shenzhen on the border with Hong Kong and Pudong, across the Huangpu River from Shanghai. These zones offered incentives to foreign firms, including low taxes, new plants, and a well-trained but cheap labor force. China had to bring its legal system more into line with international standards to court these foreign investors, but the payoff was substantial since joint ventures pumped a lot of capital into the Chinese economy.

Foreign manufacturers were attracted to the low labor costs in China, and both set up factories to produce goods for the Chinese market (such as vehicles) and contracted with Chinese manufacturers to produce consumer goods for western markets (such as clothing, toys, watches, and bicycles). Guangdong, with the best access to the financial giant Hong Kong, did especially well in the new environment. Between 1982 and 1992, 97 percent of Hong Kong's thirty-two hundred toy factories relocated to Guangdong. By 1996 China was the world's largest garment maker, accounting for 16.7 percent of world garment exports. In 1997, it manufactured 1.55 billion shirts. The market for shoes too came to be dominated by China, which in 1998 made 6.3 billion pairs of leather shoes and about 1 billion pairs of sport shoes.

Shrinking the State Sector

During the 1980s and 1990s, those who worked for the state found that reform meant they could lose their jobs. Between 1990 and 2000 some 30 to 35 million workers were shed by state-owned enterprises, under pressure to become profitable. Still, few state enterprises found it easy to compete with private or collective enterprises. The mines run by the Ministry of Coal could not compete with the eighty thousand small mines operated by local governments or private individuals. By 1992 the ministry had a debt of 6 billion yuan and needed to lay off 1 million miners. More jobs had probably been created at the small mines, but those jobs lacked the benefits and pensions of the state jobs.

The province of Liaoning in northeast China can be taken as an example. In the 1990s about half of the 10 million people who worked in state-owned enterprises there lost their jobs. The mayor of Shenyang tried to find buyers for the city's bankrupt factories, but no one wanted to take on their obligations to retirees. The situation was even worse farther north. In the cities of Heilongjiang at the end of the 1990s, up to 60 percent of the urban population was either unemployed or not being paid. Bankrupt companies paid neither salaries nor pensions, but they were not dissolved because the government did not want to take over their obligations.

The military is another part of the state sector that has shrunk considerably. The PLA peaked at 4.75 million troops in 1981. Many were later moved to the People's Armed Police, a domestic force. By 2000, soldiers on active duty were thought to number about 2.5 million. The PLA also divested itself of many of the factories it owned and operated, even many of its military

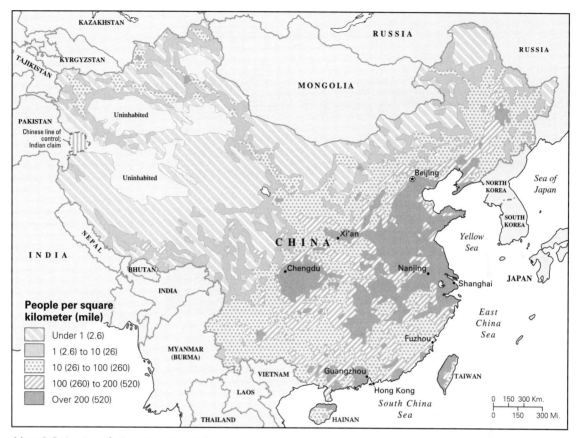

Map 29.1   **Population Density in China**

ones. Some factories that once produced tanks have been converted to produce buses or trucks; others have been abandoned.

Regional Disparities and Internal Migration

Deng Xiaoping announced early on that he was willing to tolerate growing inequalities, saying it was acceptable that "some get rich first." Because most of the industrial growth was in the coastal provinces, regional inequalities increased. (See Map 29.1.) Some regions of the country, especially ones far from good roads, remain extremely poor. In Shanxi province, the uplands are occupied by about 9 million people, a third of whom fall below the poverty line. In the late 1990s half the boys and most of the girls

in this area did not attend school. About 80 percent of the adult women were illiterate.

When internal controls on migration collapsed in the early 1980s, the coastal regions were flooded with job seekers willing to live in shantytowns or a dozen to a room to get a chance to share in the wealth that the market economy was bringing to the fortunate regions. In the 1980s, about 10 million migrated to the dozen largest cities. In 1992 city authorities estimated that 100 million migrant laborers were working away from home or roaming China in search of work. Crime in cities grew, much of it blamed on migrants. In Guangdong, internal migrants, especially those who cannot speak Cantonese, have become an exploited class, hired for the worst work, kept on the job for ten or twelve hours a day, seven days a week, unable

Migrant Workers. China's rapid economic development has brought not only prosperity to the cities, but also millions of peasants looking for a better life. Those shown here in January 2004 sit beneath a billboard waiting to be hired. *(Agence France Presse/Getty Images)*

to protest without losing their jobs. In the 1990s, as newly unemployed workers from state factories took jobs migrants had previously taken, cities began to deport larger numbers of migrants back to the countryside.

For poorer areas in the countryside, the costs of dismantling the communes have been considerable. Health care has become harder for poor people to obtain. Communes had paid the so-called barefoot doctors. Their replacements, village doctors with little more education, now have to support themselves by charging high prices for the drugs they dispense, making antibiotics beyond the reach of many peasants. Diseases that had been under control, such as hookworm and tuberculosis, have made comebacks. When poor people fall ill, their families usually have to borrow money to put down a deposit before a hospital will admit them.

There has been some trickle-down effect from the booming areas to the poorer ones. The Pearl River Delta in Guangdong imports pigs and rice from Hunan and Sichuan, helping their economies. The millions of migrant laborers from those provinces also help, sending home whatever they can spare from their wages. Yet it is often the poorer areas that are most pressed by cadres. In 1998 and 1999 peasant riots were common in Hunan, protesting the imposition of new fees and taxes by local officials.

Consumer Culture

In the early 1980s, although people began to have more disposable income, there was not yet much to buy, even in city department stores, which were well stocked with thermos bottles and inflatable children's toys but not the TVs and tape recorders customers wanted. By the 1990s all this had changed. Disposable income of urban households steadily increased, and more and more factories were turning out consumer goods. Like people elsewhere in the world, Chinese bought TVs, stereos, clothes, furniture, air conditioners, and washing machines. Shopping streets of major cities abound-

An Evening Out in Shanghai. On a Friday night in February 2002, people flock to the pedestrian-only streets of downtown Shanghai to shop, dine, and enjoy the streets. *(Bob Krist/Corbis)*

ed in well-stocked stores, with imported as well as domestically produced goods. Between 1986 and 1995, the number of refrigerators per hundred households went from 62 to 98 in Beijing, 47 to 98 in Shanghai, and 14 to 83 in Xi'an. Acquisition of washing machines made similar gains. Telephone service lagged, but Chinese responded eagerly when pagers and cellular phones became available. By 2000 there were 26 million cellular phones in China. By then there were also 8 million Internet users, with sales of personal computers ranging around 3 million per year.

In the 1990s many grew rich enough to buy imported cars, build lavish houses, and make generous gifts to all the officials they dealt with. In 1978 there had not been a single privately owned car in China; by 1993 there were over 1 million, and the number was increasing by 12 percent a year. In 1995 the government announced plans to increase car production so that by 2005 every family could own a car.

Consumer culture also came to the countryside, though there it is limited by the much lower level of disposable income. In the 1980s, as farm incomes grew, farmers began building new homes, buying better food, and purchasing consumer goods such as TVs, furniture, and clothing. Villages without electricity built small local generators. With migrant workers bringing home knowledge of city life and with television bringing everyone images of modern living, families in the countryside steadily added to the list of goods they considered essential. Chinese, like people in more developed countries, were identifying more with the goods they consumed than with politics.

SOCIAL AND CULTURAL CHANGES
Education

Education at all levels had deteriorated during the Cultural Revolution, when it was considered more important to be red than expert. An important symbolic reversal of these policies occurred in 1977 with the reinstitution of college entrance examinations. Soon those graduating from college could also apply to study abroad in Europe, the United States, or Japan, which led to a craze for studying foreign languages. In the 1990s there were as many as one hundred thousand studying in the United States at any given time.

Only a tiny proportion of Chinese reached college, however. In the 1980s there was room for only a quarter of the elementary school students to continue to middle schools, and room for only 2 percent to enter college. In the cities, the competition for middle school and college places put children under great pressure.

Educational opportunities had always been better in the cities than in the countryside, and in the 1990s the disparity seemed to grow. During the Cultural Revolution, when the educated were ousted from their jobs, teaching positions were filled by peasant teachers paid like other workers on the commune through workpoints (redeemable largely in shares of the commune's grain). With the dismantling of the communes in the early 1980s, other ways had to be found to pay teachers. The most common method was to charge parents fees, which could run 200 to 300 yuan per year for elementary school and as high as 1,000 yuan per year for middle and high school, too much for most peasants. Sometimes rural schools tried to make ends meet by having the students work, peddling apples on the streets or assembling firecrackers in their classrooms. By the end of the 1990s, universities were also charging fees, generally about 10,000 yuan per year. Like medical care, education came to be priced beyond the means of many people, especially in rural areas.

The Arts

During the decade of the Cultural Revolution, intellectuals learned to keep quiet, and ordinary people were fed a dull and repetitive diet of highly politicized stories, plays, and films. With

Cui Jian in Concert. Chinese rock star Cui Jian performs with his band for an audience of more than three thousand at New York City's Central Park on August 8, 1999. *(Getty Images)*

the downfall of the Gang of Four, people's pent-up desire for more varied and lively cultural expression quickly became apparent. A literature of the "wounded" appeared at the end of the 1970s, once those who had suffered during the Cultural Revolution found it politically possible to write of their experiences. Greater tolerance on the part of the government soon resulted in much livelier media, with everything from investigative reporters exposing corruption of cadres, to philosophers who tried to reexamine the premises of Marxism, to novelists, poets, and filmmakers who experimented with previously taboo treatments of sexuality.

Television as a cultural force expanded enormously as TV sets became a readily available consumer good and programming became diverse enough to capture people's interest. China severely restricted the showing of foreign films in theaters, but people still saw them because VCRs or DVD players became common and the pirating of videotapes and DVDs made them inexpensive. Western music of all sorts found fans, and China developed its own rock bands capable of filling a stadium for their shows. Cinema reached new artistic heights and found a large audience abroad as well as in China (see **Material Culture: China's New Cinema**).

Gender Roles

The Communist Party, from its beginnings in the 1920s, had espoused equality for women, and women were eligible to join the party on the same terms as men. Moreover, the party pushed for reforms in marriage practice that were generally seen as improving women's situations, such as giving them the right to initiate divorce. The reality never came up to the level of the rhetoric, but women did play more active roles in the revolution than they had in earlier eras of Chinese history.

After 1949 official rhetoric encouraged people to think of men and women as equal. With collectivization, women were mobilized to participate in farm work, and efforts were made to get girls enrolled in schools. Images of tough women who could do jobs traditionally done by men were part of everyday propaganda. Women did increase their presence in many jobs; the proportion of elementary school teachers who were women increased from 18 percent in 1951 to 36 percent in 1975, and continued to increase in the reform era to 49 percent in 1998.

When western scholars were first able to do research in China in the early 1980s, it was not the advances women had made that struck them most forcefully, but how far the reality lagged behind the rhetoric. Girls and women were certainly more visible outside their homes than their counterparts had been in the nineteenth century, but men still occupied most positions of power and the better-paid jobs. In rural areas, the work points women earned by working for the collective were given to the family head, not to them as individuals. The reform era seemed at that point to be taking things backward. With

fees charged by elementary schools, poorer families did not send their daughters to school for as long as their sons. New opportunities opened up by the expanding economy favored males. Young men could join construction companies and do relatively well-paid work far from home; young women could work in textile, electronic, and toy factories for lower wages. For those who did not want to leave their hometowns, employment patterns were also skewed by gender. The women often did the fieldwork while the men got the better-paid skilled work.

In the cities girls were more likely to stay in school as long as boys did, but once the state withdrew from the hiring process, their degrees were worth less. New female graduates of high schools or colleges tended not to get jobs that were as good as the ones their male classmates got, something that happened less frequently when state bureaus made job assignments. The decline in the state-owned factories has hurt both men and women, but women complain that they are the first to be laid off.

Population Control and the One-Child Family

From 1957 to 1970 China's population grew from about 630 million to 880 million. Public health measures promoted in the 1950s deserve much of the credit for reducing the death rate and thus improving life expectancy, which increased dramatically from forty years in 1953 to sixty in 1968 and sixty-five in 1984. As a consequence, population growth accelerated, and even the horrible famine of 1959–1962 could make only a temporary dent in its upward course. Mao had opposed the idea that China could have too many people, but by the time Mao died, China's population was approaching 1 billion, and his successors recognized that China could not afford to postpone bringing it under control.

Since the late 1970s, the government has worked hard to promote the one-child family in the cities and the one- or two-child family in the countryside. Targets were set for the total numbers of births in each place and quotas then

MATERIAL CULTURE

China's New Cinema

During the Mao period, feature films were produced by state-run studios under the Ministry of Culture. Particularly during the Cultural Revolution, most movies had predictable plots and stereotyped characterizations, and even within China would not have had much of an audience except for the lack of other forms of entertainment and distribution of free tickets. After the graduation of a new generation of directors from the Beijing Film Academy, beginning in 1982, films of high artistic level began to be made, and by the 1990s Chinese films were regularly screened at international film festivals. Heart-wrenching, visually stunning melodramas like *Ju Dou* (1990), *Raise the Red Lantern* (1991), and *Farewell My Concubine* (1993) often ran afoul of censors at home but found appreciative audiences abroad. Some of these

movies dramatized a long sweep of modern Chinese history, as did some quieter, less exoticized movies like *Blue Kite* (1993) and *To Live* (1994). The actress Gong Li starred in enough of these movies to gain fans around the world.

During the 1990s, Chinese filmmakers produced around fifteen hundred films, perhaps a dozen of which were widely circulated abroad. Standards of quality continued to improve, and by the late 1990s, even movies made primarily for Chinese urban audiences were gaining international audiences. *Shower* (1999), a comedy about ordinary people with no exotic past or political turmoil, won both the best picture and best director awards at the Seattle International Film Festival. *Not One Less* (2000) succeeded with children from a remote area as its main characters.

Searching Through the City. The thirteen-year old heroine of the film *Not One Less* had to figure out how to find a ten-year old boy in a large city she had never visited before. *(Kobal/The Picture Desk)*

assigned to smaller units. Young people needed permission from their work units to get married, then permission to have a child. In the early 1980s, women who got pregnant outside the plan faced often unrelenting pressure from birth control workers and local cadres to have abortions. In the 1990s, the campaign was relaxed a little, making it easier for families with only daughters to try again for a son.

The preference for boys remains so strong that China faces a shortage of young women in coming decades as female fetuses are more likely to be aborted (after being identified by ultrasound) and girl babies are more likely to be made available for adoption. In the mid-1990s China quietly began to allow unwanted children, primarily baby girls, to be adopted by foreigners, and by the end of the century, more orphans were adopted from China into the United States than from any other country.

Almost no one questions that China needs to limit population growth. The 2000 census reported a population of 1.27 billion (excluding Taiwan and Hong Kong, or 1.3 billion with them). Population control policies are not without consequences, however. By the 1990s, with increased prosperity, people talked about the pampered only children in the cities, whose parents would take them to western fast food restaurants and pay for all sorts of enrichment experiences. Not only will this generation grow up without siblings, but their children will have no aunts and uncles. Planners are already worrying about how they will take care of their aging parents, since one young couple could well have four elderly parents to support (see **Documents: Supporting the Rural Elderly**).

Family Life

Both changing gender roles and population control policies have had an impact on family organization and family dynamics. So too have many other policies put into effect by the government since 1949. Ancestor worship, lineages, and solidarity with patrilineal kin were all discouraged as feudal practices. The authority of family heads declined as collectives took over property and allocated labor. As both women and children spent much more time away from the home, the family became less central in their lives. Coerced marriages became less common, and in the cities at least, people did in fact choose their own spouses much of the time.

The reform era has not turned the clock back on these changes in family structure and authority. Scholars who have studied families in rural areas have shown that although patrilineal stem families are still quite common—the newly married couple living with or very near the husband's family—the older couple has much less power over the younger one. Even in the countryside the younger couple is likely to have decided to marry on their own and seek a companionate marriage. They may extract a hefty bride price from the husband's family, but use it to purchase things they want for their home. If a new house is built or an extension added, they will work hard to give themselves more privacy. Although the older couple may push for grandsons, the younger couple often are quite comfortable with birth control policies, happy with only one or two children, even if they are daughters. They are more concerned with the happiness of their nuclear family than with family continuity. Although divorce is still very rare in the countryside, women believe that the ability to threaten divorce gives them more voice in family decision making.

CRITICAL VOICES

From early in the reform period, people found ways to express political criticism. The first "big character" posters were pasted on Democracy Wall in Beijing in the fall of 1978. Many of those who participated were blue-collar workers with high school educations, and Deng gave them his blessing. Soon a twenty-eight-year-old electrician named Wei Jingshen courageously pasted up a call for the "fifth modernization":

What is true democracy? Only when the people themselves choose representatives to manage

DOCUMENTS

Supporting the Rural Elderly

Under Mao, scholars at universities and research institutes published relatively little, some finding the required Marxist frameworks too stifling, some wary that in the next campaign, something they wrote could be held against them. In the more open atmosphere of the 1980s and 1990s, social science disciplines were revived, and scholars analyzed Chinese society and its problems in depth.

In 1997 the Chinese journal Population Research *devoted an issue to the problem of caring for the elderly in rural areas, where traditionally people had depended on their sons to provide for them. Not only were people having fewer sons, but in the changing economy, sons were not always able or willing to provide support to their aging parents. Xu Qin, the author of the article excerpted below, stressed that the current problem will only grow worse unless the state intervenes.*

In China, a social security system has been set up only in the cities, and three-fourths of the elderly, who live in the rural areas, are almost entirely dependent on family support. . . . Respecting, loving, and supporting the elderly are traditional virtues of the Chinese nation. Since the recent reforms [1978–], however, the number of disputes over support for the elderly handled by judicial courts at all levels has risen each year, and family eldercare is becoming an increasingly salient social problem. According to a report in the *China Journal for the Elderly,* relevant units in Shanxi province have received and handled more than twenty thousand complaints from the elderly in the last four years, and Shanghai city is handling six thousand such cases every year. . . . Most of

the elderly failing to obtain support were those in the high-age bracket, the sickly, those who had no income and no spouses, and those who lived in the rural areas.

The majority of China's elderly live with their sons, but today most rural households are managed by daughters-in-law, and the relationship between mothers- and daughters-in-law has a direct bearing on eldercare. Since women have begun to participate in the labor force, they now have their own incomes and have become financially independent. Their status in the family has accordingly risen, and the relationship between mothers- and daughters-in-law increasingly favors the latter. But since the current law does not specify that daughters-in-law have the duty to support their par-

affairs in accordance with their will and interests can we speak of democracy. Furthermore, the people must have the power to replace these representatives at any time in order to prevent them from abusing their powers to oppress the people. Is this possible? The citizens of Europe and the United States enjoy just this kind of democracy and could run people like Nixon, de Gaulle, and

Tanaka out of office when they wished and can even reinstate them if they want to, for no one can interfere with their democratic rights. In China, however, if a person so much as comments on the now-deceased "Great Helmsman" or "Great Man peerless in history" Mao Zedong, the mighty prison gates and all kinds of unimaginable misfortunes await him. If we compare the

ents-in-law, arbitration is difficult when cases arise of daughters-in-law refusing to support the elderly.

The new generation of young people in rural areas have the advantage of better educations, so that their role in production is greater than that of the older generation. The declining role of the rural elderly in production, plus the fact that they were unable to accumulate any wealth before the rural reforms, has resulted in a lowering of their authority in the family. They have gradually lost control over their children providing for them; they find it increasingly difficult to resolve conflicts among their children, and frequently become scapegoats in fights among them. . . . Village cadres in charge of work related to old-age issues say that family disputes have to be resolved within three days of being reported, otherwise the elderly will have no food on the table. . . .

Currently, the state has taken a number of measures to solve the problem of family eldercare in rural areas: (1) it has launched activities for signing agreements on supporting the elderly; (2) it has promulgated the Protection Law for the Elderly and is implementing family eldercare through social intervention consisting of both ideological work and legal means; and (3) the state has begun to set up an old-age insurance system in the countryside. However, there are limitations to all of these measures. To begin with, there are no departments with authority to implement the "Eldercare Agreements." . . . Second, although the Old-Age Law has been promulgated, substantial limitations exist in the use of legal means to handle problems of family eldercare. Judicial departments have found in the course of practice that investigations and obtaining evidence are difficult, and enforcement is even more difficult when they try to resolve disputes related to family support. Last but not least, the weak economic foundations in the rural areas are a major hindrance to forming a rural old-age insurance system. . . .

On September 25, 1980, the Central Committee of the Chinese Communist Party made public the "Open Letter to All Members of the Communist Party and the Communist Youth League Concerning the Matter of Controlling China's Population Growth" and advocated that each couple should have one child. The "Open Letter" also pointed out: "Forty years after implementing the system of one child per couple, some families may be faced with a lack of persons in the family to take care of the elderly. This problem exists in many countries and we should pay attention to seeking solutions." The birth rate has fallen since then, and, with the coming of an aging society, the state should make good on its promise.

Source: From *Chinese Sociology and Anthropology* 34:2 (2002), 75–80, slightly modified.

---

socialist system of *"democratic centralism"* with the *"exploiting class democracy"* of capitalism, the difference is as clear as night and day.[1]

Wei was soon to know those prison gates from personal experience. By April 1979 he had been arrested and Democracy Wall shut down. Wei spent most of his time from then on in prison, with long stretches in solitary confinement, until he was exiled to the United States in 1997.

Wei's fate did not deter intellectuals from speaking up. In 1986 the physicist Fang Lizhi

1. Wm. Theodore De Bary and Richard Lufrano, *Sources of Chinese Tradition: From 1600 Through the Twentieth Century* (New York: Columbia University Press, 2000), p. 498.

told students that the socialist movement "from Marx and Lenin to Stalin and Mao Zedong, has been a failure" and advocated adopting the western political system.[2] That year students at one hundred fifty campuses demanded greater freedom, less corruption, and better living conditions in their dormitories. After the protests were suppressed, Deng had party secretary general Hu Yaobang dismissed from his post because he had been too conciliatory toward the students.

Debate about China's cultural and political form reached a large audience in the spring and summer of 1988 with a six-part TV documentary, *River Elegy*. It traced many of China's problems back to its ancient traditions, especially its persistent inward orientation and disinterest in the outside world. *River Elegy* attacked some of the country's most revered symbols, relabeling the Yellow River, the Great Wall, and the dragon as symbols of backward passivity, not greatness. It argued that China should move toward the outward-looking Blue Ocean civilization and away from the conservative Yellow River one.

The following spring, huge student protests erupted in Beijing. The students' protest began modestly in April with a parade honoring the memory of a recently deceased Hu Yaobang, viewed as the strongest voice in the government for political reform. Buoyed by the positive reaction of the Beijing citizenry, student leaders gradually escalated their activities and their rallying cries. They called for more democratic government: Make officials disclose their income and assets! Renounce the use of mass political campaigns! Abolish prohibitions against street protests! Permit journalists to report protest activities! End corruption! Many evoked the ideas of the May Fourth movement, claiming that China had still not achieved science and democracy. When Deng Xiaoping called the students' actions "counterrevolutionary turmoil,"

they did not tone down their rhetoric. When the momentum seemed to be flagging, a couple of thousand students staged a hunger strike to testify to their sincerity and determination.

On May 17, 1989, with the international press present to cover the visit of the Soviet premier Gorbachev, Tiananmen Square was filled not merely with students from every university in Beijing, but also from other organizations, even government ones like the Foreign Ministry, the Central Television Station, the National Men's Volleyball Team, even the Public Security Bureau Academy. There were workers in their work clothes, holding banners inscribed with the names of their factories. The formation of the Beijing Autonomous Workers Federation was announced with calls for democracy and an end to the "lawlessness and brutality of corrupt officials."

The students themselves had no experience with democracy, and the leaders who emerged often disagreed on the best tactics. Chai Ling, a female student, was one of the most zealous of the leaders. She told an American reporter in late May that she hoped for bloodshed, because the Chinese people would not open their eyes until the government brazenly butchered the people. She complained about other leaders who were talking to government officials in the hope that violence could be avoided. She claimed to feel sad that she could not tell the other students "straight out that we must use our blood and our lives to wake up the people."[3]

The public's support for the students was a humiliation to Deng and the other leaders, who declared martial law as soon as Gorbachev left and dismissed the more conciliatory Zhao Ziyang. Yet when truckloads of troops attempted to enter the city, the citizens in Beijing took to the streets to stop them. Successful against these unarmed soldiers, they were exhilarated by this evidence of "people power." On May 30 demonstrators unveiled a plaster statue of the Goddess of Democracy made by art stu-

2. Richard Baum, *Burying Mao: Chinese Politics in the Age of Deng Xiaoping* (Princeton, N.J.: Princeton University Press, 1994), p. 201.

3. Geremie Barmé, *In the Red* (New York: Columbia University Press, 1999), p. 329.

dents. Just a few days later, on June 3–4, seasoned troops were brought into central Beijing through underground tunnels, and tanks and artillery soon followed. Many unarmed citizens still tried to halt their advance, but the armored vehicles got through the blockades after bloody clashes and successfully ended both the protest and the occupation of the square. At least several hundred people lost their lives that night, many of them ordinary citizens trying to stop the soldiers from entering central Beijing.

Demonstrations against the government suppression of the Tiananmen protestors erupted in several other cities. In Chengdu, rioting led to martial law and dozens of deaths. In Shanghai a train ran into demonstrators trying to stop it. Huge rallies were held in Hong Kong. All around the world people expressed shock and outrage. Yet to party hard-liners, this bloody suppression was essential because the entire power structure was in jeopardy. In their view, allowing nonparty forces to interject themselves into the decision-making process was a greater threat to stability than corruption was. Soon Deng and the hard-liners followed up the initial military seizure of the square with the arrest and sentencing of hundreds of participants and other dissidents. Thousands of party members were expelled from the party for sympathizing with the students.

Suppression of this movement, coupled with compulsory political study classes at universities, kept political discussion subdued within China for the next several years. In the 1990s, no single issue united critics of the government. The plight of workers has prompted some to try to organize workers facing unsafe conditions or not being paid (see **Biography: Li Qiang, Labor Activist**). The government was more alarmed by the political potential of a school of Qigong teachings. Until then, the government had pointed with pride to the elderly who early each morning could be seen in parks practicing the stretching and balancing exercises called Qigong, believed to nurture the practitioners' *qi* (vital energy). Masters of Qigong often attributed all sorts of powers to their techniques. In

the 1990s one such teacher, Li Hongzhi, developed Falun Gong, a form of Qigong that drew on both Buddhist and Daoist ideas and promised practitioners good health and other benefits. Many from the party and PLA, as well as their wives and mothers, were attracted to this system of knowledge beyond the understanding of western science. When in 1999 Li organized fifteen thousand followers to assemble outside the party leaders' residential complex in Beijing to ask for recognition of his teachings, the top leadership became alarmed and not only outlawed the sect but also arrested thousands of members and sent them for reeducation. The potential of Falun Gong to reach the masses and offer an alternative to the party was seen as particularly threatening.

During the 1990s Chinese living abroad raised some of the bluntest critical voices. They publicized abuses in the legal system, such as long detentions without being charged and the use of torture to extract confessions. It is also largely activists outside China who have drawn attention to the looming crisis in China's ecology. Encouraging small rural factories has led to serious pollution problems as paper mills, chemical plants, and tanneries dump their wastes in rivers. The air quality in many large cities is very poor. In the north, so much water has been taken from the Yellow River that it runs dry for longer and longer periods each year. So much water gets brought up from underground that the water table is dropping steadily in many places. In the Yangzi region, floods have gotten worse because of tree cutting and soil erosion in recent years. Development projects of all sorts have led to the paving over of more and more arable land, leading to questions about how China will be able to feed its growing population in the decades to come. Environmentalists have been especially critical of the 600-foot-tall Three Gorges Dam project on the Yangzi River, which has required the displacement of more than 1 million people and will flood nearly 400 square miles (632 square kilometers) with more than a hundred towns.

BIOGRAPHY Li Qiang, Labor Activist

Li Qiang was born in 1973 in a small city in Sichuan. After his father died when he was eleven years old, the family had a hard time surviving on his mother's wages as a worker in the Second Construction Company. He had to quit school at age fourteen, but unable to find a job, spent much of his time reading. Li, at age sixteen, was energized by the 1989 Democracy Movement and even gave a speech in front of the city hall on justice and social inequality.

In his readings, Li had learned how the Communists in the 1920s had organized workers, and he thought workers still needed that sort of organization. In the spring of 1990, he put up unsigned big character posters calling for the right to set up independent unions. Also that spring he wrote a letter to Jiang Zemin, China's president, describing his family's plight with his mother in the hospital with hepatitis. His letter brought results. A provincial party official saw to it that his mother's medical bills were paid and a temporary job was found for Li. At the same time, the local public security office discovered that he was the author of the big character posters. He was questioned and his home searched, but they could find no evidence that he had listened to the Voice of America or had foreign contacts.

From July 1990 to December 1991, Li worked in an office for his mother's company, arranging housing for employees. The unfairness of the system angered him when he discovered that the senior cadres often had two apartments while people like his mother, who had worked there over twenty years, still did not have one. He persuaded many maltreated workers to sign letters of complaint. Not surprisingly, he was soon fired.

By this point Li had studied enough to get admitted to college and for the next two years studied law and political science. After leaving school, Li took a job in sales with a trading company, where he made a lot of money during the next two and a half years. In his spare time, he gave legal assistance to laid-off workers.

In February 1997 Li heard that an unemployed worker was planning to immolate himself in front of the city hall. The worker, over forty years old, had a wife and child and saw no hope for himself or his family. Although the worker was dragged away after pouring gasoline over himself, Li felt compelled to do something and became a full-time labor organizer. Over the next six months, he organized rallies and protests by workers at several factories as well as taxi and pedicab drivers. In December 1997 he was arrested and questioned for hours. When released the next day, he fled to Shanghai.

For the next couple of years, Li worked underground, moving from city to city, organizing strikes, protests, and demonstrations. For a while in 1999 he worked in a joint-venture factory in Shenzhen to document the long hours and inhuman treatment of workers. Fearful of being apprehended, by 2001 he had left China for the United States, where he continued to work for Chinese workers' right to set up independent unions.

TAIWAN

In 1949, when the victory of the Communist Party in the civil war seemed imminent, Chiang Kaishek and large parts of the Nationalist government and army evacuated to the island of Taiwan, less than a hundred miles off the coast of Fujian province. Taiwan had been under Japanese colonial rule from 1895 to 1945 and

Comparisons of China, Taiwan, and Other Countries

Country	GDP per Capita (in U.S. dollars)	Life Expectancy (years)	Literacy Rate	Fertility Rate
United States	35,831	77.2	97%	2.1
Japan	24,848	80.2	99	1.4
Taiwan	17,255	76.5	94	1.8
China	3,535	71.6	82	1.8
India	2,136	62.8	52	3.0
Vietnam	1,931	69.5	94	2.5

Source: World Factbook, 2002.

had only recently been returned to Chinese rule. The initial encounter between the local population and the Nationalist government had been hostile: in 1947 the government responded to protests against the corruption of its politicians by shooting at protesters and pursuing suspected leaders, killing, it is estimated, eight thousand to ten thousand people, including many local leaders. In part because of the support the United States gave Chiang and his government as the Cold War in Asia intensified, the Nationalists soon stabilized their government and were able to concentrate on economic development. After Chiang Kaishek died in 1975, he was succeeded by his son Chiang Chingkuo (Jiang Jingguo). During his presidency in the late 1980s, Taiwan succeeded in making the transition from one-party rule to parliamentary democracy.

During the 1950s and 1960s, the United States treated Chiang's Republic of China as the legitimate government of China and insisted that it occupy China's seat at the United Nations. When relations between the United States and the PRC were normalized in the 1970s, Taiwan's position became anomalous. The United States and the PRC agreed that there was only one China and Taiwan was a part of China. The United States maintained that any unification of China should come by peaceful means and continued military aid to Taiwan. China insisted that countries that wanted embassies in Beijing had to eliminate their embassies in Taiwan. As China joined more

and more international organizations, Taiwan was frequently forced out.

This loss of political standing has not prevented Taiwan from becoming an economic power. In 2002 Taiwan's per capita income for its 22 million citizens was about $17,000, placing it next after Japan in Asia and way beyond China. Several factors contributed to this extraordinary economic growth. The Nationalists started with the advantage of Japanese land reform and industrial development. They also benefited from considerable foreign investment over the next couple of decades, especially from the United States and Japan. But hard work and thoughtful planning also deserve credit for Taiwan's growth. The Taiwan government gave real authority to those with technical training. Economists and engineers, including many trained abroad, became heads of ministries. Through the 1950s, emphasis was placed on import substitution, especially by building up light industry to produce consumer goods. The 1960s saw a shift toward export-oriented industries, especially electronics, as Taiwan began to try to follow along behind Japan, moving into stereos and televisions as Japan moved into cars. In 1966 the first tax-free export processing zone was set up, attracting foreign capital and technology. By the 1980s, there was adequate wealth in Taiwan to develop capital-intensive industries such as steel and petrochemicals.

Over the past fifteen or more years, there has been increasing contact between Chinese in

Taiwan and the PRC. In 1987, when Taiwan lifted restrictions on travel, thousands of people from Taiwan visited the mainland. In 1992, 24.11 million items of mail passed between the two countries, 14.72 million phone calls were placed, and 62,000 telegrams delivered. The scale of Taiwan's investment in its giant neighbor has been a staggering $70 billion since 1987. In the early 2000s, nearly 1 million Chinese from Taiwan were living on the mainland, roughly 400,000 of them in and around Shanghai. This movement reflects the relocation of Taiwan's semiconductor and personal computer manufacturing plants to the mainland, where wages are much lower. In 2003, for the first time since 1949, charter planes carried Taiwanese home for the Lunar New Year holidays direct from Shanghai or Fujian to Taibei.

In 1996 Taiwan held its first open elections for the presidency and the National Assembly. In 2000, the Nationalist Party lost the general election for the first time, and Chen Shuibian of the Democratic Progressive Party (a party long associated with Taiwan independence) was elected president.

CHINA IN THE WORLD

After China split with the Soviet Union in the early 1960s, China severely limited its contacts with the rest of the world. It provided some assistance to African countries and to Maoist revolutionary groups, but had too great a fear of spies to encourage people to maintain ties with relatives abroad. All of this changed after Mao's death. China sought entry into international organizations, invited overseas Chinese to visit and participate in China's development, and began sending its officials on trips around the world.

It took a while for China to readjust its foreign policy. In the 1970s it supported the murderous Khmer Rouge government in Cambodia and was incensed when Vietnam invaded Cambodia. In February 1979 Deng Xiaoping ordered the army to invade Vietnam to pressure it to withdraw from Cambodia. Despite absorbing large numbers of casualties, China failed in its objectives and soon withdrew.

In the 1980s, China worked to improve its relationship with western countries, partly to reduce the threat from the Soviet Union. After the collapse of the Soviet Union, when the United States emerged as the sole superpower, China was less worried about Russian aggression, but more worried about possible independence movements among the Muslims in Chinese Central Asia. Although the United States remained a key economic partner, importing vast quantities of goods from China, China rarely supported its foreign policies and found its military might threatening.

In 1984 the British government agreed to return Hong Kong to China when the ninety-nine-year lease on the New Territories expired in 1997. China had made no attempt to take Hong Kong in 1949 and had benefited from indirect trade through Hong Kong since then, but as it took a larger role in the world, China was ready to take over Hong Kong, though it promised to let it maintain its own political and economic system for fifty years. During the 1990s, the professional and business elites of Hong Kong tried to make sure that they had alternative places to go if China imposed too draconian an order on Hong Kong, but during the first few years after the transfer, life in Hong Kong continued much as before.

To help expand its economy, China joined the World Bank, the International Monetary Fund, and the Asian Development Bank, which offered both low interest loans and various types of technical and economic advice, but also required that China report its economic situation more openly. In 2001 China was admitted to the World Trade Organization and succeeded in its bid for hosting the 2008 Summer Olympics. China's goal for so long—recognition as one of the great nations of the world—seemed finally within its grasp.

SUMMARY

How different is China early in the twenty-first century than it was at the death of Mao more than a quarter-century earlier? In the more modernized coastal provinces, the standard of living is much higher. Knowledge of the outside world is much more extensive. Inequalities are also more extreme: some Chinese have grown fabulously wealthy, while others have not been able to find work or cannot afford to send their children to school or pay for medical care. The party is no longer as dominated by a single person as forms of collective leadership have been developed, and leaders now can rise as much because of their technical expertise as their political fervor. Nevertheless, the Communist Party still dominates the government and has its hands in much of what goes on in the country. The Chinese state does not interfere in everyday affairs to the extent it used to, but it still has tremendous coercive force.

SUGGESTED READING

Post-Mao changes are considered in R. Baum, *Burying Mao: Chinese Politics in the Age of Deng Xiaoping* (1994). For specific dimensions of the politics and economics of the reform era, see S. Lubman, *Bird in a Cage: Legal Reform in China After Mao* (1999); D. Solinger, *Contesting Citizenship in Urban China: Peasant Migrants, the State and the Logic of the Market* (1999); C. Ikels, *The Return of the God of Wealth* (1996); M. Yang, *Gifts, Favors, and Banquets: The Art of Social Relationships in China* (1994); and V. Smil, *China's Environmental Crisis* (1993). Well-written journalists' accounts of China in the 1980s and 1990s include O. Schell, *Discos and Democracy: China in the Throes of Reform* (1989) and *The Mandate of Heaven* (1994); N. Kristof and S. WuDunn, *China Wakes: The Struggle for the Soul of a Rising Power* (1994); J. Starr, *Understanding China* (1997); and J. Becker, *The Chinese* (2000).

On the 1989 democracy movement, see M. Han, ed., *Cries for Democracy: Writings and Speeches from the 1989 Chinese Democracy Movement* (1990); L. Feigon, *China Rising: The Meaning of Tiananmen* (1990); and J. Wasserstrom and E. Perry, eds., *Popular Protest and Political Culture in Modern China: Learning from 1989* (1992).

On Chinese cinema in the post-Mao period, see J. Silbergeld, *China into Film: Frames of Reference in Contemporary Chinese Cinema* (1999), and S. Lu, ed., *Transnational Chinese Cinemas: Identity, Nationhood, Gender* (1997). Other facets of contemporary culture are treated in J. Lull, *China Turned On: Television, Reform, and Resistance* (1991); J. Zha, *China Pop: How Soap Operas, Tabloids, and Bestsellers Are Transforming a Culture* (1995); G. Barmé. *In the Red: On Contemporary Chinese Culture* (1999); P. Link, *Evening Chats in Beijing* (1992); J. Wang, *High Culture Fever: Politics, Aesthetics and Ideology in Deng's China* (1996); and D. Davis, ed., *The Consumer Revolution in Urban China* (2000).

Changes in the family and women's lives under the CCP are considered in M. Wolf, *Revolution Postponed: Women in Contemporary China* (1985); G. Hershatter and E. Honig, *Personal Voices: Chinese Women in the 1980's* (1988); W. Jankowiak, *Sex, Death, and Hierarchy in a Chinese City* (1993); E. Judd, *Gender and Power in Rural North China* (1994); T. Jacka, *Women's Work in Rural China: Change and Continuity in an Era of Reform* (1997); B. Entwisle and G. Henderson, *Re-Drawing Boundaries: Work, Households, and Gender in China* (2000); and Y. Yan, *Private Life Under Socialism: Love, Intimacy, and Family Change in a Chinese Village, 1949–1999* (2003). S. Brownell and J. Wasserstrom, *Chinese Femininities/Chinese Masculinities* (2002), also covers earlier periods, starting in late imperial.

CHAPTER THIRTY

Korea (1945 to the Present)

The liberation of Korea from Japanese rule was accompanied by an immediate division of the Korean peninsula in two. Stalin declared war against Japan, and Russian forces were the first to enter the Korean peninsula on August 8, 1945, six days before Japan surrendered to the United States. The United States rushed troops to Korea after the war ended on August 15, 1945, and won Soviet acquiescence to divide the peninsula at the 38th parallel to administer the surrender of Japanese forces. After Japan's defeat Soviet forces took over North Korea and U.S. forces South Korea. Korea has remained tragically divided to this day.

Both North and South formed two separate states in 1948, and the division was sealed by the bloody Korean War between 1950 and 1953, which left Korea divided at the demilitarized zone (DMZ) close to the 38th parallel. The race for superiority in military and economic strength began, but the threat of a resumption of hostilities was ever present.

Scholars have been concerned with a number of questions about this period. Was the division of Korea in 1945 simply a matter of foreign interference in Korea's affairs or an internal division? Were the leaders of North and South Korea puppets of the Soviet Union and the United States, respectively? Was the Korean War simply a North Korean act of aggression or the continuation of a civil conflict? What were the strengths and weaknesses of the North and South Korean economies? Did North Korean communism differ in any ways from Stalinist dictatorship? What were the strengths and weaknesses of South Korean developmentalism? What forces created dictatorship in South Korea under U.S. hegemony, and democracy in 1987? How successful was the U.S. role in Korea after 1945? What are the chances for Korean reunification?

LIBERATION AND NATIONAL DIVISION (1945–1949)

After liberation on August 15, 1945, both the Russians and the Americans were greeted by a spontaneous organization of people's committees (PCs) at the local level. These PCs spanned the political spectrum and demonstrated an amazing example of spontaneous democratic self-government after thirty-five years of colonial rule. Unfortunately, neither the United States nor the Soviet Union used them as a basis for an independent government and left the country. Had both sides removed their troops, Korea would most likely have ended up with a left-wing or Communist government, either peacefully or as a result of civil war, but Koreans were not left to work out their own destiny.

The Soviets used the PCs as a basis for reconstructing civilian rule, but General Hodge, who established a U.S. military government for South Korea, refused to accept them. The Soviets recruited the nationalist and socialist Cho Mansik as an interim leader in the North. In the South, the Americans brought back Syngman Rhee from the United States. Rhee considered himself above politics and parties, but he sought followers from anti-Communist collaborators with the Japanese. Kim Ku, the nationalist leader of the Korean Provisional Government (KPG), hated both the collaborators and Rhee. General Hodge disliked both Rhee and Kim Ku and sought to find the equivalent of a moderate democratic center in South Korea, but the only centrist around was the left-leaning populist, Yŏ Unhyŏng (Lyuh Woon Hyung), and he was later assassinated by the conservative police.

After Liberation, millions of Koreans living abroad in Japan and Manchuria flooded back to the peninsula, most of them radicalized by their experience during the colonial period. In North Korea, former collaborators were excluded from leadership roles, but in South Korea, collaborator businessmen and landlords formed the Korean Democratic Party (KDP). Communists jailed by the Japanese were released, and one of them, Pak Hŏnyŏng, formed the Korean

Syngman Rhee and Kim Ku. Syngman Rhee (Yi Sŭngman) on the left, nationalist leader and later first President of the Republic of Korea (1948–1960), and Kim Ku on the right, anti-Japanese nationalist and terrorist and President of the Korean Provisional Government to 1945, assassinated by one of Rhee's henchmen. *(Sajinuro ponun Choson sidae: Saenghwal kwa p'ungsok [The Choson Period in Pictures: Life and Customs] Seoul: Somundang, 1986, p. 202)*

Communist Party (KCP) in Seoul, expecting that Seoul would be the capital of a united Korea.

In North Korea, a variety of Communist groups greeted the Soviet commanders: the domestic Communists, the Yan'an Communists who had fought with Mao Zedong in the Chinese civil war, Koreans of Soviet citizenship, and the Manchurian guerrilla fighters who had fought alongside Kim Il Sung. The thirty-two-year-old Kim Il Sung and a few of his

Manchurian guerrilla fighters arrived in North Korea from Siberia on September 19, 1945. The Soviets established a northern branch bureau of the KCP and introduced Kim at a large public meeting in Pyongyang, where he praised Stalin and supported Cho Mansik. By January 1946, however, the Soviets had removed Cho Mansik from power and replaced him with Kim Il Sung. This occurred because Cho opposed Stalin's agreement with the United States to set up a trusteeship for Korea at the Moscow Conference in December.

In South Korea violent protests by workers and peasants began in late 1945. A railroad strike and mass demonstrations broke out in the autumn of 1946 in Pusan and Taegu, followed by peasant riots against Hodge's grain policies in Chŏlla and Kyŏngsang, leaving two hundred police and a thousand civilians dead. U.S. authorities quickly blamed the Communists, declared martial law, put an end to the PCs, and supported armed repression. Pak Hŏnyŏng and many Communists fled to North Korea in 1946 while landlords, businessmen, and Christians in the North moved to the South. By 1947 Syngman Rhee ruled with U.S. support.

In North Korea, Kim Il Sung became chairman of the Provisional People's Committee (PPC) and eclipsed Pak Hŏnyŏng. The PPC in 1946 carried out a popular land reform program to eliminate the landlord class and redistribute land to sharecroppers. Kim nationalized all industries without much violence because the Japanese factory owners had left the country. He reduced working hours to eight hours per day, banned child labor, created a labor federation, declared equal rights for women, established universal education through the eleventh grade, and founded Kim Il Sung University. He made his guerrilla allies from Manchuria, Kim Ch'aek and Ch'oe Yonggŏn, his chief aides and had Ch'oe create the Korean People's Army (KPA).

By 1948 the United States was locked in the Cold War against the Soviet Union. The United States supported Syngman Rhee's plan to hold national elections, but the Soviets refused to allow elections in the North because its population was only half that of the South. In April a peasant rebellion in South Korea on Cheju Island broke out against a repressive right-wing governor appointed by Rhee. Two regiments of the ROK Army assigned to Cheju also rebelled at Yŏsu on the southern coast and murdered hundreds of police and landlords. U.S. forces helped in the suppression of both rebellions. Forty-five thousand people died in the fighting on Cheju, forty thousand fled to Japan, and seventy thousand were placed in concentration camps.

Finally, a separate election was held in the South alone on May 10, 1948, and the Republic of Korea (ROK) was proclaimed on August 15. A constitution modeled on the U.S. Constitution was adopted; a National Assembly was elected, and it chose Syngman Rhee as its first president. On September 10, 1948, North Korea established the Democratic People's Republic of Korea (DPRK) with Kim Il Sung as chairman of the National People's Assembly. The Soviets withdrew their forces from Korea in December, and the United States withdrew most of its forces in 1949.

KOREAN WAR (1949–1953)

Both Kim Il Sung and Syngman Rhee began conducting cross-border raids in 1949, but the United States prevented Rhee from invading the North lest he drag the United States into a war with the Soviet Union. Kim Il Sung had a new ally in Mao Zedong after he won the Chinese civil war in 1949, but in March Kim met with Stalin in Moscow to seek support for a full-scale invasion of South Korea. Stalin refused to allow it, and Mao said that the timing for an invasion was premature.

In January 1950 U.S. Secretary of State Dean Acheson in his famous Press Club speech left South Korea out of the area that the United States would defend automatically against Communist forces. Many in South Korea and the United States castigated Acheson for inducing a North Korean invasion in June, but Kim Il Sung had already decided to invade the South. Stalin finally approved Kim's invasion plan in 1950, but he promised only to supply weapons, planes, and pilots because he wanted to avoid a direct challenge to the United States. He left Mao with the responsibility of preventing North Korea's defeat.

Mao sent perhaps as many as eighty thousand experienced Korean troops who had fought in the Chinese civil war to North Korea, and on June 25, 1950, Kim launched his invasion with seven divisions and 258 Soviet tanks against the four front-line divisions of the ROK Army, which had no tanks. North Korean forces overran the South Korean military and pushed south all the way to Pusan. Years later, the Korean novelist Sŏnu Hwi would write about the fighting in his story "Flowers of Fire" (see **Documents: "Flowers of Fire" by Sŏnu Hwi**).

President Truman viewed the invasion as a plot by Stalin to spread communism, and he dispatched U.S. forces to Korea as a "police action" rather than declare war. He also used the absence of the Russian delegate from the UN Security Council to win Security Council approval of a UN force under the command of U.S. General Douglas MacArthur.

The initial contingent of U.S. forces with remnants of the ROK Army was barely able to defend the Pusan perimeter until General MacArthur turned the tide of battle completely by launching his amphibious attack at Inch'ŏn on September 15, near Seoul. Kim was forced to withdraw his main forces north across the 38th parallel.

Truman had already signed a policy document early in 1950, NSC 48, which committed the United States to the containment of communism within its present boundaries in Asia and "where feasible" to reduce Communist power in Asia—in other words, containment with the possibility of rollback. Truman did not pause a second before choosing the rollback option and authorizing an advance into North Korea even though that action spurred Mao Zedong to commit Chinese "volunteers" to enter the war. Oblivious to Chinese signals passed through India, General MacArthur ordered his troops north to the Yalu River in his "home by Christmas" campaign on November 24, only to have his forces overrun by invading Chinese forces.

The Chinese recaptured Seoul only to lose it once again, and the fighting stabilized in 1951 along a front that eventually became the Demilitarized Zone (DMZ) near the 38th parallel (see Map 30.1). The battle raged for two more years over a few yards of territory at the cost of many casualties until an armistice was signed in 1953 by all parties except Syngman Rhee. To this day, a peace treaty has never been signed.

During the war both Presidents Truman and Eisenhower contemplated the use of atomic bombs to force the Chinese to sign an armistice. MacArthur had also wanted to bomb Chinese airfields in Manchuria, contrary to Truman's limited-war policy to prevent a third world war. When MacArthur went public with his demands, Truman relieved him of his command, a courageous decision because MacArthur was riding high in U.S. public opinion.

More than 3 million North Koreans, 1 million South Koreans, 1 million Chinese, and fifty-two thousand U.S. soldiers died in the conflict. South Koreans suffered another four hundred thousand casualties and Americans one hundred thousand. North Korean and Chinese casualties are unknown. The North was laid flat by U.S. napalm and carpet bombing and the South was devastated. Numerous atrocities were carried out on both sides, including the recently discovered massacre of Korean refugees at Nogunri by U.S. troops.

While later observers viewed it as Kim Il Sung's naked aggression against another suzerain state, one historian has argued that the Korean War was a civil war that began in 1949.[1] Because the United States stopped Syngman Rhee from invading the North, however, Kim Il Sung bears responsibility for a fruitless war that left millions dead. Many Americans condemned Truman for "losing" the war, but others believe that the United States saved South Korea for freedom and democracy. Unfortunately, it was not freedom and democracy that

---

1. Bruce Cumings, *The Origins of the Korean War*, vol. 2 (Princeton, N.J.: Princeton University Press, 1990).

DOCUMENTS

"Flowers of Fire" by Sŏnu Hwi

Sŏnu Hwi's "Flowers of Fire" was written in 1957. It tells the story of Ko Hyŏn, who was only a child when his father was shot dead by Japanese gendarmes for participating in the March First demonstrations of 1919. When his grandfather condemned his father's stupidity for losing his life and widowing his mother, Hyŏn tried to avoid dangerous commitments to survive under colonial rule. When the Japanese drafted him into the Japanese army in Manchuria, he escaped to the Chinese Communists in Yan'an. Back in Korea in 1950, North Korean troops took over his village, and the leading Communist cadre in charge was of his village was his childhood friend, Yŏnho. Yŏnho demanded he join the KPA to fight against the class enemies in South Korea, but he refused and once again ran away to the mountains. Before he did, he explained to Yŏnho why he refused to get involved.

[Hyŏn] "Capitalists, landowners, pro-Japanese, reactionaries—these are what you hate?"

"And opportunists," Yŏnho's voice rose suddenly.

[Hyŏn] "I'm not an opportunist. The object of hatred is not someone you can point to. This so-called hatred is a hatred that does nothing but produce a vicious circle of hatred."

[Yŏnho] "So?"

[Hyŏn] "The object of hatred is the absurd human condition. The poison that lurks in your breast and mine. The barbarity which oppresses others. Arrogance that pretends to have excelled others. Self-promoting, cheap, heroistic, meddling. Impudence that arrogates the right to kill or let live. . . ."

Yŏnho looked at Hyŏn with a mixture of derision and pity. The retrogression of the confused petit bourgeois grasping at a straw in muddy capitalist society!

———

Source: Peter H. Lee, ed., *Flowers of Fire* (Honolulu: University of Hawaii Press, 1974), pp. 229–230.

was defended in the ROK, but an anti-Communist dictatorship.

THE REPUBLIC OF KOREA (1953–1992): DICTATORSHIP AND ECONOMIC GROWTH

Syngman Rhee and Chang Myŏn (1953–1961)

The ROK constitution guaranteed elections and civil liberties, but Syngman Rhee proceeded to construct a dictatorship based on the police, a new army, and a centralized bureaucracy that appointed all district magistracies throughout the country. In 1949 he passed the infamous National Security Law that allowed imprisonment for treason for anyone who supported, abetted, or praised an "enemy state" (i.e., North Korea), terms so vague that Rhee immediately began to use it as a tool to repress his political rivals. It has not been significantly revised since.

Rhee railroaded bills through the National Assembly over opposition by the Korean Democratic Party. He used officials and police to intimidate voters during elections. He distributed favors to politicians, gagged newspapers,

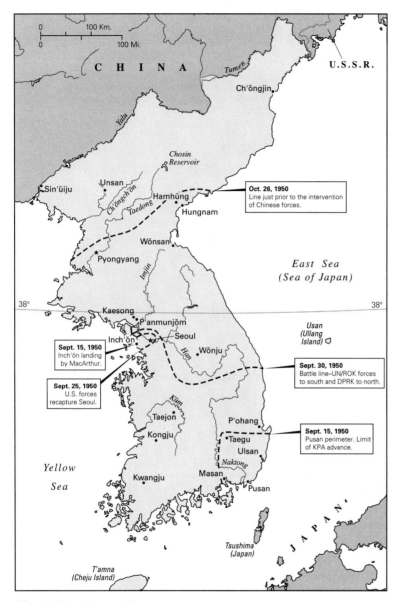

Map 30.1   **Korean War**

and jailed critics and subjected them to torture. Whatever he had learned from America about respect for law, democracy, and civil liberties he forgot once he returned to Korea.

Rhee was forced to adopt land reform during the Korean War to compete with the North. The landlord class was eliminated, but the reform created a class of conservative small property owners who henceforth voted in heavy numbers for Rhee and subsequent dictators. Eleven billion dollars of U.S. civil and military aid during the Rhee regime kept the economy above water. Rhee distributed U.S. dollars to favored businessmen in return for political contributions.

His import-substitution policy cut the cost of imported goods, but the country's economic growth rate remained very low. U.S. officials viewed the ROK as a basket case incapable of serious development and planned to turn South Korea into a supplier of agricultural products and raw materials in return for Japan's manufactured goods, but Rhee opposed beggaring South Korea for Japan's benefit.

Rhee refused to negotiate a peace treaty with Japan. He relied heavily on the United States for conventional defense, and in 1958 the United States began placing over two hundred nuclear weapons on South Korean soil, with missiles aimed at China and the Soviet Union as well as North Korea.

Finally, college students took to the streets on April 19, 1960, to protest Rhee's attempt to fix his reelection. The police fired into the crowd and killed student demonstrators, but the death knell sounded on Rhee's regime when the army refused to do likewise. American officials finally persuaded Rhee to retire in tattered dignity to Hawaii.

A revised constitution promised the arrival of democratic government, but the new premier, Chang Myŏn, was faced with anti-Communist conservatives and the old guard in his own KDP, who were incensed when he capitulated to student demands to initiate negotiations with North Korea. The economy did not thrive, and the Americans lost confidence in his leadership. He still might have served a full term had not General Park Chung Hee (Pak Chŏnghǔi) overthrown him in a coup d'état on May 16, 1961. President John F. Kennedy faced the ticklish prospect of either using force to crush the coup to preserve democracy or leave the military in command. Kennedy, fearing another DPRK invasion, chose military dictatorship rather than disrupt political stability.

Park Chung Hee: The First Decade (1961–1972)

Park Chung Hee began another dictatorial regime that began with a supreme council for

Park Chung Hee (Pak Chˇonghˇui). Army general Park Chung Hee led a coup d'état against the Chang Myŏn government in 1961 and ruled South Korea as dictator until his assassination in 1979. *(Park Chung Hee,* Toward Peaceful Unification: Selected Speeches by President Park Chung Hee *[Seoul: Kwangmyong Publishing Company, 1976])*

reconstruction staffed by military men. It lasted two years. He dissolved the National Assembly, barred the old politicians from political activity, and cracked down on civil liberties, but the Kennedy administration induced him to don civilian garb and hold presidential and National Assembly elections in 1963.

His chief deputy, Kim Jong Pil (Kim Chong-p'il), organized the Democratic Republican Party (DRP) for Park and created the Korean Central Intelligence Agency (KCIA), an all-encompassing organization that investigated, kidnapped, and tortured domestic political opponents of the regime as well as North Korean spies. Park held elections to preserve a facade of democratic procedure to please Americans, but he relied on the civil bureaucracy, police, army, and KCIA to maintain power and coerce enough voters to win the presidential elections of 1963 and 1967 and majorities for his DRP in the National Assembly. The massive migration of the rural population to Seoul and other cities, however, expanded the opposition vote until Kim Dae Jung (Kim Taejung) from Chŏlla province came within a hair of winning the presidential election of 1971.

In economic policy, Park ignored the principles of free market capitalism and adopted a developmentalist strategy similar to that of imperial Japan to expand the economy. He controlled the banks to direct foreign exchange and loans at preferential low interest rates to labor-intensive export industries like textiles to take advantage of South Korea's low wages. He allowed the most efficient companies to grow to become huge conglomerates (*chaebŏl*) and protected them from bankruptcy. Park devalued the currency to cut export prices and expand exports to America's open markets, but he also protected the economy with tariffs and nontariff barriers, banned the sale of export items on the domestic market, and prevented foreign investors from 51 percent ownership of businesses. After repressing strikes for higher wages, he created a single national trade union to block labor activism. He maintained subsistence income for the new class of smallholding farmers by buying up their rice crop at artificially inflated prices and distributing it to low-wage urban factory and white-collar workers at artificially low prices, and he socialized the cost by paying for it with tax revenue from the public. He also built multistory apartment houses for squatters and the homeless poor.

Park was able to raise $800 million in grants and loans from Japan in 1965 in return for normalizing relations against violent opposition from students and nationalists. As a result, the economy grew about 9 percent a year for almost two decades. Despite his reduction of invest-

ment in agriculture, the small landowners provided him a solid electoral base. In 1971, he established the Saemaŭl (New Village) Movement to mobilize both peasants and workers with mixed results, and factory workers struck against low wages several times between 1968 and 1971. The nation was particularly shocked in 1970 at the self-immolation of Chŏn T'ae'il, a worker in the Peace Market in Seoul, who protested worker repression.

Although close to 80 percent of women finished high school and 25 percent attended college by the 1970s, educated women were limited to secretarial or white-collar jobs. They were separated from men on the job and given lower wages for similar work. These women had no chance for promotion and were usually forced out once they married.

In the late 1960s Park feared that the U.S. commitment to defend the ROK was weakening because the United States was mired down in the Vietnam War. U.S. President Lyndon Johnson refused Park's request for military retaliation after about thirty North Korean commandoes tried to assassinate him in the presidential Blue House on January 21, 1968. Two days later, Johnson again took no action after North Korea captured a U.S. intelligence ship, the *U.S.S. Pueblo,* 15 miles offshore and kept its eighty-two crew members in detention.

Park agreed to President Johnson's request that he dispatch Korean troops to Vietnam to fight alongside U.S. forces. In return, the ROK received $1 billion in compensation for the fifty thousand Korean soldiers on the ground and the equipment supplied by South Korea for the Vietnam war effort. When Johnson decided not to run for reelection that year because of anti–Vietnam War protest, Park was convinced of U.S. weakness.

The U.S. pattern of inaction continued with the presidency of Richard Nixon. In 1969 President Nixon took no retaliatory actions when North Korea shot down a U.S. EC-121 reconnaissance plane. In July, he announced his "Nixon Doctrine," which shifted the main responsibility for self-defense to Asian nations, and in February 1970, he removed twenty thousand of the sixty-two thousand U.S. troops in Korea to cut U.S. costs. Alarmed, Park worked around Nixon by having his agents in Washington, D.C., bribe U.S. congressmen to grant more funds to the ROK—the "Koreagate" scandal. Park perceived Nixon's rapprochement with Mao's China in 1971 as capitulation to the Communist enemy, so he decided to negotiate directly with Kim Il Sung and induced him to sign a joint communiqué on July 4, 1972, for peaceful reunification. Those talks, however, soon collapsed.

Park Chung Hee: The Big Push (1972–1979)

Park now decided to carry out forced industrial development. On October 17, 1972, he proclaimed a *yusin* revitalization movement and revised the constitution to allow the president to appoint one-third of the members of the National Assembly, guaranteeing him a two-thirds majority and the ability to declare martial law at any time. Subsequently his infamous Decree No. 9 banned any criticism of the president, and he also forbade all labor union activity.

In January 1973 Park initiated his heavy and chemical industry (HCI) program to develop heavy industry, petrochemicals, and electronics for weapons production and expanded exports. He put the engineer Oh Won Chul (O Wŏnch'ŏl) in charge of the program to run it under strict military discipline from the Blue House. When the Middle Eastern oil-producing nations raised oil prices in 1973 and 1974, he refused to derail industrialization and borrowed heavily from abroad to keep the factories going. By the end of the decade, South Korea was exporting machinery, chemicals, and ships.

To eliminate his biggest political challenger, Park in 1973 authorized the KCIA to kidnap Kim Dae Jung from his hotel room in Tokyo and dump him overboard in Tokyo Bay, but a sharp U.S. protest forced Park to bring Kim back to Seoul and put him under house arrest. Park, however, regained some public sympathy when an assassin's bullet went awry and killed Park's wife, the popular Yuk Yŏngsu.

In 1974 Park began the secret Yulgok Program to develop an independent nuclear weapons program and obtained a loan for nuclear reactors from France right after South Vietnam fell to the Vietcong on July 16, 1975. President Gerald Ford immediately forced cancellation of the agreement with France, a clear example of direct intervention in ROK domestic affairs. Nonetheless, Park continued to build nuclear power plants and missiles. When Jimmy Carter of the Democratic Party became president in 1976, he was so disturbed by Park's violation of human rights that he tried to reduce the number of U.S. troops in South Korea, but members of his own administration, along with conservatives in the Republican Party, forced him to abandon the plan.

It was not until 1979 that inflation and labor protests in Pusan and the free export zone of Masan brought an end to Park's regime. Park was about to crack down on the demonstrators with military force when the head of the KCIA, Kim Chaegyu, one of the few with direct access to Park, shot and killed him on October 26 in the Blue House compound. Kim acted on his own and was arrested forthwith.

The Chun Doo Hwan Dictatorship (1979–1987)

Public expectations for the beginning of a democratic system were crushed on December 12, 1979, when General Chun Doo Hwan (Chŏn Tuhwan), chief of the Army Security Command, used a contingent of troops to seize power in Seoul. Chun declared martial law and on May 17, 1980, closed all universities, banned political activity, suspended the National Assembly, and arrested hundreds of students and opposition politicians. When students in Kwangju in Chŏlla province protested en masse on May 18 and citizens took over the city, Chun sent in troops who clubbed, bayoneted, and killed people on the streets indiscriminately. When the repression was complete the government announced 191 had died, but census officials recorded a drop of 2,000 in the population the next year. The Kwangju massacre turned a large

Kim Dae Jung (Kim Taejung), Opposition Politician and Later President of South Korea, 1997–2002. Here, on August 14, 1980, Kim Dae Jung appears on trial on the phony charge for fomenting the Kwangju uprising of May, 1980, for which he received the death penalty. *(Han'guksa vol. 19 [Seoul: Han'gilsa, 1994], p. 29)*

segment of the population against the United States for failure to prevent the bloodshed.

Chun Doo Hwan made Kim Dae Jung the scapegoat for Kwangju and had a kangaroo court sentence Kim to death. In 1980 President Ronald Reagan reached a deal with Chun to abrogate Kim's death sentence and abolish the ROK nuclear weapons program in return for a formal invitation to the White House. Kim Dae Jung was saved, but Reagan's invitation legitimized Chun's military usurpation and left many democratic activists in jail.

Chun then revised the constitution to establish a seven-year term for the presidency. He banned 567 past politicians from political activity and won a sham presidential election in February 1981. Meanwhile, Kim Il Sung in North Korea decided in 1983 that assassinating an unpopular dictator like Chun might spark a revolutionary uprising. His agents planted a bomb

in Rangoon while Chun and his cabinet were visiting Burma, and the explosion killed sixteen ROK cabinet members and officials. Kim's terror backfired when Chun was unharmed, and the tragedy only increased sympathy for Chun's regime. By 1985 Chun lifted the ban against most politicians but dismissed a half-dozen dissident professors, expelled 1,363 university students, forcibly conscripted 465 others into military service where several were murdered on duty, and subjected others to brainwashing in concentration camps. Chun took revenge on his critics in the media by dismissing about 820 newspaper and broadcast reporters, banning 172 periodicals, closing down 617 publishing companies, and taking over the Munhwa Broadcasting Corporation (MBC).

In 1987 Chun Doo Hwan gave signs of reneging on his pledge to retire at the end of his seven-year term, but the most massive demonstrations in history broke out to demand direct election of a new president in 1987. Forced to retreat, he nominated his comrade in arms, General Roh Tae Woo (No T'aeu), a commander in the Kwangju massacre, to be his party's nominee for president. He authorized Roh on June 29 to announce direct elections, restoration of freedom of the press, and reinstatement of Kim Dae Jung's right to run. Pressure from President Reagan on Chun was critical for the decision, but the main force for democracy came from the students who had fought against dictatorship for decades and elements of the urban middle class who finally joined the democratic struggle at the end.

Democracy Arrives (1987–1992)

Now that the opposition finally had a chance to replace a military leader at the ballot box, the Three Kims (Kim Dae Jung, Kim Jong P'il, and Kim Young Sam) blew the chance because personal ambition blocked them from uniting behind a single candidate. Roh Tae Woo won the election with only 35.9 percent of the vote. Regional voting was prominent as Kim Dae Jung won heavily in Chŏlla province, Kim Jong P'il in South Ch'ungch'ŏng, Kim Young Sam in Pusan and South Kyŏngsang, and Roh in Taegu and North Kyŏngsang, a pattern that remains strong. Chun had founded his own private Ilhae Foundation to control Roh after the election, but his hopes were dashed when Roh jailed fourteen of Chun's brothers and relatives for embezzlement and corruption. Chun retired in disgrace to a Buddhist monastery.

The National Assembly elections left Roh's new Democratic Liberal Party (DLP) with only a minority of seats, but once again opposition leaders Kim Young Sam and Kim Jong P'il sold out principle for power by joining Roh's DLP. Kim Dae Jung was left alone in opposition, but his reputation suffered too when it was revealed that he had accepted campaign funds from Roh. At least the workers seized the initiative to found a new, independent National Federation of Trade Unions (Chŏnnohyŏp) in defiance of the government-controlled Korean Federation of Trade Unions (KFTU). Roh, however, blocked schoolteachers from unionizing.

Roh's Nordpolitik (Northern Policy) foreign policy succeeded in achieving a breakthrough in relations with the Communist states of the Soviet Union, eastern Europe, and China. In 1988, South Korea hosted the Summer Olympics in Seoul, and Roh invited the Communist states to send athletes to the games. Kim Il Sung sought to intimidate them by sending two agents to blow up South Korean Flight 858 from the Middle East to Seoul. It killed all on board, but those nations defied Kim by sending their athletes to the games anyway.

Instead of retaliating, Roh sent officials to Pyongyang in 1989 to persuade Kim Il Sung to allow Chung Ju Yong (Chŏng Chuyŏng) of the Hyundai Corporation to open a tourist area in the Kŭmgang (Diamond) Mountain area just north of the DMZ (see **Material Culture: The Visitors' Center at the Kŭmgang Mountains**). On the other hand, he punished others under the National Security Law for traveling to North Korea without his permission to discuss peaceful reunification.

Roh induced Prime Minister Kaifu of Japan to apologize publicly for the damage done to Korea by colonial rule. He also gained Soviet and Chinese support to admit South Korea to the United Nations in 1991, forcing Kim Il Sung to abandon its previous opposition and accept admission to the United Nations as well. In short, by using carrots instead of sticks, Roh obtained most of his objectives.

CIVILIAN PRESIDENTS (1992 TO THE PRESENT)

Kim Young Sam's single-term presidency (1992–1997) solved the curse of military interference in politics by purging the high-ranking military officers who had served the dictators and stripping the Agency for National Security (the old KCIA) and the Military Security Command of their power to investigate domestic

MATERIAL CULTURE

The Visitors' Center at the Kŭmgang Mountains

The Kŭmgang (Diamond) Mountains span over 40 kilometers of land and are considered the most beautiful mountain range on the Korean peninsula. Located in North Korean territory, it has been off-limits to visitors until recently. Kim Il Sung began to allow South Korean civilians into North Korean ter-

ritory in large numbers in the 1990s. Hyundai corporation financed the construction of a visitors' center in 1998, and South Korean tourists can now come directly by land across the DMZ. The project stands as the first step to larger and more peaceful relations, perhaps reunification someday in the future.

Diamond Mountains (Kŭmgangsan). A view of the recently opened tourist center for South Korean tourists to view the Diamond Mountains (Kŭmgangsan), just over the DMZ in North Korea. *(Photonica)*

politicians. In 1995 he held the first local elections for provincial governors, city mayors, county magistrates, and local assemblies in history. Even more courageous, he prosecuted former presidents Chun Doo Hwan and Roh Tae Woo for treason, mutiny, and corruption and sent Chun to jail for life and Roh for seventeen years.

Kim suddenly became an advocate of globalization and the wholesale adoption of liberal, free market principles, but the results were dire. He reduced tariffs, and cheap imports undercut home industries. He encouraged companies to cut costs to increase efficiency, but workers were laid off. He encouraged the inflow of foreign capital, but the *chaebŏl* glutted the market with autos, semiconductors, and steel and doctored their books to hide their indebtedness from the banks. By 1996, South Korea's national debt almost doubled to $109 billion, of which two-thirds was short-term debt.

In 1997 the Asian financial crisis spread from Thailand to South Korea, and the economy crashed. Foreign lenders called in short-term loans overnight and drove a half-dozen *chaebŏl* and their suppliers into bankruptcy. South Korea was saved from defaulting on its national debt only because the International Monetary Fund (IMF) provided a record bailout package of $55 billion. When the IMF imposed a brutal retrenchment policy by raising interest rates from 12 to 27 percent per annum to stabilize the currency, more companies failed, and thousands of workers were laid off. Female workers were often the first to be fired. Kim Young Sam's popularity plummeted, even more so when several cabinet members and his two sons were sent to jail for evading military service and receiving bribes.

Kim Jong P'il split from Young Sam's party to form his own United Liberal Democratic Party, and he joined with Kim Dae Jung to ensure the latter's victory in the 1997 presidential election, the first opposition victory in ROK history. Now it was Kim Dae Jung's turn to deal with the economic crisis. He abandoned his earlier defense of low-wage workers and the unemployed by following IMF demands to allow unrestricted layoffs. The unemployment rate rose from less than 2 percent to 7.6 percent by September 1998, and national per capita income dropped from $10,000 to $7,000. Kim had to sell eleven state-owned industries, including the prized Pohang Iron and Steel Company (Posco), to private owners to raise funds.

Kim finally defied IMF dictates in the fall of 1998 by lowering interest rates to increase business investment, but the *chaebŏl* gobbled up the loan money and left small business in the lurch. When the *chaebŏl* supported unprofitable member companies, Kim Dae Jung induced foreign companies to invest in failing Korean businesses with majority ownership to save them from bankruptcy. By 2000, the economy finally began to recover.

South Korea still suffers from technological gaps and the loss of jobs to low-wage countries like China, exacerbated by *chaebŏl* outsourcing of factories to China. Kim Dae Jung's reputation hit rock bottom because his son and many officials were also prosecuted for taking bribes, and his own party took his party's chairmanship away from him.

Independents and defectors from the major parties formed a new liberal party, Our Open Party (Yŏllin uridang). Roh Moo Hyun of Kim's Millennium Democratic Party was elected president in 2002, thanks to a backlash against President George W. Bush's North Korea policy, but conservatives in his party forced him out. They then joined up with the opposition One Nation Party to impeach him for publicly endorsing Our Open Party for the upcoming April 2004 national assembly elections. Incensed by the pettiness of the impeachment, the electorate proceeded to vote the Our Open Party into a parliamentary majority, leaving the One Nation Party in a minority and the Millennium Democratic Party with only nine seats. The Three Kims were finally removed from politics.

Roh lost some liberal support when he sent troops to Iraq, but in the fall of 2004 he regained support from Our Open Party when he openly demanded abolition of the National Security Law. Possibly the victory of Our Open Party will open the path to stable party politics based on policy positions rather than shifting patron-client groups.

MODERNIZATION: CHANGES IN FAMILY LIFE, CONSUMER CULTURE, AND LITERATURE

Rapid changes have occurred in South Korean society since 1945. Arranged marriages began to decline, as marriage brokers were used for introductions only. College men and women arranged group "meetings" or group dating to enable couples to pair off for dates and "love marriages," but they still sought parental approval for marriage. Wives were still subordinated to men and mothers-in-law in marriage, but middle-class married couples obtained some distance from parents who bankrolled their large rental deposits (*chŏnse*) for individual apartments. Couples put intense pressure on their children to gain entry into the best colleges. Middle-class wives were virtually abandoned by their overworked white-collar husbands who stayed out drinking until midnight, but they took to making money in the real estate or stock markets. As women became conscious of gender discrimination and frustrated by unhappy marriages, books and movies from the 1990s began to portray (and reflect) married women seeking sexual liberation with lovers.

The growth of income and wealth led to a consumer culture and ostentatious consumption in clothing, appliances, pianos, and luxury apartments. South Koreans today continue to have wide access to goods and technology, while residents of North Korea lag significantly behind. The table on this page compares the two countries in terms of their standards of living and access to technology.

Korean poetry and literature in the vernacular came into its own in the postwar period. Many authors were consumed with the Korean War, social justice, and the evils of dictatorship.

Ch'ae Mansik's *Peace Under Heaven* portrayed an evil landlord, and the famous "Five Bandits" poem of Kim Chiha condemned bureaucrats and businessmen. Hwang Sunwŏn wrote of the poor in the 1970s, and Hwang Suk-young (Hwang Sŏgyŏng) wrote about personal problems and Korean soldiers in the Vietnam War in *The Shadow of Arms* (1985). Pak Kyŏngni's lengthy *The Land* (1980) was a best-seller, and short-story writers like Kang Sŏkkyŏng, Kim Chiwŏn, Pak Wansŏ, and O Chŏnghŭi left their mark with descriptive and contemplative stories of anomie under industrialization.

THE DEMOCRATIC PEOPLE'S REPUBLIC OF KOREA (1953 TO THE PRESENT)

The history of the DPRK in this period involves the maximization of political power in the hands of the supreme leader, a military policy based on arming the entire population backed by Soviet support to 1991, periodic terrorist acts, a revolutionary social policy, and a roller-coaster economic ride under a command economy. The collapse of communism in the Soviet Union and eastern Europe in 1991 provided a major shock to North Korea's fortunes.

Economic Growth and Political Consolidation (1953–1959)

After the end of the Korean War in 1953, Kim Il Sung relied heavily on aid from the Soviet Union and China. He invested primarily in heavy and defense industries to create the basis for economic independence and a national arms industry. He postponed the production of consumer goods to the indefinite future, called on the public to accept sacrifice for the greater good of the nation, and compensated by providing cheap housing and food, free education, and free medical treatment.

In the mid-1950s Kim embarked on a rapid farm collectivization plan aimed at converting all farmers to proletarians on wages on state farms,

A Comparison of Living Standards in North and South Korea

	South Korea	North Korea
Population	47.6 million	22.5 million
Life expectancy (years)	73.9	62.4
Infant mortality rate (per 1,000 live births)	5.0	42.0
Fixed line and mobile telephones (per 1,000 people)	1,168.0	21.1
Internet users	26.3 million	No data available
Paved roads (% of total)	74.5	6.4

Source: World Bank, http://www.worldbank.org/data/countrydata/countrydata.html.

but the plan was never fully achieved and ended with smaller collectives at the village level. Broad fields were created out of small parcels to enable the use of tractors and chemical fertilizer. Originally successful, the drawbacks of this program were not seen until decades later, particularly the shortages of foreign oil, erosion, the replacement of age-old farming experience with bureaucratic managers, and restrictions on the freedom to move or change jobs.

Industrial production in the DPRK surpassed growth in South Korea through the mid-1960s but then began to slow because of the decline in aid from the Soviet Union and China, bottlenecks in the production process, insufficient technological development, and excessive investment in weapons. Kim Il Sung's solution was to use a moral appeal to workers for greater sacrifice and undertake mass mobilization efforts like the Ch'ŏllima (the Thousand-League Horse) campaign of 1958. It was similar to the Great Leap Forward campaign in China, but was not designed to supplement factories with backyard steel furnaces and did not result in massive starvation (see Chapter 28). Workers were required to work extra hours, and students were taken out of classrooms to work.

The new proletarian state banned collective bargaining and created only single state trade and farmers' unions. Kim Il Sung borrowed Mao Zedong's "mass line" strategy in 1960 to force party cadres to consult with the workers and farmers in devising production plans. Faced with a dearth of proletarians, he ignored the Leninist party model by admitting a majority of peasants into the KWP and converting them to proletarian class consciousness by indoctrination and self-criticism. Contrary to Mao, however, he never launched periodic mass mobilization campaigns to purge party cadres and bureaucrats that had lost their revolutionary ideals.

Kim purged only members of the party who challenged his supremacy, starting with Pak Hŏnyong and the domestic Communists after the Korean War. After Stalin died in 1953 and Khrushchev denounced Stalin for creating a cult of personality in 1956, he purged members of the Russian and Yan'an factions who accused him of

doing the same thing. He also purged three generals after his military ventures against South Korea and the United States in 1968 and 1969 failed.

Foreign Relations and Expansion of Personal Power (1959–1975)

When the Soviet Union and China finally split in 1959, Kim Il Sung remained neutral and signed mutual defense treaties with both countries in 1961. He was distressed when Mao allowed President Nixon to visit Beijing in 1972 (even more so in 1979 when China normalized relations with the United States). Perhaps that was the reason that in 1972 he allowed members of families separated by the Korean War to meet for the first time since 1953 and signed a joint pledge for peaceful unification with Park Chung Hee.

In 1972 Kim Il Sung introduced a new constitution that created a new office of president, which gave him control of all government agencies. More shocking for Communists, he subordinated the KWP to his command and left it out of many of his policy decisions. As signs of his megalomania, he also built gigantic statues of himself and adopted grandiose titles like "supreme leader," "fatherly leader," "the Great Sun," and "the supreme mind of the nation."

Kim also began to displace Marxism-Leninism with *chuch'e* (self-reliance) as the leading ideology of the country. *Chuch'e* is an untranslatable term that constitutes "a subjective, solipsistic state of mind, the correct thought that will then determine correct action" in almost any imaginable situation.[2] In 1973 Kim borrowed from the dynastic tradition by grooming his son, Kim Jong Il (Kim Chŏng'il), to succeed him. He gave him responsibility for running most state affairs when he appointed him secretary of the KWP and member of the Military Commission in 1980.

Kim Il Sung divided society into a new status hierarchy. The nuclear masses included KWP party members, government officials, military officers, anti-Japanese guerrilla fighters, and

---

2. Bruce Cumings, *Korea's Place in the Sun* (New York: Norton, 1997), pp. 403–404. See also pp. 404–414.

martyrs who died in Korean War. The nonnuclear masses included nonparty workers, peasants, and clerical workers. The lowly mixed masses were outcasts with tainted backgrounds: descendants of the bourgeoisie, landlords, capitalists, and dissidents. Instead of equal treatment for all, Kim turned the status structure upside down, reviving hereditary privilege for the elite and hereditary stigma for the despised.

Kim locked all individuals into a variety of state-run mass organizations. Because of the shortage of labor, he encouraged women to work and had the state provide child care facilities for working parents. He replaced the home with communal mess halls, gave women the right to divorce, and incorporated them into the military but gave political responsibilities to only a few.

When the economy began to decline in the late 1960s, Kim opened trade relations with the West in 1972 to import advanced machinery and even fabrication plants from Europe and Japan on credit. Lacking a serious export industry, however, he defaulted on his international debt in 1975, and serious trade with the West evaporated.

After 1973 Kim Il Sung constructed along the DMZ secret tunnels into South Korea large enough to accommodate an invasion, but he attempted no large-scale attacks. The axe murder of a few U.S. troops by North Korean soldiers in the DMZ in 1976 over the petty issue of cutting down a large tree, however, created more tension. In the early 1980s President Reagan countered these challenges by shipping cruise missiles and F-16 fighters to South Korea and increased the number of troops in the joint U.S.-ROK Team Spirit military exercise of 1981.

Kim supported the Soviet Union's invasion of Afghanistan as a means of ensuring military aid. Possibly in return for that favor, a Soviet interceptor in August 1983 shot down a South Korean airliner, KAL Flight 007, that had strayed into Russian territory over Siberia. The next year the Soviets shipped more military equipment in return for docking and overfly rights, and in 1986 it promised to construct a nuclear power plant in the North.

Economic Decline After 1987

One sign of economic difficulty came in 1987 when Kim Il Sung was forced to abandon construction in midpoint on what was to be the tallest building in East Asia, the 105-story Ryugyŏng Hotel. He decided to shift investment to light industry and consumer products to improve living conditions, and he opened talks with South Korea on economic and humanitarian cooperation and sent food aid to flood victims in South Korea. In 1988 he began informal talks with U.S. representatives, but his terrorist downing of the KAL plane interrupted them. In 1990, Kim did agree with the United States to establish trade offices with consular functions in both countries.

After the collapse of communism in the Soviet Union in 1991, oil supplies to Korea dropped sharply because Russia demanded cash payment, and factories operated at only a fraction of capacity. North Korea opened a free economic trade zone in the Rajin-Sŏnbong area in the northeast in 1991, but no foreign investors responded. The floods of 1995 and 1996 and the drought of 1997 reduced the country to near-famine conditions, and perhaps 1 million people lost their lives. Denizens of Pyongyang and the army fared well, while the civilian population suffered from malnutrition and disease. For the first time, the government allowed people to leave their homes without permission to forage for food, cultivate small private plots, and sell the products in farmers' markets.

Nonetheless, illegal emigration into China increased, and refugees jumped the gates of foreign embassies in Beijing to escape to South Korea, but China cracked down on refugees and returned them home. Worldwide charitable organizations, South Korea, China, the United States, and Japan supplied perhaps a fifth of North Korea's food consumption in the 1990s. Despite the hardship, North Korea defied the prediction of foreign pundits that the regime would collapse like East Germany.

After Kim Il Sung's death in 1994, Kim Jong Il took some cautious steps to open society. He opened the Diamond Mountain tourist center for South Koreans, the Ŭiju free trade zone south of the Yalu River, and the Kaesŏng industrial park, and he permitted construction of rail and road lines across the DMZ from South Korea to Kaesŏng and the Diamond Mountains. He welcomed South Korean *chaebŏl* plans to invest in factories to hire cheap North Korean labor to export abroad, but the nuclear crisis delayed fruition.

The North Korean Nuclear Challenge

Between 1964 and 1986 North Korea received and built several gas-graphite nuclear reactors in the Soviet style at Yŏngbyŏn north of Pyongyang, for research and electrical generation. All produced plutonium as a by-product, which could be used to manufacture hydrogen bombs. In 1985 the Soviet Union induced Kim Il Sung to sign the Nonproliferation Treaty (NPT), which required inspections by the UN International Atomic Energy Agency (IAEA) to prevent military use of fissile material. The IAEA, however, never followed through on the inspections. In 1989 and 1990 North Korean officials informed Tony Namkung (Namgung Kun), an American citizen, of their desire to normalize relations with the United States and Japan, open trade with South Korea, support peaceful coexistence, reduce defense expenditures, and introduce market reforms. They also voiced their objection to the U.S. nuclear weapons on South Korean soil, the joint ROK-U.S. Team Spirit exercises, and the thirty-seven thousand U.S. troops stationed in South Korea.

In 1991, Kim Il Sung signed a denuclearization pact with South Korea, and the United States eased growing tension when it announced withdrawal of all U.S. nuclear weapons from Korean soil and cancelled the joint Team Spirit exercises with South Korea. Nevertheless, fears over the nuclear capabilities of the North continued. U.S. intelligence surmised that enough plutonium from spent reactor fuel at Yŏngbyŏn could have been extracted to make thirty plutonium bombs. That estimate was dropped to two to eight bombs, but with no concrete evidence that a single bomb had been made or tested.

Kim Il Sung offered to replace his gas-graphite reactors with new light-water reactors, which produce less plutonium as a waste product, but the United States ignored the offer and considered taking punitive action unless Kim abandoned his nuclear weapons program. A few American generals warned that a second Korean war would result in three hundred thousand to five hundred thousand military and millions of civilian Korean casualties on both sides, but Kim created a crisis when he threatened to pull out of the NPT. President Bill Clinton sent ex-president Jimmy Carter on a last-ditch effort to Pyongyang to talk directly with Kim. Carter eliminated the crisis when he appeared on CNN and announced his agreement with Kim Il Sung to freeze the processing of nuclear waste to extract plutonium at Yŏngbyŏn in return for new light-water reactors. Kim Il Sung even told Carter he was willing to carry out the North-South denuclearization agreement, pull back forces from the DMZ, match South Korea in reducing troops by 1 million men, and allow U.S. troops to remain in Korea in smaller numbers. Unfortunately, he died that year before negotiations could be expanded.

His son, Kim Jong Il, finally signed the Agreed Framework with the United States in 1994. Under this agreement, South Korea and Japan assumed the cost for the light-water reactors and the United States had to provide only 500,000 tons of heavy oil to replace energy lost from the inactive reactor. A neutral agency, KEDO (Korean Energy and Development Organization), was established to administer construction. North Korea remained a party to the NPT and promised to allow the IAEA to inspect facilities not subject to the freeze when the light-water reactors were completed but before the nuclear components were installed.

Subsequently, the United States delayed delivery of heavy oil, and the economic crash of 1997 rendered the ROK incapable of financing construction. Possibly to spur the United States to action, in 1998 North Korea fired a Taep'odong missile over Japan as a test, but that only shocked the Japanese public into consideration of abandoning the no-war clause of its constitution and American officials into contemplating North Korean nuclear-tipped missiles landing on U.S. territory.

Kim Dae Jung was elected president of the ROK in 1997 and inaugurated a new "sunshine policy (*haetpyŏtch'aek*)" based on peaceful negotiations with North Korea. When he visited President George W. Bush in Washington in March 2001 to gain support, however, Bush gave him the cold shoulder and rejected Kim's policy as appeasement. Undeterred, Kim Dae Jung "persuaded" Kim Jong Il to hold a summit meeting in Pyongyang in June 2000 and agree to solve all problems peacefully. Although Kim Dae Jung won the Nobel Peace Prize for that meeting, it was later revealed in 2002 that that he had paid a bribe of $500 million to Kim Jong Il in advance to enable the talks. When Kim Jong Il took no further measures to ease tension, Kim Dae Jung's reputation was severely damaged at home.

After the destruction of the twin towers in New York City by the Islamic terrorist al-Qaeda organization on September 11, 2001, President Bush declared his hostility to what he called the "axis of evil," a group "rogue states" that included North Korea, and he maligned Kim Jong Il for starving his own people, an obvious sign that Bush was not interested in negotiations. When U.S. intelligence discovered in 2002 the North's clandestine plan to build atomic weapons from enriched uranium (supplied by Pakistan), which the North subsequently denied, Bush cancelled all talks. He declared that the North would have to abandon its nuclear weapons program entirely before the United States offered any material aid, but Kim Jong Il refused to give up North Korea's last line of defense on a promise.

The ROK was split over Bush's policy, but the liberal Roh Moo Hyun, who supported the sunshine policy, was elected president in November 2002. When he expressed reservations about sending Korean troops to support the U.S. invasion of Iraq in 2003, the Bush administration threatened to pull all U.S. troops from South Korea in retaliation. Roh capitulated and sent the troops.

Increased Iraqi resistance to the U.S. occupation forced Bush to retreat from his threat to launch a preemptive strike against North Korea. Instead he brought China and Russia in to join the United States, South Korea, and Japan in six-nation talks with North Korea, but no progress was achieved. After Bush won reelection to the presidency in 2004, his administration resumed its harsh rhetoric.

SUMMARY

The period after 1945 was difficult for Korea: a brief liberation in 1945 followed by superpower domination by the Soviet Union and the United States, division of the country in two, and the Korean War, the worst war in Korean history. Peace was maintained between North and South Korea by a precarious armistice, with both sides heavily armed. Both the Communist North and the bureaucratic capitalist South were dominated by repressive regimes. The North Korean party dictatorship under Marxist-Leninist theory was transformed into a nationalistic, hereditary monarchy under *chuch'e* ideology, while in South Korea, Park's military dictatorship's command economy dragged the country out of poverty while trampling on human rights (see **Biography: Suh Sung and Kang Chol-hwan, Victims of Oppression**).

Students in South Korea, with the help of some intellectuals and opposition politicians, led the way in breaking the yoke of dictatorship and opening the way to democracy. The developmentalist strategy that vaulted the country to the heights of economic power began to show its flaws when the demands of the world market weakened protectionism and burst the bubble economy.

In North Korea, the Stalinist, heavy industrial economy rose initially, but fell because autarchy closed off technological innovation from external stimulation, and the collapse of communism

BIOGRAPHY Suh Sung and Kang Chol-hwan, Victims of Oppression

Both the North and South Korean governments left behind victims of oppression. Suh Sung (Sŏ Sŭng) was a Korean resident living in Japan when he traveled to Korea to complete a master's degree at Seoul National University in March 1971. Upon his arrival, he and his brother Suh Joon-shik (Sŏ Chunsik) were arrested and tortured to force a confession that they were North Korean spies. Unable to stand the torture, Suh Sung tried to commit suicide by self-immolation in April, but he survived, his face horribly disfigured. He was sentenced to death and his brother to fifteen years in prison, but his sentence was reduced to life imprisonment the next year. He was not released until 1990, after twenty-eight years in jail (his brother too, well past the term of incarceration). Suh's account of his horrific experience reveals the names of his torturers and the heroism of committed Communists or innocents who refused to confess to false charges to obtain release. Since his release, he has devoted his life to the promotion of human rights in South Korea.

The grandmother of Kang Chol-hwan (Kang Ch'ŏlhwan) migrated to Japan from Cheju Island in the 1930s at the age of thirteen. At the age of twenty, she joined the Japanese Communist Party and married a man from Cheju, who later made money from his pachinko parlor in Kyoto and became friends with the *yakuza*. Their son, Kang's father, was born in the early 1930s. In the 1960s, the grandmother persuaded her reluctant husband to move the whole family, including her brothers, to Pyongyang. They were treated as celebrities on the ship over, greeted by Kim Il Sung when they arrived, and provided a first-class apartment in the capital. The grandmother was elected to the Supreme People's Assembly, and the grandfather was appointed to the Office of Commercial Affairs. Kang's parents married in 1967, and he was born soon after.

One day in 1977, the grandfather disappeared, never to return, shipped off to a concentration camp for treason without a word to his family. Shortly after, at the age of nine, Kang returned home to find that security agents were sending him, his grandmother, his father, and his uncles to a concentration camp because of his grandfather's crime. His mother was left behind with no way to communicate with the rest of the family. They arrived at a camp where whole families were living in rags and filth, and they were placed in a hut with earthen walls and floor. The camp included two thousand or three thousand people; every year about a hundred died from hunger and disease. Minor violations were punished by a trip to the sweatbox for as long as three months. The prisoner had to crouch on his knees at all times in darkness without moving or speaking or suffer beatings for doing either. Many failed to survive.

Kang spent ten years in the camp and was able to avoid the worst punishments, but he had to carry ore from the mines and hunt rats to survive. One of his uncles attempted suicide twice. Adults worked in the gold mine for thirteen hours a day and many died from cave-ins. Women caught engaging in sex were humiliated in public or physically abused. Any babies born in the camp were taken away.

Finally, after a decade in the camp, Kang and his family were released by an amnesty, only to be subjected to strict surveillance in the countryside. Kang finally left his family behind and bribed his way across the border to China, and then to South Korea. His experiences are still being duplicated in the North.

Sources: See Suh Sung, *Unbroken Spirits* (Lanham, Maryland: Rowman & Littlefield, 2001), and Chol-hwan Kang and Pierre Rigoulot, *The Aquariums of Pyongyang* (New York: Basic Books, 2000).

in the Soviet Union robbed the country of its major material support. Both North and South had transformed their societies in different ways through social leveling and the partial liberation of women. The North turned the social order upside down, while the South created a new society of urban capitalists and white- and blue-collar workers while the farming class declined sharply. Religion was suppressed and replaced by hero worship and intense patriotism in the North, while Christianity, Buddhism, Ch'ŏndo-gyo, and new religions emerged in the South,

along with residual Confucian values and shamanism.

In the North, the loss of Soviet support and the Chinese departure from Marxist purity left nuclear weapons as the only option for defense. This forced a conversion of U.S. policy from the defense of South Korea from northern aggression to a militant policy to dismantle the North's nuclear weapons program. North Korea, however, remained fiercely committed to the kind of pugnacious independence that Korea had not experienced since the fall of Koguryŏ in 668.

SUGGESTED READING

For a general surveys of the period, see B. Cumings, *Korea's Day in the Sun* (1997); D. Oberdorfer, *The Two Koreas* (1997); and M. Noland, *Avoiding the Apocalypse* (2000).

Studies on the Korean war include B. Cumings, *The Origins of the Korean War*, vol. 2 (1990); J. Halliday and B. Cumings, *Korea: The Unknown War* (1988); S. N. Goncharov, J. W. Lewis, and L. Xue, *Uncertain Partners: Stalin, Mao, and the Korean War* (1993); and J. Chen, *China's Road to the Korean War* (1995). For an early study of the fighting, see R. Appleman, *South to the Naktong, North to the Yalu* (1961).

Studies on ROK politics include Cumings, *Origins of the Korean War*, vol. 1 (1981); G. Henderson, *Korea: The Politics of the Vortex* (1968); P. Hayes, *Pacific Powderkeg* (1990); C. K. Armstrong, ed., *Korean Society* (2002); and H.-A Kim, *Korea's Development Under Park Chung Hee* (2004).

For analysis of the ROK economy, see E. S. Mason et al., *The Economic and Social Modernization of the Republic of Korea* (1980); A. Amsden, *Asia's Next Giant* (1989); F. C. Deyo, ed., *The Political Economy of the New Asian Industrialism* (1987); C. Woo, *Race to the Swift* (1991); M. Hart-Landsberg, *The Rush to Development* (1993); R. L. Janelli with D. Yim, *Making Capitalism* (1993); P. Kuznets, *Korean Economic Development* (1994); D. Kirk, *Korean Dynasty: Hyundai and Chung Ju Yung* (1994); and H. Koo, *Korean Workers* (2001).

For South Korean literature, see P. H. Lee, ed., *Flowers of Fire* (1974), and B. and J.-C. Fulton, eds., *Words of Farewell: Stories by Korean Women Writers* (1989).

For studies on North Korea, see R. Scalapino and C. Lee, *Communism in Korea*, 2 vols. (1972); D. Suh, *Kim Il Sung* (1988); E. van Ree, *Socialism in One Zone* (1989); N. Eberstadt and J. Banister, *The Population of North Korea* (1992); B. Myers, *Han Sŏrya and North Korean Literature* (1994); M. J. Mazarr, *North Korea and the Bomb* (1995); L. V. Sigal, *Disarming Strangers* (1998); K. Oh and R. C. Hassig, *North Korea Through the Looking Glass* (2000); C. Armstrong, *The North Korean Revolution, 1945–1950* (2002); E. Cornell, *North Korea Under Communism* (2002); S. S. Harrison, *Korean Endgame* (2002); and A. Lankov, *From Stalin to Kim Il Sung* (2002).

Contemporary Japan (1965 to the Present)

Japan's desire for peace with its neighbors was marked in 1965 by demonstrations against the Vietnam War. The storms of protest provoked by public policy decisions and industrial pollution were also signs that by the late 1960s, the consequences of Liberal Democratic Party (LDP) domination and high-speed economic growth could no longer be ignored. The 1970s brought political scandals, diplomatic crises, and economic opportunities in the midst of setbacks. Minorities and working women demanded political initiatives to ameliorate their condition. Economic adjustments positioned Japanese companies to expand in export markets. In the 1980s, Japan had the world's second largest economy, but the euphoria of seemingly unstoppable growth led to a bubble in overpriced investments. When it burst in 1990, the economy deflated. Although social problems increased, most Japanese people enjoyed low crime rates, clean cities, superb public transportation, and unprecedented prosperity.

Why did the Japanese economy rise so far and fall so fast? Are protest and demonstrations worth discussing given the power of the LDP and bureaucrats? Which social trends will prove enduring, and which will prove beneficial?

POLITICAL PROTEST AND ENVIRONMENTAL POLLUTION

The 1960s saw student movements worldwide, and Japan was no exception. Students joined citizen's movements to protest Japan's support for the American war in Vietnam under the U.S.-Japan Security Treaty at the same time that they attacked educational policies. At some universities, they criticized what they viewed as assembly-line style courses. At Tokyo University, medical students protested a top-down reorganization of the program that ignored their concerns. In January 1968 they went on strike. When the university administration refused to hear their grievances and expelled their leaders, students in other departments struck in sympathy. They wanted curriculum control, amnesty for students arrested in confrontations, and no riot police allowed on campus. To make their point, they barricaded the central building. The administration cancelled entrance examinations for 1969. On campuses across Tokyo, students launched sympathy strikes. On January 19, 1969, eighty-five hundred riot police retook the campus in a two-day battle broadcast live on TV. The Diet passed a University Control Bill giving the Education Ministry enhanced authority to punish students. Radical student groups went underground.

Japan's rise to prominence in world affairs and the increase in air travel led the LDP and the Transportation Ministry to decide on a new international airport for Tokyo in 1965. Farmers who owned land at the proposed site outside Narita protested because expropriating their land destroyed their livelihood, secrecy surrounding the decision demonstrated that popular opinion counted for naught, and the airport might be used to support the American war effort in Vietnam. Farmers petitioned prefectural and national ministries; they rallied support in the Diet among the opposition parties. When these measures failed, they built barricades and fortresses; they dug ditches to trap bulldozers; they chained themselves to fences. The radical student union Zengakuren helped with agricultural work and publicity. Citizens in peace, antinuclear, and environmental movements joined them because they were fighting against government indifference to the social costs of economic growth. Plans called for the airport to be built in six years; it took twelve. The government reduced the number of runways from three to one; a proposal in 1998 to add a second also faced opposition. Having learned its lesson, the government later built

Osaka International Airport on an artificial island in the bay.

At the end of the 1960s, the left and right wings attacked capitalism and materialism. Mishima Yukio created a paramilitary organization and received permission to join Self Defense Force military maneuvers. In 1970 he called on the soldiers at SDF headquarters to remember the sacrifices made in World War II and rally behind nationalist goals by overthrowing the government. When they laughed at him, he committed ritual suicide. Between 1970 and 1972 students in the Red Army robbed banks and post offices, hijacked a plane to North Korea, and machine-gunned travelers in Tel Aviv's Lod airport in support of Maoist revolution and Palestinian rights.

Less dramatic but longer lasting, citizens' movements arose in response to industrial pollution. In the 1950s, local and prefectural governments encouraged industrial development that spread pollution from cities to towns and made Japan the most polluted nation on earth. By the early 1970s about half the population complained of suffering from pollution (see Color Plate 32). Citizens' movements mobilized hundreds of thousands of ordinarily apolitical residents to sign petitions, visit industrial sites, display posters, and launch education drives to rally support in stopping potential polluters from building in their neighborhood. They warned against trusting promises by industry and local government that a proposed factory would not pollute, and they rejected charges that fighting to protect the individual's quality of life is egotistical.

Between 1932 and 1968 at Minamata in southern Kyushu, a Chisso factory produced acetaldehyde, a key ingredient in making plastics through a process that released methyl mercury as a by-product. Dumped into the water, mercury concentrated in shellfish and other marine life and then attacked brain cells in domestic animals and humans. Although mercury can kill in a few weeks, many victims suffered progressive debilitation leading to a vegetative state and death. In 1959, a Kumamoto University research

A Victim of Mercury Poisoning. Held by her mother, this sufferer has a malformed hand along with other physical deformities characteristic of the Minamata disease. *(AP/Wide World Photos)*

team traced the cause to the Chisso factory. The team lost its government funding. With support from the Ministry of International Trade and Industry, Chisso hired researchers that proved mercury was not at fault. Workers at the plant and community leaders blamed the victims' poor diet and unsanitary living conditions for their afflictions. In 1965 another outbreak of the disease in Niigata on the Japan Sea was traced to mercury discharged by a chemical factory. Despite efforts by company officials and government bureaucrats to undermine the investigators' credibility, the Niigata outbreak lent weight to the Minamata case. The victims launched petitions, demonstrations, and sit-ins. They attracted support from doctors, lawyers, filmmakers, journalists, and academics. In 1971 they sued Chisso. The verdict against the company in 1973 brought it to the verge of bankruptcy. The victims then sued the government. The Environmental Agency refused to comply with the court's recommendation to settle. In 1995 the cabinet accepted an out-of-court final settlement that denied governmental responsibility for either the disease or the delay in acknowledging the problem.

Diseases caused by pollution in Minamata and elsewhere exposed the costs of high-speed economic growth and the way politicians and bureaucrats insulated themselves from ordinary citizens. Despite free elections and a free press, pollution victims had to protest outside regular government channels. Owing to their demands, the government instituted stringent pollution controls in the 1970s and began spending a larger portion of the gross national product (GNP) on antipollution measures than any other developed nation. By 1978 air and water pollution had declined, and manufacturers had learned how to profit from measures to keep the environment clean.

STRAINS OF THE 1970S

Having enjoyed the economic benefits of supporting the United States during the Cold War, Japan was unprepared for the international crises that punctuated the 1970s. When President Richard Nixon announced in 1971 that the United States would no longer accept fixed exchange rates that overvalued the dollar, the yen rose 14 percent. Nixon intended to make Japanese exports to the United States more expensive and less competitive. Japanese companies survived by taking advantage of lower costs for imported raw materials. Nixon's second shock came in 1972 when he recognized the People's Republic of China without notifying Japan in advance. Prime Minister Tanaka Kakuei followed Nixon to China seven months later. In 1978 China and Japan signed a peace and friendship treaty. The first oil shock came when the Organization of Petroleum Exporting Countries (OPEC) embargoed oil to countries that had supported Israel in the 1973 war. Dependent on oil for 80 percent of its energy, Japan had to pay premium prices on the world market. Inflation rose, companies reduced energy use by cutting production, and consumers stopped spending. During the remainder of the decade, Japan built nuclear power plants. Companies so rationalized energy use that when

OPEC raised prices again in 1978–1980, they had a competitive advantage over less efficient firms in their prime export markets.

To retain dominance in the Diet and cabinet, the LDP catered to its core constituencies, sometimes to the point of scandal. Tanaka Kakuei had Japan National Railroad (JNR) build a bullet train line through the mountains to his constituents in Niigata, at the cost of $60 million a mile. It provided government contracts for his cronies in the construction business and fattened the purses of real estate developers. Although all Diet members collected money from businesses and individuals for whom they did favors, Tanaka's excesses were so blatant that public outcry drove him from office in 1974. In 1976 an investigation by the U.S. Senate disclosed that President Nixon had arranged for Lockheed Aircraft Corporation to pay Tanaka almost $2 million to have All Nippon Airways buy Lockheed planes. Despite the stench of corruption, LDP politicians held on to power because voters believed that the opposition parties were too ideologically driven and fragmented to be trusted with national policy.

Industry had to make traumatic adjustments. Some arose from increasing protectionist pressures, exemplified in a 1979 report to the European Economic Community Executive Committee that called the Japanese "work maniacs who live in houses little better than rabbit hutches."[1] Nixon demanded that Japan reduce its textile imports through voluntary restraints. The increase in oil prices hurt petrochemical and energy-intensive industries. Shipbuilders saw the market for tankers decline, which hurt steel. The shipbuilding industry survived by consolidating and moving into new fields such as ocean drilling platforms. The government helped workers with wage subsidies, retraining programs, and relocation expenses. To compete with low-labor-cost countries, the steel industry developed specialty high-value-added products. Automobile and electrical manufacturing grew. In 1980, Japan pro-

duced more cars than any other country. Big electrical companies made generating plants and electric motors for trains; small firms made office equipment, household appliances, and entertainment items.

Although lifetime employment became a watchword, it covered less than half the work force. Toyota, for example, had permanent workers who received regular salary increases based on seniority and fringe benefits; during good times, it hired temporary workers, who were terminated when necessary. Over two hundred independent contractors made parts and components for cars in accordance with guidelines and timetables established by Toyota. Their workers enjoyed no job security. Women returning to the labor force after raising children typically worked at part-time or temporary jobs in small, often marginally profitable companies.

White-collar workers joined a firm straight after college and expected to stay with it for life. For indoctrination into company culture, first-year recruits lived in dormitories where they learned to maintain constant contact with their coworkers by working together and drinking together after work. Since only family men were deemed suitable for promotion, most workers soon married, perhaps to an "office lady" (OL) who understood that the company came first. Debuted in 1969, a popular movie series, *It's Tough Being a Man* (*Otoko wa tsurai yo*), commented on the conformity engineered by the straitjacket of company life through the eyes of an itinerant peddler who rejected job security for the byways of modern Japan.

Husbands and wives lived in separate worlds. Rural-based factory workers left farm work to parents, wives, and children. Only 2 to 5 percent farmed full time. For the urban middle class, a wife's job was to provide a stress-free environment for her husband. Since he had to devote full attention to his company, she managed the household, raised the children (preferably two), and did household repairs. The husband handed her his paycheck; she gave him an allowance, allocated money for food and other expenses, and saved the rest. Mothers devoted themselves

---

1. "Europe Toughens Stand Against Japan's Exports," *New York Times,* April 2, 1979, D:1, 5.

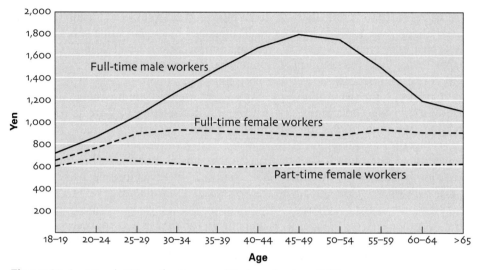

Figure 31.1   Hourly Wages for Japanese Workers, by Age, 1989
(*Mary C. Brinton,* Women and the Economic Miracle: Gender and Work in Postwar Japan
[Berkeley: University of California Press, 1992], p. 47.)

to their children's education, earning the opprobrium of being *kyōiku mama* (education mothers, implying an obsession with their children's educational success). When children needed extra help, mothers sent them to after-school schools. Mother consulted with teachers, attended Parent-Teacher Association meetings, volunteered at school, and supervised their children's nutrition, health, and homework. For the professional housewife, her child was her most important product. (See **Documents: Fujita Mariko, "'It's All Mother's Fault': Childcare and the Socialization of Working Mothers in Japan."**)

Continuing Social Issues

Women's career choices were limited. They typically worked after graduating from high school or junior college; to the mid-1980s almost 90 percent of companies rejected female graduates of four-year colleges because they had to be placed on a management track. Instead, women were hired as clerical or assembly line workers with the understanding they would retire at marriage or when they turned thirty years old. In the late 1960s women got the courts to agree that this practice constituted sex discrimination. In the early 1970s the courts forbade mandatory retirement because of pregnancy or childbirth or at a younger age than men. Women objected to being kept from managerial positions and well-meaning restrictions on the hours they could work and the kinds of work they were allowed to do. In response, the Diet passed the Equal Employment Opportunity Act of 1985. Although it urged employers to put women on the same track as men, it made no provisions for sanctions if they did not. In 1976 women's earnings stood at 56 percent of men's; in 1988 they declined to 50 percent. Companies still refuse to promote women at the same rate as men. Rather than pay women equal wages, some companies do not hire women at all. Full responsibility for home and children makes it hard for women to work past childbirth. Once the children are in school, mothers take part-time jobs. Although the working woman in Japan is imagined to be single, most are married women over age thirty-five.

Despite decades of denunciation tactics, *burakumin* still faced economic hardship and discrimination. Under the Special Measures and Enterprise Law concerning Assimilation of 1969, national and local governments put sewage systems, paved streets, better housing, schools, hospitals, and fire stations in the ghettoes. In 1976, the Justice Ministry agreed to restrict access to family registers that could be used to trace individuals back to the "new commoners" category established in 1871. Private detective agencies then published lists giving addresses for *burakumin* ghettoes. Their customers were companies, especially the largest and most prestigious, individuals, and colleges. In 1977, the overall unemployment rate was around 3 percent, but 28.5 percent of Osaka *burakumin* were unemployed. Those with jobs worked in small enterprises for low wages. Although most *burakumin* lived next to large factories, they never received more than temporary or part-time work.

Ainu and Okinawans launched movements in the 1970s to assert pride in their ethnic identities. Ainu protested that the 1968 celebration for the centenary of Hokkaido's colonization ignored them and their suffering. Kayano Shigeru opened an ethnographic museum in 1972 and wrote on Ainu language, folk tales, and practices of daily life. In 1994 he became the first Ainu elected to the Diet. He and other culturalists sought to restore seasonal ceremonies and protested plans to turn Hokkaido into an energy source for the rest of Japan with an oil-generated power station. The United States returned Okinawa to Japan in 1972, but left its bases on the islands. The local economy depended on servicing them and catering to Japanese tourists in search of a tropical experience at home. Okinawan music, dance, and crafts attracted aficionados on the mainland because they were seen as both a variant on primitive Japanese folk arts and exotic island culture. Although the national government spent lavishly on construction projects, it hired natives only in low-level jobs. *Burakumin,* Ainu, and Okinawan poverty rates and school dropout rates were higher than the national average. Negative stereotypes abounded, and outsiders tried to avoid marrying or hiring them.

Koreans resident in Japan (six hundred thirty-seven thousand in 1999) faced special disabilities in fighting discrimination. As long as Korea was part of the Japanese Empire, Koreans were Japanese citizens. The postwar constitution defined Japanese citizens as those born of Japanese fathers, and Koreans became permanent resident aliens. Although celebrities and spouses of diplomats found the naturalization process easy, working-class Koreans did not. They also suffered a division between supporters of North Korea, who followed a separatist path, and supporters of the South, who tried to preserve vestiges of Korean identity while sending their children to Japanese schools. Children and grandchildren of Korean residents who grew up in Japan and spoke only Japanese paid taxes, but they could not vote. They had to be fingerprinted for their alien registration cards. After years of protest, that requirement changed in 1991, and resident Koreans were allowed to vote in local elections. Still, Japanese refused to marry Koreans, employers to hire them, landlords to rent to them. Resident Koreans who protested were told they should go back to Korea.

Japanese nationalists ignored all evidence to the contrary in praising the virtues of their uniquely homogeneous race. The debate on Japaneseness (*Nihonjinron*) reacted to the protest movements of the late 1960s, universalizing social science theories that pigeonholed Japan solely in terms of economic development, and Japan bashing by foreigners. The more Japanese people ate, dressed, and lived like people across the developed world, the more they had to be reminded that they possessed a uniquely distinctive culture. According to *Nihonjinron,* "we Japanese" speak a language intrinsically incomprehensible to outsiders, think with both sides of the brain, and have intestines too short to digest Australian beef. "We Japanese" innately prefer consensus and

DOCUMENTS

Fujita Mariko, "'It's All Mother's Fault': Childcare and the Socialization of Working Mothers in Japan"

Various sectors in postwar society have made a fetish of conformity. This essay by a college professor provides a glimpse of how women enforce the standards for being a professional housewife. What are the conflicts between working and being a mother? How do women interact across the work divide? What is the role fathers are expected to play in child rearing?

A woman should recognize herself as the best educator of her child. An excellent race is born from excellent mothers. . . . Only women can bear children and raise them. Therefore mothers should be proud and confident in raising their children. It is also a fundamental right of children to be raised by their own mothers. . . . Employment opportunities should be given to those women who have finished raising their children and who still wish to resume working outside the home.

—*1970 Family Charter by the Committee on Family Life Problems*

I live in a small-scale *danchi* (apartment block) built for national governmental employees in the southeastern part of Nara City. The complex consists of three four-story buildings which house about 70 families. The occupants are mostly young and early middle-aged couples, though some are *tanshin-funinsha* (husbands who reside away from their families due to the relocation of their jobs). The ages of the children in this complex range from babies to junior-high-school students. There are only a handful of high school students. Therefore, the mothers' ages range roughly between 25 and 45.

Because the rent is substantially lower than in private housing, there is not much economic pressure for the wives to work. This explains the fact that the majority of wives are full-time housewives. The mothers of older children may engage in occasional part-time jobs. As far as I know, those women who work full-time are without children. If a couple has preschool children, the wives most certainly stay at home to raise them.

My contacts with my neighbors, especially the wives, are through the various activities of the *jichikai* (the voluntary association of the housing complex) such as a monthly clean-up of the common area. I also belong to one of the two Nara Citizens' Co-op groups available in the housing complex. Members of each group jointly order groceries, which the Co-op brings to the housing complex once a week. Members together divide the groceries according to each member's order.

As soon as my neighbors found out that I had a toddler, they assumed that I was a full-time housewife and mother. They never thought to ask whether I worked outside the home. Because I did have a job, they often found me walking alone without my son and they would always ask, "Where is

harmony, and we put the interests of the group above the individual.

Despite social problems, by the mid-1970s, most Japanese people enjoyed unprecedented

levels of prosperity. Income and salary disparities remained relatively narrow, and 90 percent of the population considered itself to be middle class. The proportion of total income

Hosaki today?" indicating their expectation that I would always be with my child. The situation was complicated because at the time I was a part-time lecturer at a university and I did most of my work at home. My neighbors found this kind of work pattern very difficult to understand because to them work means regular employment between 8:00 AM and 5:00 PM. Telling them that my son was at day care was tricky because they would wonder what I was doing at home during the day instead of being at work. Only after I took a full-time teaching position, which keeps me away from home most of the time, were my neighbors convinced that I was actually working.

The fact that working mothers and non-working mothers do not belong to the same circle of friends became clear to me when I spent a day with my son instead of sending him to day care. I took him to the neighborhood playground where he played in the sand box by the other children. Since he did not have toys of his own (I did not know the children were supposed to bring their own toys), a mother told her son to let my son use his toys. Several mothers were present; they talked among themselves and politely ignored me. I said a few words to them and they replied, but that was the end of our conversation. I basically watched my son, and later played with him when he wanted to play ball. After half an hour, one of the mothers finally asked me whether I lived in the same apartment complex. The question astonished me because I had frequently seen them in the neighborhood. But, as far as they were concerned, I was a total stranger.

Our son frequently became ill his first year in Japan, perhaps due to lack of immunity to the viruses he was exposed to at day care. He had hardly had even a mild cold while we were in the United States, and we were puzzled and distressed by his frequent fevers, respiratory problems, and even pneumonia. Soon after enrolling our son at Sakura Day Care, we asked the director if she had a list of baby-sitters, or if she would introduce us to people who would be willing, with pay, to take care of our son when he became sick. Her answer made us realize how unusual our request was in Japan: she was truly astonished by our question and replied that she had never heard of such people.

Our neighbors frequently offered the folk belief that "boys are more susceptible to all sorts of illness than girls when they are young" to explain my son's frequent sicknesses. But as soon as they found out that my work required me to spend two nights a week away from home, they started to use my absence to explain my son's illness. They thought Hosaki was lonely and thus became ill. No one openly criticized me for working until they found out about my absence. Then, they were quick to criticize the mother, making her absence the cause of illness, although the times of Hosaki's illness and my absence did not coincide and although his father was with him and took care of him. They sympathized with the father, who was, from their point of view, unduly burdened while the "selfish" mother was neglecting her duty of childcare.

———
Source: *Journal of Japanese Studies* 15:1 (Winter 1989): 70–71, 72–73, 80, 86, 87, 89, modified.

spent on food declined while quantity, quality, and variety increased. The older generation ate rice, vegetables, and fish. Young people ate meat, dairy products, and spaghetti. Although Japan maintained the highest savings rate in the industrialized world, people had discretionary income to eat out, go to movies, and take vacations.

THE ROARING 1980S

Japan's recovery from the shocks of the 1970s put it on a collision course with its major trading partner, the United States. Japan adjusted to oil and pollution crises by building fuel-efficient, less-polluting cars. When stricter pollution emission requirements, consumer demand for higher quality, and increased gasoline prices caught Detroit by surprise, Japan's automobile makers seized the American market. To make Japanese goods less competitive, President Ronald Reagan devalued the dollar in 1985. Japan discovered that it was twice as rich as before. The yen bought twice as much oil, and since Japanese manufacturers had already streamlined production techniques, they needed half as much to make their products as their American competitors did. When Honda raised the price of the Accord by a thousand dollars, American manufacturers raised their prices as well.

American negotiators demanded that Japan import more foreign products. Japan had lower tariffs on manufactured goods than other industrialized countries, but it protected farmers by restricting food imports. It also had nontariff structural barriers to trade—regulations to ensure quality and safety, the requirement that car buyers show proof of an off-street parking space, a multilayered distribution system, and zoning that favored shops over supermarkets and discount stores. Despite reluctance to disturb a system that provided employment and political support, the LDP and the bureaucracy gradually reduced restrictions. Australian cheese appeared in supermarkets. Shakey's Pizza, McDonalds, Kentucky Fried Chicken, and family-style restaurants invaded Japan in the late 1970s. Seven-Eleven spawned a boom in convenience stores. In 1983, Disneyland opened its first international venue near Tokyo. In 2000 it welcomed 16.5 million visitors, the largest number for any theme park in the world.

Trade surpluses and a strong currency generated more capital than Japan could absorb domestically. With unemployment rates at about 3 percent and labor costs rising, companies built factories in low-wage countries on the Asian mainland. To get around protective tariffs, antidumping measures, and quotas, they built high-technology factories in developed countries, and Toyota became a multinational corporation. In 1982, industrial plants, equipment, and capital goods constituted 43 percent of Japan's exports. Japanese capital serviced the U.S. debt. Japan became the world's largest supplier of loans to developing countries and the chief donor of foreign aid, and it supplied 50 percent of lendable capital to the World Bank.

The electronics industry had two modes of expanding overseas. In setting up production facilities, first in Southeast Asia in the mid- to late 1970s and then in developed countries in the 1980s, parent companies retained complete control of local subsidiaries. The managerial staff was Japanese; the workers were local. The U.S. Semiconductor Industry Association accused Japan of dumping in 1985; in an agreement a year later, Japan agreed to voluntary quotas. Corporations then instituted cooperative ventures with partners in the United States and Europe to develop new technology or combine specialties. Automobile manufacturers followed suit: Toyota and General Motors, Nissan, Honda, and Ford operate joint ventures and exchange components at factories from Australia to Brazil to Europe and the United States.

Japanese capital investment deepened ties with Asian neighbors, while nationalist sentiment strained diplomatic relations. Japan dominated China's Special Economic Zones and invested heavily in Korea and the Pacific Rim, leading pundits to claim that it had succeeded in creating a Greater East Asia Co-Prosperity Sphere. In 1982, the Education Ministry approved a textbook for middle school and high school students that minimized Japanese aggression in China. This led the PRC, North and South Korea, and other Asian nations to denounce resurgent Japanese nationalism. Japan's aggression and its refusal to acknowledge the suffering it inflicted on Korean women were still issues in the textbooks prepared for 2005. Asians and some Japanese criticized visits by prime ministers to Yasukuni Shrine, where war criminals are enshrined. Textbook revision and Japan's refusal to apologize for waging war roiled popular opinion even as government leaders drew closer together. When the president of South Korea visited Japan for the first time in 1984, demonstrations erupted in Seoul.

The government faced domestic problems as well. The LDP did not want to raise taxes to cover deficit spending that started in 1973. Among the culprits were subsidies for farmers, public corporations—Japan National Railroad (JNR) and Nihon Telephone and Telegraph (NTT)—and national health insurance, which initiated free care for the elderly in 1972. Following the lead of Prime Minister Margaret Thatcher in Britain, a commission set up in 1981 promoted privatizing public corporations to relieve the government of drains on its resources and undermine the strength of the railroad workers' union. Although allowed to bargain collectively, unions in the public service sector did not have the right to strike nor did they have incentive to boost productivity. In 1975, railroad workers shut down the JNR for eight days in a strike to win the right to strike.

The conservative triumvirate of the free market world consisted of Margaret Thatcher, Ronald Reagan, and Nakasone Yasuhiro, Japan's prime minister from 1982 to 1987. Nakasone privatized JNR and NTT and took the government out of the business of selling tobacco and cigarettes. Beginning in 1982, the elderly had to contribute payments for health services. Nakasone urged a return to family values, especially the obligation of the younger generation to care for their elders. He attributed Japan's economic success to its ethnic homogeneity and funded research into the foundation of Japan's distinctive identity. He also called for internationalization so that government leaders would learn how to reduce trade friction and businessmen would feel comfortable with foreigners. His promotion of corporate capitalism made Japan a major player at the Group of 7 conferences of industrialized nations while he lectured the United States on its social and economic failings exemplified in racial diversity and the lack of a work ethic.

The Good Life

For many people, old and young, the good life meant material possessions. It meant automated bread-making machines, three-dimensional TV, and self-heating canned sake. It meant laughing at Itami Jūzō's movies about funeral practices, food, tax evasion, new religions, and gangsters. The good life made it easy to buy books and magazines (1.45 billion and 4.01 billion, respectively, in 1987). (See **Material Culture: *Manga*.**) Whether a meaning for life could be found in a late capitalist society divided Japanese writers. Murakami Haruki captured the absurdity of modernity in his novels *A Wild Sheep Chase, Hardboiled Wonderland,* and *Sputnik Sweetheart.* Yoshimoto Banana's *Kitchen,* a novella popular with college students, depicted a dysfunctional family and individuals alone in a postmodern world. Nostalgia for simpler times under the Occupation sold 4 million copies of *Totto-chan, The Little Girl at the Window* by the fast-talking television celebrity Kuroyanagi Tetsuko.

Rejecting the materialism of the present meant seeking the roots of Japanese identity. A self-styled Kyoto philosopher creatively interpreted the prehistoric Jōmon era as when Japanese lived in harmony with nature and each other in a community of man and gods. Mystically transmitted through the emperor system and buried deep within every Japanese, the national essence could be recapitulated by a visit to the *furusato* (home village). JNR's "Discover Japan" and "Exotic Japan" advertising campaigns promoted visits to thatched roof farmhouses foreign to urban residents. Villages striving to overcome depopulation revived agricultural festivals to attract tourists; castle towns put on daimyo processions. On Yaeyama in the Ryukyu Islands, a new tradition of sash weaving

MATERIAL CULTURE

Manga

Japanese comics called *manga* attained their present form in 1959 when they became a source of entertainment and information for all ages.

Early *manga* were printed on cheap paper and sold at a price that the working poor could afford. The first generation born after World War II grew up reading them and continued the habit through college and into their working lives. *Manga* gave them a chance to laugh at the restrictive conditions that enforced conformity while warning them that failing to work hard and toe the corporate line would lead to mockery. *Manga* and their close cousins, animated films, became the domain of Japan's most creative minds.

From the 1960s to the mid-1990s *manga* offered escapist fantasies, often violently pornographic, for white-collar workers on their daily commute. Science-fiction *manga* appealed to children and teenagers. *Manga* taught history to students studying for entrance exams. *Barefoot Gen* graphically illustrated the horrors of the atomic bomb explosion over Hiroshima. Cookbooks and biography could be found in *manga*. *Manga* explained energy policy, the value-added tax, investment strategies, and the principles of superconductors. *Japan Inc.: An Introduction to Japanese Economics in Manga* (1986) sold over 1 million copies in hardcover.

Manga reached their peak of sales in 1994. Publishing houses devoted one-third of their total output to *manga* and sold 553 million copies a year. Shibuya, the crossroads for youth culture in Tokyo, contained *manga* superstores where the clerks dressed as *manga* characters.

Manga. Manga provided education and entertainment. "The Manga Introduction to Superconductors" explained new technology in 1987 through the eyes of three young salaried workers who visit a research laboratory. *(The Manga Introduction to Supercomputers by Takashi Hashimoto and Fumio Hisamatsu)*

Manga and the Japanese publishing industry are in decline. Their former readers on trains and in coffee shops thumb cell phones with Internet connections or play handheld computer games.

for betrothal gifts became a way to assert a folk identity and sell souvenirs to tourists.

The search for origins scarcely concealed new and to conservative eyes troubling trends among Japanese youth. In 1978 the "bamboo shoot tribe" (*takenokozoku*) of middle and high school students dressed in outlandish and expensive costumes started appearing every Sunday near trendy Harajuku in Tokyo. (See Color Plate 31.) Late at night, gangs of motorcycle riders roared through residential neighborhoods, disrupting the sleep of salary men. In

Opponents of Narita Airport. Waving staves and wearing helmets, opponents of Narita Airport battled riot police protected by heavy shields, helmets, and padded armor. *(Corbis)*

1985 newspapers started reporting an increase in incidents of bullying, some leading to murder or suicide, in elementary through high schools. The "new breed of human beings" rejected the work ethic, harmony, and consensus of their elders. They took part-time jobs that did not require the commitment of a regular position. Since many of them lived with their parents, their income bought luxury items rather than necessities. They splurged on designer clothes, meals and entertainment, and trips abroad. Married couples demanded bigger living spaces and better plumbing. They wanted a shorter work week and longer vacations. Rather than put up with low initial salaries and long hours of after-work socializing, a few workers switched jobs, and some husbands went home to their wives.

Despite these problems, Japan's economy appeared unstoppable. In 1988, its per capita GNP surpassed that of the United States. The United States cited unfair trade practices and Japan's free ride under the American security umbrella. In 1989, Morita Akio, chairman of Sony, and Ishihara Shintarō, mayor of Tokyo in 2002, published *The Japan That Can Say No*. It criticized U.S. business practices and claimed that Japan bashing was the result of racial prejudice. It also castigated the Japanese government

for fearing reform and Japanese people for being soft. Banks awash with yen urged capital on borrowers. Japanese art purchases led to an outcry that the cream of western heritage was being shipped to Asia. Mitsubishi bought Rockefeller Center in New York City. Sony bought Columbia Pictures. Real estate rose so high that land in Tokyo was valued at three times the entire United States. The tripling of the stock market inflated a speculative bubble. (See Color Plate 32.)

MALAISE IN THE 1990S

For the LDP, political problems began in 1989. The Shōwa emperor died at the beginning of the year. For having remarked that the emperor bore some responsibility for the military's behavior during World War II, the mayor of Nagasaki was shot by a right-wing fanatic. The new emperor took Heisei, translatable as "achieving peace" or "maintaining equilibrium," for his era name. Prime Minister Takeshita Noboru inaugurated a value-added tax of 3 percent that infuriated consumers. Two months later he resigned because of publicity surrounding 150 million yen he had received from Recruit Cosmo, an employment information firm with investments in real estate and publishing. LDP faction bosses had difficulty identifying an untainted successor. Uno Sōsuke lasted barely six weeks before a palimony suit by his mistress brought him down. In the election that summer, the JSP under the female leadership of Doi Takako ran an unprecedented number of women candidates and gained control of the upper house. It also did well in the more powerful lower house in 1990.

The LDP faced challenges from members of its own party. Frustrated by elderly faction bosses who monopolized the prime ministership, younger politicians split the LDP. In 1993, Hosokawa Morihiro from the Japan New Party became prime minister when the LDP suffered defeat in elections for the lower house. The worst rice harvest in two hundred years forced him to allow rice imports from Asia for the first time since World War II. Farmers were outraged. He too was caught in a financial scandal. Two more non-LDP prime ministers followed him, neither capable of dealing with Japan's economic woes. The government's tardy response to the Kobe earthquake on January 17, 1995, which killed over five thousand two hundred people and left over three hundred thousand homeless, received much criticism. In 1996, a chastened LDP returned to power, and faction bosses picked the next prime minister. In 2001, they chose a third-generation Diet member, Koizumi Jun'ichirō, who promised liberals he would make structural reforms needed to bolster the economy and pleased conservatives by his call to revise the pacifist constitution.

Koizumi inherited a stagnant economy. The speculative bubble of the late 1980s collapsed when a recession in the developed world sent sales tumbling and competition from low-labor-cost countries eroded corporations' market share. The stock market lost nearly 40 percent of its peak value in 1990 and 65 percent by August 1992. When the inflated real estate market vanished, Mitsubishi had to sell Rockefeller Center at a loss. Corporations that had borrowed billions of yen to buy land or expand their businesses discovered that their debts exceeded their rapidly depreciating assets. Banks were reluctant to lend money. The Asian economic turmoil of 1997 caused by speculators dumping Asian currencies caused another recession in Japan. Two brokerage houses and a bank went bankrupt, leading to fears of depression. Economic growth, which had limped along at barely 1 percent per annum between 1992 and 1995, went negative in 1997. In 2002, bad loans ballooned to $1.3 trillion, and government debt climbed to 150 percent of the GDP. Except for an occasional quarter of slight expansion, deflation stalked Japan.

The LDP scrambled to stimulate the economy. In the 1980s it tried to revitalize rural communities by building culture halls and art museums and encouraging production of traditional handicrafts as souvenirs. In the 1990s it poured money into dams, roads, and postmodern public buildings. In 1991 the Tokyo Metropolitan Government moved into massive new headquarters that soared above office buildings and hotels, many half empty. Koizumi halted a project to turn a saltwater swamp into farmland while the government paid farmers not to plant rice. His proposal to privatize the postal savings system threatened the Finance Ministry's control over the $3 trillion in personal savings kept outside government budgets that it used to finance public works projects, prime the stock market, and buy government bonds. Proposals to streamline the bureaucracy, reduce regulatory oversight, and eliminate positions foundered on bureaucratic inertia. Near-zero interest rates and government support for nonperforming loans failed to stimulate business investment. The Education Ministry tried to make universities more responsive to the interests of industry and eliminate irrelevant fields in the humanities and social sciences. In 2004 national universities became independent entities.

Japan faced international criticism regarding its role in world affairs. The United States grumbled when Japan refused to commit troops to the Gulf War in 1991 even though Japan's military spending ranked third below the United States and Russia. Six months after the war, Japan sent six minesweepers to the Persian Gulf amid debate fueled by antiwar sentiment in the postwar generation over whether their dispatch violated constitutional restrictions. Japan also paid $10 billion toward the cost of the war and permitted its troops to participate in peacekeeping missions in Cambodia and East Timor. After the terrorist attacks in the United States on September 11, 2001, the Diet passed an antiterrorism law that allowed Japanese troops to provide rear-echelon support for the war in Iraq in 2004.

Social Problems for the Twenty-First Century

Japan's social problems also defied easy solution. In the 1980s, American social scientists praised Japan's educational system for producing literate students who scored far higher on mathematics tests than Americans. Japanese critics feared that schools were turning out soulless automatons with weak characters and no sense of national identity, unable to think for themselves, and lacking the creativity to put Japan in the lead of technological innovation. Preteenage rebels disrupted classrooms and terrorized teachers. In a series of high-profile crimes, youths killed classmates, tortured the homeless, and murdered elderly neighbors. Labor shortages in the 1980s in the sex trade and the dangerous, dirty, and low-paying work of construction and stevedoring brought men and women from Taiwan, the Philippines, Iran, and other countries to work as prostitutes and day laborers. About half entered illegally because the Labor and Justice ministries refused to acknowledge the need for their services. Immigration of Latin Americans of Japanese ancestry was encouraged because it was thought they would assimilate to the dominant culture. In 1999, 1.56 million foreigners lived legally in Japan out of a total population of 126.6 million. Tokyo became a more cosmopolitan city, but mainstream Japanese were quick to accuse foreigners of robbery, rape, and drug trafficking.

Economic stagnation and rising unemployment had social consequences. Corporations stopped competing to hire college graduates, and unemployment rose to an official rate of 5 percent in 2001. This figure excluded part-time workers who had lost their jobs, most of them women. The government reduced the duration and value of unemployment benefits. Job security guarantees covered just over 15 percent of workers in 2002. "Pay for performance" started to replace the seniority system of merit raises. Tokyo, Yokohama, and Osaka had long had a floating population of farm men from the north who spent the winter working as day laborers and congregated in flophouses. In the late 1980s permanent dropouts started to swell their numbers. Osaka laborers caused the worst rioting in nearly twenty years in 1990 in reaction to police harassment. Homeless people appeared as well. They built cardboard cities in parks and pedestrian tunnels that surrounded train terminals except when police periodically chased them away.

The search for meaning in a materialistic world took new paths. Right-wing militants who rode sound trucks blaring martial music and decorated with posters calling for the return of the northern territories held by Russia attacked the offices of the Asahi publishing company for articles showing disrespect for the emperor. Adherents of new religions such as the Unification Church and Mahikarikyō sought a sense of community and a merging of the individual ego in a larger entity. Aum Shinrikyō attracted students from Japan's elite universities, lawyers, and businessmen. Feeling persecuted by the Justice Ministry, in March 1995 its followers released Sarin, a poison gas, in the Tokyo subway system adjacent to National Police headquarters. It killed twelve people and incapacitated thousands. The LDP tried to revise the 1951 Religious Corporations Law to bring governmental oversight to the fund-raising, educational activities, and business-related income of the 183,970 registered religious organizations. Opposition by Sōka Gakkai's political arm and other religious organizations kept the 1951 law intact.

Starting in the late 1960s, LDP politicians urged women to have more children; thereafter they lamented the selfishness of young women who put consumerism ahead of maternal responsibilities. National health insurance, a 99 percent literacy rate, sanitary housing, and nutritious diets contributed to one of the lowest infant mortality rates in the world at 5 per thousand in 1989 and longevity rates for men reaching into the mid-seventies and for women into the eighties. Women had 1.57 children apiece, well below the 2.2 necessary to maintain the population. Couples who wanted a higher standard of living or worried about the costs of their children's education limited their family size regardless of political propaganda.

In 2000, 16 percent of the population was age sixty-five or older, and Japan had the oldest population in the industrialized world. In 2015 it is projected to be 25 percent, and 25 percent of the national budget will have to be spent on social welfare. Through the 1990s, corporations had plentiful sources of investment capital at low interest rates because Japan had the highest rates of personal savings in the world. With more people retired, the savings rate will drop.

The government wants to limit its costs for hospitals and nursing homes by having children care for parents. Elder sons with the traditional responsibility for parental care have trouble finding marriage partners because women increasingly prefer to take care of their own parents. Some farmers have even sought brides in the Philippines.

Although marriage is still the norm, it too has changed. The average age of marriage for women crept from twenty-two in 1950 to over twenty-six in 2000. Crown Princess Masako delayed marriage for a career in the Foreign Ministry until she was twenty-nine. Her only child is a girl. Since the constitution defines the ruler as male, allowing this child to succeed her father will require a constitutional change, devoutly desired by Japanese feminists. So many women opt for four years of higher education that the former junior colleges have become universities even though the decline in the college age population means that more are having trouble meeting their enrollment targets. In hopes of better futures than they perceive possible in Japan, some women seek academic degrees and employment abroad. Women want careers, and they have become increasingly choosy about whom they will marry and under what conditions. Older women have been known to divorce their retired husbands because they cannot stand having "that oversized garbage" underfoot every day.

SUMMARY

Japan is a mature industrial society. Its cities are among the world's cleanest and safest, and most of its citizens enjoy a comfortable life. Japanese foods are eaten in Europe and the United States; Japanese fashions and popular music are followed in Asia. Introduced in 1980, karaoke is performed around the world. Ōe Kenzaburō won the Nobel Prize in literature in 1994 for his writings that express universal truths regarding the human condition. Japanese politicians infuriate their Asian neighbors by calling the emperor a living god and Japan a divine nation while participating in Asian economic conferences. Lingering memories of the war and Japan's wariness of China's growing economic and military strength has not prevented Japan from trading more with China than with the United States, even as it offers support for the global war on terrorism.

SUGGESTED READING

For protest against Tokyo International Airport, see D. E. Apter and N. Sawa, *Against the State: Politics and Protest in Japan* (1984).

For recent books on pollution, see J. Broadbent, *Environmental Politics in Japan: Networks of Power and Protest* (1998), and T. S. George, *Minamata: Pollution and the Struggle for Democracy in Postwar Japan* (2001).

For politics, see R. J. Hrebenar, *Japan's New Party System* (2000). For legal issues, see F. K. Upham, *Law and Social Change in Postwar Japan* (1987).

For economic issues, see R. M. Uriu, *Troubled Industries: Confronting Economic Change in Japan* (1996). For minorities, see M. Weiner, *Japan's Minorities: The Illusion of Homogeneity* (1997).

For popular culture, see S. Kinsella, *Adult Manga: Culture and Power in Contemporary Japanese Society* (2000).

For recent books on women. see Y. Ogasawara, *Office Ladies and Salaried Men: Power, Gender, and Work in Japanese Companies* (1998); R. M. LeBlanc, *Bicycle Citizens: The Political World of the Japanese Housewife* (1999); and K. Kelsky, *Women on the Verge: Japanese Women, Western Dreams* (2001).

East Asia in the Twenty-First Century

It should come as no surprise that in our increasingly global world, the countries of East Asia are now more connected than ever before. Tens of thousands of Korean, Taiwanese, and Japanese businesspeople now live in China to manage the manufacturing operations they have located there, and they regularly fly back and forth to their home countries. Thousands of Chinese now live in Japan, some as students or businesspeople; others are laborers, who often are there illegally. Huge drops in the cost of international phone calls, as well as the ubiquity of email and the Internet, make it much easier for those living outside their home countries to keep in regular contact with friends and relatives back home, creating diasporas very different from the immigrant communities of earlier times.

For two decades, Japanese, Korean, and Taiwanese tourists have been visiting China, often on package tours, and today Chinese who have prospered during the reform period are reciprocating and visiting nearby countries in increasing numbers. Popular and classical music no longer respects national boundaries, and singers and instrumentalists often have large followings throughout the East Asian countries, adding to the huge popularity of karaoke in the region. Popular TV serials are often dubbed to be shown in other East Asian countries.

Right now in Japan, there's a major Korea boom owing to the popularity of a soap opera, *Winter Sonata,* and its star, Bae Yong-joon (called in Japan Yon-sama). He has such a powerful appeal that when he visited Japan, middle-aged women were throwing themselves in front of his car and swarming his hotel. There are sev-eral Internet sites where young women who are fed up with Japanese men can try to meet Korean men (without realizing that the attitudes of Korean men are quite similar to those of Japanese men). Japan's experimental music is the world's leader in something called "noise." There are global currents in which Japan, Korea, and Taiwan participate. A Japanese wedding company is exporting Japanese-style weddings to Shanghai. In other parts of China, however, Japanese soccer players have been booed by fans still angry at Japan's wartime behavior.

Politically, East Asian countries have changed, but not necessarily toward western liberalism. After the U.S. occupation of 1945, Japan succeeded in establishing free elections and free speech and association, but it did little to reform the prewar bureaucracy, which subsequently played the leading role in devising policy for industrial development. The Liberal Democratic Party (LDP) remains the most powerful political party in Japan. Its leader-follower factions meet behind the scenes to choose prime ministers and operate to stymie initiatives for meaningful reform. The middle class has not been able to change the political system to reflect public demands, the labor movement has remained quiescent, the women's movement has not broken workplace discrimination, and the public has not demanded reform.

After forty years of student and activist struggles against dictatorial repression, South Korea held the first democratic elections for the presidency in 1987. Since 1992 the military has been subordinated to civilian control, mayors and governors and local assemblies are now elected, and two past presidents have been jailed for their crimes. In 1997, the first electoral regime change occurred. Yet the political parties have shown no lasting power and consist of many leader-follower groups that shift allegiance from one party to another. The nefarious national security law still remains on the books. Despair over economic problems since 1997 has created a conservative backlash that pines for the double-digit growth of the dictator Park Chung Hee. The country still has a long way to go before completing the democratic transition and could possibly suffer a reversal.

In Taiwan the repressive politics of Chiang Kaishek and the Nationalist Party have been replaced by democratic elections. Credit for the democratic transition goes largely to Chiang's son, Chiang Chingkuo. As president of the Republic of China he was instrumental in creating that democracy by fiat. An independence movement backed by native Taiwanese was able to elect Chen Shuibian president in 2000, but China's military threats against secession from China mean that the prospect for independence is slim. Democratic processes have gone a long way in Taiwan but for the external constraint against independence.

Although the Tiananmen massacre of 1989 scotched the democratic movement in China, there have been signs of liberal thought among students and intellectuals, who hope that economic development will lead to a larger middle class and democracy, but the regime shows little sign of liberalizing. Dissatisfaction about aspects of the new economic system has materialized in attacks against soldiers and police in several cities, strikes by workers, and rural protests against local officials for corruption. Charismatic leaders revive slogans and symbols of traditional religious beliefs to attract followers, and others appeal to Maoist egalitarianism to critique the materialism and inequality of the Deng era. If the rigid, centralized political system fails to stem corruption and meet the needs of the people, the regime might well collapse in rebellion as most past dynasties did, but not as a result of mass demand for democracy.

Finally, North Korea has maintained central control over the country with hardly a pause. Although restrictions on residence movement and occupations have eased and private plots and small private markets have been allowed under the famine conditions of the 1990s, no evidence of political protest and organization of a serious nature has been revealed. North Korea toys with the idea of adopting Deng's economic policies but is wary of doing so because liberalism and human rights threaten foreign capitalist domination and destruction of the power elite.

The 1990s were a difficult period for East Asian economies. In both Japan and South Korea, state control and protectionism caused severe economic decline. Japan had come close to surpassing the United States in a number of measurements of economic power by the late 1980s. All hopes for that were dashed, however, when the bubble economy in Japan burst in 1990, and the economy plunged into stagnation for over a decade. South Korea had a similar experience when it was the victim of the Asian financial crisis in 1997. It was bailed out eventually by the International Monetary Fund.

Meanwhile, the Chinese economy was blasting ahead at a 6 to 7 percent annual growth rate and using its low wage structure to undercut many of the labor-intensive industries of Japan, South Korea, Taiwan, and Hong Kong. China was able to escape the Asian crisis of 1997 despite an increasing rate of foreign direct investment in Chinese business because its currency is inconvertible and not susceptible to speculation. Because it has to meet foreign competition, it has had to close many state enterprises, eliminate tariff and nontariff protectionism, and admit foreign capital and investment, especially after it joined the World Trade Organization and the World Bank.

China has begun to show many of the problems that Japan and South Korea have experienced: bank loans forced by the state to insolvent companies; collusive and corrupt agreements between bureaucrats and businessmen; maintaining inefficient state enterprises as a substitute for welfare payments to workers.

The gap between rich and poor, between flourishing coastal urban regions and backward rural areas in the interior, and between skilled and unskilled workers is growing. Millions of unemployed and homeless migrant workers from the countryside fill urban slums. Strikes by workers have increased, only to be met by government repression.

North Korea's stubborn insistence on self-sufficiency and economic autarchy to prevent foreign dependency closed the country off from trade with the non-Communist world and blocked the stimulus of foreign competition to develop new technology. When communism in the Soviet Union and eastern Europe collapsed between 1989 and 1991, Russia cut off subsidized oil exports, and North Korea lacked the foreign exchange to pay for it. Without sufficient energy, its factories had to operate at less than full capacity. The country has recovered partially from the massive floods of the mid-1990s, but the population is still malnourished. Attempts at modest liberalization of the economy have been stymied by American hostility.

Despite the despair accompanying the downturn in the business cycle in East Asia, all regions but North Korea have moved away from poverty and will continue their climb toward providing decent livelihoods for their populations. There has been much talk about the possibility of creating a regional free trade bloc in East Asia like the European Community, but there are serious obstacles. The Chinese economy has by far the highest growth rate based on a huge population and low wages and stands to gain the most from unrestrained trade until its wage rates rise. North Korea needs economic assistance from China as long as its economy remains moribund, but its intense nationalism precludes domination by any foreign economy. South Korean business is shipping its factories to China, but the public fears the loss of industry and the resulting economic decline and is wary of recent Japanese hostility to North Korea. Japan has much to gain from exports of high-tech products and investment in factories in China, but lingering Chinese resentment of Japanese atrocities in World War II, official visits to the Yasukuni shrine, Japan's military alliance with the United States, and suspicion of Japanese rearmament could put a brake on further development. All nations except North Korea continue to benefit from exports to the United States and, although maybe on a smaller scale, to Europe. Trade with Southeast Asia and Latin America is growing, and the potential for exports to Russia and surrounding states in return for oil and gas could be enormous if serious political and bureaucratic obstacles to free trade in those states could be removed.

Despite economic development in most East Asian states, they all brought with them fundamental conservative traditions based on familial ties, respect for status, and male domination. Some of these traditions have been weakened by egalitarian Communist ideals, education for men and women, marriage by choice and divorce, and rising incomes, but they remain formidable obstacles against the adoption of western values.

China has undergone significant influence from the worldwide communications revolution. Cell phones and fiber optics have lowered the costs of telephones and electrical transmission. Computers have given access to about 59 million people (3 percent of the Chinese population), and the figure might grow to 250 million by 2008. Microsoft opened a research laboratory in the Haidian District of Beijing, where some eight hundred ten thousand Chinese research scientists and engineers live. Oracle, Motorola, Siemens, IBM, Intel, General Electric, and Nokia (which produces mobile phones) are running research facilities in China to develop new products as well, opening the door to innovative and independent research to young scientists.

Aware that unlimited contact with the outside world poses a political threat to the regime, the Chinese leadership has ordered operators of Internet sites to monitor government bans against rumors, libel, subversion, sabotage of national security, the promotion of cults and feudal superstition, pornography, violence, and gambling.

The movie industry has developed, and foreign movies, popular songs, and chain stores from Japan, South Korea, and the United States have penetrated the country. Whether these influences will lead to the liberalization of centralized political rule in the future remains to be seen.

Culturally, South Korea has leaped to the forefront of modern technology. It seems that everyone (including teenagers) has a cell phone. Computers and access to the Internet are widespread. The movie industry is developing rapidly, producing a generation of directors, producers, and actors. Its movies are gaining popularity abroad. Thousands of young students travel to the United States to get an education, and interest in China, Chinese language study, and tourist trips is growing rapidly. North Korea has tried to insulate itself from the communications revolution and the cultural effects of globalization, but clandestine access to the Internet has already proved subversive to the closed society by slightly opening the window of information from the world outside.

Despite stagnation in the Japanese economy, contemporary Japanese culture in the form of Japanese comics books (*manga*), computer cartoon and video games and animation (*anime*), designer clothing, pop music, new dance steps, and the paraphernalia that accompanies it for sale on the market have become major export industries. In Japan 53 million people are connected to the Internet, and cell phones are ubiquitous. Japan leads the world in new and innovative products and designs in electronics. Most of these innovations mainly affect Japanese youth and create new job opportunities outside the rigid hierarchies of big business, opening up the possibilities of individual creativity and entrepreneurship.

Signs of American culture abound in Japan, including fast food parlors; McDonald's, Burger King, Colonel Sanders, and Starbucks coffee shops are ubiquitous. Designer boutiques from the United States and Europe have taken over floors in major department stores, and Japanese designers have penetrated the West. American teenage clothing and music styles are everywhere, but no more than Japanese Nintendo games, cartoons, and the Hello Kitty fad have overwhelmed American youth. Baseball is now a Japanese national sport, albeit with its own special variations, and Japanese ballplayers have joined several American major league teams.

The tensions between the Japanese and South Korean governments have lessened somewhat over time. After 1945, the Korean government imposed a ban on all cultural imports from Japan, which included music, movies, television shows, and comic books. In October 1998, South Korean president Kim Dae Jung said that his administration would gradually reopen South Korea to Japanese cultural imports. Today, most Japanese products enter the country freely, and remaining bans on some Japanese comic books and movies are expected to be eliminated soon. The two nations agreed in 2002 to cohost the World Cup tournament, the first time that the World Cup was played in Asia and the first time that two countries had split hosting duties.

Nevertheless, suspicions about Japanese attitudes and policies remain strong. The Japanese refuse to correct distortions in Japanese textbooks about mistreatment of Koreans during the colonial period, to apologize publicly and pay reparations to the comfort women (the kidnapped sex slaves of Japanese troops), and to share advanced technology in some industries. Japanese prime ministers continue to pay homage to the war dead of the imperial period at Yasukuni shrine. The Japanese public has showed increased hostility toward North Korea and Korean residents in Japan, and proposals for rearmament are gaining strength. South Korean universities have still failed to expand Japanese language instruction and academic programs in Japanese studies.

The main question for the future of East Asia is whether peace can be maintained and war avoided. China's relations with Tibet remain troubled because of ongoing nationalistic resistance to the Chinese, but Chinese migration there has overwhelmed the smaller Tibetan population. The Chinese Muslim population in the northwest has been a problem but not a major one. Tensions with the Soviet Union and its past allies, Vietnam and India, have been eliminated because of the collapse of communism in the Soviet Union in 1991.

China supported Pakistan throughout the Cold War against India, but hostile relations with India also declined after 1991. China's relations with Indonesia were not close after the military coup in that country in 1965, but they have improved, and China's relations with the military dictators of Myanmar have generally remained close. No serious problems have emerged with other Southeast Asian states.

A major problem for East Asia is whether Japan and South Korea will remain in their dependent military relationship with the United States in the face of U.S. hostility toward North Korea. The public yearning in Japan to create a military force to establish Japan as an independent nation seems to be gaining force, but that has created serious fears in China and the two Koreas and has forced the United States to rethink its relationship to East Asia. How the United States handles the problem of a potential North Korean nuclear weapons program will make a big difference in whether peaceful trade and coexistence continue in East Asia. U.S. demands for complete and total dismantlement of nuclear weapons have been rejected by North Korea, and the United States refuses to offer incentives to the North for a negotiated solution. The possibility of unilateral U.S. military action remains despite the opposition of South Korea and China to that policy. The impasse remains.

The Japanese fear of a serious threat from a possible North Korea weapons arsenal has only served to push public sentiment toward rearmament and nuclear weapons. Six hundred books were published on North Korea in Japan, most of them extremely hostile. Prime Minister Koizumi Jun'ichirō's initial attempt to negotiate with North Korea to pay reparations for the damage during Japanese colonialism backfired when Kim Jong Il admitted kidnapping Japanese from Japan as a means of recruiting Japanese language instructors. The public, the media, and Japanese nationalists led by Abe Shinzō of the Liberal Democratic Party and Satō Katsumi of the Contemporary Korea Institute have responded with demands for a hard line against North Korea, pushing Koizumi away from a peaceful resolution of differences. While Japan might well choose to remain a junior partner in the U.S.-Japan military alliance as the best means of defense, that kind of unequal partnership cannot last forever, and hard-core nationalists are pushing for rearmament.

Japan has sought accommodation with China's economic growth, but the growth of China's military troubles Japanese leaders. At present, the Chinese military has a large army capable of defending against invasion, but its outmoded weaponry and its weak navy and air force cannot support aggressive expansion abroad as long as the United States is committed to the defense of Japan and Taiwan. Any threat against Japan would undoubtedly trigger Japanese rearmament and a Japanese nuclear weapons program backed up by a vastly superior industrial base. It seems likely that for the near future, Sino-Japanese relations will remain calm as both sides concentrate on peaceful trade and investment.

The U.S. military presence in East Asia has had a strong stabilizing effect by preventing Japanese rearmament, stemming both the growing Taiwanese desire for independence and the Chinese desire to take Taiwan by force. It has blocked both a North Korean invasion of the South and a southern invasion of the North. If it finds a way to reach a negotiated solution of problems with North Korea by not challenging its survival, it might be able to maintain a beneficial presence in East Asia. Otherwise, the United States could spark another disastrous Korean War, or East Asia may decide to solve its own problems without U.S. interference.

SUGGESTED READING

For Chinese foreign relations, see A. J. Nathan and R. S. Ross, *The Great Wall and the Empty Fortress* (1997). For the Chinese economy, see N. R. Lardy, *China's Unfinished Economic Revolution* (1998) and *Integrating China into the Global Economy* (2002). For Chinese politics and disruption, see M. Goldman and R. MacFarquhar, eds., *The Paradox of China's Post-Mao Reforms* (1999). For reform and resistance in China, see E. J. Perry and M. Selden, *Chinese Society: Change, Conflict and Resistance* (2003). For Japanese politics, see C. Johnson, *Japan Who Governs?* (1995), and R. W. Bowen, *Japan's Dysfunctional Democracy* (2003). For the Japanese economy, see B. Gao, *Japan's Economic Dilemma* (2001), and for Japan's foreign relations, see K. B. Pyle, *Japan and the Primacy of Foreign Policy: Facing New Orders in Asia* (forthcoming). For Japanese policy toward North Korea, see G. McCormack, *Target North Korea* (2004), esp. pp. 125–148.

For the two Koreas, see D. C. Shin, *Mass Politics and Culture in Democratizing Korea* (1999); B. Cumings, *North Korea, Another Country* (2003); M. O'Hanlon and M. Mochizuki, *Crisis on the Korean Peninsula* (2003); V. D. Cha and D. C. Kang, *Nuclear North Korea* (2003); and G. McCormack, *Target North Korea* (2004).

CREDITS

Chapter 16

p. 322: Fang Bao's Random Notes from Prison, from *The Search for Modern China, A Documentary Collection* by Pei Kai Cheng, Michael Lestz and Jonathan Spence. Copyright © 1999 by W. W. Norton & Company, Inc. Used by permission of W. W. Norton & Company, Inc.

Chapter 17

p. 340: Reprinted by permission of Tuttle Publishing.

Chapter 18

p. 353: Reprinted by permission of Houghton Mifflin Company. p. 362: From JaHyun Kim Haboush, transl., *The Memoirs of Lady Hyegyŏng* (University of California Press, 1996), p. 301 [ISBN: 0-520-20054-3]. Reprinted by permission of The University of California Press.

Chapter 19

p. 392: J. Mason Gentzler, ed., *Changing China: Readings in the History of China from the Opium War to the Present*. Copyright © 1977 by Praeger Publishing. Reproduced with permission of Greenwood Publishing Group, Inc., Westport, CT.

Chapter 23

p. 456: Reprinted by permission of Foreign Languages Press.

Chapter 24

p. 476: Reprinted courtesy of The Asia Center.

Chapter 27

p. 532: Reprinted by permission of The University of Scranton Press.

Chapter 29

p. 576: From *Chinese Sociology & Anthropology*, vol. 34, no. 2 (Summer 2002): 75–80. English-language translation copyright © 2002 by M.E. Sharpe, Inc. Reprinted with permission of M.E. Sharpe, Inc.

Chapter 31

p. 608: From Mary C. Brinton, *Women and the Economic Miracle: Gender and Work in Postwar Japan* (Berkeley: University of California Press, 1992), p. 47. Reprinted by permission of The University of California Press. p. 610: Reprinted by permission.

INDEX